Chicano Folklore

El Enpeloto (1998) by Ray Martín Abeyta.
Source: National Hispanic Culture Center, Art Museum, Albuquerque, New Mexico.

Chicano Folklore

A Handbook

María Herrera-Sobek

Greenwood Folklore Handbooks

GREENWOOD PRESS
Westport, Connecticut • London

Library of Congress Cataloging-in-Publication Data

Herrera-Sobek, María.
  Chicano folklore : a handbook / María Herrera-Sobek.
     p. cm.   (Greenwood folklore handbooks, ISSN 1549–733X)
  Includes bibliographical references and index.
  ISBN 0–313–33325–4 (alk. paper)
  1. Mexican Americans—Folklore—Handbooks, manuals, etc.   2. Folklore—United
States—Handbooks, manuals, etc.   3. United States—Social life and customs—
Handbooks, manuals, etc.   I. Title.
GR111.M49H47 2006
398.089'6872—dc22   2006000652

British Library Cataloguing in Publication Data is available.

Library of Congress Catalog Card Number: 2006000652
ISBN: 0–313–33325–4
ISSN: 1549–733X

First published in 2006

Greenwood Press, 88 Post Road West, Westport, CT 06881
An imprint of Greenwood Publishing Group, Inc.
www.greenwood.com

Printed in the United States of America

The paper used in this book complies with the
Permanent Paper Standard issued by the National
Information Standards Organization (Z39.48–1984).

10 9 8 7 6 5 4 3 2 1

Copyright Acknowledgments

The publisher has done its best to make sure the instructions and/or recipes in this book are correct. However, users should apply judgment and experience when preparing recipes, especially parents and teachers working with young people. The publisher accepts no responsibility for the outcome of any recipe included in this volume.

"Gente de mucha cabeza," "Dogs Allowed," and "No Comia de eso" are reprinted with permission from the publisher of *Uncle Remus con chile* by Américo Paredes (Houston: Arte Publico Press, University of Houston, 1993).

Excerpts from "Nuestra Senora de Guadalupe: The Story of Our Lady of Guadalupe" and "Coming of Age–Quincenera" are used with permission from *Una Linda Raza: Cultural and Artistic Traditions of the Hispanic Southwest*, by Angel Vigil. © 1998 Fulcrum Publishing, Inc., Golden, CO, USA.

Excerpts from *Brujas, Bultos y Brasas: Tales of Witchcraft and the Supernatural in Pecos Valley*, © 1999 by Nasario Garcia, are reprinted with permission from the publisher, Western Edge/ Sherman Asher Publishing, Santa Fe, NM.

Excerpts from *Mexican-American Legends: Songs, Festivals, Proverbs, Crafts, Tales of Saints, of Revolutionaries and More*, by John O. West. © 1989. Published by August House Publishers, Inc. and reprinted with permission of Marian Reiner on their behalf.

Excerpts from *The Kennedy Corridos: A Study in the Ballads of a Mexican American Hero*, by Dan William Dickey, © 1978, are reprinted with permission from the publisher, University of Texas Press.

Excerpts from Jose Reyna, *Raza Humor: Chicano Joke Tradition in Texas*. "Jalo." N.d P. 42. "Su mama va a cayerse" and "They Ain't Got Their Clothes On!" are reprinted with permission of the author, Jose Reyna.

Excerpts from Luis Leal, *Mitos y Leyendas de Mexico/Myths and Legends of Mexico*, 2002. "Coyolxauhqui," pp. 53-58. "Quetzalcoatl," pp. 91-98. "Aztlan," pp. 99-108. "The Return of Quetzalcoatl," pp. 109-120. "La Llorona," pp. 127-133. Reprinted with permission of the author, Luis Leal.

Excerpts from Brownie McNeil, *Corridos of the Mexican Border*, "The Kasas Contractees," 1946. P. 11, in Mody Boatright, ed., Mexican Border Ballads and Other Lore. © 1967 Texas Folklore Society. Reprinted with permission of the publisher.

Excerpts from Sara Amira de la Garza, *Maria Speaks: Journeys into the Mysteries of the Mother in My Life as a Chicana.* "La Malinche . . . La Malinalli," 2004. Pp. 105-107. Reprinted with permission of Peter Lang Publishing, Inc.

Song lyrics "Delgadina" and "Cancion Mixteca" from *La Musica de los Viejitos: Hispano Folk Music of the Rio Grande del Norte,* by Jack Loeffler (with Catherine Loeffler and Enrique R. Lamadrid), © 1999. Reprinted with permission.

Folk lyric "Corrido de Joaquin Murieta," in Philip Sonnichsen, *Texas Mexican Border Music,* 1975. From the Arhoolie CD Set 7019/20: "Corridos y Tradegia de la Fronora." (www. arhoolie.com). Reprinted with permission.

Sections from the article originally published as "Americo Parades: A Tribute" /Mexican Studies/Estudios Mexicanos/Vol. No. 16 (2), Summer 2000, pages 239-266. © 2000 Regents of the University of California, appear in chapter four.

Every reasonable effort has been made to trace the owners of copyrighted materials in this book, but in some instances this has proven impossible. The author and publisher will be glad to receive information leading to more complete acknowledgments in subsequent printings of the book and in the meantime extend their apologies for any omissions.

This book is dedicated to my son
Erik Jason Sobek

Contents

Preface

Chicano/a folklore bears the distinction of being a relatively new category of folklore and at the same time considered to be a repository and transformer of ancient European, African, and Native American traditions. The words *Chicano* (male subject) and *Chicana* (female subject) themselves are folk terms pertaining to folk speech since they were invented in the early twentieth century and popularized by the Mexican American civil rights student movement in the 1960s and 1970s. Originally *Chicano* was a pejorative term used by the Mexican American middle class for immigrants from Mexico who were poor, uneducated, and from the working class. During the 1960s, students from this ethnic group appropriated the word and used it as a badge of honor, thus transforming it into a political term to designate all Mexican Americans who were politically conscious regarding issues of race and ethnic relations in the United States. Interestingly enough, its etymology is surrounded in controversy since there is no agreement as to its precedence. The most common explanation regarding its roots or origins is that the word probably derives from the Nahuatl word *Mexica* (pronounced "meshika")— the term the Aztecs used to call themselves. The first syllable is dropped and the morpheme *xica* is left to which the syllables *ano* and *ana* are added to form the words C*hicano* and *Chicana*. This book examines the oral traditions of the Chicano people and highlights the various cultural strands that influenced its development, growth, and transformation. These folk traditions include the following genres, which are discussed in the chapters that follow:

    I. Folk narrative
      A. Myth

The first chapter explores the historical context in which Chicano folklore flourished in the United States. Chapter 2 provides an overall view of the various folk genres encompassing Chicano folklore and offers definitions and classificatory systems. Chapter 3 incorporates actual texts from the rich repertoire found in the Chicano culture, and chapter 4 focuses on the scholars that have studied, analyzed, and interpreted Chicano folklore and who have left us with excellent theoretical frameworks from which to study this cultural legacy.

Similar to other countries of the world, folklore among the Chicano people has been used and continues to be used as a source of pride and ethnic identification. Chapter 5 centers its attention on the context in which it appears and the multiplicity of areas Chicano folklore has had a significant influence. This form of cultural production is a source of ethno-nationalist pride and is often used as a political forum and platform from which grievances are articulated. Chicano folklore is a fount of inspiration for artistic expression such as films, visual arts, theater, literature, music, children's books, and other categories of human endeavor. It is an area of cultural production that delights young and old with its cleverness, wit, wisdom, beauty, and creativity.

Chicano Folklore: A Handbook also includes a filmography, a substantial bibliography, a glossary, a Web resources directory, and an index. There are an excellent number of illustrations throughout the book that add visual interest to the topics addressed in each chapter.

Acknowledgments

I want to take this opportunity to thank all the great people that helped me with the various aspects of writing this book. I thank our Executive Vice Chancellor, Gene Lucas, for his support and encouragement while working on this project. I am grateful to Melissa Byrne, Lisa Oshins, Steve Reed, Stacey Keleher and Toby Lazarowitz, our office personnel, for their support and help when I needed it. I thank my graduate student research assistants Brianne Dávila, Richard Huizar, Michelle Baca, and José Anguiano for their outstanding work in typing, scanning images, and other research assistance they provided for me during the long process of writing this volume. I am most appreciative of Professor Luis Leal who, at 98 years of age, continues to publish and teach; I am constantly learning from him, and this time he helped me scan some of the myths from his book *Mitos y Leyendas de México/Myths and Legends from Mexico*. I thank him and all the other scholars and artists whose work I cite and use with their permission.

Funding resources are always essential to have when writing a book. I am indebted to the Chicana and Chicano Studies Department for their continued support of my research through the yearly renewal of the Luis Leal Endowed Chair funds. My heartfelt thanks to all my colleagues: Chela Sandoval, Mario García, Guisela Latorre, Jonathan Inda, Ralph Armbruster Sandoval, Tara Yosso, Edwina Barvosa-Carter, Gerardo Aldana, Francisco A. Lomelí, and Horacio Roque Ramírez, *gracias!* Sincere thanks to Denise Segura, Director of the University of California, Santa Barbara UCCLR (University of California Chicano/Latino Research) project, and Carl Gutiérrez-Jones, Director of the Center for Chicano Studies. I am grateful for the research funds granted.

I am most appreciative of my husband, Joseph G. Sobek, and my son, Erik Jason Sobek, for their love, support, and understanding.

One
Introduction

Chicanos and Chicanas, or Mexican Americans, trace their European roots in the United States to the late 1520s and 1530s, when Alvar Núñez Cabeza de Vaca first explored the South and Southwest. Of course, their indigenous roots extend even deeper into past centuries to the various Native American groups living in the Southwest and Mexico such as the Aztecs, Mayas, Zapotecs, Mixtecs, Totonacs, Otomí, Yaqui, Pima, Navajo, and Pueblo Indians and numerous other autochthonous peoples from the Americas. Chicanos/as inherited their rich folklore traditions from three principal cultural strands: indigenous, European, and African. Middle Eastern traditions can also be included, because the Arabs were in Spain for 700 years and Middle Eastern groups migrated to Mexico also. In addition, Anglo-American incursions in the Southwest after the 1846–48 United States–Mexican War brought Mexicans in direct contact with Anglo-American traditions, and these continued to enrich the European cultural heritage first introduced by the Spaniards. This is particularly apparent in the linguistic changes that took place with the introduction of the English language; however, it also manifested in the other customs and traditions introduced to the Southwest by this new ethnic group, such as the celebration of Thanksgiving in November and the celebration of Independence Day on the fourth of July.

The great tripartite cultural legacy is evident in the numerous folklore genres such as myths, folktales, legends, jests, folksongs, folk theater, traditional customs, folk beliefs, medicine, festivals, folk celebrations, children's songs and games and riddles. It is also exhibited in the superb culinary traditions— such as tamales, tortillas, mole, chocolate, tequila, and atole—as well as in the arts and crafts, architecture, traditional dances, and costumes extant in the culture. Other folk genres particularly salient in Chicano/a oral traditions are those related to speech. Linguistic dexterity is highly valued in Chicano-Mexican culture, as is evident in the extensive repertoire of expressions found in the Spanish language such as proverbs, proverbial exaggerations, proverbial comparisons, proverbial expressions, *caló,* tongue twisters, and the infinite forms of specialized vocabularies found in the culture.

The numerous Chicano/a traditions that have been passed from generation to generation throughout the centuries are not static but continue to be dynamic and ever-changing, and are treasured gifts of artistically marked information. Scholars in the late nineteenth century coined the term *folklore* to identify this particular type of cultural heritage extant in all world cultures. This chapter provides a historical context in which Chicano/a folklore developed and thrived from the Spanish colonial period to the present. There are seven major historical periods marking specific events of importance that gave rise to new categories of folklore or exploded those that were present in nascent forms:

    I. The Spanish Colonial Period (1492–1821)

    II. Mexican Period (1821–1848)

    III. United States–Mexican War and U.S. colonization and settlement of the Southwest (1848–1910)

    IV. The Mexican Revolution of 1910–1921 and World War I

    V. Mexican American Assimilation and Acculturation (1921–1930)

    VI. Repatriation and Deportation of Mexicans and Mexican Americans (1930–1942)

    VII. The Bracero Program (1942–1964)

    VIII. The Chicano/a Movement (1965–present)

These periods highlight specific moments in Chicano historiography that stimulated the expansion, development, and transformation of folklore genres.

I. THE SPANISH COLONIAL PERIOD (1492–1821)

The Spanish colonial period commenced on October 12, 1492, when the Spaniards first arrived in the Caribbean Islands and proceeded to colonize the various islands, including what is now Cuba, the Dominican Republic, and Puerto Rico. From these Caribbean islands, explorations began immediately into surrounding areas—one of the most prominent being Hernán Cortez's expedition departing from Cuba in 1519 to explore the Mexican coast. Previous to Cortez's three ships expedition, there had been others attempting to navigate the Mexican coast and enter the mainland, but these attempts had ended in failure; they had been unable to enter inland into the territory of the Mexica Coluha or Aztec Empire. During these early forays two Spanish sailors, Jerónimo de Aguilar and Gonzalo Guerrero, were shipwrecked for several years in Yucatan; they were left there stranded from the failed expeditions. No doubt Spanish oral traditions began to be implanted into the Maya cultural landscape through these two men (Díaz del Castillo 1967, 40). In fact, Gonzalo Guerrero actually married a Mayan woman and had several children with her. He became assimilated into the Yucatan culture and refused to join Cortez when he and his men attempted to "save" the two shipwrecked sailors. Cortez picked up Jerónimo de Aguilar, one of the stranded sailors, who did agree to join him. After picking up Aguilar, who proved to be invaluable as a translator, the ships continued their journey down the coast of Yucatan north toward what is today the city of Veracruz.

There Cortez established a friendship with the local *cacique,* or chief, who in a strategic move in planning for the future, offered Cortez 20 Indian maidens as gifts to serve as wives or servants. Among the 20 maidens was a young woman, originally a princess or belonging to the ruling class but who had been sold into slavery: Malintzin Tenépal, later known as Malinche and baptized in the Catholic faith as Marina. She was formally called Doña Marina as a sign of respect by the Spaniards, who held her in high regard due to her intelligence, linguistic skills, and diplomatic and political abilities. Malinche has come down in history as the second Eve for supposedly having betrayed the Indian nations by aiding Cortez in the conquest of Mexico. Chicana writers, for good reason, have contested the negative simplistic view heaped on Malinche by nineteenth-century nationalist Mexican historians and have provided a revised vision of Malinche's role in the conquest. Malinche has become a source of myth and legend, and an overall fount of inspiration for Chicana feminist political theory and for visual artists and literary authors. She is one of three great colonial period female figures, together with the Virgin of Guadalupe and La Llorona, or the Wailing Woman, who continue to exert tremendous influence in the production of Chicano/a folklore and in other areas of cultural production as well as political and philosophical thought.

Cortez's landing in the Gulf of Mexico in the area of what is today the city of Veracruz was the beginning of a cultural *mestizaje,* or mixing, writ large, since he eventually proceeded with his 500 men, thousands of Indian allies, horses, and military equipment on to the Aztec capital, Tenochtitlan, conquered the Aztec empire, and laid the foundations for the settlement and expansion of the Spanish Empire in the American mainland. The Spaniards carried with them their own cultural traditions, which they began to impart to all Native Americans in Mesoamerica and later to the whole American continent. These cultural traditions included the major genres of folklore cited earlier. Particularly salient and important was the implantation of the Catholic faith in the Native American populations and all that religious belief system entails, such as festivals, life rituals, foods, saints' narratives, belief systems, and religious songs, theater, and art.

Nevertheless, the Native American populations were not static, empty vials in which information was being poured into but were in fact the possessors of rich cultural legacies. The numerous Indian groups had and continue to have their traditions, language, belief systems, and so forth. With the confluence of the two major cultural strands, European and indigenous, a massive transformation began to transpire in the cultural production of these two major groups, and new incarnations of old myths and icons surfaced in all aspects of daily life. The *mestizaje,* or mixing, was not only in the verbal and material area of cultural production but in the biological realm of the two races as well.

A third important strand of cultural legacy and of biological and cultural *mestizaje* is the African one. African slaves arrived in the Americas as early as Columbus's first trip and continued to be imported both as personal servants and later as slaves to work the huge agricultural haciendas, the mines, the sugar factories, and *latifundios* (great landed estates used for agricultural production and/or cattle) as well as for other tasks related to the colonization project. African slaves were imported by the thousands, as is evident by the statistics the German scientist and explorer, Alexander von Humbolt, compiled and published for the different racial groups living in Mexico in the nineteenth century (Lafaye 1998, 81):

Indian Natives	2,500,000
Whites/ Spaniards	
Creoles	1,025,000
Europeans	70,000
Black Africans:	6,100
Castes of mixed blood	1,231,000
Total:	4,832,100

This great number of Africans meant that their cultural capital traveled with them and was added to the folklore landscape of the new continent. The areas of the Mexican Caribbean coast and the Acapulco Pacific coast were particularly impacted with the African population in Mexico. This mixed population came to the Mexican northern territories in what is today the Southwest during the colonial period. For example, there were various Afromestizos accompanying the expeditions that went into New Mexico, Texas, Florida, and California.

The Spanish colonial period (1492–1821) for the Chicano/a population is by far the most significant historical period in the establishment of Chicano folklore. It was during this intensive era of conquest and colonization in the Southwest that Spain not only planted its flag in the northern territories but disseminated its cultural heritage and language system in the newly conquered lands. The Spaniards brought with them their folk narratives, their family and religious rituals, their festivals and celebrations, their folk speech, art, theater, music, songs, food, belief systems, children's songs and games, dress, as well as architecture and technology (cattle, horse, and agricultural tools), weaving, carving, and metallurgy. So for three centuries, from 1492 to 1821, the three cultural strands (African, European, and indigenous), intermingled, fused, converged, diverged, and produced new elements. The Spanish, being the more powerful political force, dominated the other strands. The prominence of the Spanish language and the Catholic faith among Chicanos/as is a testament to this fact. Of particular interest and as models of outstanding *mestizaje* are the three legends inherited by Chicanos/as from the Spanish colonial period: La Malinche, La Llorona, and the Virgin of Guadalupe.

Malinche's biography reads like a fairy tale: An evil mother, having remarried after her husband's death, sold her young child to Maya merchants so that her son from her second marriage could inherit the patrimony her first husband had left her daughter. The daughter was of Aztec stock and had grown up to the age of seven or so around the Nahuatl-speaking population, so her native tongue was Nahuatl. When she was sold to Maya merchants, she soon learned the Maya language as well. Cortez was able to capitalize on her linguistic skills (she learned Spanish very quickly, evidencing a particular knack for languages) and she proved to be invaluable to him in the conquest of Mexico. Malinche's role as Cortez's translator, confidant, and advisor has been highly frowned upon and, during Mexico's nationalist movements of the nineteenth century it earned her the reputation of being a traitor, of betraying her people. Malinche has become symbolic of those who prefer the foreign to the autochthonous, and in fact a word (folk speech) bearing her name was coined to depict such despicable people: *malinche* or *malinchista*. She has also been incorrectly attributed as being the mother of the mestizo race for being the first to bear a mestizo child in Mexico since she bore Cortez a son, Martín Cortez. However,

"La Llorona," The Wailing Woman (1979) by Alvaro Suman.
Source: Courtesy of Alvaro Suman.

recall that Gonzalo Guerrero had already sired mestizo children in the Yucatan Peninsula. Malinche in fact was not the first Indian woman in Mexico to bear a mixed-blood son.

La Llorona, the Wailing or Weeping Woman, another figure from the colonial period, proceeds from two major cultural influences: European and indigenous. The basic kernel of the La Llorona narrative is that she was a mestizo woman who, having been jilted by her Spanish lover, in revenge kills her children by drowning, according to one variant. For this heinous crime, God punished her to roam the world looking for her murdered children. La Llorona appears at night wailing, *"Ayyyyy mis hijos!"* [Ohhhh my children!]

usually around waterways such as canals, rivers, lakes, streams, water pools, and irrigation ditches. The Native American strand from the Aztec tradition is related to the Goddess Cihuacóatl, who takes children at night while asleep in their cribs, leaving an obsidian knife behind. A second version, as told by Sahagún (1953–1982), is that La Llorona was a woman who just before the conquest could be seen and heard wailing at night: "She appeared before men, she was covered with chalk, like a court lady. She wore earplugs, obsidian earplugs. She appeared in white, garbed in white. . . . pure white. Her womanly hairdress rose up. By night she walked weeping, wailing . . ." (Book I, ch. 6, II; see also Leal 2005, 136). Mexican Americans have invariably used the folk legend to socialize their children into proper behavior, a sort of Chicano boogey man which was especially effective in urging children to go to bed at night or else the Llorona would take them away.

The third, and possibly most important icon in Chicano/a folkloristics is that of the Virgin of Guadalupe, who, according to legend, appeared four times to an Indian by the name of Juan Diego during December 9–12, 1531, at the Cerro del Tepeyac in Mexico City. The legend narrates how a young Indian neophyte is in a rush to fetch a doctor for his uncle, who is ill in bed. On his way to the doctor an apparition manifests itself in the guise of the Virgin of Guadalupe (i.e., the Virgin Mary) at the Hill of Tepeyac. She informs Juan Diego she wants him to deliver a message to the Archbishop of Mexico: She desires a church be built at the site where she is appearing. Juan Diego is reluctant and gently reminds the beautiful, brown-skinned lady that he is only an Indian and that the Archbishop will not listen to him. He implores her to send someone more important. She insists that he should be the one to carry the message, that she specifically has chosen him because he is a humble Indian.

When Juan Diego arrives at the cathedral to inform the Archbishop of the Beautiful Lady's wishes, he is denied an audience with the prelate. After another attempt, the Indian messenger is finally able to communicate the Virgin's wishes to the Archbishop. However, the Archbishop does not believe Juan Diego and sends him away requesting some proof. Juan Diego returns to the Hill of Tepeyac and informs the Virgin of Guadalupe that the Archbishop has asked for a sign. The Virgin agrees and orders Juan Diego to pick some roses that are on the hill. Juan Diego is skeptical, being that it is early December (December 12), when flowers do not normally bloom on the hill. He obeys the Virgin's orders and goes around the hill, where, to his surprise, there is an abundance of roses. (The Virgin's apparition is also known as the Miracle of the Roses.) He picks a bundle of roses and journeys once again to Mexico City to deliver the sign the Virgin has sent to the Archbishop. When Juan Diego appears before the Archbishop again and proceeds to show him the roses the Virgin of Guadalupe has sent, an image of the

Virgin is seen imprinted on the white cotton *tilma* or robe the Native American is wearing. All kneel in front of the cloth, and today that piece of cloth is framed, mounted, and displayed at the Villa de Guadalupe church in Mexico City.

The folklore and popular culture surrounding the Virgin of Guadalupe is infinite—from folk narratives to personal experience narratives, *casos* [miracle stories], jokes, miracles, songs of all kinds, folk art, folk belief, folk medicine, theater, popular culture such as movies, *telenovelas* (soap operas), and so forth, the icon has had a tremendous impact and influence. Today she continues to be a rich source of cultural production (and commerce).

The colonial period was a most productive era for the introduction of Spanish folklore in its myriad manifestations, the *mestizaje* of folkloric forms, and the production of new folklore icons and items. The indigenous strand was particularly important in folklore production during the colonial period in the area of foodways, because there were numerous food products not known to the European world, such as chocolate and maize, as well as hundreds of fruits and vegetables known and grown in the American continent only. African contributions were significant also in the area of food, particularly food preparation, as well as in folk belief systems and in the area of music. The three strands produced the marvelous cultural *mestizaje* that is the legacy of the Chicano people.

II. MEXICAN PERIOD (1821–1848)

The Spanish colonial period came to an end in 1821. The Spanish colonies in the American continent were becoming more and more dissatisfied with Spanish colonial rule. For one thing, the bureaucracy was overwhelming: All kinds of paperwork and permits had to be filled out for any business transaction that took place. The Spaniards were meticulous about keeping accurate records of everything that transpired in the colonies. The *criollos,* or Spaniards born in America, resented the many laws instituted for the governing of Nueva España, or New Spain, as well as the other South American colonies, including the laws that prohibited them from holding important government positions. Self-government and self-determination were not perceived by the *criollos* to be a hallmark of Spanish colonial rule. The burden of heavy taxation without proper representation was particularly galling to the colonists, as were all the restrictions on trade imposed by the mother country.

The liberation models projected by the United States in 1776 and later by the French Revolution in 1789 provided the impetus that led to the Wars of Independence in 1810 in Mexico and throughout Latin America.

The battle cry of Miguel Hidalgo y Costilla of *"¡Viva México!"* [Long live Mexico!] followed by *"¡Viva la Virgen de Guadalupe!"* [Long live the Virgin of Guadalupe!] inspired not only the *criollo* elite class but the Indians, mestizos, and blacks to join the insurgents and fight for Mexican independence. The battle for independence lasted 11 years, until 1821 when the insurgents finally and decisively defeated the Spanish forces. After 1821, what was known as New Spain became the Republic of Mexico. The *criollos* took the name *Mexico* from the ancient Mexica or Aztecs, which their ancestors had defeated in 1521, precisely 300 years before.

The newly minted Mexican nation, wishing to colonize and populate the distant territories to the north of Mexico City, began offering settlers from the United States opportunities to obtain huge land grants in what was then the province of Texas. Stephen Austin was one of these enterprising easterners granted land. Soon a steady flow of Anglo-American settlers from the East and the South began to pour into the Texas area. Some Anglo-Americans had also been exploring the coast of California, and the Lewis and Clark Expedition had made exploratory incursions into the land west of the Mississippi River. The granting of land to Euro-American settlers proved to be a huge mistake for the young Mexican nation; after its independence from Spain, it was teetering on the brink of several civil wars due to the infighting between liberals and federalists. A major bone of contention with the Texas settlers developed with respect to the slave issue. After its independence in 1821, Mexico abolished slavery, and the new Anglo-American settlers, many of them who came from the slaveholding states of the South, saw these antislavery laws as a direct violation of their property rights. State rights became a big issue, and by 1833, there was a definite segment of Texans who wanted to secede from the Mexican nation. By 1836, after fierce and bitter battles between Texans (including Texas Mexicans) and Mexicans with Santa Ana at the head of Mexico's troops, Texas gained its independence, and the Texas Republic was created. Mexico was never happy with Texas's self-declaration of independence and did not recognize the Lone Star Republic of Texas. The United States immediately recognized Texas as an independent country, and there was soon talk of Texas joining the Union. A second major conflict that led to the United States–Mexico War was the problem of territorial boundaries. Texas claimed the Rio Grande River as its territorial boundary, whereas Mexico insisted the boundary lay farther north at the Nueces River. Soldiers were stationed on both sides of the Rio Grande River border. Eventually gunfire erupted between the two forces, and the U.S.–Mexico War exploded in 1846, lasting until 1848. The United States was victorious in this conflict and Mexico, as the defeated country, had to cede huge portions of its Mexican territory. Texas, Arizona, New Mexico, California, Colorado, Utah, Nevada, and parts of Oregon and Oklahoma were ceded to the United States as part of the Treaty of Guadalupe Hidalgo signed in 1848. The United States, although the victor in this war, paid $15 million for the lands to Santa Ana.

The conflict between the United States and Mexico resulted in the production of folklore. Legends regarding fighters on both sides of the border emerged. The Alamo is a gold mine for legends depicting Mexican fighters as well as Mexican victims. Legends surrounding the figure of Santa Ana also arose, as well as narratives depicting the valor or cowardice of other leaders on both sides of the conflict. Songs are also part of this rich repertoire of folklore emanating from the two great conflicts: the Texas war with Mexico and the U.S. war with Mexico. Américo Paredes, a Chicano scholar from Texas, asserts that cultural conflict between Anglo-Americans and Chicanos is the main fount of inspiration for the production of Chicano/a folklore. The culture clash between the groups was bound to produce folk genres such as the *corrido* tradition and folk heroes such as Gregorio Cortez, Jacinto Treviño, and Joaquín Murieta.

In fact, folklore during the Mexican period 1821–1848 arose through not only the culture conflict between Mexicans and Anglos but also the close proximity between the two groups. Mexicans and Anglos, with their different cultural systems (i.e., one English, the other Spanish; one Catholic, the other Protestant) commenced to have influences on each other aside from the cultural clash that differences in worldview elicited. Thus, Chicano foodways were soon adopted by Anglo settlers and Chicanos/as also transformed their own culinary traditions. Barbacoa (barbeque), chili con carne (most popularly known as chili) are but two salient examples of Anglos adopting Mexican cuisine and adding their own individual stamp on the products. Chicanos also adopted Anglo-American food products, which transformed food preparation systems—for example, using yellow cheese (longhorn and cheddar) and Monterey cheese instead of white Mexican cheese (*asadero, panela* and fresh Mexican cheese). The Mexican period also witnessed the beginning of transferring Mexican folk knowledge as it related to cattle and horse husbandry. This ethnic group possessed a great store of knowledge with respect to cattle and horses since these animals had been introduced by their Spanish forefathers to the Americas and in particular to the Southwest. Thus, the Mexican *vaqueros,* or cowboys, possessed excellent skills with cattle and horses, not only in riding and working with them but also in the folk traditions of tanning hides, working with leather, drying and salting beef for food consumptions (beef jerky), and other aspects of folk technology related to ranch life including the Spanish guitar and cowboy singing.

III. UNITED STATES AND COLONIZATION (1848–1910)

The date 1848 marks more than the end of the United States–Mexico War; it is also a transition period in Chicano/a history when Mexican citizens became U.S. citizens. 1848 is also the date the California Gold Rush began, which, as had previously happened in Texas, produced a tremendous influx of Anglo-Americans from the East Coast and Europeans from the old continent. This new influx of European and Anglo-Americans elicited a culture conflict between native Californios and other Latinos (mainly Chileans and Peruvians). The conflict arose out of the competition for the mining of gold. Euro-Americans resented the skill and expertise U.S. Latinos and Californios exhibited in the prospecting and mining of gold. This skill and expertise was acquired during the 350 years of experience in working the mines in Mexico, a country rich in silver and gold, and Chile and Peru, two countries rich in mineral deposits (silver in Peru and copper in Chile). The U.S. Latinos competed more than favorably against the newly arrived Europeans and Anglo-Americans, who had scant experience, having recently arrived from Paris, London, Oslo, Stockholm, Frankfurt, and so on, which are not necessarily known for their metal mining tradition. The inevitable happened and laws directed against Latinos were instituted. Particularly onerous was the foreigners' tax law, in which Californios and Latinos were forced to pay $20 tax per month for the privilege of mining. Euro-Americans were exempt from this law, since the law applied to Latinos and Californios, who were perceived as foreigners; in contrast, by mutual consent, newly arrived Europeans were granted immediate "American" status. Soon a paradigmatic folk hero among the Latinos arose representing their extreme frustration at the oppressive laws targeting them: Joaquín Murieta.

Joaquín Murieta surfaced during the turbulent years of the Gold Rush in 1848. He became a figure celebrated by the folk in *corridos* and legends, and hated by the establishment. There are various versions of the Murieta story and what propelled him to a life of crime. According to a fictionalized account of his life written by John Rollin Ridge, *The Life and Adventures of Joaquín Murieta: Celebrated California Bandit* (1854) Murieta was a Mexican miner from Sonora, California who was resented for his skills in the mining of gold. He was living a quiet life when his brother was killed and his wife was raped and murdered by an Anglo mob. Joaquín himself was humiliated in front of his family when he tried to intervene. This terrible string of misfortunes is said to have motivated Joaquín to seek revenge and bring justice to the death of his brother and wife. Thus began the outlaw life of Murieta, who became a highway Robin Hood–type of robber, stealing from the rich to give to the poor. During the many stage holdups he is said to have killed numerous Euro-Americans.

The California state legislature offered $5,000 for the head of Joaquín Murieta. Mexican American legislatures objected to this reward offering, stating that a basic principle of United States law—innocent until proven guilty—was being violated. They further pointed out the danger in such a call for the head of Murieta, since no one knew what he looked liked; therefore, anybody could kill a Mexican man, cut his head, and claim it was Joaquín. There would be no way to prove such a head belonged to the celebrated bandit. This objection was disregarded, and the publicity for the reward went out. An officer by the name of Capitan Love went out with his soldiers to hunt for Joaquín's head, soon thereafter brought in what was purported to be the head of the much-maligned Joaquín, and received the reward. The celebrated bandit's head was pickled and placed in a clear jar. It was exhibited with traveling circuses throughout the state of California. The pickled head eventually landed in a bar in San Francisco but was lost after the 1907 San Francisco earthquake and fire that devastated the city.

Joaquín Murieta can be rightly classified as a social bandit if we keep in mind the characteristics outlined by Hobsbawn (1969). Hobsbawn first provides three major categories for the classification of a social bandit: noble robber, or Robin Hood; resistance fighter, or guerrilla; and avenger (Hobsbawn 1969, 42). He further adds nine major characteristics associated with social banditry:

1. The noble robber begins his career of outlawry not by crime, but as the victim of injustice, or through being persecuted by the authorities for some act that they, but not the custom of his people, consider a criminal.

2. He "rights the wrongs."

3. He "takes from the rich to give to the poor."

4. He "never kills but in self-defense or just revenge."

5. If he survives, he returns to his people as an honorable citizen and member of the community. Indeed, he never actually leaves the community.

6. He is admired, helped, and supported by his people.

7. He dies invariably and only through treason, since no decent member of the community would help the authorities against him.

8. He is—at least in theory—invisible and invulnerable.

A rendering of Joaquín Murieta from the cover of *The Life and Adventures of Joaquin Murieta: The Celebrated California Bandit,* by John (Yellow Bird) Rollin Ridge.
Source: Copyright © 1955 by the University of Oklahoma Press, Norman, Publishing Division of the University. All rights reserved. Reprinted by permission of the University of Oklahoma Press.

9. He is not the enemy of the king or emperor, who is the fount of justice, but only of the local gentry, clergy, or other oppressors (Hobsbawn 1969, 42–43).

Murieta's life story produced a cottage industry of folklore and popular culture. A play based on Murieta's life was written by Charles E. B. Howe titled *Joaquín Murieta de Castillo, the Celebrated California Bandit* (1858), and a year later a pirated version appeared as *The Life of Joaquín Murieta, Brigand Chief of California.* Novels also appeared, including *Joaquín, the Terrible* (1881), by Joseph E. Badger, Jr.; The *Pirate of the Placers; or Joaquín's Death-Hunt* (1882) also by Badger. As late as 1932 Walter Noble Burns wrote a novel based on Murieta's life bearing the title *The Robin Hood of El Dorado.* This was followed years later by Pablo Neruda's play *Splendor and Death of Joaquín Murieta* (1972). Most recently a documentary was done, titled *Behind the Mask of Zorro* (2005), and a couple of scholarly books have been published.

A *corrido* detailing the life of Joaquín Murieta is still being recorded today. The *corrido* celebrates the life and exploits of the social bandit; he was perceived as one righting the wrongs visited on the common Mexican people. Murieta's exploits and folk status initiated the second half of the nineteenth century and marked the emergence of the Mexican American resistance fighter. This resistance fighter reacted against the atrocities (e.g., lynching of Mexicans, segregation, beatings, property confiscated or outright stolen by the law of Squatter's Rights, incarcerations) committed against the Mexican population who had chosen to stay in their ancestral lands under the new regime and the supposed protection of the Treaty of Guadalupe Hidalgo. The Treaty was supposed to have guaranteed them their rights as new American citizens under Article VIII, which stipulated:

> Mexicans now established in territories previously belonging to Mexico, and which remain for the future within the limits of the United States, as defined by the present Treaty, shall be free to continue where they now reside, or to remove at any time to the Mexican Republic, retaining the property which they possess in the said territories, or disposing thereof and removing the proceeds wherever they please; without their being subjected, on this account, to any contribution, tax or charge whatever.
>
> Those who shall prefer to remain in the said territories, may either retain the title and rights of Mexican citizens, or acquire those of citizens of the United States. But, they shall be under the obligation to make their election within one year from the date of the exchange of ratifications of this treaty: and those who shall remain in the said territories, after the experiation of that year, without having declared their intention to retain the character of Mexicans, shall be considered to have elected to become citizens of the United States.
>
> In the said territories, property of every kind, now belonging to Mexicans not established there, shall be inviolably respected. The present owners, the heirs of these, and all Mexicans who may hereafter acquire said property by

contract, shall enjoy with respect to it, guaranties equally ample as if the same belonged to citizens of the United States. (Bevans 1972, 791–806)

The Treaty of Guadalupe Hidalgo in no uncertain terms spelled the right of property ownership and the right of Mexicans to retain their lands owned previous to the United States–Mexican War. Nevertheless, Mexicans soon lost their lands by various means, including the U.S. court system; oftentimes deeds and grants were invalidated by the Anglo-American courts.

The second major folk hero representing the tail end of this tumultuous era was Gregorio Cortez, who emerged as a hero in the Mexican American community at the end of the nineteenth century in 1901 in the Southeastern part of Texas near San Antonio. Cortez was the hero-protagonist of more than 20 *corridos* penned in his honor in addition to the multiple legends associated with his clash with Anglo-American authorities. According to Paredes (1958), Cortez was a man minding his own business and living with his family in his small ranch. The local sheriff came looking for a man that had traded a horse (which was Rumaldo, Cortez's brother), and due to a language misunderstanding the sheriff fired and mortally wounded Rumaldo. Cortez then shot the sheriff and fled. A manhunt ensued and eventually Cortez was captured, tried in court, and sent to jail. Cortez's defense lawyer used the "right to self defense" argument, but to no avail.

Rebels, resistance fighters, insurgents, revolutionaries, or bandits, as the established order and the ruling classes preferred to call them, were not the only class of folk groups that emerged in the Wild West of the 1850s–1900s. This period was a time when the United States was building the infrastructure for the development of the West, and this was being undertaken at a furious pace. Labor was needed to build the great railroads that were to deliver the beef, fruits, vegetables, cotton, copper, timber, and other products from the rich western lands long desired and now newly acquired. The cowboy (both Mexican and Anglo-American) crystallized as a definite figure at this point in time and according to Paredes, the *corrido* genre also crystallized as a vigorous and dynamic tradition in the second half of the nineteenth century.

Corridos narrating the long cattle drives to Kansas have been rescued from the period. Paredes cites two such corridos in his book *A Texas Mexican Cancionero: Folksongs of the Lower Border* (1976) "Corrido de Kiansas I" and "Corrido de Kiansas II." Depicted in the lyrics of these songs are brave and skillful Texas Mexican cowboys who amaze the Anglo-Americans with their knowledge, techniques, and strategies for managing cattle and horses. Cowboy outfits, work-related clothes (e.g., the lariat, saddle, big hat for the sun and for hauling water, leather chaps, the indispensable cowboy boots, and even the guitar) and tools are all part of the Mexican tradition in the United States that was acquired by the Anglo-American cowboys and became the archetypal American figure in American folklore.

The railroad worker was another key figure in the development of the American West and once again major figures in this saga, although hardly acknowledged in railroad history books, were the Mexican railroad workers. The Chinese railroad worker is more readily recognized as an important racial group that participated in the building of the railroads. However, the Chinese Exclusion Act 1882 put a stop to Chinese immigration due to Anglo-Americans' fear of Asian overpopulation—the "yellow peril." The Mexican worker became even more desirable because he was perceived to practice the "homing pigeon" syndrome, which was to work in the United States and returned to Mexico when the work was completed. *Corridos* about Mexicans being recruited by American companies once again detail this important aspect of American history. There are numerous corridos such as *"Del Interior o los Enganchados"* [From the Interior or the Contract Laborers], *"De 'La Maquinita' o de 'El Emigrante'"* [The Little Machine or the Immigrant], *"Corrido de Pensilvania"* [The Pennsylvania Corrido], and others that narrate the Mexican worker coming to build American railroads. There is also a hilarious novel by Daniel Venegas titled *Las aventuras de don Chipote o cuando los pericos mamen* (The Adventures of Don Chipote, or When Parrots Suckle Their Young) (1928), written in a style that is very folklore oriented (i.e., with folk speech liberally interspersed throughout the narrative and folk characters as protagonists).

It was during the second half of the nineteenth century that the development of the acculturation and assimilation process of the Chicano people in the United States became manifest. Because there was a significant itinerant population of migrant workers, railroad workers, and the others, now terribly impoverished, that chose to stay in the United States after the United States–Mexico war, a traveling type of folk theater, reminiscent of medieval traveling theaters, flourished during these decades. It was popularly known as *teatro de carpa* or "tent theater" because it was associated with traveling circuses and tents were the main setting in which these itinerant theaters performed. The scenery was minimal and the performances consisted of skits and one-act plays. Here one type of folk theater is performed, and it is also here that the use of *caló*, or speech related to the working classes, the lumpen proletariat, and the delinquent elements is used. It is in this setting that we also see the development of code-switching in English and Spanish in particular to form the basis of humor, be it through bilingual jokes or in the text of the skit itself. The *teatro de carpas* yearly toured the Southwest, stopping at the barrios or

Mexican neighborhoods in major cities as well as smaller towns and rural areas where the Chicano population tended to reside.

While California was developing at a rapid pace and constant immigration was pouring in, displacing the old Californio ranchos and hacienda way of life, New Mexico was not perceived as being as lucrative for Anglo-American settlers as California and therefore was able to preserve its traditions for a longer period of time. New Mexico did not become part of the Union until 1912 in part due to Anglo reluctance to admit a state with such a high number of Hispanics/Mexican Americans. It was not until the 1920s–1940s that New Mexican authors began to write about their disappearing traditional way of life. New Mexican traditions in all genres of folklore are legendary and are particularly noticeable today in its architecture, its cuisine, its religious festivals, and the preservation of seventeenth-century Spanish vocabulary and idiomatic expressions. In particular, New Mexico is famous for the conservation of its folk theater such as the *pastorelas* (Christmas nativity plays), the *Matachines* dance, and *Los Comanches* (depicting a famous battle between Spanish soldiers and Pueblo Indians that took place in the eighteenth century).

In Texas, while the culture clash continued unabated, the development of Chicano folklore as distinct from Mexican folklore continued to grow. In particular, the Mexican-Texan musical traditions (Tex-Mex) began to be greatly influenced by the new German and Slavic (Polish and Yugoslavian) settlers who brought with them their own cultural traditions from Europe. The accordion became a major musical instrument in Chicano musical traditions such as the polka and the corrido. What has become known as *música tejana*, or Tex-Mex music, crystallized in the second half of the nineteenth century. The Texas-Mexican cuisine continued to develop during this period also and has acquired international distinction. Its effect on Anglo-American folk traditions has been phenomenal, as is evident in the hundreds of barbeque festivals in Texas (and the South) as well as the chili cook-offs, the barbeque grills in every back yard, the *fajita* phenomenon, the *jalapeño* jellies and eating contests, the *nachos,* and tortilla chips and other culinary delights the Texas Mexicans created and disseminated.

IV. THE MEXICAN REVOLUTION OF 1910–1921 AND WORLD WAR I

The Mexican Revolution of 1910–1917 had a profound effect on Mexican immigration to the United States since the violent upheaval to the south produced untold grief, suffering, and destruction in the Mexican population. Numerous individuals and their families from the middle and working classes picked up their belongings and left for the United States. The large influx of immigrants, many from Mexican urban centers, settled in the large U.S. cities such as Los Angeles, San Francisco, Chicago, and San Antonio, and initiated the development of small Mexican neighborhoods or "little Mexicos."

The United States during this period had a more or less open border for Mexicans since the building of the infrastructure to sustain a fast-growing population necessitated the strong arms and bodies of workers. In 1907 the curtailment of Japanese immigration with the passing of the Gentlemen's Agreement Act (again due to the fear by the Anglo-American population of a yellow peril or fear of Asian overpopulation) once again encouraged Mexican immigrants to come and work in the United States.

A second major factor affecting Mexican migration to the United States was this country's entrance in the European conflict known as World War I in 1914–1918. The war-torn European countries needed food supplies for they were unable to grow their own crops given the violent state of affairs. The United States, particularly the states of California and Texas were poised to feed Europe with the fertile and bountiful agricultural lands that were ready to produce all types of fruits and vegetables. The completion of the railroad linking east to west and the invention of the refrigerated railroad cars provided the means by which the produce from the western states could be safely carried to the East Coast. Mexican workers were constantly recruited by American companies in what were called *enganches*—literally "hooks," because the Mexican worker was "hooked" to go work in the United States with promises of making plenty of dollars. The *corridos* of this period detail the numerous train trips from the interior of Mexico to the United States. Employment agencies eagerly recruited Mexicans. For example, there is one *corrido* in which the *enganche* of Mexican workers takes them to the steel mills of Pennsylvania; this song is titled *"Corrido de Pensilvania."*

V. MEXICAN AMERICAN ASSIMILATION AND ACCULTURATION (1921–1930)

The *corrido* is the main musical folk genre that surfaces during the Mexican Revolution and continued to flourish thereafter in both Mexico and the United States. Other traditions had already been firmly established in the past centuries although these traditions were not static but continued to expand and evolve particularly with the constant flow of new immigrants from Mexico who kept replenishing the old traditions and bringing in new ones from the different states in Mexico from which they came.

A second genre that developed in the 1920s was folk speech, as English was having a considerable effect on the Spanish language. New forms of expressions and vocabulary using both English and Spanish (code-switching) were introduced, as well as new words invented using English words and transforming them into Spanish words such as *cuora* ["koura"] for quarter, *nicle* ["nikle"] for nickel, *traque* [trake] for railroad tracks, and so forth. This mixture of Spanish and English infuriated Mexicans in Mexico, and the pejorative term *pocho,* referring to Mexican Americans, began to gain currency during this period. It is a term used to designate Mexicans born or raised in the United States and especially those who have lost the traditions and customs associated with being Mexican. Nevertheless, Mexican Americans continued to assimilate and acculturate, particularly during the 1920s, when new generations were being born—the offspring of the immigrant generations that had migrated during the Mexican Revolution.

VI. REPATRIATION AND DEPORTATION OF MEXICANS AND MEXICAN AMERICANS (1930–1942)

A rude awakening began to set in by the late 1920s. The tremendous immigration from Southern Europe (darker skinned peoples) brought in a sense of panic to the nativist Anglo-American population who feared the darker "races." In 1924 the Border Patrol was instituted, and the U.S. Congress passed the Quota Act of 1924. Mexicans were not included in the Quota Act due to strong pressure from agribusiness leaders, who felt they needed the Mexican workers for their agricultural fields. Nevertheless, by the late 1920s an economic depression began to set in, and Mexicans began to be targeted for deportations. The 1930s brought a full-fledged economic depression, and Mexicans began to be deported en mass. Some Mexican Americans, even though they were citizens, were also deported or "encouraged" to go to Mexico.

The Mexican government reacted by instituting a Repatriation Program in the late 1920s and 1930s in order to manage the huge influx of Mexicans and Mexican Americans who were being deported and basically dumped at the border cities of Mexico. There is a significant repertoire of *corridos* depicting this painful era, many of which detail the travails of being deported to Mexico. These folk songs provide important historical account of what happened to Mexicans and American citizens of Mexican descent during the 1930s decade. Such corridos as *"Deportados"* [Deportees], *"El Emigrado"* [The Immigrant"], *"Los Repatriados"* [The Repatriated Ones"], and *"Corrido de la Triste Situación"* [The Ballad of the Sad Situation] are excellent examples. Another genre of folklore that gained impetus was the *canción* [song] and

Tex-Mex music [Texas-Mexican]. Because a portion of the Mexican American population from the state of Texas dated their ancestry from the 1700s, many were settled in their small plots of land who survived the immigration raids and deportations, which tended to target urban areas. During the 1930s what has become known as ethnic or race records began to be produced by small companies owned by Chicanos. A small cottage industry arose, particularly in the Rio Grande Valley and San Antonio area. Eventually this led to the rise of *conjunto* music (a small group of musicians composed of guitar, accordion, and drums) which is best known for polka music and country style songs (*canción ranchera*).

Nevertheless, the deportations had a deleterious effect on a Mexican American folk genre. For example, by the early 1940s, the *teatro de carpas* [tent theater], which concentrated its efforts in urban centers, areas that were the hardest hit in terms of deportations, had basically disappeared.

VII. THE BRACERO PROGRAM (1942–1964)

The 1930s economic depression dealt a hard blow to Mexican immigration. However, this state of affairs did not last long. In 1942, the United States entered another world conflict even larger than the first one in 1914–18: World War II. Once again Europe was in great need of food supplies, and the U.S. agricultural lands needed workers to harvest the crops. The railroads too needed workers to keep the tracks in good physical condition. Mexico, however, was very reticent about sending workers to the United States after the 1930s deportations. It wanted guarantees that its workers would be protected and would not be summarily expelled once they were no longer needed. Therefore, before agreeing to allow Mexicans to enter the United States, the Mexican government insisted certain conditions had to be met. An agreement between the United States and Mexico was hammered out in 1942, and the accord for the importation of Mexican laborers became known as the Bracero Program. Workers by the thousands came to work in the agricultural fields, as well as the railroads, and they labored not only in the Southwest but in such states as Wyoming, Idaho, Washington, Minnesota, Wisconsin, Colorado, Utah, and many other states of the Union. Again, *corridos* depict this era when once again the urban areas as well as rural areas were replenished with the Mexican population. The Bracero Program was supposed to end after World War II ended, but agribusiness was so pleased with the workers that the Program was renewed repeatedly. This went on until 1964, when it finally ended partly because of the pressure exerted by César Chávez and the United Farm Workers' Union.

The influx of Mexican immigrants who came mainly from rural areas stimulated the growth of Tex-Mex music, with its lively polka beat and working-class performers. The new immigrants brought with them Mexican culture and traditions, and this reinforced the Mexican traditions that had been in the United States for centuries. Each wave of new immigrants, then, has prevented Mexican oral traditions from disappearing. Thus foodways continued to thrive and expand, the Spanish language has repeatedly been reinforced, Mexican songs in vogue in central and southern Mexico were introduced to the Southwest, and belief systems kept on being replenished. The 1950s also saw a rise in new consciousness with respect to Mexican American rights as citizens. The GI Forum, which consisted of Chicano veteran soldiers who had fought in World War II and in the Korean conflict, united to form a group that began to articulate grievances such as segregated schools, restaurants, and cemeteries in Texas.

In academia, Américo Paredes, through his scholarship in folklore studies, challenged stereotypical perceptions of Mexican Americans. His book "*With His Pistol in His Hand*": *A Border Ballad and Its Hero* (1958) is a landmark in *corrido* and Chicano folklore studies. It is an outstanding analysis of one *corrido* (and its variants): the "Ballad of Gregorio Cortez." He initiated contemporary Chicano folklore scholarship with the publication of dozens of articles focusing on the Chicano population.

VIII. THE CHICANO/A MOVEMENT (1965–PRESENT)

The date 1965 is commonly acknowledged as the beginning of the Chicano civil rights movement and the Chicano/a literary renaissance. It is the birth of the Teatro Campesino initiated by Luis Valdez and his group of actors. The Teatro Campesino derived much of its form from the folk *teatro de carpas,* which needed very little scenery and was devoid of fancy theater buildings. Much of the Teatro Campesino's repertoire was heavily influenced by folklore, and the *corrido* was one of its most commonly used forms of musical expressions. In addition, the one-act plays or skits utilized had much to do with stock characters such as *la muerte* [death], the devil, the good farm worker, and the evil contractor and/or patron or boss.

The renaissance of the *corrido* also occurred in 1965, since the farm workers union organizer, César Chávez, used *corrido* singing as a form of entertainment and for rousing the crowds at their frequent strikes, meetings, demonstrations, and boycott gatherings. There are numerous *corridos* whose principal theme is César Chávez and the farm workers organizing efforts.

The student-led Chicano movement in the 1960s was also imbued with folklore elements. There was a new emphasis on recapturing the Chicanos/ as' indigenous past, and Mesoamerican myths of the Aztecs and the Mayas served as rallying points for the nationalist movement of the 1960s and early 1970s. The myth of Aztlán was reintroduced and elaborated upon, not only by Chicano scholars and political leaders of the student movement, but also by the poets, fiction writers, and visual artists who somehow felt very much connected to this myth. The Aztlán myth is related to the history of the Aztecs who migrated from a place in the north (in a mythical place called Aztlán) and traveled south to found their empire in Tenochtitlan (present-day Mexico City). The Chicano movement reconnected to the ancient gods and goddesses of the Aztec, Toltec, and Mayan worlds. Most important among these gods was Quetzalcoatl, or the Plumed Serpent. The chapters that follow examine these folklore genres in detail and provide ample examples.

REFERENCES

Bevans, Charles I. ed. 1972. *Treaties and Other International Agreements of the United States of America, 1776–1949.* Vol. 9. Washington, DC: Department of State, 1972.

Díaz del Castillo, Bernal . 1967. *Historia verdadera de la conquista de la Nueva España.* [1632].Mexico City: Editorial Porrúa.

Hobsbawn, Eric. 1969. *Bandits.* New York: Delacorte Press.

Lafaye, Jacques. 1998. "Mexican Casta Painting: Caste Society in New Spain." *Artes de México: La Pintura de Castas.* 2 (8):81–83.

Leal, Luis. 2005. "The Malinche-Llorona Dichotomy: The Evolution of a Myth." In *Feminism, Nation and Myth: La Malinche,* ed. Rolando Romero and Amanda Nolacea Harris, 134–38. Houston: Arte Público Press.

Paredes, Américo. 1958. *"With His Pistol in His Hand": A Border Ballad and Its Hero.* Austin: University of Texas.

Ridge, John R. (Yellow Bird). 1854. *The Life and Adventures of Joaquín Murieta, the Celebrated Bandit.* San Francisco.

———. 1986. *Joaquín Murieta.* Norman: University of Oklahoma Press, 1986.

Sahagún, Fray Bernardino. 1953–1982. *Florentine Codez: General History of the Things of New Spain,* 2nd ed. Trans. Arthur J. O. Anderson and Charles Dibble. Salt Lake City: University of Utah/ Santa Fe, NM: The School of American Research, Museum of New Mexico.

Two
Definitions and Classifications

FOLKLORE

The term *folklore* has been defined in different ways throughout the centuries by scholars interested in this particular area of cultural production. In its early stages of development, folklore was conceptualized in England as the study of "antiquities" or "popular literature." It was not until 1846 that William Thoms suggested using the term *folklore* as a more fitting replacement for these two terms and provided an enumerative type of definition by listing the various genres included within the general concept of the term. While Thoms' definition was enumerative, it nevertheless contained the basic kernel that was to be used up to the present century and that is the emphasis on the "oral traditions" component. One of the most comprehensive definitions of *folklore* is Alan Dundes's, which appeared in his article "What Is Folklore?" published in 1965. His definition provides a fairly exhaustive list of the forms of folklore:

> Folklore includes myths, legends, folktales, jokes, proverbs, riddles, chants, charms, blessings, curses, oaths, insults, retorts, taunts, teases, toasts, tongue-twisters, and greetings and leave-taking formulas (e.g., See you later, alligator). It also includes folk costume, folk dance, folk drama (and mime), folk art, folk belief (or superstition), folk medicine, folk instrumental music (e.g., fiddle tunes), folk-songs (e.g., lullabies, ballads), folk speech (e.g., slang), folk similes (e.g., as blind as a bat), folk metaphors (e.g., to paint the town red), and names (e.g., nicknames and place names). Folk poetry ranges from oral epics to autograph-book verse, epitaphs, latrinalia (writing on the walls of public bathrooms), limericks, ball bouncing rhymes, jump-rope rhymes, finger and toe rhymes, dandling rhymes

(to bounce children on the knee), counting-out rhymes (to determine who will be "it" in games), and nursery rhymes. The list of folklore forms also contains games; gestures; symbols; prayers (e.g., graces); practical jokes; folk etymologies; food recipes; quilt and embroidery designs; house, barn, and fence types; street vendor's cries; and even the traditional conventional sounds used to summon animals or to give them commands. There are such minor forms as mnemonic devices (e.g., the name Roy G. Biv to remember the colors of the spectrum in order), envelope sealers (e.g., SWAK—Sealed With A Kiss), and the traditional comments made after body emissions (e.g., burps or sneezes). There are such major forms as festivals and special day (or holiday) customs (e.g., Christmas, Halloween, and birthday). (Dundes 1965, 3)

In addition, the word *folkloristics* was also coined in the 1960s to differentiate the forms of folklore from the study and theorizing about these forms themselves. In other words, in the 1950s and 1960s there was a general shift from merely collecting folklore items to critically analyzing, theorizing about, and interpreting this important area of cultural production. It should be pointed out that in Latin America and Mexico the term *tradiciones populares* [popular traditions] and *cultura popular* [popular culture] are used interchangeably with the word *folklore*, which is sometimes spelled *folclore or folclor*. Popular culture for folklorists in the United States is another area of study that includes films, television productions, cartoons, magazines, contemporary songs written by professional song writers, amusement parks, popular works of fiction such as the romance and western fiction genre, and in general that culture produced by the mass media and contemporary society.

This chapter focuses on the definitions and classificatory systems extant for the major genres or categories of Chicano/a folklore. These genres include folk narratives (myths, legends, folktales, and jests); folk songs (*corrido, canción ranchera,* and *décima* and conjunto music), folk speech (proverbs; proverbial expressions such as comparisons, exaggerations, jargon or *caló*; riddles; and tongue twisters); folk dance and folk costumes; folk belief; folk medicine and folk ailments; folk food; folk arts and crafts; folk theater; children's songs and games; and folk celebrations.

FOLK NARRATIVE

Included under the general category of folk narrative are myths, folktales, legends, and jests. I have provided a useful table conceptualized by William Bascom in "The Forms of Folklore: Prose Narratives" (1965, 6). The table highlights the differences and similarities among myths, legends, and folktales.

William Bascom's Table for Differentiating Prose Narratives

1	Formal features	PROSE NARRATIVES		
2	Conventional opening	None		Usually
3	Told after dark	No restrictions		Usually
4	Belief	Fact		Fiction
5	Setting	Some time and some place		Timeless, placeless
5a	Time	Remote past	Recent past	Any time
5b	Place	Earlier or other world	World as it is today	Any place
6	Attitude	Sacred	Sacred and secular	Secular
7	Principal character	Non-human	Human	Human or non-human
	Form of prose narrative	Myth	Legend	Folktale

Myths

Myths are sacred stories that narrate the lives of the gods before the universe and the world had been created or at that point when the universe was being formed. They are told in mythic time (i.e., indefinite time, in the time of the gods). The Chicano people have inherited their myths principally from the Aztecs and the Mayas. Some of the most popular myths include the myths related to Aztlán, the Priest-God Quetzalcóatl, the Moon Goddess Coyolxauhqui, the Sun-War God Huitzilopochtli, the Fifth Sun, the Earth Mother Goddess Coatlicue, the Mother Goddess Tonantzin, and the Water God Tlaloc. The classificatory system used for classifying motifs devised by Stith Thompson and known as *Motif Index of Folk-Literature: A Classification of Narrative Elements in Folktales, Ballads, Myths, Fables, Mediaeval Romances, Exempla, Fabliaux, Jest-Books, and Local Legends* (revised and enlarged 1955) is applicable to the classification of motifs for the pre-Columbian myths. These include:

A. Mythological motifs

A0–A99	Creator
A100–A499	Gods

A500–A599	Demigods and Culture Heroes
A600–A899	Cosmogony and Cosmology
A900–A999	Topographical Features of the Earth
A1000–A1099	World Calamities
A1100–A1199	Establishment of Natural Order
A1200–A1699	Creation and Ordering of Human Life
A1700–A2199	Creation of Animal Life
A2200–A2599	Animal Characteristics
A2600–A2699	Origin of Trees and Plants
A2700–A2799	Origin of Plant Characteristics

FOLKTALES

One of the major characteristics of the folktale is that the action of the tale occurs in undefined period of time. The popular formula "Once upon a time . . ." indicates this particular identifying characteristic of the genre. The Spanish formula *"En aquellos tiempos . . ."* also frames the action of the tale in an undefined period of time, although both formulas indicate the time period the action took place a long, long time ago. The geographic setting is in this world, although for the most part it is also in an undefined geographic area; for example, the tale might state "in a kingdom by the sea." The characters or protagonists of the tales may be human beings, animals, or supernatural beings (e.g., fairies, ogres, monsters, the devil, ghosts). Another major identifying characteristic is that these tales are not believed. People are aware that these types of tales are derived from the imagination as opposed to the corpus of myths belonging to a group of people who may believe them to be sacred stories which are true.

The classificatory system for the folktales of the world was devised by two scholars: Antti Aarne from Finland and Stith Thompson from the United States. Aarne published his classificatory system under the title *Verzeichnis der Märchentype* (*Index of Folktale Types*) in 1910, and Thompson published his work as *The Types of the Folktale* (1928). The combined classificatory systems are known as Aarne-Thompson Folktale Types (A-T) and are categorized with the following numbering system:

I. Animal Tales

1–99	Wild Animals
100–149	Wild Animals and Domestic Animals
150–199	Man and Wild Animals
200–219	Domestic Animals

| 220–249 | Birds |
| 250–274 | Fish |

II. Ordinary Folktales

300–749	A. Tales of Magic
300–399	Supernatural Adversaries
400–459	Supernatural or Enchanted Husband (Wife) or Other Relatives
460–499	Superhuman Tasks
500–559	Supernatural Helpers
560–649	Magic Objects
650–699	Supernatural Power or Knowledge
700–749	Other Tales of the Supernatural
750–849	B. Religious Stories
850–999	C. Novelle (Romantic Tales)
1000–1199	D. Tales of the Stupid Ogre

III. Jokes and Anecdotes

1200–1349	Numskull Stories
1350–1439	Stories about Married Couples
1440–1524	Stories about a Woman (Girl)
1525–1874	Stories about a Man (Boy)
1875–1999	Tales of Lying
2000–2399	Formula Tales
2400–2499	Unclassified Tales

Equally useful in folktale research is Thompson's motif-index cited previously (*Motif-Index of Folk-Literature*). The motif-index provides a classificatory system of motifs, which then allows for the comparison of folktales throughout the world via the motifs included within their plot. Major categories of motifs are as follows:

A. Mythological Motifs	(A0–A2799)
B. Animals	(B0–B799)
C. Tabu	(C10–C961.1)
D. Magic	(D0–2145.1.1)
E. The Dead	(E0–E780.1)
F. Marvels	(F0–F1035)
G. Ogres	(G10–G532)
H. Tests	(H0–H1538)

J. The Wise and the Foolish	(J0–J2661.4)
K. Deceptions	(K0–K2371.1)
L. Reversal of Fortunes	(L10–L435.2.1)
M. Ordaining the Future	(M211–M372)
N. Chance and Fate	(N2.2–N831.1)
P. Society	(P15.1–P312)
Q. Reward and Punishment	(Q2.–Q502.1)
R. Captives and Fugitives	(R11.1–R311)
S. Unnatural Cruelty	(S11.–S431)
T. Sex	(T11.4.1–S431)
V. Religion	(V361)
W. Traits of Character	(W111.1–W111.3.2)
X. Humor	(X111–X1020)
Z. Miscellaneous Groups of Motifs	(Z0–Z311)

In addition to European folktales inherited via Spain, Mexico, and Anglo-American culture, Chicanos have also inherited folktales from the indigenous groups in Mexico as well as from Native Americans in the Southwest. Many of the animal tales, such as the coyote cycle of tales, are derived from Native American oral traditions from the Southwest. Thus, Chicanos have a rich repertoire of folktales from numerous cultural traditions. Some of the well-known scholars who have collected, classified, and/or written about Chicano folktales include Aurelio Macedonio Espinosa, José Manuel Espinosa, Juan Rael, Arthur L. Campa, Stanley Robe, Américo Paredes, and Luis Leal.

Fairy tales are a subgenre of the folktale. These fairly large corpus of narratives tend to include a fairy within the plot of the story such as in Cinderella. Although fairies are not a sine qua non of the fairy tale. Chicano folklore has inherited its large collection of fairy tales from the Spanish, Mexican, and Anglo-American tradition. Therefore, most narratives under the heading of fairy tales are found in the Chicano oral tradition. The same is true for the compendium of stories under the heading of "Mother Goose" stories as well as those found in the collections of the Brothers Grimm, Hans Andersen's fairy tale collections, and Aesop's collection of moral fables. European folk narratives are part of the cultural heritage of the Chicano people, whether in English or Spanish.

LEGENDS

Legends are defined as folk narratives whose action takes place in historical time in a specific geographic space on earth and with protagonists that may be human or supernatural. Examples include legends about haunted houses, geographic spaces, bodies of water, ghosts, werewolves, vampires, the devil, saints, ogres, monsters, animals, and other supernatural beings. Legends can also be about persons or events such as folk healers and historical figures as Francisco Villa, Emiliano Zapata (both Mexican heroes from the Mexican Revolution of 1910–1917). Other culture heroes include Joaquín Murrieta, Gregorio Cortez, and Jacinto Treviño. Three of the most famous legends from the Mexican/Chicano cultural complex are the Virgin of Guadalupe, La Malinche, and La Llorona. All of these figures date from the 1500–1531 period. Legends also can be classified by using Stith Thompson's motif-index of folk literature.

JESTS (JOKES)

Chicano humor shares many similarities with Mexican and Hispanic humor in general. However, due to their unique socio-historical and political position in the United States, Chicanos/as have developed a joking pattern that identify such humor as expressly Chicano or Mexican American. Within folkloristics, jokes have been classified under the category of folk narratives but differ from the other categories such as myth and legend because of the main characteristic of this genre: the humorous elements. Américo Paredes posited that numerous Chicano jokes are derived from the intercultural experience between Anglo-American and Mexican Americans. The culture clash between the two groups has given rise to a large corpus of jokes in which the Mexican American bests the Anglo or in which the Anglo appears in a ridiculous or humiliating position. There are many other jokes, however, deriving from a single protagonist or from events. Some of these joke categories are detailed in the following sections.

Political Jokes

Political jokes are important because they offer insights into the worldview and political interest of the joke narrator as well as the political atmosphere extant in a nation. Through humor, joke narrators reveal attitudes toward such things as the voting process and the high or low regard they have for politicians and government services such as the welfare system, the schools, the police, and national symbols such as the flag. An example of this is evident in the following joke told by Mexicans regarding the Mexican and American flag:

¿Qué le dijo la bandera mexicana a la Americana? [What did the Mexican flag tell the American flag?]

¡Por pendeja te estrellaste! ¡Pónte águila como yo! [Because of your stupidity you were shattered. Be a sharp eagle like me.]

The joke makes reference to the stars and stripes of the American flag and the eagle on the Mexican one. This attitude of wit and intelligence on the part of the Mexican and stupidity on the part of the American is reiterated in a number of jokes. Paredes attributes this to the political tensions the two countries have had for hundreds of years and posits the theory of culture clash as a major element in the cultural production of Chicanos.

Religious Jokes

The relationship between human beings and their god(s) is a significant component of a culture. This relationship, however, has many variables and is difficult to ascertain by a simple analysis of the formal religious beliefs and rituals of a people. Furthermore, this socio-spiritual dimension is not static but is in continuous flux. An excellent source of information shedding light on this aspect of human endeavor is the joking patterns exhibiting religious themes. Most Chicanos/as belong to the Catholic Church. It is surprising to note, therefore, that a large number of jokes reveal a tendency toward the erotic when dealing with religious orders and the priesthood in general. The following joke told by a Chicano student exemplifies this:

> There are two . . . three nuns coming to heaven and Saint Peter opens the door and he asks . . . he tells them they cannot come in to heaven today because heaven is completely full. But that they could go back to earth and . . . do anything they wanted to do and they could come back without this counting against them. So after Saint Peter says that, the nuns start smiling. So Saint Peter asks one of them what she was going to do when she went back to earth. And she said, "Well, I am going to be Brigitte Bardot for a night." Saint Peter said, "Oh, that's pretty good." Then he asked the other one what she was going to be when she went back to earth. She said she wanted to be for one night Gina Lollobrigida. "Hmmm," he said (Saint Peter). Then he asked the last nun what she was going to be and she said, "I'm going to be Iraca Papolini." Saint Peter's reaction is kind of confused. He said, "I never heard that person before." The nun said, "Yeah, just look!" She takes out a newspaper clipping which says: "Iraq pipeline laid by 100 men."

Mexican Immigrant Jokes

The political boundary erected between the United States and Mexico has been ineffectual in curtailing the flow of people traveling in and out of both countries. This never-ending human migration taking place for more than

150 years has given rise to a corpus of folklore related to the difficult and not infrequently painful experience of crossing the United States–Mexican border, either legally or undocumented. In this type of jokes the Mexican immigrant is featured as the main protagonist. Many of these humorous narratives are based on a play on words between English and Spanish or a misunderstanding of one language or the other. These jokes are generally told by Mexican immigrants living in the United States. They therefore serve the function of objectifying the painful experience of being an immigrant and not knowing the language, thus relieving the anxiety associated with this condition.

Mother-in-Law Jokes

Mother-in-law jokes are a favorite topic for American television and nightclub stand-up comics. The image of the mother-in-law in American humor has tended to be extremely negative. She is usually domineering, insensitive, overly concerned with cleanliness and tending to overstay her welcome at a couples' home. A visit by a mother-in-law is viewed as one of the worst disasters befalling a couple. Her lack of tact is clearly exposed in her desire to accompany the couple on their honeymoon. Mexican American humor tends to share some of these features when it comes to mother-in-law jokes. Mother-in-law jokes is a category that highlights the interrelationship between family members.

Pepito Jokes

Pepito jokes have as their principal protagonist a young boy around six or seven who is sexually precocious. Pepito jokes have a high sexual content and are extremely popular throughout Mexico, Spain, and Latin America. These jokes seem to be closely related to Greek Bobo jokes, which also feature the often sexually oriented adventures of a child.

Don Cacahuate Jokes

The Don Cacahuate [Mr. Peanut] jokes' main protagonist, Don Cacahuate, is usually displayed as a rather naive man but one who gets his point across in a humorous manner. He often has his wife, Doña Cebolla [Mrs. Onion] with him. Both characters come across as being quite clueless and naïve.

Pedro de Urdemalas

In this complex of jokes Pedro de Urdemalas [Peter Who Does Mischief], as the name implies, is always into some kind of mischief. The humor is derived from Pedro getting away with all types of misadventures and getting the best out of other people. He is a trickster type of figure.

Jokes about Women

Gender issues are often encountered in Chicano jokes. There is a whole complex of jokes related to women. These jokes are usually misogynist in nature and portray women in a disparaging manner.

El Colmo Jokes

There is a complex of jokes that were popular in the 1970s–1990s period and were called *chistes del colmo*. The word is difficult to translate, but it has more or less the meaning of the "last straw" type of event or action. The jokes were in the form of a riddle in which the key word *colmo* appears. These jokes exhibit a question and answer structure, and the humor lies in the double meaning of the words involved (either in the question or in the answer or both) or in the absurdity of the response. Examples:

Question: *¿Cuál es el colmo de la fuerza?* [What is the epitome of being strong?]

Answer: *Doblar una esquina.* [to fold (turn) a corner.]

Ethnic Jokes

Ethnic jokes reveal important attitudes regarding self and others. This type of jokes was common in the United States previous to the Civil Rights Movement of the 1960s and 1970s. Due to the pressure from ethnic minorities, they have generally fallen out of favor today. Chicanos, nevertheless, have in their repertoire jokes in which the main protagonist and/or secondary characters in the narrative belong to various racial groups. Popular among Chicanos are jokes in which three men of different nationalities are engaged in some type of contest. Usually an American appears among the contestants. Other nationalities commonly mentioned are the French, English, and Russians. As can be expected, the Mexican American triumphs in these events. Likewise Chicano jokes about Anglos usually pit a Chicano and an Anglo in some sort of confrontation. Again, the Chicano usually makes the Anglo appear ridiculous or gets the better of him or her through ingenuity and wit.

FOLK SONGS

The Mexican and Mexican American cultures have one of the richest traditions of folk music in the world. In part this is due to the large number of indigenous groups living in Mexico, each having their own splendid musical heritage. For example, the Yucatan peninsula has a marvelous cultural heritage because of the numerous groups of Maya Indians making their home there. And the Queretaro, Jalisco, the Huasteca area, Central Mexico, and Veracruz region all have distinct indigenous cultures and musical traditions. In addition, Mexico has experienced extensive European and African immigration; the French and Spanish influences having been well documented. However, the German, Polish, and Anglo-American influence on Chicano music has not been thoroughly studied, although some Chicano scholars such as Manuel Peña have delved into this important area of Mexican American cultural folksong influence. Among the multiplicity of folksong genres we can include the *corrido, canción, canción ranchera, indita, décima, vals,* polka, schotiz, *alabado, romance, balada, mambo,* rock and roll, cha cha cha, *canción tropical,* bolero, tango, *valona, son, cuando, salsa, cumbia, merengue, bachata, quebradita,* conjunto music (also known as Norteño music or Tex-Mex music), *banda,* and several other categories too numerous to mention. All of these are part of the musical traditions of the Chicano people. One of the most important genres, however, is the *corrido,* or Mexican ballad, in terms of quantity and in terms of socio-political and cultural importance it has had and continues to have in the community.

The Rise of the Corrido

Merle Simmons, in his excellent article "The Ancestry of Mexico's *Corridos*" (Simmons 1963), delineated the *corrido*'s historical journey from *romance* to its present form. Simmons found that traditional Spanish ballads approximating the structure and thematic manner of the *corrido* existed throughout the colonial period in the years preceding the resurgence of these songs. Simmons (1963) gave rise to a scholarly debate between Simmons and Américo Paredes, the Chicano folklore scholar and *corrido* foremost authority. Although recognizing the *corrido*'s ancestry in the romance, Paredes's writings distinguish between "traditional ballads," which he views as "survivals of a moribund tradition tentatively evolving into something else," and a ballad tradition, the second implying "a crystallization of those survivals at one particular time and place into a whole ballad corpus, which by its very weight impresses itself on the consciousness of the people" (Paredes 1958, 104). Both scholars agree, however, that the *corrido* is a vigorous ballad tradition which emerged in the second half of the nineteenth century after its long gestation in the colonial period and proved to be the form par excellence that met the political and expressive needs of both an ethnic group in the United States (i.e., the Chicanos/as) and the Mexican nation.

A second scholarly dispute arose between Paredes and Vicente T. Mendoza, the eminent Mexican folklore scholar, related to the rise of the *corrido*. The discussion revolves around the chronological states of this genre's supposed rise and "fall." Mendoza suggests three phases of *corrido* production: (1) its emergence as a political weapon of protest against the dictatorship of Porfirio Díaz (1880–1910); (2) its explosion during the years of the revolution (1910–1917), when *corrido* production reached its nadir both in quality and quantity, and (3) the post-1930 period of decline (Mendoza 1974,15–16). Américo Paredes, on the other hand, postulates that there was indeed a hiatus in the colonial period when *corrido* production was at a minimum. However, Paredes theorizes that the *corrido* was reborn in the Northern part of Mexico and the Southern part of Texas, (what is known as the Rio Grande Valley area or "Lower Texas-Mexican Border"), as a result of the culture conflict that ensued after the United States–Mexico War of 1848. The Texas-Mexican scholar posits that "border conflict, a cultural clash between Mexican and American, gives rise to the Texas-Mexican *corrido*. The Lower Border produces its first *corrido* hero, Juan Nepomuceno Cortina, in the late 1850s. By 1901, ten years before the beginning of the epic period of Greater Mexican balladry, the heroic tradition is fully developed in the Rio Grande area in such ballads as *"El Corrido de Gregorio Cortez"* (Paredes 1958, 104).

It was the clash of cultures between Anglo-Protestant America and Catholic-Latino Mexicans, asserts Paredes, that provided the classical historical conditions for the rise of a ballad tradition such as the one found between the English and Scottish border, and that of the frontier romances of the Christians and Moors (Paredes 1958, 241–247). Rural Texas-Mexicans, lacking the means of production, sang of their heroes *"defendiendo su derecho"* (defending their rights), as the *corrido* puts it, from the encroaching American colonizers. These incipient-protest *corridos* provided the paradigms on which Mexican rebel texts of the 1880s patterned themselves. If we are to accept Mendoza's and Paredes's arguments, two separate creative processes were taking place in Mexican society with respect to these musical compositions: one in Greater Mexico proper, and one in the Lower Texas-Mexican Border. Both traditions eventually produced classic *corridos* such as "Gregorio Cortez" in Texas and "Heraclio Bernal" in Northern Mexico. Mendoza and Paredes both agree on the characteristics of typical *corrido* protagonists: They are mostly male heroes (women appear in these songs mostly as secondary characters). The *corrido* is a predominately masculine form of literary musical expression that narrates principally the deeds, activities, aspirations, and adventures of male protagonists or male-related events such as war, battles, horse racing, and bullfighting. In spite of being a male-dominated genre, women have played and continued to play an important part in its development both in terms of singers and protagonists.

Both Mendoza and Paredes posited a decline of the *corrido*. However, I have posited in various writings that the *corrido* did not disappear, as had been predicted in various writings but that in fact the *corrido* experienced a "renaissance" in the 1960s, when César Chávez led the drive towards farm worker unionization and the Chicano movement saw new interest in oral traditions. The *corrido* has experienced a resurgence with the rise of Mexican immigration to the United States as well as with the rise of drug trafficking: the *narcocorrido* phenomenon.

The Mexican Revolution (1910–1917) and the Corrido

Historical events in the early twentieth century in Mexico supplied the *corridista* [*corrido* composer and singer] with the protean matter to fashion his or her excellent musical compositions. This is particularly true during the turbulent years of the Mexican Revolution (1910–1917) since with each new general rising from the ashes of a battle, a *corrido* was born to commemorate the event. The following chronological outline of Mexican history highlights important events that have been immortalized in *corridos* and are part of both the Chicano/a and Mexican cultural landscape.

The Revolution of 1910

1910. November 20. Revolution breaks out both in northern and southern Mexico.

1911. January 30. Ricardo Flores Magón and other socialists lead revolt in Baja California.

March 5. Francisco I. Madero defeated in northern Mexico.

March 6. U.S. President orders military soldiers to the Mexican border.

April 1. President Porfirio Díaz proposes a constitutional amendment for non-reelection of the President and Vice-President of Mexico.

May 25. President Porfirio Díaz resigns as president of Mexico.

October 15. Francisco Madero elected Constitutional President.

November 6. Madero inaugurated as President.

November 28. Emiliano Zapata publishes his *"Plan de Ayala."*

1913. February 22. President Madero and Vice-President Pino Suárez murdered.

March 26. Venustiano Carranza writes the "Plan of Guadalupe," appoints himself as First Chief of the Constitutionalist Revolution.

1914. April 2. City of Torreón surrenders to Constitutionalist troops under Francisco Villa.

April 21. American troops land at Veracruz.

July 15. President Victoriano Huerta resigns.

August 16. Venustiano Carranza enters Mexico City as First Chief of the Constitutionalist Army

November 1. The Aguascalientes Convention resolves that Carranza be removed from the post of First Chief and Villa from that of Commander-in-Chief of the northern armies (División del Norte) he led.

November 14. American troops leave Veracruz.

1915. April 16. Battle of Celaya and defeat of Francisco Villa.

1917. May 1. Carranza inaugurated as Constitutional President of Mexico.

(Zabre 1969, 51–53)

The Cristero Rebellion (1926–1929)

The Cristero Rebellion (1926–1929), a peasant-led movement protesting the anticlerical laws promulgated in the Mexican Constitution of 1917 (Articles 3, 5, 24, 27, and 130), similarly produced hundreds of *corridos* depicting the various events taking place during that blood-drenched period. Alicia Oliveira de Bonfil, in her study *La literatura cristera* (1970), divides the literary production of these years into three stages:

1. Period of Protest in which literary production is characterized by short verses, prayers (*oraciones*) and protest songs.

2. The Rebellion proper, where *corrido* production emerged as the main literary vehicle of expression.

3. Post-Rebellion period in which prose genres took over; the novel, the legend, the "relato."(Bonfil 1970, 2)

The Cristero rebellion was the result of devout Catholic *campesinos'* dissatisfaction with what they perceived as infringement of their civil and religious liberties and, more significantly, the slowness with which agrarian reform measures promised by the Mexican Revolution were being, or rather not being, implemented. The major geographical areas of rebellion were in the north central states of Jalisco, Guanajuato, and Zacatecas, and it was these areas that produced a large number of *corridos* detailing the various battles and events related to the Cristero conflict. Bonfil classifies the *corridos* produced during this conflict as follows: I. *Corridos* relating the heroic deeds of Cristero heroes, II. Cristero *corridos*, III. *Corridos* describing important Cristero battles, IV. *Corridos* describing historical events, V. *Corridos* describing political figures (Bonfil 1970, 26). The Cristero rebellion proved to be a fertile ground for *corrido* production.

1930s to 1964

While *corrido* production and creativity was ebbing in Central Mexico after the 1930s there was a resurgence in northern Mexico and the American Southwest, particularly in Texas. Philip Sonnichsen denominates the years between 1929 and 1935 the "Golden Age of the Recorded *Corrido*." Sonnichsen states, "It seems to me that the recorded tradition did indeed sustain the *corrido* tradition, as *corridos* were frequently expanded to fit both sides of a 78 rpm record" (Sonnichsen 1975, 1). Chris Strachwitz, who worked closely with Sonnichsen, attributes the "Golden Age" of the recorded *corrido* to the radio's phenomenal popularity in the 1920s and the consequent decline in regular record sales. Strachwitz deduces that these events forced the record companies to look into other available markets for possible sales, one of these markets being the ethnic and "race" one. Record companies initiated extensive ethnic talent recruitment in order to record those songs popular and marketable to specific regional groups. Mexican Americans proved to be a profitable ethnic minority who had a wide variety of musical groups available for recording and were willing to spend their money on the records (Strachwitz 1975). Strachwitz adds that although the years of the Great Depression brought *corrido* production almost to a halt,

> A strong resurgence of regional music took place at the end of World War II when returning GIs and well paid factory workers demanded 'down-home' music—or the music with which they had grown up. Record shop owners and juke box operators, finding that the major labels were unwilling or unable to supply this music, started small labels all over the country. In South Texas Ideal Records was perhaps the first local label to specialize in Mexican music although several firms like Globe and Imperial from Los Angeles were already involved. Falcon Records soon joined to help make almost every popular musician a recording artist in the area. Corridos began to appear once again—not only the commercial ones from Mexico's Tin Pan Alley, but regional ones, from Texas. (Strachwitz 1975, 30)

Some of the more popular recording companies were Ideal Records from south Texas and Globe, Imperial, and Falcon Records from Los Angeles.

César Chávez and the Renaissance of the Corrido, 1964–2005

The *corrido* experienced a renaissance with the rise of the farm workers' unionizing activities under the leadership of César Chávez in the 1960s. Chávez was trying to form a labor union in the agricultural fields of California so that farm workers could get better wages and better overall treatment, such as having sanitation facilities in the agricultural fields where the farm workers toiled, adequate drinking water, and other guarantees that other workers in the United States took for granted. It was not an easy task to unionize farm laborers, given the great number of them and their poverty level, but his organizational skills led him to include music in the various meetings, gatherings, and later the protest marches and boycotts he held to force agribusiness to recognize the United Farm Workers Union. The *corrido* became an excellent tool in Chávez's organizing efforts, and soon ballads began to be written detailing the benefits of the union and the rationale for forming a labor union.

Coupled with Chávez's unionizing drive, Luis Valdez and the Teatro Campesino became associated with the labor organizing activities and the education of the farm worker. The Teatro Campesino performed in the agricultural fields of California, on top of truck flatbeds, and in the migrant camps; they performed at the various marches, demonstrations, protest drives, and boycott activities. For the Teatro Campesino the *corrido* was a staple of their performance repertoire since the genre lent itself well to narrating the message the Teatro wanted to publicize. In this manner, the *corrido* became known for these very important aspects of the Chicano civil rights movement of the 1960s and turned into the form par excellence that could be used to inform the general population of the travails, injustices, oppression, and exploitation suffered by the Chicano people at the hands of hegemonic society. Thus, such balladeers as Rumel Fuentes from Texas and Francisco García attained some prominence as *corrido* writers during these 1960–1980 decades.

A second important element in keeping the *corrido* tradition alive and energized has been the continued influx of Mexican immigrants coming to the United States in search of jobs in the 1960s after the Bracero Program was terminated in 1964. This migration pattern did not decrease with time but in fact has been steadily increasing up to 2006. There has been much press coverage of the "illegal immigrant" or undocumented worker, as he or she is now called, both in Mexico and the United States. The intense focus on the "problem" of undocumented immigrants crossing the border has stimulated the Mexican immigrant *corrido* genre not only by buying these songs but by promoting the writing and singing of them. In addition, immigrants bring Mexican *corridos* as part of their cultural heritage, thus expanding the repertoire in the United States and aiding in their diffusion in this country. Immigrants provide the raison d'être for the subgenre of Mexican immigrant *corridos*.

The Narcocorrido [Drug-Smuggling Corrido]

The *corrido* continues to be an extremely popular form of musical entertainment and continues to evolve, producing new categories such as the *narcocorrido*. The *contemporary narcocorrido* traces its roots to the smuggling ballads dating from the 1880s. When Mexico lost the war with the United States in 1848, it also lost almost half of its territory, including the land encompassing the present states of California, Texas, Arizona, New Mexico, Nevada, Utah, and Colorado. These states were carved out of the territory ceded to the United under the terms of the Treaty of Guadalupe Hidalgo signed in 1848. From one day to the next people living on the northern side of the newly created U.S–Mexican border found themselves to be the new citizens of the United States. Nevertheless, since the borderline dividing California, Arizona, and New Mexico from Mexico was not a physical one and the borderline in Texas was the Rio Grande, people continued to go about their business as they had been doing prior to 1848. Technically, carrying products back and forth across the river or the imaginary line dividing the two nations was smuggling. In the 1880s "smuggling" consisted of textile goods that were ferried across the Rio Grande into Mexico. Later, during the Mexican Revolution in 1910–1917, smuggling consisted of guns and ammunition that were smuggled into Mexico to aid revolutionary soldiers in their quest for freedom from the 30-year dictatorship of Porfirio Díaz. The 1920s Prohibition Laws in the United States brought a new phase of Mexican smuggling; this time it was hard liquor—mainly tequila. There is a whole series of *corridos* depicting the exploits, apprehension, and incarceration of bootleggers, as they were called, such as *"Los Tequileros."* Smuggling consisted of bringing in tequila or other alcoholic beverages from Mexico into the United States, which at that time prohibited the production and selling of alcoholic beverages. After the Prohibition Laws were abolished, marijuana began to be smuggled into the United States. Nevertheless *corridos* dealing with narcotic smuggling did not come into their own until the 1970 with the hit *corrido* *"Contrabando y Traición,"* better known as *"Camelia La Tejana"* written by Angel González and performed by the Tigres Del Norte, a *corrido* singing group who became famous both in Mexico and the United States after their initial hit. *Narcocorrido* production continued to rise in the 1980s, as drug smuggling intensified and drug traffickers became wealthy and famous. These drug lords demanded *corridos* be written about them and their exploits; thus, several *corridos* depicting the adventures and misadventures of famous drug smugglers became extremely popular. Some of these *corridos* include *"Corrido de Miguel Angel Felix Gallardo," "Corrido de Caro Quintero," "Corrido de Pedro Aviles,"* and *"Los Gallos de Sinaloa."*

There are six major stages in the evolution of the *narcocorrido*:

1. Exemplum type *narcocorridos*: Early *narcocorridos* exhibited strong moralizing tendencies. They were more in line with the exemplum type *corrido* of an earlier period where the disobedient son or daughter is punished for misbehaving. In this *corrido*, the drug trafficker comes to a bad end; that is, he either dies or ends up in prison.

2. Commissioned *narcocorridos*: These *corridos* were generally commissioned by the drug lords. They wanted *corridos* to glorify their deeds and valor, so they paid *corridistas* to sing their praises.

3. *Narcocorridos* glorifying the trade: These *corridos* glorify the trade—that is, the money and power gained by drug trafficking.

4. *Narcocorridos* glorifying the actual use of the drugs: These *corridos* glorify the use of the various drugs that are commonly smuggled to the United States such as cocaine, heroine, marihuana, and so forth.

5. *Narcocorridos* using obscene words: The use of obscene or cursing in the lyrics is a recent phenomenon dating from the 2000s.

6. *Narcocorridos* with women involved in drug trafficking

Jenni Rivera, one of the few women who sing *narcocorridos*, has several *narcocorridos* in which the protagonist is a woman.

One of the more startling changes in the lyrics of the *corrido* and that is associated with the *narcocorrido* is the obscene words incorporated in the lyrics of these songs. The lyrics of *narcocorridos* have become increasingly permeated with curse words. In the past, *corridos* were basically free of curse words, but with the introduction of the *narcocorrido* drug lord as protagonist, the lyrics began to use obscene words related to the drug trafficking business. The *narcocorridos* have become so controversial that some states in Mexico, such as Chihuahua, passed legislation prohibiting the playing of these ballads on the radio. On the other hand, in the Los Angeles area, there was a radio station in 2004–2005 that had a daily program dedicated to playing *narcocorridos*.

This brief introduction highlights the historical and social factors effecting *corrido* production. It is obvious that the *corrido* has not disappeared and that the early predictions of its demise by Vicente T. Mendoza have not come to pass; indeed, the *corrido* tradition is as vigorous as ever with new ballads being composed by the hundreds and hitting the radio, television, film, stereo, iPod, and video waves daily.

Classification of the Corrido

Scholarly work on the classification of the *corrido* was done by Vicente T. Mendoza in the period encompassing the decades 1930–1960. His system was based on the thematic content of the *corrido* such as historical, revolutionary figures, agrarian reform movement, the Cristeros Rebellion, political, lyrical, execution of men, *corridos* depicting valiant men, *corridos* depicting bandits, prisoners, kidnappings, crimes, scandals, giving a hex, fatality, crimes of passion, accidents and disaster, horses, related to cities, parricide-type *corridos*, bull fighters, religious, biblical, moral type *corridos*, and "miscellaneous type *corridos*." *Corridos* can be written on any topic whatsoever and are thus difficult to classify since categories are constantly cropping up, as is the case with recent immigrant type *corridos* and the *narcocorrido*.

Formal Structure of the Corrido

In the next section the formal aspects of the *corrido* are highlighted, focusing on the flexible nature of its structure, a characteristic that in part explains the *corrido's* ability to survive and to please such a large segment of the Mexican and Chicano population. The *corrido's* meter, rhyme and strophe structure have been diligently studied by Danial Castañeda in his work *El corrido mexicano: su técnica literaria y musical* [The Mexican *Corrido*: Its Literary and Musical Structures] (1943). A brief overall view of the varied meters employed in the *corrido* demonstrates its flexibility and the ease in which numerous themes can be transformed into appropriate subject matter for *corridos*. Castañeda divides poetic rhyme into two major categories: (1) stanzas composed of one meter and (2) stanzas composed of two or more meters in various possible combinations. In the first category the stanzas are variously

1. octosyllabic
2. hexasyllabic
3. heptasyllabic
4. dodecasyllabic [with the syllabic rhyme scheme of (6–6), (8–4), (4–8), (5–7)]
5. decasyllabic syllabic rhyme scheme [(5–5), (4–6), (6–4), or (4–6), again alone or in combination)]
6. tridecasyllabic [(5–8) or (8–5), alone or in combination].

In item numbers 4, 5, and 6, the syllabic rhyme scheme may appear alone or in combination with the others.

The second category (stanza composed of two or more meters) yields similar possibilities. Some of these include

1. octosyllabic meter + hexasyllabic meter
2. octosyllabic meter + dodecasyllabic meter
3. octosyllabic meter + dodecasyllabic meter—both combined with an octosyl-labic meter such as:

   a. (12–8-12–8) and (8–8-8–8)
   b. (12–8-12–8) and (8–8-8–8)
   c. (12–8-12–8) and (8–8-12–8)

Castañeda has likewise devised a typological scheme for classifying the large variety of strophes found in the *corrido*:

Type 1: Stanza formed by one quartet

Type 2: Strophe formed by one quintet

Type 3: Strophe formed by one sextet

Type 4: Strophe formed by one octave

Type 5: Strophe formed by one *décima*

Type 6: Combination type strophe formed by two quartets, quintets or sextets (the meter may vary or be a combination thereof)

Language Register and Audience of the Corrido

The language used in the *corrido* is characterized by its archaic and *campesino* (farm worker) flavor. The colloquialisms or nonstandard Spanish words found in Mexican ballads generally show the same linguistic traits that are characteristic of other nonstandard Spanish dialects present throughout the Spanish-speaking world.

Corridistas generally belong to the lower strata of Mexican and Chicano society: their language register, or forms of expression, therefore, reflects their class origins. Colloquial expressions serve three major functions: (1) as a means of social identification, (2) to introduce humor and levity in the unfolding drama of the *corrido*, and (3) structural component.

With respect to the first function, that of social identification, the troubadour is aware of his or her audience's humble origins and opts for a style that reflects this reality. The choice of the colloquial style serves to imbue the lyrics of the ballad with a realistic *campesino* flavor. By utilizing the dialect variety of a word, the *pueblo* [people] identify more readily with the lyrics, insuring, to a certain extent, its popularity. The colloquialisms integrated in the lyrics identify, in turn, the balladeer as a bona fide member of the audience's social class. In employing a rural oriented dialect, composers and singers are implicitly asserting they are one of "them." This direct verbal identification with the common folk provides the balladeer with the right to expound on any subject concerning the people; to comment, satire, eulogize, and so forth political events and, most significantly, possess the freedom to flatter or discredit heroic figures. In fact, in order to be a successful *corridista* it is de rigueur for the poet to be psychologically attuned to the *pueblo*'s feelings. In conveying the political or social message of the *corrido*, he or she must meticulously avoid introducing any personal feeling that might cognitively and/or affectively clash with the people. Many learned poets have tried to imitate the style of the *corrido*. However, it is largely the unskilled use of colloquialisms that betray them as not belonging to the *pueblo*. It is indeed difficult, if not impossible, for a learned *"corridista"* to fool the pueblo.

A second function of interspersing colloquial words and expressions in the lyrics of the Mexican ballad is to inject humor in the text. Colloquial words often introduce a note of levity, since formal Spanish is put aside and this in turn provides an opportunity for humor. The *corrido* text generally carries a serious message, which, of course, can produce great anxiety in the audience. The introduction of colloquial words opens up a space for laughter and thus prevents the audience from becoming too depressed. The *corridista*'s aim, aside from delivering a message and to inform the public, is to entertain. Colloquial words provide an escape valve that lets out the pent-up emotion built up by the narrative of the *corrido*.

An equally important function of colloquialisms in the *corrido* is a structural one. The structural function can be divided into meter and rhyme. In structuring the meter of the *corrido,* the writer finds colloquialisms and ready-made proverbial expressions particularly useful. The lyrics of the *corrido* are generally composed of eight syllables per line. Therefore, if the author has one syllable too many, he or she can delete a syllable by using the colloquial variant of Spanish. For example, in the *"Corrido de Don Venustiano Carranza"* there are several instances of this technique:

¡Ora sí, señor Carranza,	Now, Mr. Carranza,
hasta aquí puso una raya	you have placed a demarcation line

pa' que no corra más sangre	so that no more blood shall flow
en los campos de batalla!	in the battlefields.

(Mendoza 1974, 39)

By using the colloquial words *ora* (*ahora* = now and *pa* = *para* = for) the author structures an eight-syllable line without destroying the meaning. Most *campesinos* and unlettered people commonly use *ora* and *pa*.

The second structural function that colloquialisms serve is that of providing rhyme to a line. For example, in *"El corrido de los combates de Celaya"* we have:

Y decían los carrancistas:	And the Carrancistas said:
Ahora de aquí no salemos,	"Now, from this place we can't get out
que si llegan los villistas	If Villa's men should come
aquí nos acabaremos.	We shall all perish here!"

(Mendoza 1974, 56–60)

By the insertion of *salemos* instead of the standard *salimos* (to go out; to exit) the rhyme is accomplished.

It is evident from the preceding analysis that colloquialisms present in the *corrido* are not there solely by chance or by mere whim of the *corridista* but are significant entities both in the structural configuration of the folksong as well as its social importance. The troubadour for the most part consciously selects a colloquial word for aesthetic purposes as well as social acceptability and humor.

Canción

The word *canción* is a general category for the classification of songs that can encompass any musical composition. It is similar to the word *song* in English, which is generic for any musical text. However, when one wants to be more specific, other categories come into play, and the word *canción* then refers to a very specific type of song. The *canción* is a musical composition that is lyrical in nature; it expresses deep emotions, profound sentiments, and tender, lyrical feelings, although at times the *canción* can express powerful emotions related to despondency from rejection by the loved one. The *canción* is derived from European and, most specifically, Spanish and Italian traditions dating from the Middle Ages. Recall that the Spaniards brought with them their musical heritage and taught them to the indigenous populations. Thus, the harp, the piano, the guitar, the *vihuela*, the violin, and other European instruments became part of Mexico's national legacy. Nevertheless, the Native American populations across the Americas had their own musical traditions, and therefore Mexican/Chicano music exhibits the influences of numerous indigenous peoples. A third important musical heritage is derived from the African cultures imported into Mexico via slavery and/or immigration. However, Vicente T. Mendoza asserts that for the *canción*, the Spanish and Italian influence are the most pronounced (Mendoza 1961).

There are literally thousands of *canciones;* therefore, a classificatory system has been difficult to devise. Mendoza has classified the *canción* in his book *La canción mexicana: Ensayo de clasificación y antología* [*The Mexican Canción: An Essay on Classification and an Anthology*], written in 1961, not by using a single vector but using various parameters for its classification. Following is Mendoza's classificatory system (Mendoza 1982, 19–21) [my translation].

    I. By chronological order

    II. By its classic structure: Mexican, romantic and sentimental

    III. By its musical form

    IV. According to the verse's meter

    V. According to the sentiments expressed in the text

    VI. (A). According to the type of text exhibited

    VII. (B). *Canciones* according to the type of text exhibited

    VIII. (A). According to its regional origin

    IX. (B). *Canciones* according to the geographic region from where they originate

    X. Foreign origin

    XI. According to the function of the song or the time in which it is sung

    XII. According to the form and style in which they are sung

    XIII. According to the rhythm and musical instruments used

    XIV. Songs related to various occupations, work, and circumstances

    XV. According to the elements employed

    XVI. Miscellaneous

Mendoza provides 314 examples of *canciones* to illustrate the 16 categories he posited in his book on the classification of these musical compositions. Some examples include "*Los ojos de Pancha*" (# 46); "*La Jesusita*" (#146); "*La rielera*" (#148); and "*Canción Mixteca*" (#301), among others. A more satisfactory classificatory system needs to be devised for the Mexican/Chicano *canción*.

Of particular interest for Chicanos is the *canción ranchera* (country music type songs). The *canción ranchera* and the *corrido* are the two most popular genres of musical compositions with the general Chicano population, particularly with the older population and adults. The *canción ranchera* (CR), as its title indicates, targets audiences from the countryside, the provinces of Mexico and the working class both in Mexico and the United States. Factory workers, agricultural workers, the lower middle class and indeed even the middle class of the Chicano population enjoy these types of songs. The CR, as opposed to the *corrido,* focuses more on the lyrical side and emotional side of human sensibilities. The *corrido's* major characteristic is that it is an epic-narrative type of musical composition: It tells a story via music. The CR centers the majority of its topics on the love/hate relationship between lovers. It either gushes with fervent love for the beloved, for the sweetheart, or encapsulates words of jealousy, disdain, loss of love, loss of faith in love, loss of innocence, and a sense of betrayal, even rage at the lover's unfaithfulness and inconstancy. The CR may also encompass satirical verses, particularly directed at the unfaithful beloved or at the new suitor. It uses plain, direct language, although it is also known for its beautiful metaphors and philosophical insights about love and life in general. One of its most successful composers and performers was José Alfredo Jiménez, born in 1925 in Dolores Hidalgo, Guanajuato, Mexico, and raised in Mexico City. His songs, such as *"Amarga Navidad," "El rey," "Camino de Guanajuato," "Cuatro caminos," "De un mundo raro," "Despacito," "Ella," "La mano de Dios," "La media vuelta," "La que se fue," "Pa' todo el año," "Si nos dejan," "Si tú también te vas," "Tú y las nubes," "Virgencita de Zapopan,"* and *"Yo,"* are some of the most popular songs with the Mexican/Chicano public.

The interpreters or performers of the CR and the *corrido* can be a single person; such famous singers as Pedro Infante, Jorge Negrete, Vicente Fernández, Lola Beltrán, and Irma Serrano have aided immensely in disseminating and popularizing both the *corrido* and the CR. Duets, trios, and other groups of singers can also perform *corridos* and *canciones.* Of particular note are musical performers such as the mariachi ensemble and the Texas-Mexican *conjuntos.*

The Mariachi

The mariachi is a group of musician-singers from three to more than a dozen who perform Mexican songs, particularly, but not exclusively, CRs, *canciones románticas, corridos,* and *boleros.* The state of Jalisco is credited with being the birthplace of the mariachi. No one has ascertained definitively the etymology of the word, but there is an interesting story explaining its origin.

The word is supposedly derived from the French *mariage* since it was believed that during Emperor Maximilian's attempt to form an empire in Mexico he particularly liked this type of group of musicians and frequently had them over to play for his festivities, including weddings. Thus the musical group became identified with the word *marriage,* and the word *mariachi* was born. A second version asserts the word *mariachi* is derived from the Nahuatl-speaking Indians belonging to the Coca tribe living in the Cocula and near Guadalajara, Jalisco. A third theory associates the word *mariachi* with a wood known as mariachi and from which string musical instruments were made. The string instruments made from the mariachi wood, and the musicians playing them became associated and thus the word for the Mexican mariachi was derived (Vigil 1998, 121). The mariachi musicians wear the *charro* costume associated with Jalisco. The ensemble includes musicians that play the guitar, the violin, the trumpet, the horn, the harp, guitarrón or large guitar, and the vihuela. Mariachis are popular with the Chicano people and they are frequently seen playing at weddings, baptisms, anniversaries, birthdays, *quinceañeras* (15-year-old young woman's presentation to society) and even at burials. They are ever present at political events such as rallies, festivals, and any gathering calling for happy, energetic, lively music. Politicians love to use them because they attract the general public with the cheerful, loud music and project an image of energy, happiness, and vigor.

The Texas-Mexican Conjunto

The Texas-Mexican conjunto is a group of musicians or ensemble of musicians who play a particular style of music known as conjunto music. The consensus among conjunto scholars, such as Manuel Peña, and other musicians is that it originated in Texas in the Rio Grande Valley (the most southeastern part of Texas by the Gulf of Mexico and the Mexican border) and San Antonio area in 1936, although the precursor of the conjunto style was already in evidence in the 1880s and 1890s. Peña proposes the date 1936 as the birth of conjunto music, as this was the date the first polka, *"La chicharronera,"* was recorded by one of its greatest performers, Narciso Martínez. Martínez is thus considered the "Father of Conjunto Music" (Peña 2001, 15). Other outstanding musicians disseminating and concretizing the conjunto style of music in Texas in the 1930s were Pedro Ayala and Santiago Jiménez. This style of music is characterized by the prominence of one of the instruments the music is played with: the accordion. There is not complete agreement as to whether the accordion was introduced in Texas by the new German and Polish immigrants entering and settling Texas after the

U.S.–Mexican War of 1848 or whether it came from Mexico. According to one viewpoint (e.g., Pedro Ayala; see Peña 2001, 14), Mexican Americans enjoyed the accordion music brought in by the German and Polish settlers and began to make it their own; others point to Monterrey, Mexico, as the area that introduced the accordion to the Texas-Mexican people.

The first generation of conjunto musicians set the basic conjunto style in the 1930s and continued to expand and develop the genre in the 1940s and 1950s. The conjunto ensemble evolved into having four basic musical instruments: the accordion, the *bajo sexto* (12-string guitar), the contrabass (*tololoche*), and later the addition of drums in the 1950s. A new group of accomplished musicians joined the ranks of the first generation of conjunto performers: Valerio Longoria, Tony de la Rosa, Paulino Bernal, and Daniel Garcés who, according to Peña (2001, 19), in the late 1940s and 1950s "propelled conjunto music into the next level of development." Peña juxtaposed conjunto music and orchestra-type music, positing a class division between middle and upper class and poor, working class. The two musical traditions bisected the Mexican American population in the 1930s–1950s, with orchestra music appealing to the affluent wealthy (high society) and conjunto music serving the needs of the working class. Peña (1985) delineates how conjunto music was not just a form of entertainment for the working class but was a source of cultural resistance and ethnic working class solidarity. Racism was quite pervasive throughout the state of Texas; indeed, it was rampant in the Southwest and through-out the United States. Segregation of the races was still legal and continued to thrive even after it was outlawed in the 1950s. The rise of conjunto music in the 1940s and 1950s can be perceived as the assertion of a people against hegemonic society's pressure to assimilate. The divide between upper-class and working-class Chicanos/as intensified after World War II, with the expansion of urbanization stimulated by returning servicemen and women in need of housing. Upwardly mobile middle-class Mexican Americans did not want to identify with the working-class sector and thus rejected the conjunto style music associated with them. Peña is correct in positing his theory regarding the relationship between music and social structure, because for Chicanos/as this type of music served to sustain them against cultural annihilation. Thus, conjunto music became for the working class a weapon of cultural resistance and as a means of cultural survival in an environment that threatened their cultural specificity. Conjunto music became extremely popular during the 1950s, and musicians expanded the popularity of this genre by touring all over the Southwest and other areas containing large numbers of the Chicano population such as Chicago and other parts of the Midwest. Conjunto music continued evolving but the new musicians tend to keep in mind the classic conjunto style and try to preserve this musical tradition. In the last decade it has achieved international fame with performers touring Europe (particularly Germany) and the United States to appreciative audiences and aficionados. Women have also become part of the conjunto tradition; some performers achieving national fame, such as Eva Ybarra and Lupita Rodela, who had her own group of musicians in the 1980s.

WOMEN IN THE MUSICAL TRADITION

The musical world in Western civilization has been dominated by male musicians both in classical music and folk music. Nevertheless, women always have been involved with music whether at the margins or front center stage. Most significantly, women consistently are major players within the contents of songs, albeit oftentimes in a negative or pejorative sense, as in the song *"Mujer Paseada"* [Woman Who Has Been Around]. In this section a brief overview of important women singers from Texas and California who perform *corridos* and/or *canciones* are highlighted.

Historically, most of the important Mexican American women singers have come from Texas and California. During the late nineteenth century *teatro de carpa*, or tent theater and vaudeville theater included women singers, comedians, *vedettes* [dancers], and chorus girls. In Los Angeles, as early as 1904, Charles Loomis recorded more than 40 noncommercial cylinder recordings of the sister duet Rosa and Luisa Villa who accompanied themselves with guitar and mandolin. The Villa sisters were followed by the Herrera sisters in the mid-1920s; they recorded for the Sunset Label in Los Angeles. Numerous other sister duet acts ensued. However, it was the Hermanas Padilla from Los Angeles who in the 1930s began to make national and international news.

These two women, Margarita and María Padilla, sang *ranchera*-type or rural-working class songs and, according to Zack Salem, Jim Nicolopulos, and Chris Strachwitz (1991, p. 3), the Padilla sisters "pioneered a vocal style that widely influenced ranchera singing and created a demand for other female vocal duets." Nicolopulos and Strachwitz underscored the differences between the musical tradition emanating from Los Angles and the one surfacing in Texas. In Los Angeles, Mariachi music dominated the Mexican American entertainment scene whereas in the Texas/Mexican border in the region between San Antonio, Texas, and Monterrey, Nuevo León the Música Norteña or Tex-Mex music prevailed.

In the 1920s and early 1930s major recording companies such as Columbia had been involved in recording Mexican and Mexican American singers. However, with the advent of the Great Depression and later with the inception of World War II, mainstream companies ceased recording local talent. The demand for Mexican American music continued to expand, particularly from the sector of the jukebox industry that needed the records for their restaurants and bars. It is at this time (in the 1940s) that the jukebox entrepreneur Armando Marroquín began to record for Discos Ideal. This small mom-and-pop recording company based in the

Picture of Lydia Mendoza from the dust jacket of the DVD *Chulas Fronteras* and *Del Mero Corazon,* two films by Les Blank and Chris Strachwitz.
Source: Brazos Films, BF-104, DVD, 2003.

Lower Rio Grande Valley in Texas became actively engaged in recording hundreds of singers from Alice, Falfurrias, San Benito, Brownsville, and other communities in the area.

One of Marroquín's first recordings was that of a duet act composed of his wife and sister-in-law, Carmen and Laura Hernández. The Hernández sisters were born in Kingsville, Texas, in the 1920s. Carmen was married to Marroquín and was involved with her husband in the jukebox industry. When recordings from mainstream companies dried up due to World War II restrictions, Carmen and Marroquín began to record the Carmen and Laura duet singing act. The first major "hit" of the Carmen and Laura singing performance was the song *"Se me fue mi amor"* ["My Love Has Gone"], which narrates the pain of leave-taking as the woman's sweetheart goes off to war. The song is interesting because it describes the action from the perspective of the woman. Rosita Fernández was another major voice in the musical scene in the 1930s and 1940s. She starred in movies but is best known for her role as star performer for the summer-long Fiesta Noche del Río in San Antonio, Texas. Rosita and Laura were another women's singing duet important during this same era. Their song *"La Traidora"* [The Treacherous Woman"] is paradigmatic of the recurring figure of the Treacherous Woman.

The most outstanding woman singer from Texas is Lydia Mendoza. Born in Houston, Texas, in 1916, she covered a span of six decades and recorded more than 1,000 songs in many different genres. Lydia Mendoza's mother is credited with launching her daughter's career into music. Because of the family's precarious economic situation, Lydia was forced to sing at a very early age. According to Clark (2002, 112), "The Familia Mendoza performed regularly in San Antonio's Plaza de Zacate alongside and in competition with duos, trios, and quartets of male Mexican singers, guitarists, accordionists, and fiddlers." Clark attributes the success of the Mendoza family in San Antonio to various factors: (1) excellence of the female Mendoza voices—especially Lydia's, (2) their wide-ranging repertory of popular songs (some composed by Leonora) and more traditional songs and instrumental music, (3) mother Leonora's financial astuteness, and (4) the novelty of the female youthful group in competition with more common male groups.

Another major Tejana singer who achieved fame in more recent times is Selena Quintanilla. Born in 1971 and killed tragically in 1995, Selena also had a wide repertoire of musical styles—from *cumbia norteña*, to mariachi, to mainstream pop. Her songs *"Como la flor"* and *"Amor prohibido"* (1994) achieved national and international success.

The *corrido* and the *canción ranchera* chronicle reality as it exists in our society. Chicana women have been involved both as performers of these songs as well as protagonists in the lyrics of these musical compositions. Nevertheless, both as performers and as sex objects represented as the Other in both *corridos* and *canciones* women encounter a patriarchal system that is difficult to eradicate. Contemporary *narcocorridos* singing groups, for example, exclude women and make it difficult for them to perform in the tightly knit male-oriented bands. The songs sung by these male groups continue to portray women as sex objects. Fortunately, strong women such as Lydia Mendoza and more recently Jenni Rivera, a contemporary singer of *corridos* and *narcocorridos*, are able to break the barriers and succeed in a very difficult male-dominated environment.

FOLK SPEECH

The folklore genre encompassing folk speech includes proverbs, exaggerations, comparisons, idiomatic expressions, tongue twisters, riddles, and jargon or specialized vocabulary related to groups of people. It also encompasses all the linguistic variation studies in dialectology and the field of linguistics. The Chicano population privileges verbal dexterity and in particular enjoys playing with both English and Spanish, since a large percentage of them are bilingual. Therefore, some of the categories of folk speech pertaining to the Chicano population often include bilingual structures. Furthermore, knowing the various registers of a language is considered a positive attribute in a person. Folk speech in the Chicano community is therefore characterized by a rich spectrum of folk items.

Proverbs (also known as Dichos, Proverbios, and Refranes)

Scholars have found it difficult to provide a satisfactory definition for the proverb. Mieder (1997, 661) gives the following definition: "A concise traditional statement expressing an apparent truth with currency among the folk. Defined more inclusively, proverbs are short, generally known sentences of the folk that contain wisdom, truths, morals, and traditional views in a metaphorical, fixed and memorizable form and that are handed down orally from generation to generation." Perhaps a more simple definition that is easy to grasp is this: A proverb is a succinct statement that encompasses a wise message. It is often structured in metaphoric language with a subtle dose of humor. It is generally structured with two clauses: For example, *Camarón que se duerme se lo lleva la corriente* [A shrimp that falls asleep is taken by the stream's current]. The message inscribed within the statement is that one should be alert at whatever one is doing, otherwise a misfortune can happen. There are literally thousands of proverbs and many published collections are in existence.

Proverbial Phrases

Proverbial phrases, also known as idiomatic expressions, are short phrases that are metaphorically constructed and are not complete sentences—for example, "You are pulling my leg," that is. "You are lying to me, you are fooling me." The Spanish equivalent is *"me estás tomando el pelo,"* which literally translated means "You are taking my hair."

Proverbial Exaggerations

Proverbial exaggerations are short sentences that exaggerate a particular attribute or characteristic of a person, place, or thing. They have a formulaic structure: *"Es . . . tan . . . que."* For example: *"Es tan tacaño que no da ni los buenos días."* [He is such a tightwad that he will not even give you a greeting.]

Proverbial Comparisons

Comparisons are sentences that compare one object with another. These are also formulaic in their sentence structure. *"Es como . . .* [He/she/it is as]; *"Es . . . como"* [He/she/it is . . . like]. For example: *"Es como el mar: grandote y alborotado."* [He is like the ocean: big and noisy.]

Caló

Chicano *caló* is composed of standard Spanish, nonstandard Spanish, standard English, and nonstandard English in various combinations. For example, the phrase *"hay los vidrios"* literally means "There the broken glass is," but in *caló* it means "See you later." It is a play on words between *ver* (to see) and *vidrios* (glass or broken glass). The sentence uses standard Spanish but with a totally different meaning.

Jargon

There is also specialized jargon used by truck drivers, policemen, cooks, drug-smugglers, and other groups of people who develop their own vocabulary pertaining to their work or profession.

Riddles (Adivinanzas)

The riddle, or *adivinanza,* is composed of two parts: an interrogative (at times implied) and an answer (e.g., "*Una vieja larga y seca que le escurre la manteca?*" [What is an old lady that is long and grease drips down on her?] Answer: the candle) A more elaborate definition is found in Mieder (1997, 728): "The riddle is generally agreed to consist of a description and its referent—the first posed by the riddler, the second guessed by the respondent. The enigma comes from the incorporation of a 'block element' in the description: an ambiguity that prevents the description from being obvious. The ambiguity may occur at any level of the linguistic code from the phonological to the semantic, and it is often presented as an opposition or paradox within the description."

The classification of Spanish language riddles is based on the subject matter, such as riddles related to fruits, riddles related to vegetables, erotic riddles, and so forth.

Tongue Twisters

Tongue twisters are playful forms of entertainment practiced by both children and adults. The tongue twister relies on the repetition of sounds and similar sounding sounds in the same phrase or sentence in order to "confuse" or trick the tongue into making an error.

FOLK THEATER

Chicano folk theater has a long tradition dating back to 1598 when Captain Juan de Oñate crossed the Rio Grande River at the El Paso, Texas area. The crossing of the river was quite dangerous and in order to offer thanks to the Almighty, Captain Oñate requested a mass to be performed. After the mass was over, two dramas were performed: an auto sacramental or religious drama and a play written by one of the soldiers accompanying the Oñate expedition. Religious plays as well as secular plays were part of the various ceremonies and festivals frequently taking place in the newly conquered lands of New Mexico. Arthur L. Campa and Juan Rael have done extensive research in folk theater and collected several texts especially from the state of New Mexico. Campa divided the religious dramas into two categories: those exhibiting plots from the Old Testament and those taking their subject matter from the New Testament. Some of the religious plays include the following:

    I. Old Testament Dramas

      Adán y Eva

      Caín y Abel

II. New Testament Dramas

Los Pastores

Los Reyes Magos

La Pastorela

El Auto de Los Pastores

El Nacimiento

El Coloquio de los Pastores

El Niño Dios

Los Pastores Chiquitos

Camino de la Pastorela

El Niño Perdido

El Coloquio de San José

III. Passion Plays

La Pasión

Enactment of biblical scenes related to Jesus Christ and his crucifixion were also very much a part of the folk theater of New Mexico. However, no texts have been collected since the enactment of the Stations of the Cross was mostly visual, accompanied by the singing of *alabados* [religious songs].

III. Secular Dramas

Los Comanches

Los Tejanos

Los Moros y Cristianos

Las Cuatro Apariciones de Nuestra Señora La Virgen de Guadalupe

Los Matachines

Many of the folk dramas cited here, such as *Los Pastores, Pastorelas, Los Comanches, Los Matachines,* and *Las Cuatro Apariciones de la Virgen de Guadalupe,* are performed in New Mexico. *Pastorelas* and *Las Cuatro Apariciones de la Virgen de Guadalupe* are more commonly performed throughout California, whereas the *Pastorelas* and *Los Matachines* are frequently performed in Texas. *Pastorelas* are also performed in Arizona. Luis Valdez and the Teatro Campesino alternate each year in performing *La Pastorela* and *Las Cuatro Apariciones de la Virgen de Guadalupe* at the Mission of San Juan Bautista in California.

In addition to the plays listed here dating from the colonial period, the *teatro de carpa* developed quite strongly during the nineteenth century and continued its trajectory up until the 1940s. It is the precursor of the Teatro

Campesino. The *teatro de carpa* [tent theater] was so named because this type of theater was a traveling vaudeville type of performance, and the dramatic events were often inside a tent *[carpa]*. The *teatro* consisted of one-act plays, usually humorous skits that entertained the working class.

The Teatro Campesino developed in 1965 under the leadership of Luis Valdez. Its major format was the short skit or *actos* (acts), which were performed on the flatbeds of trucks in the agricultural fields of California. The *actos* were political in nature and were designed to raise the consciousness of farm workers so that they would demand better wages and working conditions in the fields of California. The Teatro Campesino worked in conjunction with the unionization project initiated by César Chávez. Folk elements were very much a part of the Teatro Campesino. Thus the stock characters such as Death, the Devil, the poor farm worker, and the evil contractor were very much a part of the *actos*. Folk music such as the *corrido* and the *canción ranchera* were also an integral part of the Teatro's performances and entertainment project.

CHILDREN'S SONGS AND GAMES

Chicano children's songs and games have been inherited from Spanish, Mexican, and Anglo-American traditions. Children's songs and games can be divided into various categories:

    I. *Canciones de cuna* (lullabies)
   II. Hand and finger games such as "This Little Piggy Went to Market"
  III. Counting out rhymes
   IV. Children's songs
    V. Singing games
   VI. Miscellaneous games such as tag, hide-and-seek

Children's songs and games are used to teach language skills, socialize children into proper behavior, and socialize them into group activities. Patriarchal structures are very much evident in these texts and socialize the children into established gender roles.

FOLK BELIEF

Previous to the 1960s, folk belief was classified under the value-ridden and pejorative category of "superstitions." After the 1960s a reevaluation of folk beliefs and a more enlightened view of this area of folklore production emerged. Folk belief is that area of folk knowledge in which people seek to explain the world around them. Folk beliefs include beliefs in witches, the afterlife, supernatural beings, werewolves, vampires, ogres, ghosts or revenants, and poltergeists. There are folk beliefs related to good and bad luck, and there are objects that can help you achieve good luck or alternatively ward off bad luck. Folk beliefs are classified according to topic, such as folk beliefs related to the weather, death, childbirth, pregnancy, menstruation, foods, the devil, marriage, weddings, illnesses, agriculture, planting, harvesting, evil spirits, the hereafter, health, children, the saints, and numerous other subjects.

FOLK MEDICINE AND FOLK AILMENTS

Both folk ailments and folk remedies are derived from indigenous, Spanish, Mexican, as well as African traditions. Folk ailments such as *susto* [emotional shock], *empacho* [a type of indigestion], and *aire* [cold draft] all have their respective folk remedies to cure them.

FOLK DANCE

Chicano folk dancing is derived from Mexican, Spanish, and possibly Anglo-American folk dancing traditions. During the 1960s in particular there was a revival of Mexican folk dancing by Chicano students, who demanded from educational institutions that their cultural traditions be taught at all levels of the school systems from primary grades to colleges and universities. Thus a renaissance of Mexican folk dancing came about during the Chicano movement and continues to be a very visible and much-enjoyed part of the education of students. Towns and cities also display during the various festivals Mexican folk dancing. The folk dances are typical of the major cultural areas in Mexico: Veracruz, Chiapas, Yucatán, Tehuantepec, Nayarit, Central Mexico, the Huasteca region, Jalisco, Zacatecas, Northern Mexico (Sinaloa, Tamaulipas, Sonora, and Chihuahua), and other Mexican states and regions. The dances are characterized by the colorful, bright costumes. The major dancing step is the *zapateado*, which is heavy heel and toe footwork.

FOLK COSTUMES

Folk costumes are related to folk dances. Each region in Mexico has a very specific type of dress inherited from a mixture of Spanish and indigenous

Raíces de mi Tierra, a student folk dance organization at the University of California, Santa Barbara.
Source: Courtesy of *Raíces de mi Tierra.*

traditions. The *charro* [Mexican cowboy] outfit, with its characteristic wide-brimmed, embroidered hat from the Jalisco area is a favorite. The *charro* outfit is only worn by mariachi musical ensembles in the United States. During the Chicano movement, wearing indigenous types of clothing was popular; many Chicanas wore embroidered blouses and the men wore Mexican ponchos. However, the majority of Chicanos and Chicanas wear typical American clothes. A popular form of dress, particularly for men in Texas, is the Tejano outfit which consists of Texas style boots, jeans, cowboy shirts, and a cowboy hat.

FOLK CELEBRATIONS

Chicano/a folk celebrations can be divided into three categories: religious, secular, and personal. Some of the religious and personal celebrations interconnect. Religious celebrations are related to the Catholic Church calendar, such as Easter in the spring, *Día de los Muertos* [Day of the Dead], and Thanksgiving in the fall, the Día de La Virgen de Guadalupe [Holy Feast of the Virgin of Guadalupe],

December 12, and Christmas in the winter. Secular celebrations include New Year's Day, Cinco de Mayo, Fourth of July, and 16th of September. Personal celebrations include birthdays, a person's Saint's Day, confirmation, communion, *quinceañera* (15th birthday), marriage anniversaries, and death.

FOLK ARTS

The folk art area of cultural production can be divided into religious folk art and secular arts. The religious folk art is produced by *santeros* and *santeras*, traditional wood carvers. The *santeros/as* carve out and paint sacred images of God, the Virgin Mary, and the saints from the Catholic pantheon. Other folk arts include architecture, furniture, weaving, quilting, tinwork, ironwork, silverwork, gold jewelry and filigree, and leather work.

FOLK FOOD

In an analogous manner to the other genres, Chicano folk foods have been influenced by indigenous Anglo-American and Spanish culinary traditions. Some of the folk foods that are popular today include the following: *tamales, enchiladas,* corn tortillas, flour tortillas, barbecue, *chiles rellenos, carne asada,* green chile stew, red chile stew, salsa, *bizcochos, sopaipillas, empanadas, buñuelos, churros, tacos, cabrito, menudo, atole, capirotada, mole, quesadillas,* nachos, *fajitas, chicharrones, carne seca* [beef jerky], *pozole, caldo de pollo, caldo de res,* and *nopalitos.*

CONCLUSION

The great confluence, or *mestizaje,* of cultural traditions in Mexico and later in the United States have provided Chicanos/as with a rich cultural heritage. Chicano/a literary folklore as well as material culture exhibit an enormous variety of folklore items and are astonishing both in terms of quantity and quality. Chicanos and Chicanas have taken the various traditions inherited and given them their own originality, their own imprint. Due to the confluence of Spanish, Mexican, African, and Anglo-American cultures, the Chicano people's folklore can truly be called one of the richest in the world.

REFERENCES

Bascom, William. 1965. "The Forms of Folklore: Prose Narrative." *Journal of American Folklore* 78 (307): 3–20.

Bonfil, Alicia Oliveira de. 1970. *La literatura cristera.* Mexico City: Instituto Nacional de Antropología e Historia.

Castañeda, Daniel. *El corrido mexicano: su técnica literaria y musical.* México: Editorial Sucro, 1943.

Clark, Walter Aaron, ed. 2002. *From Tejano to Tango: Latin American Popular Music.* New York: Routledge.

Dundes, Alan. 1965. "What Is Folklore?" In *The Study of Folklore,* ed. Alan Dundes, 1–3. Englewood Cliffs, NJ: Prentice-Hall.

Mendoza, Vicente T. 1974. *El corrido mexicano.* Mexico City: Fondo de Cultura Económica.

———. 1982. *La canción mexicana: Ensayo de clasificación y antología.* Mexico City: Fondo de Cultura Económica.

Mieder, Wolfgang. "Proverbs." In *Folklore: An Encyclopedia of Beliefs, Customs, Tales, Music and Art Vol. II,* ed. Thomas A. Green, 661–67. Santa Barbara, CA: ABC-Clio, 1997.

Paredes, Américo. 1958. *"With His Pistol in His Hand": A Border Ballad and Its Hero.* Austin: University of Texas.

Peña, Manuel. 1985. *The Texas-Mexican Conjunto: History of a Working Class Music.* Austin: University of Texas Press.

———. 2001. "Conjunto Music: The First Fifty Years." *Puro Conjunto: An Album in Words and Pictures.* San Antonio, TX: Guadalupe Cultural Arts Center, 13–30.

Salem, Zack, Jim Nicolopulos, and Chris Strachwitz. 1991. *Roots/Raíces Tejanas: The Women (1946–1970).* El Cerrito, CA: Arhoolie Productions, CD-343, 3–26.

Simmons, Merle E. 1963. "The Ancestry of Mexico's *Corridos.*" *Journal of American Folklore* 76: 1–16.

Sonnichsen, Phillip. 1975. "Texas-Mexican Border Music." Vol. 2 and 3 *Corridos Part I and II,* Liner Notes. Berkeley, CA: Folklyric LP9004.

Strachwitz, Chris, 1975. "The 'Golden Age' of the Recorded Corrido." Liner Notes in *Texas-Mexican Border Music, Vols. 2 and 3; Corridos Parts 1 and 2.* Folklyric Records. Berkeley, CA: Arhoolie Records, 29–30.

Vigil, Angel. 1998. *Una Linda Raza: Cultural and Artistic Traditions of the Hispanic Southwest.* Golden, CO: Fulcrum Printing.

Zabre, Alfonso Teja. 1969. *Guide to the History of Mexico.* New York: The Pemberton Press.

Three

Examples and Texts

MYTHS

Coyolxauhqui

Beside the town of Tula there is a mountain chain called Coatepec. There lived a goddess named Coatlicue, mother of the four hundred Mimixcoa, the warriors representing the stars and brothers and sisters of the Moon goddess, Coyolxauhqui.

The goddess Coatlicue did penance by sweeping the mountains of Coatepec every day. One day, as she swept, a little ball of feathers descended upon her, a ball not unlike a skein of yarn. The goddess liked the little ball so much— the feathers' colors were bright and beautiful that she picked it up and tucked it between her breasts, beneath her clothes. And after having finished her chores she wanted to look at the bright little ball, but did not find it when she reached for it. And they say that the little ball caused her pregnancy.

When her children the Mimixcoa found out that their mother was with child, they became infuriated. "Who got our mother pregnant?" "Who shamed and embarrassed us?"

And their sister Coyolxauhqui said to them, "Brothers and Sisters, let us kill Mother who has shamed us by letting someone impregnate her in secret."

When the goddess Coatlicue found out that Coyolxauhqui and her brothers and sisters were plotting against her, it pained and frightened her. But the child that she carried inside her womb, who was the god Huitzilopochtli, consoled her and said, "do not fear; for I know what I must do."

Those words restored Coatlicue's calm and she shed the worry that had come over her.

Since the Mimixcoa had accepted Coyolxauhqui's advice to kill Coatlicue for the shame and dishonor she had brought upon them, they armed themselves for the fight, twisting and tying up their hair as brave men do.

One of the Mimixcoa, Quauitlicac, who turned out to be a traitor, told Huitzilopochtli, yet in his mother's womb, what their brothers and sisters were devising. Huitzilopochtli answered him with these words: "Oh, my uncle! Pay full attention to what your brothers and sisters do and listen to what they say for I know what I must do."

As the four hundred Mimixcoa had already resolved to kill their mother, they departed to the mountains of Coatepec, their sister Coyolxauhqui leading them. And they went well armed and dressed with rattles and darts just as when they went to battle.

The traitor Quauitlicac got ahead of them, scaled the mountains, and told Huitzilopochtli how the Mimixcoa were already on their way to kill him. And Huitzilopochtli said to him, "Watch their position."

And the traitor responded, "They come upon the place called Tzompantitlan."

And Huitzilopochtli asked the traitor again, "Where are the Mimixcoa now?"

Quauitlicac responded, "They have arrived at Coaxalapa."

One more time Huitzilopochtli asked the traitor, "And now, how far are they?"

Quauitlicac answered that they had reached Apetlac.

Huitzilopochtli asked again, "And now, how far are they?"

The traitor responded that they were in the middle of the land.

One more time Huitzilopochtli asked the traitor, "Where are they now?"

Quauitlicac responded that they were very close and that at their head marched the goddess Coyolxauhqui.

In the instant that the Mimixcoa arrived where Coatlicue was, Huitzilopochtli burst forth from the womb. He carried with him a shield, a dart, and a blue shaft. He had his face painted, and in his hair he wore a feather. On his thin left leg he also wore feathers. His arms and his thighs were painted blue.

Huitzilopochtli ordered a certain Tochancalqui to light up a firebrand, a snake called xiuchcatl. His orders were carried out, and with that xiuchcatl he wounded Coyolxauhqui, who died totally dismembered. Her head remained in the mountains of Coatepec.

Huitzilopochtli got up, armed himself, and departed in pursuit of the Mimixcoa. He fought with them until he expelled them from Coatepec. The Mimixcoa could not defend themselves, for their weapons were nothing to Huitzilopochtli. Thus, they were defeated and many died. Even though they begged Huitzilopochtli not to kill them, the Sun God had no compassion.

Very few escaped, and those who managed to save themselves retreated to the place called Huitzlampa.

As a result of his triumph over Coyolxauhqui—a triumph that symbolizes the triumph of the sun over the moon and the stars (respectively Coyolxauhqui and the Mimixcoa), a triumph that repeats itself every morning as the sun comes out—the Mexicans began to worship Huitzilopochtli and they became the People of the Sun. They considered him also the God of War because he gave them great bravery in battle. The manner and the customs by which Mexicans served and honored Huitzilopochtli were taken from those practiced in the mountain chain still known as Coatepec.

- Luis Leal. *Mitos y Leyendas de México/Myths and Legends of Mexico*. Santa Barbara, CA: University of California, Santa Barbara, Center for Chicano Studies Publications, 2002, 53–58.

Commentary

The myth of Coyolxauhqui has been re-visioned by Chicana visual artists and creative writers such as Cherríe Moraga and Irene Pérez. Since the battle between Coyolxauhqui and her brother Huiztilopochtli is interpreted to mean the triumph of patriarchy over matriarchy, Chicanas are calling for a healing process to take place between men and women. The re-membering of Coyolxauhqui (i.e., putting her back together again after being totally dismembered in battle) is a beginning for the process of healing. Therefore, artists such as Irene Pérez portray Coyolxauhqui totally reconstituted; whole and healthy again.

Quetzalcóatl, or the Lost Paradise

According to ancient legends, during the third age of the universe, a white, tall, robust man with a wide forehead, large eyes, long black hair, and a thick, beard came from the East to Anahuac. They say that out of modesty he always wore a long tunic; some red crosses adorned his fine cape. That person was not a human; he was a god that some experts identify with the god of the air, and others with Saint Thomas; his name was Quetzalcóatl, which means literally "feathered serpent" and allegorically "very wise man."

In Tula, where the Toltecs worshiped this god, the principal priest was given the name Quetzalcóatl. One of these priests became very famous, and the people loved him like a god, for he taught them how to cultivate corn and other plants. He was very industrious and invented the art of smelting metals and cutting stone. He was a man of mild manners and did not tolerate talk of war in his presence. He was, in addition, a prudent lawmaker, a fact well

Coyolxauhqui—Líbrate Aztlán by Ìrene Pérez.
Source: Courtesy of Irene Pérez.

demonstrated by the laws that he gave his people. And above all, his life was simple and exemplary. When he wanted to publicize a law, he would send a town crier to the Mount of Trumpets—a hill near the city of Tula where Quetzalcóatl lived—from which his voice could be heard for 300–400 miles around.

They say that in his day corn grew so abundantly that one plot sufficed to satisfy the needs of a family. The squash were as big as a human body, and dyeing cotton was not necessary because it grew in every color. All the other grains were also of comparable proportions. The trees and the land bore tasty and abundant fruit. During that time an incredible number of birds of beautiful plumage sweetened the days of the townspeople with their soft melodies. The Toltecs believed that Quetzalcóatl had governed with such wisdom that no better life in this world was possible.

But as every garden of paradise has its weed, Tezcatlipoca—a proponent of human sacrifices, a practice that Quetzalcóatl prohibited—arrived in Tula for the purpose of expelling Quetzalcóatl from the country. This political and religious conflict would eventually cause the downfall of Quetzalcóatl.

Tezcatlipoca practiced black magic. One day he transformed himself into an old man and in that form he went to the palace of Quetzalcóatl and said to the servants, "I want to see the king and speak with him."

The servants responded, "Go, old man, you cannot see him for he is ill and you would leave him angered and sorrowful." Then the old man said, "I must see him."

The servants, seeing the persistence of the old man, answered, "Fine. Wait here." One of the servants went to tell Quetzalcóatl that an old man wished to see him and speak to him, and he added, "Sir, we tried to kick him out of the palace, but he won't leave."

Quetzalcóatl then said, "Let him enter. Tell him that I have been waiting for him for many years."

The servants called the old man and he entered into Quetzalcóatl's chambers and told him, "My son, how are you? I have a medicine here for you to drink."

Quetzalcóatl responded, "Welcome, old man, come, for I have been waiting many years for you."

Then the old man asked Quetzalcóatl, "How is your health? How is your body?"

Quetzalcóatl replied, "I am not well. I cannot move my hands and feet."

Then the old man said to the king, "I have medicine here that I brought for you. It is good and healthy; it intoxicates all who drink of it. If you were to drink and get drunk, you would be cured and your heart will grow young again. And remember the fatigues of death and that you must go to Tlapala."

Quetzalcóatl responded, "Oh, old man, where do I have to go?"

The old man told him, "You have to go to Tlapala, where another old man awaits you. You will speak with him, and after your return, you will be like a young man, even like a boy." Quetzalcóatl heard the words of the old man and became excited. Then the old man, without pausing for a moment, continued, "Quetzalcóatl, drink this medicine."

Quetzalcóatl replied, "I do not want to drink it."

The old man insisted, saying, "Drink it now, because if you do not, you will crave it later. Drink, even if only a little."

Quetzalcóatl finally gave in and tasted medicine, and he liked it. He kept on drinking and said, "What is this? It seems to be very good and tasty. It has cured me and taken away my illness. I am fine now."

The old man repeated, "Drink again, because this medicine is good and healthy, and you will feel better."

Quetzalcóatl drank again and got drunk. He began to speak sadly, deeply moved by the trickery that the evil wizard disguised as an old man had used against him.

What he drank was no medicine, it was pulque, the intoxicating drink from the juices of the maguey. Tezcatlipoca, who hated the Toltecs, had triumphed by conquering Quetzalcóatl, who had drunk the pulque with hopes of regaining his youth. And Quetzalcóatl, right after tasting the pulque, felt strong desires to go to Tlapala.

Quetzalcóatl, accompanied by many Toltecs who celebrated the journey with music, started on his way immediately. They say that near the town of Tlalnepantla he left an imprint of his hand on a rock that the Mexicans would later show to the Spaniards after the Conquest. When Quetzalcóatl arrived in Cholula, the townspeople received him with many festivities and they entrusted their government to him. The town of Cholula had heard news of the virtues of Quetzalcóatl and his intolerance for any type of cruelty— an aversion so great that he would not even permit talk of war in his presence. According to tradition, the people of Cholula owe their art of foundry to Quetzalcóatl, an art that later distinguished them. They also credit him for the laws by which they governed themselves ever since, the rites and ceremonies of their religion, and the invention of the calendar.

After residing in Cholula for long years, Quetzalcóatl continued his journey to the Kingdom of Tlapala. But before abandoning Cholula he said to the people that they could count on his returning to govern them again. The Cholultecas consecrated him as the greatest god of Anahuac. Cholula spread and popularized devotion to him far and wide throughout all of the nations of the region, where he was revered as the God of Air. Devotion to him reached as far as Yucatan, where the Mayans adored him by the name of Kukulcán. The festivals dedicated to him, especially in Cholula, were great and splendid.

The people of Anahuac never forgot the prophecy of Quetzalcóatl, and everyone awaited his return. They even knew when he would be back; he told them that it would be in the year of Ce Ácatl.

According to myth, Quetzalcóatl turned into the planet of Venus which, being an evening star, would die in the West every night and then reappear, transformed, as the morning star.

Quetzalcóatl o el Paraiso Perdido (1999) by Alvaro Suman.
Source: Courtesy of Alvaro Suman.

• Luis Leal. *Mitos y leyendas de México/Myths and Legends of Mexico.* Santa Barbara, CA: University of California, Santa Barbara, Center for Chicano Studies Publications, 2002, 91–98.

Commentary

The myth of the return of Quetzalcóatl was disastrous for the Aztecs since their belief that Quetzalcóatl was to return led them to believe the Spaniards might be their god returning to Mexico and were hesitant to harm the Spaniards in any way. This gave the Spaniards a great advantage since they had no qualms about engaging in battle with the Mexica (Aztecs), eventually conquering them, and demolishing their empire. Chicanos, in the early stages of the movement, admired Quetzalcóatl for his wise leadership, his kindness, and genius. He appears in many Chicano murals and in poetry and fiction.

Aztlán

They say that Moctezuma, surrounded by a glorious empire and with so much wealth, decided to find out where his ancestors lived, and to search for the seven caves so often mentioned in their history. With this in mind, he called his advisor, Tlacaélel, and said to him, "I have resolved to send several men in search of our ancestors and in search of the mother of our god Huitzilopochtli, who may still be alive."

Tlacaélel replied, "Powerful Lord, most knowledgeable Lord. You must know, great Lord, that what you wish to do is not for men of strength and valor, neither for people of war, nor for captain generals, for they are not going to conquer, but rather to discover where our ancestors lived. And for this, it is better to send witches or wizards and sorcerers who are apt to know how to find those places. For according to our history, getting to that place requires passing over great deserts and lagoons as well as thick reed swamps. For these reasons, my Lord, take my advice and seek out the people that I speak of, and they will discover your ancestors for you and bring you word of them. The stories say that the place the Aztecs originally came from was very pleasant and wonderful. There the people were serene, living many years without aging or tiring or needing anything. But when they left there, everything became thorns and thistles; the rocks became sharp enough to hurt them, the plants pricked, the trees became thorny and everything turned against them so that they would never be able to return."

Moctezuma, following the advice of Tlacaélel, called Cuauhcóatl, a royal historian and elder of many years, and told him, "Elderly father, I want to know what you remember of the seven caves that our ancestors inhabited, and where our god Huitzilopochtli lived, and from where he brought our grandparents."

Cuauhcóatl answered him, "Powerful Lord, what I know of what you ask is that our grandparents lived in that happy and blessed place of Aztlán, which means whiteness. In the middle of a body of water there rises a great hill named Culhuacan because its peak is twisted somewhat downward. On that hill are some caves where our ancestors lived for many years. There the

Mexitin, or Aztecs, lived peaceably, for flocks of ducks, herons, and other beautiful birds as well as a great variety of fish abounded. There they enjoyed refreshing coolness from the woodlands and attractive springs. There they traveled in canoes and made floating platforms on which they planted corn, chile, tomato, beans, and all types of seeds. But after they left that paradise, everything turned against them. All was overrun by snakes and serpents and other venomous animal. This is what our predecessors told me and what I have recorded in my ancient histories, powerful Sir."

The king replied that it must be true because Tlacaélel had told him the same story. Soon he gave the command to search for all of the magicians and wizards of the provinces that could be found, and sixty elders—men and women who understood the supernatural—were brought before him.

Moctezuma told them, "Venerable elders, I have decided to find out where the Mexican people came from and also to find out if the mother of our god Huitzilopochtli yet lives. For these reasons I want you all to go and search for Aztlán."

After receiving many gifts from the king the wizards departed in search of the mother of their god. First they gathered together on the hill known as Coatepec located in the Tula province; here they invoked the gods to ask them to show them the way to proceed. Then they covered their bodies with a magical ointment that allowed them to take the shape of animals. Some transformed themselves in lions, others into tigers, others into coyotes, and yet others into mountain lions.

Transformed in this way, they arrived at a large lagoon with a large island in the middle—the hill called Culhuacan. There they turned back into human form, and immediately they saw people in canoes who called to them in their own language. When they approached, those in canoes asked them where they were from and why they had come. The envoys responded, "Sirs, we are from Mexico and we are sent by our king to look for the place that our ancestors once inhabited."

The people in canoes asked them, "What god do you worship?"

"We," they answered, "adore the great Huitzilopochtli. We were sent by our king Moctezuma and by his advisor Tlacaélel. We seek the mother of Huitzilopochtli, who was called Coatlicue, and the place that our ancestors came from, which was called Chicomoztoc. And if she still lives, we bring gifts for the grand lady Coatlicue."

The canoeists asked them to wait while they went to see the advisor of Coatlicue, to whom they said, "Admirable sir, some people have arrived that say that they are Mexican and that they bring gifts for the mother of their god Huitzilopochtli."

The elder said to them, "Let them be welcomed. Tell them to come here."

Then the messengers returned in their canoes and escorted the new arrivals to the great hill of Culhuacan, the upper half of which they say is of fine sand and cannot be climbed. Upon entering the old man's house at the foot of the hill, they greeted him with much courtesy and reverence. He told them, "Welcome, my children. Who sent you here?"

"Our Lord Moctezuma and his advisor Tlacaélel."

"Who is Moctezuma and who is Tlacaélel? Those names are not from here, they are not names of the seven men who guided each community that came from here."

The Mexicans responded, "Sir, we confess to you that we did not know the seven gentlemen. Nobody remembers them because they have all died."

The elder, bewildered, responded with great amazement, "Oh, Lord of creation! Who killed them? All of us who remained here are still alive. Nobody has died. So, who are the ones who live now? Before leaving Mexico, did you see the god Huitzilopochtli? Didn't he tell you when he would return? Before he left he told his mother that he would be back, and today the poor thing still waits tearfully, for no one can console her."

The wizards responded, "Sir, we did what our lords commanded and we bring presents for the great lady."

"Well then, come with me," said the elder.

The wizards, carting their gifts, followed the old man, who began to climb up hill with great agility. They followed in the sand with great effort. The elder saw that the sand reached their knees and they could not climb. A bit later they were up to their waists in sand. The old man said to them, "What's wrong, Mexicans? What do you eat over there in your land that makes you so heavy? Give me the gifts and I will bring the lady down so that you can see her."

The old man took the gifts and climbed up as though the packages were made of straw. A little bit later he came back with an elderly woman crying bitterly who told the Mexicans, "Welcome, my children. You must know that since my son Huitzilopochtli left, I am in tears and great grief awaiting his return."

The Mexicans humbled themselves before Coatlicue and said to her, "Great and Powerful Señora, our king Moctezuma and his advisor Tlacaélel sent us to find our ancestors and ordered us to kiss your hand and to give you these gifts, which are the goods and riches of your son, Huitzilopochtli."

"This is all well and good, my children," answered Coatlicue, "but tell him to have pity on me and the difficulties I face without him. Tell him to remember that when he left he told me, 'I will not be away long; I will be back as soon as I take these seven communities to the Promised Land, where they will settle.' But it seems that he does not remember his sad mother, nor does he seek her, nor does be pay attention to her. Therefore, I order you to tell him that the time has come for him to return. Take him this fiber-spun shawl and this sash for him to wear."

The Mexicans took the shawl and the sash and began to climb down the hill. When they were at the foot of the mountain Coatlicue called to them and told them, "Wait! You should see how in this land people do not age. See my old assistant? Well, let him descend and you will see that when he arrives down there he will be a young man."

The old man—indeed old—began to descend the slope and the lower he got, the younger he became. When he arrived where the Mexicans were, he looked very young. Then he told them, "Look how young I am. Well then, I will walk halfway up the hill and you will see how much older I get."

So he did, and when he turned around, he looked like a 40-year-old man. He climbed up barely a few steps above the foot of the hill, and he looked very old when he turned around. Coatlicue told the Mexicans, "See now, my children, how this hill has such a power that if an old man wants to be young he goes down to where it seems right to him, and he can return to the age of his choice. And if he wants to be a child again, he goes all the way down, and if he wants to be a youth, he just climbs up a bit beyond the midpoint. And so we live many years, this is how it is, nobody dies."

Before bidding farewell, Coatlicue gave the Mexicans some gifts to give to Moctezuma and Tlacaélel. They took the gifts and, after casting the same spell as in their departure from Mexico, they assumed the same animal forms as they had in their coming. Walking in this guise, they arrived at the hill of Coatepec, where they gathered. But when they took their own human forms and counted the group, they discovered that 20 of them were missing. Surprised to see their numbers so diminished—for one-third of them were gone—they concluded that some of the beasts that they had encountered must have eaten those who were missing. And they say that it took them 10 days to travel out and only 8 days to return.

Once they had recovered from the trip, they went to see Moctezuma and gave him the gifts that Coatlicue sent. They told him, "Sir, Our Lord, we have completed that which you commanded. We inform you that we have seen that land of Aztlán and that hill of Culhuacan where our parents and grandparents lived and migrated from, and we brought you samples of plants which grow and are cultivated there."

They also told him of all of the things that the mother of Huitzilopochtli had told them, how people could get young again by climbing the hill, and how in that land nobody died. They also reported the great grievances that ue had about Huitzilopochtli, her son, and how she awaited him still for she knew that after a certain time, he would be expelled from this land.

The king sent for Tlacaélel and had the wizards repeat in front of him all that they had said.

When they finished the story, Moctezuma and Tlacaélel began to cry, remembering their ancestors and the desire they had to see that place. They also cried because their god Huitzilopochtli would have to abandon them one day. And if their god left them, what would become of them?

- Luis Leal. *Mitos y leyendas de México/Myths and Legends of Mexico*. Santa Barbara, California: University of California, Santa Barbara, Center for Chicano Studies Publications, 2002. pp. 99–108.

Commentary

The myth of Aztlán is one of the most important myths in Chicano/a mythology. It is a foundational text that situates the Chicano population in the United States more than 30,000 years ago. This provides a legitimacy of origins; i.e. that the Chicano population in the Southwest are not foreigners as commonly perceived but that they have a right to be here since their ancestors, the Aztecs originally resided in this area of the United States. Aztlán then becomes the primordial land of origins; it is the lost paradise that Chicanos in a reverse migration are recuperating.

Aztlán appears in Chicano historical texts, political tracts as well as literary texts of all kind. It is also highly visible and frequently used in Chicano/a visual arts such as murals and paintings. Aztlán is a powerful myth that galvanized the Chicano movement in its early stages (1960s and 1970s) and gave Chicanos a definite sense of belonging in the Southwest.

The Return of Quetzalcóatl

One day a mysterious man arrived at Moctezuma's palace in the Great City of Tenochtitlan and told the guards that he wished to speak to the king. Once in his presence, Moctezuma observed that the man had no ears or fingers. He barely looked like a human being.

When the king asked him where he was from, the man told him that he was from the Land of the Mountain of Fire. When he asked him who had sent him, he told him that he had come on his own to tell him of the things that he had seen on the coast. The earless man told him that one day he saw a round hill that moved upon the water of the sea and that this thing had neared the rocks and the beach. He said that he had never seen the likes of this in his life, and that he was still frightened and amazed.

Moctezuma called one of his subjects and ordered him to go to the coast to investigate whether this stranger told the truth or lies. He also ordered his envoy to take the governor of the coastal province to task for his carelessness and for his lack of alertness.

The subject, accompanied by a slave, embarked on the journey and soon arrived at the governor's palace. After he had reprimanded the governor for his carelessness he ordered him to send messengers to find out if there was really a mobile hill off the coast.

The governor issued the order and sent some messengers to the coast; they did not take long in coming back and saying with great trepidation that they had seen a horrible round thing in middle of the waters, that it moved to and fro, and that some men appeared upon it from time to time.

The governor and Moctezuma's subject decided to go to the sea themselves with the purpose of satisfying their king's wishes.

When they arrived at the coast they hid behind some rocks so as not to be seen by the strangers. Soon they realized that all they had been told was indeed the truth. To better observe the strangers they climbed up into a tall tree, and from there they watched the men on the mysterious object lower a canoe into the water into which a few of them stepped and they began to fish near the rocks. Later, the canoe returned to the floating house.

Once Moctezuma's orders bad been carried out, the subject returned to Tenochtitlan without a moment's delay to tell the news to his king and recount what he had seen.

Upon arriving in the presence of Moctezuma the subject said, "Oh, powerful Sir, you may imprison me or put me to death, but what the mysterious man said is true. I myself, my Lord, wishing to see with my own eyes but what he told was true, climbed up a tall tree to see better, and here is what I saw: a house in the middle of the water from which emerged white men with white faces and white hands, and long, thick beards. Their dress, of every color: white, yellow, red, green, blue, and purple. Upon their heads they wear something round. I saw them put a canoe in the water and some of them got in and prepared to fish near the coast. At dusk they returned to their house on the sea. This is all that I can tell you now."

Moctezuma bowed his head and, without a word, he covered his mouth with his hand. He remained this way for a long while. It seemed as though he were mute for he was unable to offer any reply. Finally, after much time had passed, he gave a deep sigh and told the subject that he had brought him fatal news.

"Who can I believe if I cannot believe you? What do I gain by sending another messenger if you, with your own eyes, have seen the things of which you speak? I believe it is time to act."

Moctezuma called an assistant right away and told him to set free the man from the coast who was being held in custody, the man from the Land of the Mountain of Fire. When the assistant arrived at the prison cell, he found it mysteriously empty; the prisoner had escaped without a trace.

Once Moctezuma heard that, he said that he had suspected that the man had been a magician, and that he was glad that the prisoner had escaped for he had told the truth. The king quickly called one of his officials and ordered him to bring two silversmiths, two lapidaries, and two feather-weavers. The order was to be carried out in total secrecy under penalty of death.

When the artists arrived, they were given gold, precious stones, and beautiful feathers. The jewelers were ordered to make beautiful jewels, the lapidaries, to polish the precious gemstones, and the feather-weavers, to prepare ceremonial ornaments of rich colors.

Moctezuma told his subject, who was one of his favorites, "I have ordered that jewels be made, and that precious gems and feathers be worked, and I want you to take them as a gift to those who have arrived in our land. I want you to discover who sent them here, for that is the person who should receive the gifts. You must find out with absolute certainty if their chief is the one that our ancestors called Topiltzin or Quetzalcóatl. Our history tells us that when he left our land he said that he would return to govern this nation and recover the gold, silver, and the jewels that were hidden in the mountains. According to these histories, they will come to take all the riches that we now possess. If it is really Quetzalcóatl, make him welcome in my name and give him these gifts. You should also tell the governor to make all types of foods available to him: well-seasoned poultry and deer meat, well-baked bread, as well as fruit and chocolate. All this should be placed upon the beach and should then be taken to the house on the water where they stay. You should hand all these foods over to him so that he, his children, and his companions may eat. Pay close attention to see if he eats or if he refuses the food before him. If he eats and drinks, he is Quetzalcóatl for sure for this would indicate that he is familiar with the native dishes, that he had eaten them before, and that he has come back to taste them again. You must also tell him to wait until I die. When this occurs, he will be welcome in this land to take possession of his kingdom, since it is his. We know that he left it in charge of my ancestors to govern for him. I have always known that my dominions do not belong to me, that I only had them on loan. Tell him to permit me to finish my days here, and that then he can come and enjoy his properties. Do not go in fear or anxiety, and do not fear that they will kill you, I swear to you that I will provide for your children and give them my treasures and also make them part of my council. If for any reason he does not like the food that you are going to offer him and he shows craving for human meat and for eating you, let him eat you. I assure you that I will honor my promise of caring for your wife, your children, and all of your family."

The subject, obedient to his king, answered that he would gladly go. Accompanied by assistants carrying all of the presents, he left Tenochtitlan in secret under the shield of night. When they arrived at the governor's palace, he ordered him to have a variety of foods prepared. Once the dishes were ready, they took them to the coast where the white men could still be seen on their floating house.

The Aztec emissaries, without being seen, placed the food near the edge of the sea. The faithful subject waited there, accompanied by one of his assistants. In order to better observe what was happening, they climbed the same tree from which they had previously spied the white men during their earlier journey, and they saw many of them fishing in a canoe. As it was late, the two Aztecs decided not to call to them, but instead waited until the next day.

One hour before dawn, they took the foods that had been prepared to the coast and left them on top of some rocks close to where the white men fished. There they sat and waited; and when the sun came out, they saw that some of the men were out on deck. From the ship the soldiers were able to distinguish the two Aztecs sitting on the rocks, and they immediately lowered the canoe and four of them went out on the sea. When they disembarked, each greeted the other in his own language, but were unable to make themselves understood. The subject, by means of signs, made them understand that they could take the food to their floating house. The white men understood them and put everything into the boat. The Aztecs went with them.

On the ship, the Aztecs admired the strong construction, the spacious deck, and the numerous bunks. Their surprise was so great that they thought that all of it must be supernatural.

Once they overcame their curiosity, they asked to be taken to the chief. They were not able to make themselves understood, but finally one of the white men pointed to a man who stood on the bridge, leaning on a rudder, with his hand upon his cheek. The subject of Moctezuma, seeing that this man wore nicer clothes than others, understood that he was the chief. The subject cautiously approached him and, prostrating himself humbly before him, he presented the well-dressed man with the jewelry, the precious gems, and the art objects made from the beautiful plumage. When they saw these things, the bearded men were filled with joy. The objects were admired and passed from hand to hand.

Moctezuma's subject managed to communicate with signs to the leader of the white men that his king had sent those gifts and that he lived in the Great City of Tenochtitlan. Also by signs, the subject was able to indicate that the leader should partake of the food that he had brought for him. He tasted everything but he most enjoyed the chocolate, which he found refreshing and flavorful. The sailors shared his opinion.

After tasting some of the food that the white men offered them and after having drunk a liquid that they liked very much and that the men on the ship called wine, the two Aztecs—returned to the beach and prepared to depart on their journey back to Tenochtitlan to inform their king of all that had come to pass and to present to him the gifts and foods that the chief had sent.

When they arrived in the presence of Moctezuma, they told him all that they had seen. They described the ship, the appearance the white men, and the foods and drinks that they had tasted. Moctezuma refused to eat the crackers that they brought, saying that they were the food of the gods and that to eat them would be sacrilege. He called one of his priests and told him to take those foods to the city of Tula and bury them in the temple of Quetzalcóatl.

The chief of the white men had eaten and drank what the vassal had offered him. Quetzalcóatl had returned to reclaim his lands and his riches. The gods had abandoned Moctezuma!

- Luis Leal. *Mitos y leyendas de México/Myths and Legends of Mexico.* Santa Barbara, California: University of California, Santa Barbara, Center for Chicano Studies Publications, 2002. pp. 109–120.

Commentary

The Return of Quetzalcóatl refers to the promise Quetzalcóatl made his people that he would return someday. The Aztecs when they first spotted the Spaniards in their big ships on the Gulf of Mexico did not know what to think of it and thought that perhaps Quetzalcóatl, their long gone God, had returned. The myth above narrates the terrible conundrum in which Moctezuma found himself: are those people Gods who have returned or are they enemies who must be banished from Mexico? The hesitancy that Moctezuma displayed was eventually to cost him dearly—his empire.

FOLKTALES

The Enchanted Frog

Once a poor man and woman had three sons. The first son told his parents he wanted to go and find a life for himself, the second said the same, and the youngest also said he wanted to go find himself a life. The father and mother didn't want them to go, but finally they gave them permission and a blessing, and the sons set out.

The oldest went ahead of the others and he came to a resting place by a cottonwood tree, and a frog was singing there. He liked the song and shouted from below, "Why don't you come down here so that I can marry you?"

"No, no, I can't come down," the frog replied. "You couldn't make a life with me."

Finally, after the boy had tried for a long time to get her to come down, the frog jumped and fell into the boy's cape. When the boy saw her, he said, "What do I want with a frog?" And he threw her away and went on.

Later the second brother arrived there, and when he heard the frog singing so beautifully he said, "Come down so that I can marry you."

"No, sir," the frog said. "Yesterday a boy came by here and made me come down from my chamber, and when I came down he scorned me and threw me away."

The boy said he wouldn't do that. He said he really would marry her, and he spread out his cape for her to jump down. So the frog jumped down but when he saw it he said, "Uy, how disgusting! What do I want with a frog?" And he threw her away just as his brother had done, So then finally the youngest brother came along and like the others he heard the enchanted Frog singing in the cottonwood tree. The boy told her to come down from the cottonwood because he wanted to meet her.

"No, I can't do that," the frog told him. "Two boys have come by here and both have asked me to come down, and then they scorned me and threw me away." But the boy keep begging for her to come down until the frog said, "All right, spread out your cape for me to jump down." The boy spread out the cape and the frog hopped and fell in the cape, and the boy took her and put her in his pocket. Then he went on down the road.

He came to the town where his two brothers were living. They were married now and were very proud, and the youngest brother was married too—to the frog. When they were all reunited, they wrote to their parents to tell them they were married and to send them presents. And wives of the older brothers also wrote, but not the frog. The frog couldn't write. And the parents wrote back saying they wanted to receive gifts from the wives. They told them to send them three embroidered kerchiefs.

The youngest brother was heartsick, and when he got home to his frog he told her what his parents had written. "Don't worry," the frog told him. "Throw me into the sea." So he went to the sea and threw her in, and the frog came out with a little cape made of a single cloth embroidered with pure gold.

"Send this little cape to your parents," she told him. The sons all sent their gifts and the parents were amazed by the gift from youngest son's wife— a little cape made of a single cloth embroidered with pure gold.

But then the parents sent word to say that they wanted to meet their sons' wives, and told the sons to bring their wives for a visit. The sons all agreed to go to visit them with their wives, but the youngest was very worried and said to himself, "What am I going to do now? The frog doesn't even look like a woman." But when he went home and told the frog about it, she told him not to worry, that she would go too.

And since the frog knew that the wives of her brothers-in-law were spiteful, she went and started washing her hair with lye. The envious wives saw her and decided they were going to wash their hair with lye too. They washed their hair with lye and it all fell out and they were bald.

And then that night the frog told her husband, "Now take me and throw me into the deepest part of the sea. Leave me there and come for me in the morning."

The boy did that, but he was very sad because he didn't think he would see his frog ever again. The next day he got up very early and went to look for her at the place where he had thrown her into the sea, and there on the bank of the sea he found a princess in an elegant carriage.

"Here I am," she told him. "I'm free from my enchantment. Now let's go visit your parents." And they started out because the other brothers and their wives were already on their way.

They all arrived, and the parents were pleased to see their sons and their wives. The wives of the older two had their heads covered so no one could see they were bald. The parents were so pleased that they gave a banquet that night.

And when they were eating, the princess pretended she was stuffing garbanzos and eggs down the front of her dress, but she was really putting in money. But the bald-headed wives really did stuff garbanzos and eggs into their dresses.

After the banquet they all went to dance, and everyone's eye was on the beautiful princess and everyone said she was the prettiest woman they had ever seen. And with each turn she took as she was dancing she scattered pesos and silver coins. But the envious wives scattered the garbanzos and eggs they had stuffed into their bosoms when they were eating. The people ran to get the money, and the dogs ran to get the garbanzos and eggs!

- J. Manuel Espinosa. *Cuentos de Cuanto Hay/Tales from Spanish New Mexico.* Trans. Joe Hayes. Albuquerque: University of New Mexico Press, 1998. Pp. 103–106.

Commentary

As in other folktales such as "The Horse of Seven Colors," "The Enchanted Frog" follows a similar pattern of having three sons going out to seek their fortunes. Again the youngest one is the one that gets the best wife for he does not disdain the ugly frog but marries her. This is a reverse of the frog who is really a prince and until a princess kisses him he becomes free of the enchantment and assumes his human form. In this case it is a woman who has been enchanted and becomes human after she finds someone to marry her. The folktale was collected from Alensio Chacón (Age 58, Alcalá, New Mexico).

LEGENDS

La Llorona

Attention, ladies and gentlemen, for I am going to tell you the story of La Llorona, the mysterious woman dressed in white who eternally searches for her children.

It is said that after the Conquest of Mexico by the soldiers of Hernán Cortés the dwellers of the city, which was known as the Great Tenochtitlan, would hear at midnight—usually when the moon was bright—sad, moaning wails that seemed to be the cry of a woman in great pain.

During the first months, the citizenry of the city, when hearing the mournful cry, would cross their hearts and lock the door and windows for they thought that it was an afflicted soul in search of salvation. Not even the bravest of the conquistadores dared to go out into street after midnight, the hour when the terrifying cries were most often heard.

The lament went on night after night, but curiosity began to overcome fear for some people. Anxious to unravel the mystery, they began opening their windows to see what went on in the street. Others opened their doors, and some even stepped out of their houses when they heard the cries. They all wanted to be the first to discover the source of the mournful moaning.

Before having seen anything, and without knowing for certain, most thought that it was a ghost, for the cries, which came from a great distance, were always clear and did not seem to be human. Some said that they had seen the ghost—but deathly afraid, they could not tell what they saw. Some even went totally mad.

After many attempts, they finally determined that the cries came from a woman dressed in white who covered her face in her thick white shawl. Without knowing for certain who the mysterious woman was, they named her La Llorona—the Wailing Woman, and this is what we still call her today.

Soon they found out that La Llorona was a woman who had lost her children. According to some, she herself killed them, and now, in repentance, she searches for them to no avail.

They also say that La Llorona, not finding her children in Mexico City, began to appear in the streets of other cities; always with the same dress and the same shawl covering her face, the face that no one has gazed upon. And what is most extraordinary is that she could appear at the same time in various cities in Mexico, Central America, and Aztlán—where they tell me she is greatly feared.

Not everyone believes that the woman dressed in white murdered her children. The indigenous people of Mexico fear her because they think she is the goddess Cihuacóatl who, since the days of King Moctezuma, roams crying through the streets of the city, saying, "Oh, my children! Woe is me for now I must abandon them!"

They also say that one night, a few years after the Conquest, when Martín Ecatl governed Tlatelolco, the goddess Cihuacóatl showed up at a humble home and stole a baby whose mother had left him alone in the cradle.

If La Llorona is the goddess Cihuacóatl for the indigenous people, for the mestizo she is none other than Doña Marina, Malinche, the woman who helped the Spaniards conquer Mexico and by whom Hernán Cortés had children. They say the Conqueror wanted to take their children to Spain, but that La Malinche, to keep him from it, put them to death and threw them into one of the numerous canals that ran through Mexico City in those days. Doña Marina has never repented, and since then she roams the streets by night in search of her children.

Others say that La Malinche does not search for her children, but that she comes from the other world in torment, rueful for selling out her people by taking sides with the conquistadors.

Men in particular fear La Llorona for they say that she has the power to lure them, take them to unknown places, and kill them there. To fool men, she appears to them with the face of a girlfriend, a wife, or a beautiful young woman impossible to resist. She is always wearing white, has black hair, a thin build, and penetrating eyes that hypnotize those who dare look at them directly.

Word has it that an army officer was once walking in front of a church at night in Mexico City, and that he suddenly came upon a woman dressed in white with her face covered in a shawl of the same color. Since it is not common to see women alone at such hours, for it was very late, he stopped the woman, wanting to know who she was. The officer, who was on his way back from a party, was feeling quite lightheaded. When he detained the woman in white, he said,

"Take off your shawl so I can see if you are pretty. If you are, I will walk with you."

La Llorona, for the woman he had stopped was none other, uncovered her face—what the soldier set eyes on froze his blood. Instead of seeing a beautiful woman, what he saw was more a skull-face. Although a bit inebriated, the soldier fell to the ground unconscious. When he came to, he had lost his mind. La Llorona had again wreaked vengeance, appearing with the semblance of death.

A friend of mine in Guanajuato told me that one night a young man on horseback was crossing a river and heard the weeping of a woman. He and his horse, both surprised at hearing those cries, stopped in their tracks. The horse raised its ears, a sign that it had been spooked. It would not move forward no matter how hard the young man tried to spur it on. When the young man at last was able to get out of the river, the horse took off in a gallop at great speed, unrestrained. The young man then realized that a woman dressed in white was chasing him, her long hair flowing behind her. She seemed to be flying in his pursuit. The horse kept on madly galloping, and, at a turn in the road, the young man was thrown from the horse, the animal bolted in a mad race. Fortunately the horseman did not die. But the next morning, when some peasants came upon him, he seemed to have lost his mind. They took him to his house, for he was able to tell them who he was, and when he told his mother what had happened, she told him this:

"You most certainly encountered La Llorona. Give thanks to God that she did not kill you, as she tends to kill all men who cross her path in the night."

I for one, ladies and gentlemen, do know why La Llorona tricks and kills men to avenge what a man once did to her, leaving her abandoned with no means of protection. Unable to support the children that the man had left her, she had to kill them and throw them into one of the many canals in Mexico City.

Children are the ones who fear La Llorona most, and they will not go out at night especially when the moon is high. Even though mothers always tell their children, "Behave yourselves! For if you don't, La Llorona will come and take you away with her!" many children disobey and misbehave. Then La Llorona takes them into the winds, and they are never seen again.

This is the legend of La Llorona. As far as I am concerned, my friends, I do not believe that La Llorona is just any ghost, or the goddess Cihuacóatl, or La Malinche, or even a woman seeking to avenge her mistreatment by men, nor do I think that she is a bogeyman invented to scare children and make them obey their parents. I believe that she is death in person, and that she roams in search of those who will soon die and don't know it. If this were not the case, how could she stay alive for so many years? This is why we hear her on moonlit nights, and most of all, when someone is about to die. I also believe it is La Llorona whom the dogs bark a night, not the moon, as some say. When people in small towns hear dogs bark they say, "The dogs are howling at the moon, who is nearing death? Could it be Pedro, the rich man?"

This, for me, is the true legend of La Llorona. But you can figure it out yourselves.

This is how the story teller spoke, and those who hear him—men, women, and children alike—go home to their houses by the light of the moon with more fear than usual. Before lying down to rest, they lock the doors and windows just in case.

- Luis Leal. *Mitos y leyendas de México/Myths and Legends of Mexico.* Santa Barbara, CA: University of California, Santa Barbara, Center for Chicano Studies Publications, 2002, 127–133.

Commentary

La Llorona is one of the most common legends found in Chicano and Mexican culture. There are literally thousands of variants of La Llorona legends since people generally "know" of a particular case where the Llorona appeared to someone. Therefore, if you ask a person if they know who La Llorona is they will describe her as the woman that scares children into good behavior. They will usually tell you of an uncle or cousin or other relative who saw La Llorona. Professor Luis Leal provides the basic kernel of La Llorona legend but in addition expands on the notion that La Malinche is La Llorona. La Llorona appeals to Chicanos due to their identification with La Llorona's children. Metaphorically speaking the Chicano population has felt bereft of a mother country since neither Mexico nor the United States claimed them as lawful, authentic citizens. La Llorona appears in murals and painting as well as literary works.

The Wailing Woman (La Llorona)

People were accustomed to saying that all of my people around here used to hear the Wailing Woman. As for me, I never heard her, nor did I believe in it. One time I did read a book about the Wailing Woman, just so I could find out for myself what the Wailing Woman was all about, where she came from, or why people claimed that they could hear the Wailing Woman.

In this book it says that during the thirteenth century they used to kill the persons who were supposedly witches. And this one particular woman, they tied her to a post so as to burn her alive because people claimed she was a witch. All of this came from Spain. When they tied her to the post to burn her, as I understand it, they burned an innocent person who was not a witch. And if they burned an innocent woman, those who burned her, as well as their descendants, were going to hear her cry for centuries to come. On the night that they burned her, some of their relatives, 20 miles away, heard her cry.

And from that time onward, until right this very moment, they've heard her wail—so say the people—throughout all parts of the world that the Spaniards conquered. So there's people scattered all over the globe who are descendants of those persons who burned this woman, who up until today can hear her wail.

I don't believe it. I guess I'm not a descendant of hers because I haven't heard her.

- Nasario García. *Tales of Witchcraft and the Supernatural in the Pecos Valley.* Santa Fe, New Mexico: Western Edge Press, 1999, 94–95.

Commentary

"The Wailing Woman" is an unusual version of La Llorona. However, there seem to be as many variants as there are people since each person has personal, individual knowledge of a Llorona tale. The above is interesting for the tracing of its origins in Spain in the thirteenth century.

La Llorona

La Llorona was a woman who was in love with a Spaniard. She had several children from him. One day he decided to marry a woman from Spain and to leave his lover. The jilted woman in a fit of rage killed her children. She was punished by God for killing her children to roam the waterways, canals, rivers, lakes in search of her children. She wails at night as she looks for her children: "*AAAyyyy mis hijos!*" ("OOHHH my children!")

- As told by Susana Escamilla de Tarango, to the author.

Commentary

This legend provides a basic kernel for the La Llorona legend.

Omens Related to La Llorona from Sahagún

Omen number six: "At night you will hear the anguished wailing of a woman who cries: 'Oh, my sons, your destruction is near.' and 'Oh my sons! Where shall I take you so that you will not perish?'"

Commentary

Sahagún provides the Mesoamerican strand of La Llorona legend since it is believed by many that it is not purely a European legend but is also an indigenous one. The two strands, i.e. European and Mesoamerican have converged and given birth to the Mexican and Chicano Llorona.

Cihuacóatl as La Llorona

The principal goddess was called Cihuacóatl goddess of the Xochimilca and, although she was the particular deity of the Xochimilca, she was venerated in Mexico and in Texcoco. The goddess Cihuacóatl was made of stone. She [. . .] was dressed [. . .] all in white—skirt, blouse, and mantle. If [her priests] saw that eight days had passed and no one had been sacrificed, they took a baby's cradle and put in it a sacrificial flint knife, called "The Child of Cihuacóatl" [. . .] They wrapped it up in cloth. They would give the cradle to a woman so that she might take it on her back to the market place. They would instruct her to go to the most important merchant woman. She would carry the cradle to the market [. . .] asking her to look after it until she came back. [. . .] Surprised that, not having nursed all day, the baby had not cried [. . .], the merchant woman would then open the cradle and find in it the sacrificial knife, the "child" of Cihuacóatl.

The people, on seeing this, cried out that the goddess had come and had appeared in the market place. They would say that she had brought along her child to show her hunger and to reproach the lords for their neglect in feeding her.

- Fray Diego Durán. *Historia de las Indias de Nueva España*, 1579.

La Malinche

How Doña Marina Was a Ruler [Cacique] and the Daughter of
Important Rulers Governing Villages and Populations and in the
Manner in Which She Came to Be in Tabasco

Before I begin the story of the Great Montezuma and his great Mexico
and Mexicans, I want to say that which pertains to Doña Marina, since from
childhood she was a great lady and ruler of villages and of populations; and
it is in this manner that I begin my story: Her father and mother were rulers
and chiefs of a town called Painala and they also had other towns that were
under their domain about eight leagues from the Ville of Guazacualco. Her
father died leaving the little girl and her mother widowed. Her mother married
another chief who had not been previously married and they had a son from
this union. And according to the story, they loved him very much, that is,
the son they had after they were married. They [Malinche's mother and step
father] agreed between themselves to give the inheritance to their new son after
they died and so that there would not be any question as to the new heir they
gave away the young girl, Malinche, to some Indians from Xicalango during
the night so no one would see. Then they spread the word that she [Malinche]
had died. And during that precise moment another child died who happened
to be the daughter of one of their slaves and they announced that she [the
slave's daughter] was the heir i.e. Malinche, who had died. In this manner,
the Indians from Xicalango gave her [Malinche] to the Indians from Tabasco
and the Tabascans gave her to Cortés. And I met her mother and her brother,
the son of the old lady. He was by now a grown man and was the ruler of
his villages since the second husband of the old lady had died also. And after
they became Christians, the old lady took the name of Marta and her son
became Lázaro. This I know very well because in the year of 1523, after having
conquered Mexico and other provinces, there was an insurgent movement
led by Cristóbal de Olid in the Hibueras. Cortés went there and passed by
Guazacualco. The majority of the people in that town went with him, as I will
narrate later on in its proper place and time, and since Doña Marina in all the
wars in New Spain and Tlaxcala and Mexico was such an excellent woman and
a great tongue [translator] as I will narrate later. For this reason Cortés took
her with him everywhere he went. And at the time of that journey she was
married to Juan Jaramillo, whom she had married in a town called Orizaba in
front of certain witnesses, one of which called himself Aranda, a person who
was from Tabasco. And he [Aranda] told us about the marriage and it was not

in the manner narrated by the Chronicler Gómara. Doña Marina had a great presence and was absolute ruler over all the Indians in New Spain.

When Cortés was in the town of Guazacualco, he sent for all the caciques [chiefs] from that province so that he could talk to them regarding our Sacred Doctrine and about their good treatment. It was then that Doña Marina's mother and half brother, Lázaro came together with the other caciques. Days before, Doña Marina had told me that she was from that province and had been the ruler of the town. Cortés knew this very well as did Aguilar, the other interpreter. So when the mother and brother came they recognized each other since clearly Doña Marina was her daughter for she looked just like her mother. The mother and brother became fearful because they thought they had sent for them so that they could be killed and so they were crying. When Doña Marina saw them crying she consoled them and told them not to be afraid; that when they sent her away with the Xicalango Indians they did not know what they were doing. That she forgave them. She gave them many gold jewels and clothing and she told them to return to their town, that God had been kind to her—had saved her from worshiping idols. He had granted her the grace to become a Christian and to have a son from her master Cortés and to be married to a gentleman such as was her husband Juan Jaramillo. That even if they offered her to be a cacique of all the surrounding provinces in New Spain, she would not accept for she preferred to serve her husband and her master, Cortés, more than anything else in the world. [. . .] And returning to our story, Doña Marina knew the language from Guazacualco, which is the same as the Mexican [i.e. Aztec] language. She also knew the language from Tabasco just as Jerónimo de Aguilar knew the language from Yucatan and Tabasco, which is one and the same [i.e. Maya]. They, Doña Marina and Aguilar, understood each other well. Aguilar would translate Maya into Castilian Spanish to Cortés. This was a great start for our conquest, and it was thus that all things would happen, thanks be to God, very easily. I have wanted to declare this because without having Doña Marina we could not understand the language of New Spain and Mexico [i.e. Nahuatl the language of the Aztecs].

- Bernal Díaz del Castillo's *Historia verdadera de la conquista de la Nueva España.* [1632] Mexico City: Editorial Porrúa, 1967, pp 56–57. (My translation)

La Malinche. . . La Malinalli

The historical legend goes like this: Malinalli was given up by her parents at an early age and she lived throughout her youth in the southern region of Mexico acquiring the languages of the many different tribal peoples among whom she lived. When Cortés arrived to Mexico, a gift was given to him of many women, and among them was Malinalli. In very little time, the Spaniards discovered Malinalli's gift with languages, and her ability to translate and speak on behalf of Cortés made her his favorite consort. She traveled everywhere with him, and is mentioned many times by the famous Spanish chronicler, Fray Bernal Díaz de Castillo (1992) [sic]. There are codices painted by the Aztec scribes enslaved by the Spaniards in which she appears, dressed in native robes, standing by the side of Cortés, with the traditional symbol for wind, or speech, coming out of her mouth. She became Cortés' lover and, in time, has a son from him. This is where the notion of her as *la chingada,* the "fucked one," the "raped one," comes from. In his book, *The Labyrinth of Solitude,* Octavio Paz (1959) writes a brilliant description of how we, as Mexicans, have identified with this notion of being *chingados* because of our historical cultural origins.

This is when the legend becomes polysemic, when the multiple meanings begin to jump out, when the various political interest latch onto the narrative to make her story theirs.

- Sarah Amira de la Garza. *María Speaks: Journeys into the Mysteries of the Mother in My Life as a Chicana.* New York: Peter Lang, 2004, 105–107.

The Virgin of Guadalupe

Nuestra Señora de Guadalupe: The Story of our Lady of Guadalupe

On one cold winter morning in December, 1531 an Aztec Indian man named Juan Diego was walking to church. It had been ten years since the mighty battles with the men of Cortés had ended. The soldiers and warriors had put down their weapons and now peace had returned to his land, Juan himself had recently converted to Christianity. It was his habit to go to the church for religious instruction.

His church was not in his village but in Tlatelolco, a village just outside of Mexico City. His usual path took him by the houses in the village but this morning for some reason he decided to walk over the hill of Tepeyac.

As he neared the top of the hill he heard voices singing. Now he had heard the voices of people singing the holy praises to the Lord in church but he had never heard such beautiful music as this in all his life. He heard the tinkling of bells and the voices moved around him like the wind itself. He thought that this must be what the voices of heavenly angels sound like.

As he reached the top of the hill the beautiful singing voices and music stopped. Everything became very still and Juan no longer even felt the coldness. He heard his name being called, "Juan, Juan."

A traditional depiction of The Virgin of Guadalupe.

Suddenly he saw a bright cloud with the shafts of a colorful rainbow coming out of it. The cloud came to a stop before him and when the cloud split in two there was a woman standing there. The woman looked like a beautiful Aztec princess. Her clothes shone like the sun and she was surrounded by the heavenly light. When she spoke Juan heard the heavenly music he had heard before. He knew it was a miracle so he fell to his knees to pray.

"Juan," the heavenly woman said, "I have chosen you to deliver a message to the bishop at the cathedral."

"But beautiful woman," answered Juan, "I am a poor Indian. I am not worthy to deliver a message to the bishop. Why have I been chosen?"

With a soothing kindness in her voice the woman answered, "I am the Blessed Virgin Mary, the mother of the Lord Jesus Christ. Just know that I have chosen you to be my messenger on this earth. Go to the bishop and tell him that he is to build a church for me here on the top of this hill. The church is to be a shrine which will show my love for all my people. Go, give the bishop my message."

Juan ran faster than ever to the cathedral to give the Virgin's message to the bishop. When he arrived at the cathedral he knocked on the door to the bishop's quarters. The bishop's helpers opened the door and asked Juan what he wanted. He told them, "I have a message for the bishop from the Virgin Mary, the Mother of God."

When they heard this they could not help but laugh to hear a poor Indian tell such a story. But Juan was persistent and eventually they let him in to see the bishop . The bishop listened to Juan's story but did not believe him. He told him, "Juan, your story is incredible. Imagine the Virgin appearing to you on a hill with a message for me to build a church! Go for now and we'll think about it."

Juan left feeling like a failure. He knew the bishop's helpers had laughed at him and that the bishop had not believed his story. He felt that he had let the Blessed Virgin down. When he returned to Tepeyac he once again saw the Virgin. She floated on air as if nothing were holding her up except her heavenly powers.

"O Holy Mother. I have failed you. The bishop did not believe me. I knew I was not worthy."

"Juan, do you not know that now you are within my graces? I have chosen you and I will make it be as it should. Go back to the bishop and give him my message again. A church must be built in my name on this hill."

Juan returned to the bishop a second time. Again the bishop did not believe Juan. He said, "Juan, if you have truly seen the Blessed Virgin Mary, bring back a sign that the miracle is real. If not, then never come to me with this story again."

On his way back to tell the Virgin that he needed a sign Juan received the news that his uncle was dying of typhoid fever. Juan immediately rushed to the side of his uncle but when he arrived he found out that it was almost too late. His uncle asked him to bring the priest because he knew he would not last for another day.

Juan rushed to the Virgin to tell her what the bishop had said and to ask forgiveness for not coming right back. "O, Blessed Virgin. I was late because my uncle is dying and is not expected to last another day. Also, the bishop requires a sign that you really spoke to me. Please help Blessed Mother."

"Juan, do you not know that I am here to help you? I have already cured your uncle. He will live. Now go to the top of the hill where only the cactus grows. There you will find a rose bush in bloom. Take those roses to the bishop and he will believe."

Juan went to the top of the hill and there was a beautiful rose bush in full bloom. When Juan saw the roses on that cold winter day he knew it was a miracle and he knelt down to pray. He knew that when the bishop saw the roses that had bloomed in the middle of winter and smelled their beautiful fragrance, he would believe his story. Juan gathered the roses in his *tilma,* which is a kind of

Juan Diego y la Virgen (1999) by Alvaro Suman.
Source: Courtesy of Alvaro Suman.

poncho. He showed the roses to the Virgin and she said, "Now take these to the bishop and tell him to build the church in my honor."

When Juan arrived at the cathedral for the third time the bishop's helpers refused to let him see the bishop. Juan told them that he had the sign the bishop had asked for. They said, "If you have the sign let us see it. Let us see the sign of a miracle. Then you will see the bishop."

Juan opened his *tilma* and roses tumbled onto the floor. Roses fell out of the *tilma* like snow falling to the ground. Beautiful, fresh roses lined the inside of the *tilma*. In their astonishment the bishop's helpers reached out to touch the roses and felt their soft, smooth petals. They knew that it was indeed a miracle.

When Juan showed the bishop the roses the bishop also knew that it was a holy sign from heaven. As Juan opened his *tilma* more roses fell to the ground. Even more miraculously, inside Juan's *tilma* was the image of the Holy Mother as Juan had seen her on the hill of Tepeyac. The bishop and his helpers fell to their knees at the sight of the holy image and prayed to the Virgin.

The bishop built a church on the site Juan showed them on the hill of Tepeyac. Now the site is called Guadalupe. To this day Juan's *tilma* with the image of the Holy Mother is inside the shrine to the Blessed Virgin. Prayerful worshipers can look at the *tilma* and be reminded of the love the Holy Mother has for her people. For all eternity the shrine to Our Lady of Guadalupe is a reminder of the miraculous apparition that appeared to Juan Diego many years ago.

- Retold by Angel Vigil *Una Linda Raza: Cultural and Artistic Traditions of the Hispanic Southwest.* Golden, CO: Fulcrum Publishing, 1998, 47–49.

The Devil at the Dance

This man who ran around was a good-looking man, and all of the women were after him. And then he went and asked a young lady to dance and shortly after they started dancing, by chance the girl happened to look behind him and saw a tail and saw that he also had hoofs. Then the girl got scared and left him, and suddenly there was a cracking noise. The cracking noise sounded loud and he disappeared. It was the evil spirits.

- Nasario García. *Tales of Witchcraft and the Supernatural in the Pecos Valley.* Santa Fe: Western Edge Press, 1999, 63.

Commentary

"The Devil at the Dance" is a very popular tale which seems to resurface periodically. In the 1970s at the height of discotheque popularity there was a rumor that the devil had appeared at a discotheque in Tijuana, Mexico.

The rumor that the devil was appearing all along the border at Mexican discotheques became quite common. See my article: "The Devil at the Discotheque: A Semiotic Analysis of the Devil Legend." In *Monsters with Iron Teeth: Perspectives on Contemporary Legend, III.* Edited by Jillian Bennet and Paul Smith. Sheffield, UK: Sheffield Academic Press, 1988, 147–158.

The Devil at the Dance

There were these two sisters who wanted to go to the dance being held at the village that night. They asked their parents if they could go but the parents refused to give them permission. The young ladies wanted to go to the dance very badly so after their parents went to sleep they sneaked out of the house and went to the dance. One of them began to dance with a handsome man. She danced with him all night. When the clock struck twelve she happened to look at his feet and he had the claws of a rooster instead of human feet. The girls were frightened to death and went right home. They realized that one of them had danced with the devil all night.

- As told to the author by grandmother Susana Escamilla de Tarango.

"Look Daddy, I Already Have Teeth!"

There was this man who was on his way to visit his girlfriend. And on the way, he heard a baby crying and headed in that direction and he found him. He picked him up and got on the horse with him. When he got on the horse, the baby said to him: "Look, daddy, I already have teeth!" It was then that he saw the baby's teeth, and he tossed the baby down and took off and he never again went to see his girlfriend at night. During the day, yes, but not at night.

- Nasario García. *Tales of Witchcraft and the Supernatural in the Pecos Valley.* Santa Fe, NM: Western Edge Press, 1999, 63.

The Ball of Fire

This is the story about a neighbor that we had. It was late at night when he was on his way home from playing pool. It happened right here in Villanueva, and on his way home right in front of our house. Dad saw a very strong light go by next to our neighbor. It was a ball of fire. And Dad claims that it was none other than a witch who passed by the neighbor. And he never ever again played pool late at night, let alone go out at night. Those balls of fire that jumped from one side of the ditch to the other, right here in Villanueva, were witches, according to some people.

- Nasario García. *Tales of Witchcraft and the Supernatural in the Pecos Valley.* Santa Fe, NM: Western Edge Press, 1999, 63.

The Disobedient Son

This is the story about a very disobedient son who didn't obey his father. It's true because my grandma used to tell us about it. She saw it back when she was a girl. The father used to head down this one road, but the boy didn't like it. One day the son got angry and he raised his arm in anger to strike his father. As he did so, his hand shriveled up, and at the same time the ground swallowed him up to his waist. Then the people began to pray and pray, but they couldn't free him, so then they tried to dig him out. The more they dug, the farther down he went, not to mention the fact that the dirt was holding him back until he dried up from the waist down. Then the son promised God that if He got him out, he would roam the four corners of the earth for the rest of his life, preaching the word of God and what had happened to him with his father so that sons and daughters of other parents wouldn't be mean to their parents—and would obey them. If not, they would suffer the same fate as he had. After God opened up the earth and the son was set free, he kept his promise. He roamed the four corners of the earth until he died.

- Nasario García. *Tales of Witchcraft and the Supernatural in the Pecos Valley.* Santa Fe, NM: Western Edge Press, 1999,. 69.

Commentary

The "Disobedient Son" tale is a very popular one. It is used by parents to warn their sons and daughters not to be disrespectful for if they are punishment can come swiftly in the form of having your arm wither or the earth swallowing you. Chicano author Tomás Rivera wrote a vignette in his novel "*. . . Y no se lo tragó la tierra/ . . . And the Earth Did Not Part.*" (Berkeley, California: Quinto Sol Publications, 1972), related to this notion of supernatural punishment. In Rivera's novel, the punishment does not come to pass.

JOKES (JESTS)

"Jaló!"

Bueno. Este era un siñor. Era un americano. Y 'taba un mexicano . . .'taba componiendo su carro. Y cada vez que lo prendía no jalaba. Y, pos, si americano creía que podía decir 'hello' en español. Y li ijo:—¡Jaló!
Y li ice el mexicano:—Pos, qué ti importa si jaló o no jaló?

[Well. There is this man. He was an American. And there was this Mexican . . . he was fixing his car. And each time he tried to start the car it would not start. And, well, this American man thought he could say "hello" in Spanish and he said: "*Jaló!*" (meaning in Spanish "Did it start?"). And the Mexican man told him: "What do you care if it starts or does not start?"]

- José Reyna. *Raza Humor: Chicano Joke Tradition in Texas.* San Antonio, TX: Penca Books, n.d. [My translation.]

"Su Mamá Va a Cayerse" *[Your Mother Is a Jersey Cow]*

Iba un señor en una carretera y iba la pobrecita . . . llevaba la mamá sentada, la ancianita, pa' allá (cayéndose). Pasa un americano que estaba en, este, aprendiendo español. Y le . . . y por quedar bien, le dice al señor:—¡Oiga, señor! ¡Su mamá va a cayerse! ¡Su mamá va a cayerse! (Vaca Jersey).

Y le dice:—¡Condenado, éste!, dice. ¡Pos, la tuya será brema! (Vaca Brahma).

[There was this man driving on the highway and he had his elderly mother sitting on the seat but falling to the side. An American man who was learning Spanish thought he would do a good deed, so he yells to the driver: "Listen Mister, your mother is going to fall down." However his Spanish sounded like he was saying "Your mother is a Jersey cow." So the driver yells back: "Well, your mother is a Brahma cow!"]

- José Reyna. *Raza Humor: Chicano Joke Traditions in Texas.* San Antonio, TX: Penca Books, n.d., 42

Commentary

The Spanish words *"Va a caerse"* are conflated as *"vaca jersey"* by the English-speaking man. This joke belongs to the general category of verbal confusion between English and Spanish or Spanish and English. This category includes the mispronunciation of one word that makes it have a totally different meaning in the other language, that is, in Spanish or in English. In addition, the jokes present the tensions between Anglos and Chicanos and oftentimes provide an excuse for the Chicano/a to berate or curse the Anglo-American who appears stupid in the joke.

"They Ain't Got Their Clothes On!"

Hablando de los Aggies, iban dos Aggies caminando, eh. Y estaba una cerca muy alta. Una cerca, pero de palo, tú sabes, pero bien alta. Y le dice un Aggie al otro:——Qué habrá áhi?

———*Pos, no se.*

———*¿Por qué no te subes?*

____*Orale, pos, dale. Dame . . . gimme a footlift, áhi.*

Se pone el otro bato y la da un footlift y se sube el bato, y le dice:———*Oye, bato. Andan encueraos! tú sabes.*

———*Y, ¿qué son? mujeres o hombres?*

———Goddamn, don't be stupid man! They ain't got their clothes on! How can I tell?

[Speaking about the Aggies (Texas A&M students). There were two Aggies walking, ok. And there was this fence that was very high. This wooden fence but, you know, very high. And one Aggie says to another: "I wonder what's on the other side?"

"Well, I don't know."

"Why don't you climb up and see?"

"OK. Give me a footlift, here."

So the other guy gives him a footlift and the dude climbs up and says: "Listen dude. There are some nude people here!"

"And what are they, men or women?"

"Goddamn, don't be stupid man! They ain't got their clothes on! How can I tell?"]

- José Reyna. *Raza Humor: Chicano Joke Tradition in Texas.* San Antonio, TX: Penca Books, n.d. [My translation.]

Commentary

This joke belongs to the "Stupid Aggie" category of jokes. It provides an opportunity to laugh at the Texas A&M students who have the reputation among the other university students of being stupid since the school was originally an agricultural school.

"Pedro de Urdimales y la esposa del Diablo"

Pedro de Urdimales jue a trabajar con el diablo, y era . . . era tan curioso así, que un día onde andaba trabajando, le mandó un jarro de atole el diablo, que no lo empinara ni le metiera la mano y que se comiera el atole. Entonces le hizo on abujero en el fondo, y le ponía el dedo, ves, y le quitaba el dedo y se pegaba el chorro de atole en la boca y la volvía a tapar con el dedo.

———*Pero, hombre, dijo, éste está . . . tá muy vivo, dijo. Yo creo que yo lo voy a matar. Dijo:*———*Sabes que a la noche, dijo, vamos a ir yo y mi mujer y tú, dijo, a recibir un ángel que vive, dijo, en el voladero fulano, dijo, allí nos vamos a acostar en la orilla pa' recibir el ángel.*

Bueno. Pedro, siempre redingando (?), verdad, fue y se acostó en la orilla del . . . del voladero, ves. Entonces pensó, y dijo:—Lo que quiere el diablo, dijo, es matarme. Se durmió la diabla, la esposa del . . . del diablo y la cambió pa la orilla y él se hizo contra el diablo. El diablo se levantó y agarró a la vieja y la aventó pa' abajo. Creía que era Pedro, y el diablo por eso, yo creo, no tiene mujer. Porque se la mató Pedro de Urdimales.

[Pedro de Urdimales went to work for the devil and he was very curious, so one day when he was working, the devil sent him a glass of gruel. The devil told him not to drink from it; not to put his hand in it or drink the gruel. Then [Pedro] made a hole at the bottom of the glass the size of his finger. He would take his finger off the bottom of the glass and drink from it.

"Man, this guy is too smart," said the devil. "I think I am going to kill him." He told Pedro: "You know, tonight we are going—you and I and my wife—to meet an angel who lives by the cliff such and such. We are going to sleep by the cliff's edge to greet the angel."

"Very well." Pedro, who was always griping, "ok", went to lie down by the edge of the cliff, see. But then he thought: "What the devil wants to do is to kill me."

The devil's wife went to sleep and Pedro moved her to the edge of the cliff and he went to sleep next to the devil. The devil got up and grabbed his wife and threw her down the cliff. He thought it was Pedro. And the devil, that is why I think, he does not have a wife. Because Pedro de Urdimales killed her.]

- José Reyna. *Raza Humor: Chicano Joke Tradition in Texas.* San Antonio, TX: Penca Books, n.d. [My translation.]

Commentary

Pedro de Urdimales, which literally means Peter the Evildoer, is a trickster figure in Hispanic folklore. He is always playing jokes on the other characters and always getting the best of them including the devil, as the above joke demonstrates. Pedro de Urdimales is known all over Spain, Latin America, Mexico, and the Hispanic United States.]

Gente de Mucha Cabeza

Andaba un turista en México y oyó a un joven, "¡La cabeza de Pancho Villa, la cabeza de Pancho Villa!" Y otra vez, "¡La cabeza de Pancho Villa!"

Y la compra el turista, "Pos hombre, es una gran cosa. Pues en México la han buscado y nunca la han podido encontrar y yo la voy a comprar." La compró.

Llega acá a la frontera y viene otro chamaquillo, "¡La cabeza de Pancho Villa, la cabeza de Pancho Villa! ¡Barata! ¡La vendo, la cabeza de Pancho Villa!"

Le dice el pelado chingado, el turista, "¡Qué cómo la cabeza de Pancho Villa! Mira, aquí la traigo. Ya la compré."

"Ah," dice, "pero ésa es cuando era viejo y ésta es de chamaco. Mire. Está más chiquita que la que trae usté."

[There was a tourist in Mexico, and he heard a young man yelling: "The head of Pancho Villa! The head of Pancho Villa!" And once again: "The head of Pancho Villa!" (The young man was selling the head of Pancho Villa.)

And the tourist bought it: "Well man, this is a great thing! In Mexico they have been searching for it and have never been able to find it. I am going to buy it!" So he bought it.

When he arrives at the border another kid yells: "The head of Pancho Villa! The head of Pancho Villa! Cheap! I am selling the head of Pancho Villa!"

So the damned guy—the tourist says: "How can you say you are selling the head of Pancho Villa! Look, I have it here. I already bought it!"

"Oh," the kid says, "but that one is when he was an old man and this one is when he was a child. Look. This one is smaller than the one you have."]

- Américo Paredes. *Uncle Remus con Chile.* Houston: Arte Público Press, 1993, 70–71. Author's translation.

"Dogs Allowed"

Now that you mention these little towns in central Texas. There was one in which they had a restaurant with a sign that said, "No Dogs or Mexicans Allowed."

So down the street just a little ways was another restaurant run by some Mexican people, and they put up a sign: "Dogs Allowed. Gringos Too."

- Américo Paredes. *Uncle Remus con Chile.* Houston: Arte Público Press, 1993, 43.

Commentary

The joke is a sad commentary on the discrimination and segregation practiced in Texas and other parts of the United States previous to the 1960s civil rights movements. It turns the tables around and make the "gringos," or Anglo-American people appear in the eyes of the Mexican American population to be a notch below dogs.

"No comía de eso" [He Did Not Eat That]

Fue un mexicano a un restaurante por allá en el centro de Texas. Entró y se sentó en una de las mesas. "Let me see the menu."

Entonces viene un mesero, "I'm sorry," *dice,* "but we don't serve Mexicans here."

"What the hell!" *dice.* "I don't eat Mexicans!"

[A Mexican went to a restaurant in Central Texas. He went in and sat down in one of the tables. "Let me see the menu."

Then the waiter came over, "I'm sorry," he said, "but we don't serve Mexicans here."

"What the hell!" he says, "I don't eat Mexicans!"]

- Américo Paredes. *Uncle Remus con Chile.* Houston: Arte Público Press, 1993, 43. Author's translation.

Commentary

The joke depicts the discrimination and segregation suffered by Mexican Americans previous to the civil rights movements that outlawed segregated facilities. The humor deflects the pain by turning a depressing situation into a joke. This text is an excellent example of how some people handle racism or a painful situation—by joking about it.]

Jesus Christ Joke Cycle

When Jesus was at the last supper together with all his apostles, he raises his goblet of wine and very sadly exclaims: "Verily I say unto you that one of you will betray me."

To which Judas quickly responds: "Jesse, whenever you start drinking right away you want to pick a fight."

- Personal collection: folklore class University of California, Irvine, 1978.

#2. Jesus is nailed to the cross at Calvary flanked by the two thieves. Jesus turns to one side and asks one of the thieves: "Are you ready?" And the thief answers: "Yes."

He turns to the other side and he asks the second thief: "Are you ready?" And the second thief answers: "Yes."

"O.K." (Jesus then starts humming and tap dancing "Tum, de, dum . . ." "Tea for Two." with arms outstretched.)

- Personal collection: folklore class University of California, Irvine, 1978.

Commentary

Jesus Christ jokes were popular in the 1960s–1980s. Although many factors play an important role in the acceptance and dissemination of the Jesus Christ joke cycle among Chicanos/as, the most significant element in their popularity was the overall cultural revolution of the above decades. The jokes reflect a philosophical preoccupation of the "God is death" generation, the challenging of authority by the civil rights movements of the 1960s and the questioning of the status quo by the Radical Left. The counter-culture generation sought a more personal and involved God and tried to debunk the cold, detached figure of an earlier era. The jokes in this cycle describe an all too human God. Moreover, this God created in our own image, possesses some of the more negative human attributes—in some jokes he is a picaresque figure, in others he is presented as a drunkard and a trouble-maker while still in other narratives he is mercilessly ridiculed in his sufferings. It is clear that the Vietnam War and subsequent events in world history such as Watergate contributed to the demythification of various power structures and long-revered institutions such as the Church. This demythification is once again made evident in the content of the Jesus Christ jokes cited above.

FOLK SONGS

Romance

Delgadina	**Delgadina**
Delgadina se paseaba	Delgadina was strolling
en su sala muy cuadrada,	in her well-squared hall,
con su manto de hilo de oro	with her mantle of golden threads
que en su pecho iluminaba.	that illuminated her breast.
"Levántate, Delgadina,	"Arise, Delgadina,
ponte tu falda de seda,	put on your silken dress,
porque nos vamos a misa	because we are going to mass
a la ciudad de Morelia."	in the city of Morelia."

Cuando salieron de misa
su papá le platicaba,
"Delgadina, hija mía,
yo te quiero para dama."

When they left mass,
her father said,
"Delgadina, my daughter,
I want you as my mistress."

"No lo quiera Dios, papá,
ni la Virgen Soberana.
Es ofensa para Dios
y traición para mi mamá."

"God would not wish that, father,
nor the Sovereign Virgin.
It is an offense against God
and treachery against my mother."

"Luego que lleguemos a casa.
yo te pondré en castigo
por hija desobediente
no a vedar lo que te digo."

"After we get home
I will start your punishment
for being a disobedient daughter
who should not deny what I ask."

"Júntense los once criados,"
dice el padre de Delgadina.
"Enciérrenla en un
*   cuarto oscuro*
donde la voz sea ladina.

"Bring forth my eleven servants,"
says Delgadina's father.
"Confine her in a dark room

where her voice will sound foreign.

Si le dieran que comer
la comida muy salada
si le dieran que tomar
la del agua su rostro dada."

If you feed her
give her very salty food,
and if you give her drink,
throw water in her face."

"Madrecita de mi vida,
tu castigo estoy sufriendo.
Regálame on vaso de agua
que de sed me estoy muriendo."

"My dearest mother,
I am suffering your punishment.
Give me a glass of water
for I am dying of thirst."

"Júntense los once criados,"
dice la madre de Delgadina.
"Llévenle agua a Delgadina
en esos vasitos de oro,
sobre bordados de China."

"Bring forth my eleven servants,"
says Delgadina's mother.
"Take water to Delgadina
in these golden glasses,
on Chinese embroidery."

Cuando le llevaron el agua
Delgadina estaba muerta
Como gallo, boca arriba

When they took her the water,
Delgadina was dead,
like a rooster face up,

Tenía su boquita abierta.	With her little mouth open.
La cama de Delgadina	Delgadina's bed
De ángeles está coronada	with angels was crowned,
Y la de su papá el rey	while that of her father the king
De demonios apretada.	Was crowded with demons.
Ya con ésta me despido	With this I take my leave
Por los azahres de lima,	by the blossoms of a lime tree
Aquí se acaba cantando	here I cease singing
La obediente Delgadina.	Of the obedient Delgadina.

• Jack Loeffler, Katherine Loeffler, and Enrique R. Lamadrid, eds. *La Música de los Viejitos: Hispano Folk Music of the Rio Grande del Norte.* Albuquerque: University of New Mexico Press, 1999, 3–4.

Commentary

This is a romance (collected from folk singer Crescencio M. García) that has been traced to the sixteenth century in Spain, Portugal, Northern Africa, and all over Latin America and the U.S. Southwest. Its topic is sexual incest since the father of young Delgadina requests that she be his lover. Delgadina refuses and she is severely punished. There are numerous versions of this romance that is known today as *"El Corrido de Delgadina"* ["The Ballad of Delgadina"]. Its long lasting survival may be due to the fact that it touches upon a problem that is still very much with us today. In the 1980s and 1990s the secret was exposed in the United States with a series of cases that came to light. Studies undertaken revealed that the problem of incest was quite common but families normally kept the secret hidden from the world due to the shameful nature of the act. See my article "'La Delgadina': Incest and Patriarchal Structure in a Spanish/Chicano Romance-Corrido." In *Studies in Latin American Popular Culture Journal* 5(Spring 1986), 90–107.

Décima	**Décima**
Qué largas las horas son	How long the hours are
en el reloj de mi afán!	In the timepiece of my desires!
¡y qué poco a poco dan	And how little do they give
alivio a mi corazón!	Solace to my heart!

Para mi no hay sol ni luna	For me there is no sun or moon
no hay tarde, noche,	No afternoon, night or day
no hay día,	
tan solo estoy, vida mía,	I am only thinking of you, my love
pensando en tí desde la una;	Ever since one o'clock
ha quedado mi fortuna	My good fortune is to be found
a las dos con atención,	At two o'clock since
se alivia mi corazón	My heart will find relief
a las tres diciendo: suerte,	At three o'clock I shall say: luck
y así, mi alma para verte	And in that manner to see you my love.
¡qué largas las horas son!	*How long the hours are!*
De buena fe te idolatro	With good intentions I adore you
y con buenas excelencias	And with good thoughts
pues, mi alma, las	For you see my love, the Three Powers
tres Potencias	
me tienen en pie a las cuatro;	Have me standing here since four o'clock
a las cinco, con recato,	At five o'clock with good manners
mis sentidos en ti están,	My thoughts are with you
pensando siempre que dan	Always thinking that it will be
las seis, sin ver tu hermosura;	Six o'clock and I shall not see your loveliness
y así, no hay hora segura	And so there is no sure hour
en el rejoj de mi afán.	*In the timepiece of my desires.*
No hay hora que me sujete,	There is no hour that can keep me
vida mía, de ti el desvelo,	My beloved for you I am sleepless
porque la luz de tu cielo	Because the light from your heaven
en pie me tiene a las siete,	Has me standing since seven
a las ocho me promete	And at eight there is a promise
que mis penas cesarán	That my grief will come to pass
y que las nueve serán	And that at nine o'clock
mis caricias bien pagadas.	My endearments will be well paid
¡Ah, qué horas tan dilatadas!	Oh how slow time goes by
¡y qué poco a poco dan!	And how little do they give!
En fin, cuántas horas ves	In all how many hours do you see
que el día y la noche tiene,	That day and night possess
otras tantas me entretienen,	An equal amount do entertain me
mi bien, te ofrezco a las diez,	My love, I offer you at ten o'clock
a las once pienso que es	At eleven o'clock I think it is

bien pagada mi afición	Going to be well paid my affliction
y cuando las doce son	And when twelve o'clock is here
te deseo con más anhelo;	I desire you even more
porque la luz de tu cielo	Because the light from your heaven
de alivio a mi corazón.	Gives solace to my heart.

- Vicente T. Mendoza and Virginia R.R. de Mendoza. *Estudio y clasificación de la música tradicional hispánica de Nuevo México.* México City: Universidad Nacional Autónoma de Mexico, Instituto de Investigaciones Estéticas: Estudios de Folklore #5, 1986, 309–310.

Commentary

The décima, or 10-line strophe poem (or song, since the décima could be recited or sung), was the form par excellence during the eighteenth and nineteenth century in the Southwest, particularly in New Mexico. The form had a specific structure of a *planta* or initial 4-line strophe followed by a 10-line strophe in which one of the lines from the 4-line strophe gave closure to the first 10-line strophe. There were a total of four strophes with a rhyme scheme of (a/bb/aa/cc/dd/c). In the second half of the nineteenth century the corrido overtook the décima in popularity. Today the décima is still very much in vogue in the Caribbean, Colombia, Venezuela, Central America, and the Gulf Coast states of Mexico, particularly Veracruz. However, in the United States mainland it is not a popular form today, except with Puerto Ricans.

Corridos

Joaquín Murieta

Joaquín Murieta

Yo no soy Americano	I am not an American
pero comprendo el inglés.	But I do understand English.
Yo lo aprendí con mi hermano	I learned it with my brother
al derecho y al revés	Forward and backward
A cualquier Americano	And any American
lo hago temblar a mis pies.	I make him tremble at my feet.
Cuando apenas era un niño	When I was barely a child
huérfano a mi me dejaron.	I was left an orphan.
Nadie me hizo ni un cariño	No one gave me any love,
a mi hermano lo mataron	They killed my brother,

y a mi esposa Carmelita:	And my wife Carmelita,
cobardes la asesinaron.	The cowards assassinated her.
Yo me vine de Hermosillo	I came from Hermosillo
en busca de oro y riqueza	In search of gold and riches.
Al indio pobre y sencillo	The Indian poor and simple
lo defendí con fiereza	I defended with fierceness
Y a buen precio los sherifes	And a good price the sheriffs
pagaban por mi cabeza.	Would pay for my head.
A los ricos avarientos	From the greedy rich,
yo les quité su dinero.	I took away their money.
Con los humildes y pobres	With the humble and poor
yo me quité mi sombrero.	I took off my hat.
Ay, que leyes tan injustas	Oh, what unjust laws
fue llamarme bandolero.	To call me a highwayman.
A Murieta no le gusta	Murieta does not like
lo que hace no es desmentir.	To be falsely accused.
Vengo a vengar a mi esposa,	I come to avenge my wife,
y lo vuelvo a repetir	And again I repeat it,
Carmelita tan hermosa,	Carmelita so lovely
como la hicieron sufrir.	How they made her suffer.
Por cantinas me metí	Through bars I went
castigando americanos.	Punishing Americans.
"Tú serás el capitán	"You must be the captain
que mataste a mi hermano.	Who killed my brother.
Lo agarraste indefenso	You found him defenseless,
orgulloso Americano."	You arrogant American."
Mi carrera comenzó	My career began
por una escena terrible.	Because of a terrible scene.
Cuando llegué a setecientos	When I got to seven hundred (killed)
ya mi nombre era temible.	Then my name was dreaded.
Cuando llegué a mil doscientos	When I got to twelve hundred
ya mi nombre era terrible.	Then my name was terrible.
Yo soy aquel que domina	I am the one who dominates
hasta leones africanos	Even African lions.

JOAQUÍN MURIETA
The California Bandit

Depiction of Joaquín Murieta in *The Life and Adventures of Joaquin Murieta: The Celebrated California Bandit,* by John (Yellow Bird) Rollin Ridge.

Source: Copyright © 1955 by the University of Oklahoma Press, Norman, Publishing Division of the University. All rights reserved. Reprinted by permission of the University of Oklahoma Press.

Por eso salgo al camino	That's why I go out on the road
a matar americanos	To kill Americans.
Ya no es otro mi destino	Now my destiny is no other,
¡Pon cuidado, parroquianos!	Watch out, you people!

Las pistolas y las dagas	Pistols and daggers
son juguetes para mi.	Are playthings for me.
Balazos y puñaladas	Bullets and stabbings
carcajadas para mi	Big laughs for me.
Ahora con medios cortados	With their means cut off
ya se asustan por aquí.	They're afraid around here.
No soy chileno ni extraño	I'm neither a Chilean nor a stranger
en este suelo que piso	On this soil which I tread.

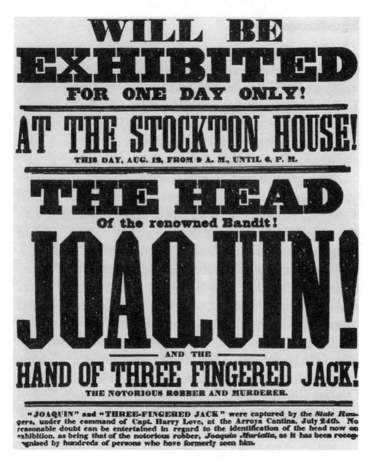

Poster announcing the one-day display of Joaquín Murieta's head.
Source: Courtesy of the Huntington Library, Art Collections, and Botanical Gardens, San Marino, California.

De México es California	California belongs to Mexico
Porque Dios así lo quiso	Because God wanted it that way,
y en mi sarape cosida	And stitched to my serape,
traigo mi fe de bautismo.	I carry my baptismal certificate.
Qué bonito es California	How pretty is California
con sus calles alineadas,	With her well-laid-out streets,
donde paseaba Murieta	Where Murieta passed by
con su tropa bien formada,	With his well-aligned troops,
con su pistola repleta,	With his loaded pistol,
y su montura plateada.	And his silver-plated saddle.
Me he paseado en California	I've had a good time in California
por el año del cincuenta	Through the year of '50
Con mi montura plateada,	With my silver-plated saddle
y mi pistola repleta,	And my pistol loaded
Yo soy ese mexicano	I am that Mexican
de nombre Joaquín Murieta.	By the name of Joaquín Murieta.

- Phillip Sonnichsen. "Texas-Mexican Border Music." Vols. 2 and 3 Corridos part 1 and 2 Liner Notes. Berkeley, California: Folklyric LP9004, 1975.

Commentary

The "Corrido de Joaquín Murieta" is an important song which details the conflict between Mexicans/Californios and the recently arrived Anglo-American settlers in 1848. See chapter 1 for a discussion of Murieta and his role in the history of California during the Gold Rush era.

El Corrido de Gregorio Cortez The Ballad of Gregorio Cortez

En el condado de El Carmen	In the county of El Carmen,
miren lo que ha sucedido,	look what has happend
murió el Cherife Mayor,	the Major Sheriff is dead,
Quedando Román herido.	leaving Román badly wounded.
En el condado de El Carmen	In the county of El Carmen
tal desgracia sucedió	such a tragedy took place:
murió el Cherife Mayor,	the Major Sheriff is dead;
no saben quién lo mató.	No one knows who killed him.

Se anduvieron informando *como media hora después,* *supieron que el malhechor* *era Gregorio Cortez.*	They went around asking questions about half an hour afterward; they found out that the wrongdoer had been Gregorio Cortez.
Ya insortaron a Cortez *por toditito el estado,*	Now they have outlawed Cortez throughout the whole of the state;

Rendering of Gregorio Cortez from *With His Pistol in His Hand: A Border Ballad and Its Hero* by Américo Paredes.
Source: Courtesy of University of Texas Press. Copyright © 1993.

que vivo o muerto se aprehenda
porque a varios ha matado.

let him be taken, dead or alive,
for he has killed several men.

Decía Gregorio Cortez
con su pistola en la mano;
—No siento haberlo matado,
lo que siento es a mi hermano.

Then said Gregorio Cortez,
with his pistol in his hand,
"I don't regret having killed him;
what I regret is my brother's death."

Decía Gregorio Cortez
con su alma muy encendida:
—No siento haberlo matado,
la defensa es permitida.—

Then said Gregorio Cortez,
with his soul aflame,
"I don't regret having killed him;
self-defense is permitted."

Venían los americanos
más blancos que una amapola,
de miedo que le tenían
a Cortez con su pistola.

The Americans were coming;
they were whiter than a poppy
from the fear that they had
of Cortez and his pistol.

Decían los americanos,
decían con timidez:
—Vamos a seguir la huella
que el malhechor es Cortez.

Then the Americans said,
and they said it fearfully,
"Come, let us follow the trail,
for the wrongdoer is Cortez."

Soltaron los perros jaunes
pa' que siguieran la huella,
pero alcanzar a Cortez
era seguir a una estrella.

They let loose the bloodhounds
so they could follow the trail,
but trying to overtake Cortez
was like following a star.

Tiró con rumbo a Gonzales
sin ninguna timidez:
—Síganme, rinches cobardes,
yo soy Gregorio Cortez.—

He struck out for Gonzales,
without showing any fear:
"Follow me, cowardly rinches [Texas Rangers];
I am Gregorio Cortez."

Se fue de Belmont al rancho,
lo alcanzaron a rodear,
poquitos más de trescientos,
y allí les brincó el corral.

From Belmont he went to the ranch
where they succeeded in surrounding him
quite a few more than three hundred,
but he jumped out of their corral.

Cuando les brincó el corral,
según lo que aquí se dice,

When he jumped out of their corral,
according to what is said here,

se agarraron a balazos
y les mató otro cherife.

they got into a gunfight,
and he killed them another sheriff.

Decía Gregorio Cortez
con su pistola en la mano:
—No corran, rinches cobardes,
con un solo mexicano.—

Then said Gregorio Cortez,
with his pistol in his hand,
"Don't run, you cowardly *rinches*,
From a single Mexican."

Salió Gregorio Cortez,
salía con rumbo a Laredo,
no lo quisieron seguir
porque le tuvieron miedo.

Gregorio Cortez went out,
he went out toward Laredo;
they would not follow him
because they were afraid of him.

Decía Gregorio Cortez:
—Pa' qué se valen de planes?
No me pueden agarrar
ni con esos perros jaunes.—

Then said Gregorio Cortez,
"What is the use of your scheming?
You cannot catch me,
even with those bloodhounds."

Decían los americanos:
—Si lo alcanzamos qué hacemos?
Si le entramos por derecho
muy poquitos volveremos.—

Then said the Americans,
"If we catch up with him, what shall we do?
If we fight him man to man,
very few of us will return.

Allá por El Encinal,
según lo que aquí se dice,
Le formaron un corral
y les mató otro cherife.

Way over near El Encinal,
according to what is said here,
they made him a corral,
and he killed them another sheriff.

Decía Gregorio Cortez
echando muchos balazos:
—Me he escapado de aguaceros,
contimás de nublinazos,—

Then said Gregorio Cortez,
shooting out a lot of bullets,
"I have weathered thunderstorms;
this little mist doesn't bother me."

Ya se encontró a un mexicano,
le dice con altivez:
—Platícame qué hay de nuevo,
yo soy Gregorio Cortez.

Now he has met a Mexican;
he says to him haughtily,
"Tell me the news;
I am Gregorio Cortez."

—Dicen que por culpa mía
han matado mucha gente,
pues ya me voy a entregar
porque eso no es conveniente.—

"They say that because of me
many people have been killed;
so now I will surrender,
because such things are not right."

Cortez le dice a Jesús:	Cortez says to Jesús,
—Ora sí lo vas a ver,	"At last you are going to see it;
anda diles a los rinches	go and tell the *rinches*
que me vengan a aprehender.—	that they can come and arrest me."

Venían todos los rinches,	All the *rinches* were coming,
venían que hasta volaban,	so fast that they almost flew,
porque se iban a ganar	because they were going to get
diez mil pesos que les daban.	the ten thousand dollars that were offered.

Cuando rodearon la casa	When they surrounded the house,
Cortez se les presentó:	Cortez appeared before them:
—Por la buena sí me llevan	"You will take me if I'm willing
porque de otro modo no.—	but not any other way."

Decía el Cherife Mayor	Then said the Major Sheriff,
como queriendo llorar:	as if he was going to cry,
—Cortez, entrega tus armas,	"Cortez, hand over your weapons;
no te vamos a matar.—	we do not want to kill you."

Decía Gregorio Cortez,	Then said Gregorio Cortez,
les gritaba en alta voz	shouting to them in a loud voice,
—Mis armas no las entrego	"I won't surrender my weapons
hasta estar en calaboz.	until I am in a cell."

Decía Gregorio Cortez,	Then said Gregorio Cortez,
decía en su voz divina:	speaking in his godlike voice,
—Mis armas no las entrego	"I won't surrender my weapons
hasta estar en bartolina.	until I'm inside a jail."

Ya agarraron a Cortez,	Now they have taken Cortez,
ya termina la cuestión,	and now the matter is ended;
la pobre de su familia	his poor family
lo lleva en el corazón.	are keeping him in their hearts.

Ya con ésta me despido	Now with this I say farewell
a la sombra de un ciprés,	in the shade of a cypress;
aquí se acaba el corrido	this is the end of the ballad
de don Gregorio Cortez.	of Don Gregorio Cortez.

• Américo Paredes. *A Texas-Mexican Cancionero: Folksongs of the Lower Border.* Urbana: University of Illinois Press, 1976, 64–67.

Commentary

"The Ballad of Gregorio Cortez" is a key folk song depicting the culture clash between Anglo-Americans and Chicanos in the late nineteenth century. See chapter 1 for a detailed discussion of this *corrido.*

Los reenganchados a Kansas	**The Kansas Contractees**
Un día tres de septiembre	One day the third of September,
Ay, ¡qué día tan señalado!	Oh, what an unusual day
Que salimos de Laredo	When we left Laredo
Para Kansas reenganchas.	Signed up for Kansas,
Cuando salimos de Laredo	When we left Laredo
Me encomendé al Santo Fuerte,	I committed myself to the strong saint,
Porque iba de contrabando	Because I was traveling illegally
Por ese lado del puente.	On that side of the bridge.
Uno de mis compañeros	One of my companions
Gritaba muy afanado:	Shouted very excitedly:
—Ya nos vamos reenganchados	"Now we are going under contract
A trabajar al contado.	To work for cash,"
—Corre, corre, maquinita,	Run, run, little machine,
por esa línea del Quiri,	Along that Katy line,
Anda a llevar este enganche	Carry this party of laborers
Al estado de Kansas City.	To the state of Kansas City.
Salimos de San Antonio	We left San Antonio
Con dirección a Laguna,	In the direction of Laguna,
Le pregunté al reenganchista	I asked the contractor
Que si íbamos para Oklahoma.	If we were going to Oklahoma.
Respondió el reenganchista:	The contractor replied:
—Calle, amigo, no suspire,	"Quiet, friend, don't sigh,

Pasaremos de Oklahoma	We shall pass through Oklahoma
Derechito a Kansas City.	Right straight to Kansas City."

—Ese tren a Kansas City	That train to Kansas City
Es un tren muy volador,	Is a flying [speedy] train
Corre cien millas por hora	It travels one hundred miles per hour
Y no le dan todo el vapor.	And it's not going full steam.

Yo les digo a mis amigos:	I tell my friends:
—El que no lo quiera creer,	"Let him who doesn't believe me
Que monte en el Santa Fe,	Get aboard the Santa Fe
A ver a donde está al amanecer.	And see where he'll be at dawn.

—Al llegar a Kansas City	Upon arriving at Kansas City
Nos queríamos regresar,	We wanted to return
Porque nos dieron el ancho	Because they gave us a raw deal
con las veras de alinear.	With the aligning of the railroad tracks.

Decían los americanos	The Americans said
con muchísimo valor:	With a great deal of bravery:
—júntense a los mexicanos	"Round up the Mexicans
Para meterlos en la unión.	So they can join the union."

—Nosotros le respondimos:	We replied to them:
—Lo que es a unión no entramos	"We will not join the union,
Esta no es nuestra bandera.	This is not our flag
Porque somos mexicanos.	Because we are Mexicans.

Si nos siguen molestando	"If you continue to bother us
Nos vamos a regresar	We will go back
para el estado de Tejas	To the state of Texas
Donde hay en que trabajar.	Where there is work."

—Agarramos un volante,	We got in a flier (gang).
Trabajamos noche y día	We worked night and day,
Nomás daban de comer	All they gave us to eat
Solo purita sandía.	Was plain watermelon.

Vuela, vuela, palomita,	Fly, fly, little dove,
Párate en ese manzano,	Light on that apple tree,

Estos versos son compuestos	These verses are composed
A todos los mexicanos.	For all the Mexicans.
Ya con ésta me despido	Now with this (verse) I bid farewell
Por la flor del granado	With the flower of the pomegranate,
Aquí se acaba cantando	Here one stops singing
Los versos de los	The verses about the contractees.
reenganchados.	

- Brownie McNeil. "Corridos of the Mexican Border." In *Mexican Border and Other Lore,* ed. Mody Boatright, 1–34. Austin: Southern University Press and Texas Folklore Society, 1946, 11.

Deportados	**Deportees**
Voy a contarles, señores,	I am going to tell you, gentlemen,
voy a contarles, señores,	I am going to tell you, gentlemen,
todo lo que yo sufrí,	All about my sufferings
cuando dejé yo a mi patria,	When I left my native land,
cuando dejé yo a mi patria,	When I left my native land,
por venir a ese país.	In order to go to that country.
Serían las diez de la noche,	It must have been ten at night
serían las diez de la noche	It must have been ten at night
comenzó un tren a silbar;	When a train's whistle was heard
oí que dijo mi madre	I heard my mother say
Ahí viene ese tren ingrato	"Here comes that hateful train
que a mi hijo se va a llevar.	That will take my son away."
Por fin sonó la campana,	Finally they rang the bell
por fin sonó la campana;	Finally they rang the bell
vámonos de la estación,	"Let's go on out of the station;
no quiero ver a mi madre	I'd rather not see my mother
llorar por su hijo querido,	Weeping for her dear son,
por su hijo del corazón.	The darling of her heart."
Cuando a Chihuahua llegamos	When we reached Chihuahua,
cuando a Chihuahua llegamos,	When we reached Chihuahua,
se notó gran confusion,	There was great confusion:
los empleados de la aduana,	The customs house employees,

los empleados de la aduana
que pasaban revisión.

Llegamos por fin a Juárez,
Llegamos por fin a Juárez
ahí fue mi apuración
qué dónde va,
qué dónde viene
cuánto dinero tiene
para entrar a esta nación.

Señores, traigo dinero,
señores, traigo dinero
para poder emigrar,
su dinero nada vale.
su dinero nada vale,
te tenemos que bañar.

Los güeros son muy maloras,
los gringos son muy maloras,
se valen de la ocasión,
y a todos los mexicanos,
y a todos los mexicanos,
nos tratan sin compasión.

Hoy traen la gran polvadera,
Hoy traen la gran polvadera
y sin consideración,
mujeres niños y ancianos
los llevan a la frontera
los echan de esa nación.

Adios, paisanos queridos,
adios, paisanos queridos,
ya nos van a deportar
pero no somos bandidos
pero no somos bandidos
venimos a camellar.

The customs house employees,
Were having an inspection.

We finally arrived at Juárez,
We finally arrived at Juárez,
My big worries came there
"Where are you going,
Where are you coming from,
How much money have you,
In order to enter this country?"

"Gentlemen, I have money,
Gentlemen, I have money,
Enough to be able to emigrate."
"Your money is worthless,
Your money is worthless,
We'll have to give you a bath."

The blonds are very unkind:
The gringos are very unkind.
They take advantage of the chance
To treat all the Mexicans
To treat all the Mexicans
Without compassion.

Today they are rounding them up
Today they are rounding them up
And without consideration
Women, children, and old folks
Are taken to the border
And expelled from that country.

So farewell, dear countrymen,
So farewell, dear countrymen,
They are going to deport us now,
But we are not bandits
But we are not bandits
We came to work.

Los espero allá en mi tierra,	I'll wait for you in my country
los espero allá en mi tierra,	I'll wait for you in my country
ya no hay más revolución;	Now that there is no revolution;
vamonos cuates queridos	Let us go, brothers dear,
seremos bien recibidos	We will be well received
en nuestra bella nación.	In our own beautiful land.

- Paul S. Taylor. "Songs of the Mexican Migration." In *Puro Mexicano,* ed. J. Frank Dobie. Dallas: Southern Methodist University Press, 1969, 234–37.

Commentary

The song "Deportees" depicts the travails Mexican immigrants experienced during the 1930s when the United States decided to deport all Mexicans who did not have proper documents to Mexico. Documentation for the crossing of the border had not been a serious matter, for the United States had needed workers in the past decades. All that had been needed was a piece of paper noting that they had paid the crossing toll which at times consisted of ten dollars. Since Mexican had been crossing the border for many years, many did not keep the stub that proved they had paid the toll and thus were technically "illegal." Mexican Americans who could not have their U.S. birth certificates at hand (for what person carries his/her birth certificates at work or while shopping, for example?) were caught in the raids and deported also. Children who were U.S. citizens but had Mexican parents were also deported to Mexico. Numerous songs written during the 1930s narrated experiences from this painful historical epoch.

Canto del bracero	**The Bracero's Song**
Cuando yo me fui pa'l norte	When I left for the North
me colé por California.	I slipped through California.
Yo no tenía cartilla ni pasaporte	I did not have a card or a passport
ni amigos ni palancas en migración,,	Neither friends nor an "in" with immigration
pero me colé con resolución.	But I slipped in with great resolve.
Recorrí varios estados	I traveled through various states
de la Unión Americana	Of the American Union.
en Arizona y Texas y por Luisiana	In Arizona and Texas and through Louisiana

siempre sentí la falta de estimación	I always felt a lack of respect
quesque [que es que] dicen que es discriminación.	Which they say is called discrimination.
Ay que triste es la vida	Oh how sad is life!
que triste vida la del bracero	How sad the life of a bracero!
ay cuanta decepción,	Oh how many disappointments, how
cuanta desolación.	much desolation.
Lejos de nuestros padres	Far from our parents
y de la novia y el compañero	and far from one's girl and one's friend
dan ganas de llorar	I feel like crying
no más de recordar.	by just remembering.
Al pasar por Minesota	When I passed through Minnesota
y por Clivelan y Ojayo	And through Cleveland and Ohio,
cuánto le suspiré	How I sighed
al rancho del Pitayo	over the Ranch of the Pitayo,
rancho que abandoné	The ranch I left behind
por aventurar	to seek adventure,
y al pensar en el fue para llorar.	And thinking about it was enough to make me cry.
Si tú piensas ir detente,	If you are thinking of going, stop.
o si estás allá regresa	Or if you are there, return
donde está tu cariño y está tu gente	To where your beloved resides and your people too
y el rinconcito aquel que te vio nacer	And that small corner of the world where you were born,
donde está el amor que pueden perder.	Where there is a loved one you might lose.

• *Libro de Oro de la canción.* Mexico City: n.d., 12.

Commentary

When the Great Depression of the 1930s ended with the coming of World War II, Mexican workers were again highly desirable and courted. The

United States begged Mexico who was now hesitant to encourage its workers to emigrate to the North to allow Mexican workers to come to the United States and work on the agricultural fields and railroads in particular. Mexico decided to be a "good neighbor" and entered negotiations for the importation of Mexican labor to the United States. This was the Bracero Program, in which the United States and Mexico signed an agreement guaranteeing a series of rights to the Mexican workers. The Bracero Program initiated in 1942 ended until 1964 because employers in the United States were very much in favor of it. It was not until César Chávez and the farm workers union exerted pressure on the U.S. government that this particular type of guest worker program ended.

Dallas, Noviembre Veintidos   Dallas, 22 November

(by Martín Rosales, recorded by Juan Cabral y su Conjunto)

Los rayos del sol tejano	The rays of the Texas sun,
lo vieron caer, llorando	Saw him fall, weeping
en los brazos de su amante,	In the arms of his beloved
fiel esposa y compañera.	His faithful wife and companion.
El veintidós de noviembre	On the twenty-second of November
cuando en tus horas triunfantes,	When you were triumphant in life.
pasastes [sic] por Dallas, Texas,	You passed by Dallas, Texas
por complacer semejantes.	In order to please your people.
Cuando llegaron a Texas	When you arrived in Texas
en español nos hablaron,	You spoke to us in Spanish
cómo íbamos a hacer menos	How were we to ignore
el honor que nos brindaron?	The honor you bestowed on us?
[Viniste] tú, el Presidente,	You, the President came
amado por mucha gente,	Beloved by so many people
te nos fuistes [sic] de repente	You left us all of a sudden
por hombre honrado y valiente.	You an honest and valiant man.
Los tejanos te quisieron,	The Texas Mexicans loved you
tú quisiste a los tejanos,	And you also loved them
no fue un tejano el cobarde	It was not a cowardly Texas Mexican
que detonó los disparos.	That fired the bullets.

Me da orgullo ser tejano	I am proud to be a Texas Mexican
y por eso me da pena,	And that is why I am saddened
que en Dallas haigas	That you were in Texas
[sic] estado	
cuando sucedió la escena.	When the event took place.
Ya con esta me despido	With this I bid farewell
llorando del Presidente,	Crying for the President
Juan Kennedy se llamaba,	John Kennedy was his name
amado por mucha gente.	Beloved by many people.

- Dan William Dickey. *The Kennedy Corridos. A Study of the Ballads of a Mexican American Hero.* Austin: University of Texas, Center for Mexican American Studies, 1978, 97

Corrido de Juan F. Kennedy	**The Ballad of John F. Kennedy**
By Arnulfo Castillo (oral version)	
Año de mil novecientos	It was the 1900s
muy presente tengo yo,	I remember it well
murió un hombre valeroso	A great man died
de energía y de corazón.	Full of energy and a good heart.
Hombre que no tuvo miedo	A man that was not afraid
porque no lo demostró,	He never showed [fear]
anduvo por donde quiera	He traveled everywhere
de ese mundo alrededor.	In this whole world.
Y escuchen este corrido	And listen to this ballad
de gran tristeza y dolor,	Full of sadness and pain
es la tragedia más grande	It is the worst tragedy
que en Dallas aconteció.	That happened in Dallas.
Era la una de la tarde	It was one in the afternoon
por la voluntad de Dios,	God willing
cuando nos llegó el alarma	When we heard the news
que el mundo se estremeció.	That shook the world.
Johnny Kennedy se ha muerto	Johnny Kennedy has died
sin comprender la razón,	No one knows the reason

sólo una mano asesina	Only the murderous hand
de un hombre sin corazón.	From a man without a heart.
Kennedy llegó a este estado	Kennedy came to this state
como invitado de honor,	As a guest of honor
lo trataban como hermano	They treated him like a brother
sin recelo y sin rencor.	Without suspicion or hate.
Kennedy con su familia,	Kennedy with his family
también el Gobernador,	Also the Governor
con una dulce sonrisa	With a sweet smile
saludaba a su nación.	Greeted the nation.
Cuando una mano asesina	When a murderous hand
de un balcón le disparó,	From a balcony fired the shot
Kennedy murió en seguida	Kennedy died instantly
y por poco el Gobernador.	And the Governor almost died too.
Su esposa muy aflegida [sic]	His wife very saddened
nos oculta su dolor,	Hides her grief from us
con un abrazo muy tierno	With a tender embrace
lo estrecha en su corazón.	She holds him to her heart.
Llorando le dice al cielo	Sobbing she implores the heavens
"Diosito, Kennedy, no,	"God, not Kennedy, no
si sólo busca en tu suelo	He only wants for this earth
la paz pa' [para] nuestra nación."	Peace for our nation."
"Dios mío, por qué te lo llevas,	"God why are you taking him
siendo un hombre superior,	He is such a great man
siendo un hombre tan sincero,	He is such a sincere man
y de tan noble corazón?"	And with such a noble heart?"
Vuela, vuela, palomita,	Fly, fly little dove
párate en aquel panteón,	Go fly to that cemetery
ve y lleva estas florecitas	Go and take this flowers
donde Kennedy quedó.	Where Kennedy was laid to rest.
No digas que se haya muerto	Do not say he has died
porque agrandas el dolor,	Because you increase our grief

diles que se haya dormido	Go tell them he is only sleeping
descansando con honor.	Resting in peace with honor.
Johnny Kennedy no ha muerto	Johnny Kennedy has not died
Diosito se lo llevó,	God took him
para guardarlo en el cielo	To keep him in heaven
como de administrador.	As an administrator.
Dispénsenme este corrido,	Please excuse this ballad
y al pobre compositor,	And the poor composer
es que se halla entristecido	It is just that he is sad
concédanme la razón.	Please grant me this favor.
Johnny Kennedy no ha muerto	Johnny Kennedy has not died
Diosito se lo llevó,	God took him with him
y del cielo nos 'ta [está] mirando	And from heaven he is seeing us
para cuidarnos mejor.	In order to take better care of us.

• Dan William Dickey. *The Kennedy Corridos. A Study of the Ballads of a Mexican American Hero.* Austin: University of Texas, Center for Mexican American Studies, 1978, 109–110.

Commentary

The two corridos depicting the tragedy of the assassination of President John F. Kennedy demonstrate the great love Mexican Americans had and continue to have for this American president. Kennedy appealed to Mexican Americans because he was the first presidential candidate that directly campaigned in Mexican American neighborhoods and asked for their vote. He made the Mexican American community visible when they had been for the main part invisible to Anglo-American society. The corridos narrate the tragedy and in the process make explicit the great affection and admiration Chicanos had for Kennedy.

El Corrido de César Chávez	**The Ballad of César Chávez**
En un día 7 de marzo	On the 7th day of March
Jueves Santo en la mañana	Good Thursday in the morning
salió César de Delano	César left Delano

César Chávez with María Herrera-Sobek.
Source: Courtesy of the César E. Chávez Foundation.

componiendo una campaña.	Organizing a campaign.
Componiendo una campaña este va a ser un ejemplo esta marcha la llevamos hasta mero Sacramento.	Organizing a campaign This is going to he an example This (protest) march we'll take To Sacramento itself.
Cuando llegamos a Fresno toda la gente gritaba	When we arrived in Fresno All the people chanted

César Chávez with María Herrera-Sobek.
Source: Courtesy of the César E. Chávez Foundation.

y que viva César Chávez
y la gente que llevaba.

Nos despedimos de Fresno
nos despedimos con fe

Long live César Chávez
And the people that accompany him.

We bid good-bye to Fresno
We bid good-bye with faith

para llegar muy contentos	So we would arrive safely
hasta el pueblo de Merced.	To the town of Merced.
Ya vamos llegando a Stockton	We are almost in Stockton
ya mero la luz se fue	Sunlight is almost gone
pero mi gente gritaba	But the people shouted
sigan con bastante fe.	Keep on with lots of faith.
Cuando llegamos a Stockton	When we arrived at Stockton
los mariachis nos cantaban	The mariachis were singing
que viva César Chávez	Long live César Chávez.
y la Virgen que llevaba.	And the Virgin of Guadalupe.
Contratistas y esquiroles	Contractors and scabs
ésta va a ser una historia	This is going to be your story
ustedes van al infierno	You will all go to hell
y nosotros a la gloria.	And we will go to heaven.
Ese Señor César Chávez	That Mr. César Chávez
el es un hombre cabal	He is a very strong man
quería verse cara a cara	He wanted to speak face to face
con el gobernador Brown.	With Governor Brown.
Oiga Señor César Chávez	Listen, Mr. César Chávez,
su nombre que se pronuncia	Your name is well known
en su pecho usted merece	On your chest you well deserve
la Virgen de Guadalupe.	The Virgin of Guadalupe.

- Written by Francisco García and Juanita Saludado. *Las voces de los campesinos.*
  FMSC-1 (1976).

Commentary

César Chávez had a great impact in corrido production since he began to use these songs to rally the farm workers at their meetings, demonstrations, protest marches, and boycotting activities. There are several *corridos* depicting the great deeds Chávez accomplished and the love and respect farm workers had for him.

Canción Mixteca

Qué lejos estoy del suelo
donde he nacido.
Intense nostalgia invade
mi pensamiento.

Y al verme tan solo y triste
cuál hoja al viento,
quisiera llorar,
quisiera morir de sentimiento.

¡Oh, tierra del sol,
suspiro por verte,
y ahora que lejos vivo
sin luz, sin amor!

Y al verme tan solo y triste,
cuál hoja al viento,
quisiera llorar,
quisiera morir
de sentimiento!

Song from the Mixtec Region

How far away I am from the land
Where I was born.
An intense nostalgia invades
My thoughts.

And seeing myself so alone and sad
Like a leaf blowing in the wind
I feel like crying,
I feel like dying of nostalgia.

Oh, land of the sun
I sigh to see you
And now that I live far away
Without light, without love!

And seeing myself so alone and sad
Like a leaf blowing in the wind
I feel like crying
I feel like dying
Of nostalgia!

- *Cancionero mexicano Tomo I.* Mexico City: Editores Mexicanos Unidos, S.A., 1992, 186.

La Llorona

Todos me dicen el
    Negro, Llorona
negro pero cariñoso.

Todos me dicen el Negro,
    Llorona,
negro, pero cariñoso.

Yo soy como el chile verde,
    Llorona,
picante pero sabroso.

The Wailing Woman

Everyone calls me the Black man, Llorona

I am black but very affectionate.

Everyone calls me the Black man, Llorona

I am Black but very affectionate.

I'm like the green hot pepper, Llorona

spicy hot but very tasty.

Yos soy como el chile verde,
    Llorona,
picante pero sabroso.

¡Ay, de mi, Llorona,
Llorona de azul celeste.
¡Ay, de mi, Llorona,
Llorona de azul celeste.

Aunque la vida me
    cueste, Llorona
no dejaré de quererte.

Aunque la vida me
    cueste, Llorona,
no dejaré de quererte.

Si al cielo subir
    pudiera, Llorona,
las estrellas te bajara.

Si al cielo subir
    pudiera, Llorona,
las estrellas te bajara.

La luna a tus pies
    pusiera, Llorona,
con el sol te coronara.

La luna a tus pies
    pusiera, Llorona,
con el sol te coronara.

¡Ay, de mí! Llorona,
Llorona llévame al río,
¡Ay, de mí! Llorona,
Llorona llévame al río,

Tápame con tu rebozo,
    Llorona,
porque me muero de frío.

I'm like the green hot pepper, Llorona

spicy hot but very tasty.

Oh, my Llorona
Llorona of the sky blue.
Oh, my Llorona
Llorona of the sky blue.

Even if I lose my life, Llorona

I will not stop loving you.

Even if I lose my life, Llorona

I will not stop loving you.

If I could climb to heaven, Llorona

I would bring you the stars.

If I could climb to heaven, Llorona

I would bring you the stars.

The moon at your feet I'd place, Llorona

And crown you with the sun.

The moon at your feet I'd place, Llorona

And crown you with the sun.

Oh, my Llorona
Llorona take me to the river.
Oh, my Llorona
Llorona take me to the river.

Cover me with your shawl, Llorona

Because I'm so cold I could die.

Lizard Bride by Maya González.
Source: Courtesy of Maya González.

Tápame con tu rebozo, Llorona, porque me muero de frío.	Cover me with your shawl, Llorona Because I'm so cold I could die.
No sé qué tienen las flores, Llorona, las flores del camposanto.	I don't know what the flowers have, Llorona The flowers from the cementery.
No sé qué tienen las flores, Llorona, las flores del camposanto.	I don't know what the flowers have, Llorona The flowers from the cementery.

Que cuando las mueve
  el viento, Llorona,
parece que están llorando.

That when the wind blows, Llorona

Que cuando las mueve el
  viento, Llorona,
parece que están llorando.

They look like they are crying.

¡Ay de mí! Llorona,
Llorona tú eres mi shunca.

That when the wind blows, Llorona

¡Ay de mi! Llorona
Llorona tú eres mi shunca.

They look like they are crying.

Oh woe is me, Llorona
Llorona you are my sweetheart.

Me quitarán de quererte,
  Llorona,
pero de olvidarte nunca.

Oh woe is me, Llorona
Llorona you are my sweetheart.

Me quitarán de quererte,
  Llorona,
pero de olvidarte nunca.

They may force me to stop loving you,
  Llorona
But forget you, never.

Las campanas claro dicen,
  Llorona,
sus esquilas van dobando.

They may force me to stop loving you,
  Llorona
But forget you, never.

Las campanas claro dicen,
  Llorona,
sus esquilas van dobando.

The bells are clearly saying,
  Llorona
The bells are tolling

Si mueres, muero contigo,
  Llorona,
si vives te sigo amando.

The bells are clearly saying,
  Llorona
The bells are tolling.

Si mueres, muero contigo,
  Llorona,
si vives te sigo amando.

If you die, I die with you,
  Llorona
If you live, I'll keep loving you.

If you die, I die with you,
  Llorona
If you live, I'll keep loving you.

• Public domain.

Commentary

The folk song "La Llorona" is one of the most beautiful haunting songs in Mexican and Chicano folk tradition. It is a folk song originally from Oaxaca but is found in all parts of the Mexican republic and the Chicano population.

Contrabando y Traición o Camelia la Tejana

By Angel González

Salieron de San Ysidro
procedentes de Tijuana
y traían las llantas del carro
repletas de hierba mala
eran Emilio Varela
y Camelia la Tejana.

Al pasar por San Clemente
los paró la migración
les pidió sus documentos
les dijo ¿dónde son?
ella era de San Antonio
una hembra de corazón.

Una hembra si quiere
    a un hombre
por él puede dar la vida
pero hay que tener cuidado
si esa hembra se encuentra herida
la traición y el contrabando
son cosas incompartidas.

A Los Angeles llegaron
a Hollywood se pasaron
en un callejón oscuro
las cuatro llantas cambiaron
allí entregaron la hierba
y allí mismo les pagaron.

Emilio dice a Camelia
hoy te das por despedida
con la parte que te toca
ya puedes rehacer tu vida
yo me voy pa' San Francisco
con la dueña de mi vida.

Sonaron siete balazos
Camelia a Emilio mataba
la policia sólo halló

Contraband and Treachery or Camelia The Texan

They left San Ysidro
They were coming from Tijuana
And they had the wheels of the car
Full of bad weed
It was Emilio Varela
And Camelia the Texan.

Upon passing by San Clemente
The immigration stopped them
They asked them for their documents
And asked them where they were from.
She was from San Antonio
A strong hearted woman.

A woman when she loves a man

She will give her life for him
But one must be careful
If that woman is wounded
Betrayal and contraband
Are incompatible actions.

They arrived at Los Angeles
And went on to Hollywood
In a dark alley
They changed the four tires
They delivered the weed [marijuana]
And received payment right there.

Emilio tells Camelia:
Today we say our farewells
With the money you received
You can remake your life
I am going to San Francisco
With the love of my life.

Seven bullets rang out
Camelia was shooting at Emilio.
The police only found

una pistola tirada	A gun left behind.
del dinero y de Camelia	Of the money and Camelia
nunca más se supo nada.	No one knows their whereabouts.

- Luis A. Astorga. *Mitología del 'Narcotraficante' en México.* 2nd ed. Mexico City: Plaza y Valdés, 1996,. 127–128. [My translation.]

Commentary

"Contrabando y Traición o Camelia la Tejana" [Contraband and Treachery or Camelia The Texan] also known as "Camelia La Tejana," released in 1970 was a major hit of the musical group known as Los Tigres del Norte. The song skyrocketed them into stardom and became the first major narcocorrido hit which in turn launched the *narcocorrido* phenomenon. There had been narcocorrido ballads previous to *"Contrabando y Traición"* but this *corrido* was at the right place and the right time since drug trafficking had begun to be a major international concern in the United States, Mexico and Colombia. After *"Contrabando y Traición"* numerous other hits appeared. In fact, the song was so popular that it spawned derivatives such as *"Ya Encontraron a Camelia,"* [They Have Found Camelia], *"El Hijo de Camelia"* [Camelia's Son] and other songs including a movie based on *"Contrabando y Traición."* See María Herrera-Sobek. "The Transnational Imaginary and 'Narcocorridos'—Violence, Drugs and Transgressive Discourse in Mexican Ballads." In *Violence and Transgression in World Minority Literatures.* Edited by Rüdiger Ahrens, María Herrera-Sobek, Karin Ikas, and Francisco A. Lomelí. Heidelberg, Germany: Universitätsverlag Winter GmbH Heidelberg, 2005, 83–99.

FOLK BELIEF

Witches

And that business of witches, this also is what happened to another woman. They say that she was bewitched through her own flowers. The woman had them arranged in a bouquet of six. And this lady folk healer cured her, not here in New Mexico, but in another place, and she told her who the person was who had her in this state of perpetual illness. She told her that she would be able to tell who bewitched her just by putting water in a pan. The folk healer left her alone watching the pan of water, and six cotton balls showed up. Then the sick woman knew who had bewitched her using the flowers on the windowsill. The flowers dried up, and the figure six showed up. She remembered who the person who had bewitched her was, but she was already dead. Later on the woman would pick flowers, but they wouldn't last. The dead person had put an evil spell on the flowers forever. And the woman was never able to pick flowers and put them inside on the windowsill because they would dry up. Outside, yes, but not inside.

- Told by Lala Gallegos in Nasario García. *Tales of Witchcraft and the Supernatural in the Pecos Valley.* Santa Fe, New Mexico: Western Edge Press, 1999, 65.

Bewitched

This is the story about a woman who was bewitched, but she didn't know where or why. She went to a female healer to be cured—and she was cured—but she didn't know who had cast an evil spell on her. The healer told her she couldn't tell her the name of the person who had bewitched her, but that she would cure her. In the process she would have a bowel movement and she would pass something unpleasant. Then she got nauseated and she passed a bunch of chicken feathers. The woman with the spell then remembered who it was who had bewitched her.

I myself did cast the evil eye on a little boy, but the evil eye can be cured very easily, if you catch it in time. If it goes beyond a Friday the little boy will die. The person responsible for casting the evil eye alone can cure it by giving the afflicted baby water by mouth, although many people claim that it's not always good to do that. But you put a glass of water right underneath the baby's crib, with an egg in the glass of water, and then you place a small stalk or straw underneath on top of the glass. Everything has to be underneath the crib where the baby is sleeping. If the egg floats to the top, it's because the baby has the evil eye. And if the egg stays at the bottom, the baby doesn't have the evil eye.

The way to cure a little baby, if the egg floats to the top, is by giving it water by mouth. That's how I also cured my little dog, twice.

- Told by Lala Gallegos in Nasario García. *Tales of Witchcraft and the Supernatural in the Pecos Valley.* Santa Fe, NM: Western Edge Press, 1999, 65–66.

Someone Cast a Spell on My Hair

And speaking of the evil eye, someone cast a spell on my hair. Once, when perms were becoming fashionable, I went to Pecos. Some people from here in San José lived over there, relatives of ours. And I told them here: "I'm going to Pecos to get a perm. Anyway, I have a place to stay there, so I won't be back until tomorrow." So I took off. My husband Roman wasn't here; he was working far away. Anyway, I went and I got a perm. Then my hair started growing. This was when my son Roberto was about to be born. He was born on September the eighth. My hair was really getting long. It kept growing, but I have always had a natural curl, I don't like it. So I get a perm. In any case, my hair was really long, and it was brownish, very beautiful hair. It came down to my waist, but it still had a little curl at the end, so the lady didn't cut it. Then someone cast an evil-eye spell on my hair and it fell out right here above my forehead. It looked like they had cut it very smooth with a straight razor. I was advised to seek treatment from a Juan or a Juanita, for him or her to spit on me three successive Fridays at the same time, but using *cachana*. It's a root, and the person who's supposed to cure you would toast it, put it in her mouth and chew it. Then she would spit on your hair at the same time for three Fridays in a row. My hair grew back out.

Just because of pure jealousy for my hair, someone had cast the evil-eye spell on it, and then there's the question of who's going to get you well, but I was told that a Juan or a Juanita could do it. A woman or a man, whomever I had most confidence in. My aunt Juanita Tafoya lived around here in San José, right close to where my *comadre* Manuelita lived, I went and spoke to her, "Why of course! Bring me some *cachana,* and I'll get you well, but for three Fridays in a row you have to come so I can spit *cachana* on you."

Well, I did as she said, and do you know that my aunt Juanita cured me?

- As told by Clara S. Ortiz in Nasario García. *Tales of Witchcraft and the Supernatural in the Pecos Valley.* Santa Fe, NM: Western Edge Press, 1999, 143–144.

Indigestion (Empacho)

One time my daughter, the one who lives in Albuquerque, got indigestion. She was about four years old. Oh! She wouldn't let us sleep at night. She cried and cried and she didn't want to eat, so we took her to the doctor. Her stomach just kept hurting. We took her to a doctor who was quite young at the time. My husband Román was working there at the Dead Horse Ranch, or someplace close by. The doctor said; "She has something stuck in her stomach, but I don't know what it is." But he gave her some medicine.

The indigestion is born in the intestine and that's where it grows. Water, candy, and many other foods also are the cause, but candies and water are the worst ones for indigestion. That I know because of experience.

Román came home and he said, "I'm going to call my Uncle Manuel Sánchez." And since you have a short fuse and can't hold back your tongue when you're young, I said to him:

"Humbug! What does that old man know?"

But he went and called on him, Roman didn't pay any attention to me. He brought him to the house. "Oh my little one," and he would rub his hands this way and that way. "Why, look at the electricity in my hands. I'll massage your precious daughter in just a little bit."

All I could do was listen. Well, he massaged her back, and she remained very silent. He massaged her and her back cracked, because that's what happens to your back. Many times they'll rub you with an egg. I never did that. I only rub with my hands and then I pull the skin. I pull the skin and I snap it. The child had quite a case of indigestion.

Well, no sooner had Uncle Manuel come and gone when Roman asked for something to eat because he hadn't eaten since he had arrived from the Dead Horse Ranch. For my daughter I made her some *atole,* blue-corn gruel, which is good for your stomach.

"What did I tell you, Clara? The old man's okay, isn't he?" So said Roman, rubbing it in.

And it's a good thing I paid close attention. My mother also gave massages for indigestion. That's how I learned and so I taught myself. That's why I used to give massages. They would bring me these little girls, quite often in fact, from there in San Juan, with all types of indigestion. And I used to massage them.

"And how much are you going to charge me?" they'd say to me after I finished.

"No. One doesn't sell the remedy," I used to tell them. "All that's important is for the little girls to get well, and that's it."

I would massage them first, you see? I'd rub them until the indigestion would loosen up and then I'd snap the skin and if it didn't crack they weren't suffering from indigestion. The skin has to crack when you snap it. The poor children complained, because it hurt. When it cracks, it's because the indigestion (the ball) has cut loose from the intestine. After the massage I would give them a teaspoon full of bluing with salt, but a lot of salt, followed immediately with a glass of water. That serves as a good laxative so as to get rid of the indigestion. Later on I used to use quicksilver.

- As told by Clara S. Ortiz in Nasario García. *Tales of Witchcraft and the Supernatural in the Pecos Valley.* Santa Fe, NM: Western Edge Press, 1999, 145–146.

I've Been Bewitched So Many Times

You can't imagine the number of times I've been bewitched, but some of them have been really horrible. Two of them have been so awful that they've practically sent me to the grave, but the good spirits keep coming back. Whenever they see me about to drop dead, they revive me, and that's what happened to me this one time. I won't say where, but it occurred in 1950, when my lungs collected a lot of blood. Huge globs of blood from my lungs! The doctor gave me three days to live. Three days! I remember that it was a Tuesday and then on Wednesday I went to a female folk healer. Then I was to die on the following day. That's what the doctor himself had told me, and then the folk healer told me the same thing. I didn't say anything to the folk healer, all the while spitting blood. And I guess I was terribly weak; I weighed less than 90 pounds.

Then I went and bought some powder herbs from this particular folk healer. The herbs were all mixed together: alfalfa, cocklebur, chamomile, all of the herbal remedies that are used nowadays, but they were all mixed together. I still have the two little boxes. The folk healer gave them to me to drink like a tea. In less than six days I was well again.

- As told by Lala Gallegos in Nasario García. *Tales of Witchcraft and the Supernatural in the Pecos Valley.* Santa Fe, NM: Western Edge Press, 1999, 69–70.

A Doll Made of Pure Hair

This is the story about this man who had a witch's tiny doll inside his stomach and the folk healer took it out. That's true because I saw it with my own eyes. I'm not going to name the place either, but this man was bewitched, and then a folk practitioner, a healer, came and he told the man more or less who the evil persons were who had put on the spell. The folk healer came and dug a small hole right in the driveway; he was a spiritualist and wise. He dug a hole and from there he took out a jar. It was a pint-size jar like one used for canning green chile, and inside the jar was a witch's doll made out of real woman's hair. The hair was long, and the doll was well-made, just as a doll should be, and then sewn with leather-type shoestrings. Then the healer took it out and told us to burn it. We burned it, and once we had finished burning it, the skeleton turned out to be that of a tiny bird, or that of a mouse. That's the evil that had been cast on this man. That's what was torturing that man, and it wasn't tormenting him badly, just a little bit at a time. This happened on or about the month of June, and by December of that same year he would have been dead if the woven-hair doll had not been taken out in time.

By that time he wouldn't have even been able to breathe. They were going to kill him. There were three women who had him suffering like that.

It was in the driveway, where we used to park the truck day after day, night after night. This man was inflicted with the evil spell here in Villanueva, but his family lived outside Villanueva, in another state. But the spiritualist came and took out the evil spirit so that the man wouldn't suffer here anymore. He himself took him over there where the evil spirit was.

We went and checked things where we used to park the truck because the healer was going to show up at four o'clock in the afternoon. That dirt was hard as if it were solid cement. We had to pour more and more water so that the dirt softened up. The sick man dug first and then the healer dug last so that he would be the one to take out the witch's doll. And he warned the sick man not to go get scared, and for him to pray as much as he could, because what he was about to see was frightening. And that's what he dug up—a witch's doll. It was the figure of an old woman and her hair was black and gray, salt and pepper like. It was a real witch's doll with little hands, little feet, and a head, and very thin. Then we burned it, and the sick man was cured.

- As told by Lala Gallegos in Nasario García. *Tales of Witchcraft and the Supernatural in the Pecos Valley.* Santa Fe, NM: Western Edge Press, 1999, 71–72.

Folk Beliefs

- Don't eat fruit found around the house (especially if there are no orchards or fruit trees); somebody may be trying to bewitch you.
- Don't play with fire or matches before bedtime or you'll wet the bed.
- When speaking of someone who is dead, say, "May s/he rest in peace," lest that person come and pull at your feet while you're in bed.
- Be sure to make the sign of the cross when going past a church or bad luck will come to you.

- Be sure to take off your hat when passing by (in front of) a church or God will punish you.
- If a bird flies into your home, someone is going to die.
- If a person admires a baby too much, it can become the victim of the evil eye.
- If you break a mirror, you'll be faced with several years of bad luck
- Never look at the host in church or God is going to punish you.
- Strike your father and your arm's going to shrivel up or
- Strike your father and the ground will swallow you up to the waistline and you'll roam the four corners of the earth for the rest of your life.
- If you see someone eating something (e.g., dessert) you wish you could have, but can't, you'll develop a sore at the tip of your tongue.
- Should you see a dog peeing, you're going to get a sty in one eye.
- If you sleep next to an open window, you'll wake up with one eye shut.
- Wash your face every morning with cold water and you won't get wrinkles.
- Wash your face with cold water every morning and you'll live longer.
- If a ghost appears before you (at night), make a cross using your thumb and index. finger (right hand), utter the words, *Póngate las cruces* [put the crosses on], and it will disappear.
- If you drop a spoon on the floor, someone's coming to visit you.
- If you pray for rain, but none comes, punish the santos (saints) (e.g., make them face the wall) and they'll respond.
- If the sky is full of sheeplike clouds, it's because it's going to rain a lot.
- When the clouds are rosy red, it's because it's going to be windy.
- Frogs will appear in lagoons after heavy rains or thunderstorms.
- *A* falling star will destroy the earth if it hits the ground.
- If a cat washes its face, people are coming to visit.
- Wet the top of your head on a hot summer day before swimming or you'll get a sunstroke.
- Whenever you have a nose bleed, put a coin (a penny) on your forehead to make it stop.
- If a rooster crows during the day, the weather's bound to turn nasty.
- Don't tickle the baby on the bottom of his feet or he'll lose his breath.
- Don't cut the baby's fingernails or else you'll cut off its circulation.
- If you want your rheumatism to go away, put on a copper bracelet.

- If you cut your finger, put a cold knife (the blade) on the cut to stop the bleeding.

- If you wish to catch the witches, turn your t-shirt inside out.

- Don't eat pork for supper or you'll hear pig's noise in bed all night long.

- Nasario García. *Tales of Witchcraft and the Supernatural in the Pecos Valley.* Santa Fe: Western Edge Press, 1999. Pp. 214–217.

FOLK MEDICINE AND FOLK AILMENTS

The Curandera

The *curandera* was also an important figure in the lives of those who lived in little *placitas*. It was she who doctored the sick and attended at the birth of the babies. They were not only called *curanderas*, but *parteras* [midwives] also.

They were middle-aged or old women whose mothers, grandmothers, or aunts had been *curanderas* before them, and from whom they had learned about *remedios,* and what each one was good for. There were good *curanderas*, and others who were not so good. They were busy most of the time, being sent from far and wide, especially so if they had the reputation of being good *curanderas*.

Some would go for them in wagons, others on horseback or burros. Those on horses would let the *curandera* sit on front on the *silla* or saddle, while the man mounted on behind, the two riding the same horse. Before she left home, she gathered all the remedios [remedies] she thought might be needed, and took them with her. She stayed at the patient's bed side treating them with the *remedios,* until the sick one either got better, or died. She would use one *remedio* after another, and sometimes two or three at the same time. If the sick got well, she was praised for it. If she or he died, it was because God willed it so, and she was not to blame. The *curandera* never charged for her work. When asked how much was owed her—they knew she would not charge them—she would reply that it was nothing, "just what you want to give me."

And those who appreciated what had been done for them gave her in pay or *correspondencia* [reciprocal] things like flour, corn, beans, chili, and sometimes fifty cents or a dollar. Then they would take her home again. But there were others who had no gratitude and just said *gracias* [thanks], and let the *curandera* walk, or get back home any way she could.

Some of the *remedios* that were used by the *curanderas* were gathered at home, along the rivers, fields, and on the mesas. Some were grown in gardens. Like *anis* [anise seed]—this was not only used for *remedio,* but for flavoring little cookies (*biscochitos*). Then there was *jilantro* [cilantro], *mostasa* [mustard], *alegría* [cockscomb], *polello* [pennyroyal], and *yerba buena* [peppermint].

Some *remedios* that grew in the north were brought back by the chili sellers, and those that could only be found in the south were brought, and sold to the *curanderas* by the freighters. Then there were some *remedios* that were brought from Mexico; these were bought at the little *tiendejons* [stores] in town, such as *coral molido* [ground coral] and *oro bolador* [gold leaf].

The *remedios* that grew in the Sierra, such as *altamisa* and *oshá* roots, some man would make a special trip to get these for the *curandera*. Also, when hauling wood pitch and cedar bark, other *yerbas* would be brought home.

Here are some of the *remedios*, and what they were used for by the old *curanderas*.

For *calentura* [fever], *flor de sauco* [elderberry] flowers were placed in a jar of water, soaked for twenty-four hours, and then strained through a cloth, and the water given to the sick one. This was used either fresh or dry.

Polvos de coyote is like a small tomato bush. In the spring it has a white flower, later a small green berry, which looks like a tiny tomato, about the size of a small marble. In the fall this berry dries up into a pod, and inside this is a grey powder. This powder was blown into the ears to cure *sordera* [deafness]. The reason for its name, *polvo de coyote*, is that it grows on the mesa, where the coyotes roam.

Yerba de la golondrina [swallow's herb] was used as an *ungüente* [salve]. This *yerba* was picked green and hung up to dry. When dry, it was ground into a powder and mixed with sheep tallow for a salve. It was used for wounds, cuts, and sores. *Yerba de la golondrina* grows close to the ground, has small round leaves, and looks like a small fern. The reason for the name is that the swallows eat the leaves of this *yerba*.

Yerba de la golondrina grows only in the southern part of the state.
SUBJECT: The *Curandera* (WPA: 5–5.52 #70) (collected November 19, 1940)

- "The Curandera." *Women's Tales from the New Mexico WPA: La Diabla a Pie.* Edited by Tey Diana Rebolledo and María Teresa Márquez. Houston: Arte Público Press, 2000, 26–27.

Remedios [Folk Remedies]

These are some of the remedios that were used by the old *curanderas*.

Canutillo (some called it *carrizo* grass) grows on river bottoms and looks like tall jointed grass. This *canutillo* was boiled and the tea from it drank three times a day for kidney trouble.

Then there was a cure for hives or *gervor de sangre* [*hervor de sangre*]. Cedar bark from small cedar trees was also boiled, and the water used to bathe in; also the water was given as a drink.

Pagua was for *inchasón (hinchazón)* [dropsy]. This was mashed when green, into a pulp, then a poultice of this was bound on the joints—ankles, knees, elbows, and wrists. In about three days, the skin would break, and the water drained out. After the swelling went down, an *ungüento* was made from soil pitch, from pinion trees and the yolk of an egg mixed, and applied to the joints to heal the sore places.

Pagua grows in *vegas* [river deltas] where it is damp. This *yerba* was also used for stomach trouble, by boiling it for tea to drink.

Copper rings and bracelets were worn by those suffering from neuralgia. headaches, and rheumatism. These were made by the old *plateros* [silversmiths]. The copper they used was bought in towns, where it had been brought in by freighters from the different mining towns. Copper was also brought in from Chihuahua. And sometimes old copper kettles, that were battered up and not used, were bought by the old *platero*, and cut up for rings. These old *plateros* made silver rings also. But silver being more expensive than copper, there was less sale for them.

The prices were twenty five cents for a ring, and fifty cents for a bracelet. But mostly they were traded for the same amount in products.

Sometimes when the *platero* had a number of these rings and bracelets made, he sold them in other placitas [town squares]. For he also waited until fall, then in his wagon or on his burro would take his wares to sell or trade to those who had no *platero* close. These copper rings were kept to use only in case of pain, and were loaned to neighbors and friends who suffered and did not have any of their own.

These rings were called *anillos de corimiento* (neuralgia rings).

Alegría (cockscomb) was grown at home in gardens. It grows about from two, to three feet high, and has a large red leaf. These leaves were mashed or squeezed, and the juice rubbed around the eyes. This was supposed to cure weak or sore eyes. It was used by the young girls for rouge. In those days the cheeks were painted but not the lips. Alegría was also used in making dyes for blankets and clothing.

Cota is a tall grass—like weed that grows in corn and bean fields. This was used for a blood purifier. The weed was boiled and the tea drank three times a day. The tea from *cota yerba* is red and bitter. It was also used as a wash for wounds and sore eyes. Many of the old people drank this tea with their meals instead of coffee or *atole*. *Cota* was gathered in the summer months, and hung on the *vigas* [rafters] in the storerooms to dry for use in winter.

When babies became ill, and none of the *curanderas' remedios* helped them, and they lost weight, and would not eat, it was called *tristeza* or *melarchico* (sadness or melancholy). So to cheer and make them well again, red wool strings were tied on their wrists and ankles so that baby could look at these gay strings, and forget its tristeza, and brighten up again.

Babies were harmed by *mal de ojo* (evil eye). It was said that some persons could hurt babies with evil eye or *mal de ojo* unconsciously. When baby was made sick by anyone who had *mal de ojo*, the mother called the *curandera*, who would ask who had last played with the baby. When told, she would send for, and tell this person to give the baby water, rub salt on its head, and hold it in his or her arms while a prayer was said. Then the baby would get well at once.

To protect little children from *mal de ojo*, strings of coral beads were tied around their necks. And when anyone played with a baby, they were supposed to give it a little slap on the head to break the spell, in case they might have *mal de ojo*.

Orégano del campo (wild sage) was boiled and the tea drank for colds and coughs. It grows wild on the mesa and foothills. When it comes up in the spring and is still tender, many of the native people cook it for greens, especially on ranches where vegetables are scarce.

The curandera made little woolen cords, some white, others colored, and, on San Blas Day (Saint Basil), the twenty-seventh of February, had them blessed. These cords were to be tied around children's necks to prevent sore throat or any other throat ailment during the year. And the mothers would send her gifts in *correspondencia*, like cornmeal, flour, or whatever they had.

SUBJECT: *Remedios*. WPA: 5–5-53 #3 November 26, 1940

- *Women's Tales from the New Mexico WPA: La Diabla a Pie*. Edited by Tey Diana Rebolledo and María Teresa Márquez. Houston: Arte Público Press, 2000, 28–30.

FOLK TRADITIONS AND CUSTOMS

SUBJECT: *Casorios*. WPA: 5–5-52 #67 (collected December 10, 1940)

Casorios [Weddings]

When a young man wanted to marry a certain girl, he went to his father, and told him he wanted him to ask for her. His father would tell him to wait until fall when the crops were all in.

Sometimes the boy and the girl were secretly engaged, he having asked the girl through his sister. So in the late part of October or early November, when all the crops were in, the boy's father went to the young man's *padrino* (godfather) to tell him that his godson (*ahijado*) wanted to marry. After finding out who the girl was, the *padrino* would set the date for the asking, and write the letter. If he could not do it himself he would get someone who could.

When the day arrived, father, godfather, and an uncle or two went to the girl's home, usually after supper, when they were sure her father would be home. When they arrived, and were asked in, and sat down, they would talk about the weather, crops, or any other subject except the one which their visit was made for.

After staying an hour or more, they would get up and leave. As the boy's father bid the girl's father good night, he handed the other the letter, which he had in his pocket all the time. When the company had left, the father read the letter. If he could not read, he got some friend or neighbor who could to read it for him, and talked it over with his wife. The next day the girl's *madrina* was sent for, and told that her godchild had been asked for in marriage, and by whom. The *madrina* then took the girl in a room by herself and told her she had been asked for, and asked if she wanted to marry.

If the girl was bashful, she would not reply then, but when her *madrina* left, would tell her little sister or brother to tell her mother and father that the answer was yes, or no. If the answer was no, the family waited a week *"Ocho días,"* then her father would write or have a letter written, saying his daughter had refused the offer, and give it to some male member of the family to take to the young man's father.

This was called giving the *calabasa* [squash], meaning his offer had been squashed. The boy would be disappointed, but soon would try his luck somewhere else. Sometimes he would ask for four or five girls before he was accepted.

But when the girl's answer was yes, the father and mother would wait, usually two weeks, sometimes longer, to answer.

In the meantime, the house was cleaned from top to bottom, the walls white-washed with *yeso,* and the patios all swept, and the bride-to-be fitted out in a new dress. Then, a letter was sent saying their daughter had accepted the marriage offer, and that the young man, and his family could come on a certain day—about three days after the answer was given—and receive her.

On the day of the *prendorio* (receiving the bride), the girl's family prepared a fiesta. About sunset the boy's family arrived, with all their close relatives, and the *madrina* and *padrino* [godfather]. They brought with them the *donas* (gifts for the bride). This consisted of a *colchón de lana* (wool mattress), blankets, pillows filled with wool, and a trunk in which there were clothes for the bride, rich as calicos, ginghams, shoes, and the wedding dress, veil, and wreath of wax flowers. And sometimes she was given money, ten or twenty dollars.

After supper when all had feasted, there would be a *baile,* and they'd danced until daylight. The next morning the house would be turned over to the groom's family, they doing all the work and bearing all expenses of everything until the wedding was over. The bride's family had nothing to do, or worry about, but were treated like guests.

About three days after the *prendorio,* on the wedding day, which was any day of the week except Tuesday (that day was considered unlucky, and the saying was *"Los martes no te cases ni te embarques,"* [on Tuesdays never marry or go on a journey]), the bride was dressed by her *madrina de casorio* [matron of honor] whom she had selected. Usually a married couple acted the part of a best man. Before leaving for church, both bride and groom knelt, and received their mother's and father's blessing, then left for the church where they were to be married. Just the four went, bride, groom, *madrina,* and *padrino.* The families stayed home, and never went to see their children get married.

After the ceremony they came back to the bride's home, where a wedding feast was served; this lasted all day. At night there would be a *baile,* where they danced until dawn. After the dance, relatives, neighbors, and friends, with the *músicos,* would accompany the bride, and groom back to her parents' house. There the bride would be given to the groom's family and the groom to the bride's family.

This was called *la entregada de los novios* [the giving away of the bride and groom]. After this, breakfast was served to all, and as each left for home, they wished the bride and groom *munchos [muchos] años de vida y felicidades* [many years of life and happiness].

- *"Casorios* (Weddings)." *Women's Tales from the New Mexico WPA: La Diabla a Pie.* Edited by Tey Diana Rebolledo and María Teresa Márquez. Houston: Arte Público Press, 2000, 34–36.

El Abuelo—The Whipping Man

Catalina Gurulé, age 45, the granddaughter of Nicholas Gurulé, tells this story of the old days of her grandfather.

Long time ago the people of the village chose an old man, called an *abuelo*, to whip their lazy and disobedient children. So in the darkness of the night the old man went about the village, his face stained with bright colors and his chin masked with a long beard made of wool. He carried a whip made of long, narrow thongs of leather which cut stinging stripes on the backs and legs of the lazy, disobedient children. He would come quietly up to the door and knock loudly on it.

"Who is there?" the father or the mother would ask.

"El Abuelo" would come the answer, and the door would lay open and there he was. "Any bad, lazy children in the house?" he would ask, flourishing his whip.

The father or mother would say, "Juan (or whatever the child's name might he) would not do his work today."

The culprit would quake with fear when the *abuelo* would turn upon him.

"Dance and sing if you promise to do your work and mind your parents, and kiss the feet of El Abuelo," commanded the old man.

If the guilty one was repentant and made his promise, he stepped out to the middle of the floor and lifted up his hands and danced while he sang:

Baile, Paloma, Señor Gorrundú	Dance, Dove, Sir Clown
Alza las alas y baila tú.	Up with your wings and dance yourself.

Then he would stop his dance and kneel down and kiss the feet of El Abuelo, who would then vanish quickly into the dark. If the culprit did not sing and dance, he received the cut of the lash.

- "*El Abuelo*—The Whipping Man." *Women's Tales from the New Mexico WPA: La Diabla a Pie.* Edited by Tey Diana Rebolledo and María Teresa Márquez. Houston: Arte Público Press, 2000, 14.

FOLK CELEBRATIONS

Baptisms

Baptisms are a cause for celebration since it involves the ritual of formally presenting and officially making the infant a member of the

Catholic Church. A *padrino* and a *madrina* [godfather and godmother] are required to take the infant to church and be given the official rites of baptism by a catholic priest. The infant is dressed in a beautiful white lacy gown and the parents, relatives, and *padrino* and *madrina* are all dressed in their Sunday best. After the baptism the *padrinos* may throw coins at the children waiting outside the church. A celebration is in order here and all go to the parents house to eat, drink, and listen to music played by hired musicians or if too poor to hire musicians, played by a CD player.

• María Herrera-Sobek. Personal recollection.

Confirmation

The confirmation of a child (around seven years old) is also a cause for celebration and basically the same type of festivities are done as for a baptism. A *madrina* [godmother] is required for a girl and a *padrino* [godfather] for a boy. The rite of confirmation involves taking the child to church where a bishop formally inducts the older child into the Catholic Church.

Rite of First Holy Communion

The child is presented to the church by a *madrina* (for a girl) or a *padrino* (for a boy) after the child has learned the basic precepts of the church via studying the catechism. A family celebration follows.

• María Herrera-Sobek. Personal recollection.

Coming of Age—Quinceañera

Many cultures have the coming of age ceremony to mark the passage from adolescence to adulthood and to initiate the adolescent into the adult world. This rite of passage is an important part of the structure of a society, for it establishes membership in the adult society. It also is important for it conveys to the adolescent the responsibilities of adulthood. These celebrations also signal to all witnesses that the culture will continue as one generation joins another in keeping the traditions alive.

Cultures throughout the world have various rites of passage. In the Jewish culture it is the *bar mitzvah* and *bat mitzvah*. In the Navajo culture it is the *kinaalda*. In American Anglo culture it is the debutante ball. In Hispanic culture it is the *Quinceañera*, the celebration of a young girl's 15th birthday. The name *Quinceañera* is a combination of two Spanish words, *quince* for 15 and *años* for years. The *Quinceañera* is an affirmation of religious faith and it signifies the entrance of a young woman into adulthood in society and the church.

The *Quinceañera* has stronger roots in Mexican culture than in southwestern Hispanic culture. But, as is true whenever two cultures influence each other, the practices of Mexican culture have influenced American culture, and it is common to find both Mexican and Mexican American families celebrating the *Quinceañera*.

The preparations for a traditional *Quinceañera* often take months. The planning can be as involved as a formal wedding and the celebration itself can be as expensive as a wedding. In older, more traditional times, the girl's parents determined many of the decisions concerning the *Quinceañera*, but in modern

Maritza Jiménez at her quinceañera celebration.
Source: Courtesy Pinedo's Studios.

Maritza Jiménez at her quinceañera celebration.
Source: Courtesy Pinedo's Studios.

Maritza Jiménez at her quinceañera celebration.
Source: Courtesy Pinedo's Studios.

practices the girl has more say in the decisions. Typical decisions involve the buying or making of the fancy dress to be worn, the date of the celebration, the guest list, the banquet menu, the arrangements for the Mass and the members of the attendant court. The extended family is especially important in these decisions for they often are responsible for various aspects of the celebration and help with the expense. The celebration of the *Quinceañera* consists of two parts. The first is the church ceremony. During the church ceremony the girl is escorted by a court of honor. The court consists of fourteen *damas,* young women, each one representing a year in the honoree's life. Fourteen *chambelanes,* young men, escort the *damas.* The honoree herself represents the fifteenth year and is escorted by the *chambelán de honor.*

The church Mass is a continuation of the religious events the girl has previously experienced. The Mass serves as a rededication to the religious faith expressed in the girl's baptism, Holy Communion, and confirmation. The Mass also is the girl's rededication to the spiritual aspects of her life. Often the Mass includes a sermon stressing the values of family and the religious life and asks for the blessing of the girl's patron saint. The priest instructs the young woman to seek positive role models, noting that the Blessed Virgin Mother is an excellent role model for religious women. During the religious ceremony of the *Quinceañera,* the girl's god- parents will often give her gifts of special significance. Common gifts are a cross, a ring, a religious medal, and flowers. The cross represents her Christian faith. The ring is a symbol of the responsibilities the young woman has to her community and her church. The religious medal is another symbol of her Christian faith. As a symbolic act of devotion, the girl will take the gift of the flowers and lay them at the feet of the statue of Our Lady of Guadalupe in the church. As an accompanying symbol to these gifts, the young woman will wear a white dress as a symbol of her purity.

After the Mass the *Quinceañera* moves to its second part, the fiesta. Either after the Mass or later in the evening the family hosts a reception in honor of the young woman. The reception begins with the introduction of the parents and the honoree, as well as members of her family. In this manner the *Quinceañera* is the introduction of the young woman to society. The first dance is a waltz in which the young woman dances with her father. Next she dances with her *chambelán de honor.* Then the celebration continues with toasts, food, music and more dancing.

The *Quinceañera* can vary from an event as simple and modest as the repeating of one's baptism vows to a celebration rivaling the most grand formal wedding. The young woman's *padrinos* often help the parents with the expenses and the arrangements of the *Quinceañera.* In some *Quinceañeras* the *padrinos* each provide one element of the event, such as the cake, flowers, etc.

The heart of the celebration is the rite of passage of a young woman into the adult world of the church and society. One often performed *Quinceañera* ritual is for the young woman to throw a doll into a crowd of young girls, symbolizing her departure from childhood.

The *Quinceañera* serves to confirm the importance of the family and the culture that sustains the family. Its final message is the affirmation of the adult role the young woman is to play in her family, the church and society.

- Angel Vigil. *Una Linda Raza: Cultural and Artistic Traditions of the Hispanic Southwest.* Golden, CO: Fulcrum Publishing, 1998, 23–24.

Weddings

This is a very elaborate festivity celebrating the marriage between a man and a woman. In this case there are various sets of *madrinas* and *padrinos* since they help with the different expenses of the wedding. There are a large number of chamberlains and bridesmaids accompany the bride who is dressed in a beautiful, long white gown. After the wedding ceremony all retired to a fancy reception and dance where dinner is served and toasts are plentiful wishing the bride and groom a happy life. There are live musicians playing at the reception which then turns into a dance. The father dances with the bride the first dance and the groom dances the second dance. There is a custom of pinning money to the bride's gown to help them get started in their new life.

Silver and Golden Wedding Anniversaries

Silver and golden wedding anniversaries are celebrated by going to church with friends and relatives and then coming home and having a celebratory meal. Gifts are given to the couple celebrating their anniversary. Silver anniversaries celebrate 25 years of marriage; golden anniversaries celebrate 50 years of marriage.

Birthdays

There are two types of birthdays in the Chicano/a folk tradition: the actual date of birth (cumpleaños) and the feast day of the Saint or holy Virgin whose name one bears or has been named in his or her honor (Día de Santo). For example, say a woman's name is Guadalupe and she was born August 1. She would normally celebrate her birthday August 1. However, she can also celebrate her Saint's name, which would be December 12, the feast date of the Virgin of Guadalupe.

Birthday celebrations and *Día de Santo* celebrations can be elaborate or simple. A birthday cake is always in order, and food may be traditional such as mole or simple, such as hot dogs and hamburgers (i.e. a barbecue in the backyard). The old custom of bringing *mañanitas* or mariachi singers to sing happy birthday songs is dying out, although still celebrated in some parts of the United States, mainly in Chicano/a neighborhoods. A more common way of celebrating is to have the birthday in a restaurant and hire a mariachi group to sing to the person celebrating his/her birthday. This is usually done as a surprise and the usual song sung as the mariachis stroll in to the party is "Las Mañanitas."

- María Herrera-Sobek. Personal experience and recollections.

FOLK SPEECH: PROVERBS, EXAGGERATIONS, COMPARISONS, JARGON

Proverbs

A buen hambre no hay mal pan. (If one is hungry there is no bad bread). A hungry person will find any food delicious.

A caballo dado no se le busca colmillo. (Don't look a gift horse in the mouth). Do not be fussy about a gift that is given.

A cada santo se le llega su función. (Each saint has his feast day). Your day will come.

A falta de pan buenas son semitas. (When one does not have bread wafers are good). (If you do not have anything to eat any food will do and taste good).

A gato viejo; ratón tierno. (For an old cat give him a young mouse). Said when an old man has a young wife or girlfriend.

Amor de lejos; amor de pendejos. (Love that is far away is stupid). A lover that lives far away tends to be unfaithful.

Camarón que se duerme se lo lleva la corriente. (The shrimp that falls asleep is taken away by the current). Don't fall asleep at the job because bad things will happen to you.

Dime con quien andas y te diré quien eres. (Tell me with whom you hang around and I will tell you the type of person you are). One tends to acquire the characteristics of those one keeps company with.

Después del conejo ido pedradas al matorral. (After the rabbit is gone you throw stones trying to catch it). Said of one that is late doing something that should have been done in time.

Dios dice ayúdate que yo te ayudare. (God helps those who help themselves). Literally: God says help yourself and I will help you.

El muerto al pozo y el vivo al negocio. (The dead man goes to the hole and the live one goes on with business as usual.). No sooner is one dead then one is forgotten.

El muerto a la sepultura y el vivo a la travesura. (The dead man goes to his tomb and the live one goes to have fun). No sooner is one dead then one is forgotten.

El muerto y el arrimado a los dos días apesta. (Fish and company smell by the second day). Company is a nuisance after the second day. Literally: the dead person and company smell by the second day.

El que amanece dios lo ayuda. (God helps he who gets up early). Get up early if you want to prosper.

El que come y canta; loco se levanta. (he who eats and sings at the same time will go crazy) Do not talk with your mouth full.

El que con niños se acuesta; mojao [mojado] amanece. (He who sleeps with children wakes up wet). If you hang around bad company you are going to get burnt.

El que con lobos anda a aullar se enseña. (He who hangs around with wolves will learn how to howl). If you hang around with bad company you will learn their bad habits.

El que hambre tiene atiza la olla. (He who is hungry tends the fire). A person who is interested in something gets involved in it.

El que nace para tamal del cielo le caen las hojas. (He who is born to be a *tamal* the leaves fall from heaven). The stars rule your destiny—your life is predetermined and you can't change it.

El que por su gusto es buey hasta la coyunta lame. (He who likes the bad life follows it).

El sordo no oye pero compone. (He who is deaf does not hear but makes up what he does not hear). Said of someone who did not hear something well and makes up something to compensate.

En la cama y en la carcel se conocen los amigos. (In sickness and in jail you will know who your friends are). True friends do not let you down when you are in trouble.

Están más cerca mis dientes que mis parientes. (My teeth are closer then my relatives). Meaning: I come first. Said when someone eats the food available and does not save any for the rest of the people.

Hombre prevenido vale por dos. (A man who is prepared is worth two). A person who comes prepared for a job is better than having many who are not prepared.

La mejor salsa es el hambre. (The best sauce is hunger). When one is hungry any food will taste great.

Los niños y los locos dicen la verdad. (Children and crazy people tell the truth). You will hear the truth from a child's mouth and a naive person.

Más da el duro que el desnudo. (A person who is stingy will give more money than one who does not have any money at all).

Más sabe el diablo por viejo que por diablo. (The devil knows more because he is old rather than because he is smart). People who are old are wise.

Más vale malo por conocido que bueno por conocer. (It is better to have someone around who one knows even though he/she is bad rather than have someone new who one does not know).

Más vale pájaro en mano que ver un ciento volar. (It is better to have a bird in hand than two in the bush). Better to have something small but secure than to gamble on something bigger but that may not happen. Literally: Better to have a bird in hand than to see one hundred flying.

Más vale solo que mal acompañado. (It is better to be alone than to be with someone who is bad for you).

No hay loco que coma lumbre. (There is no one crazy enough to eat fire). No one will do something that will really harm them.

No hay mal que dure cien años ni enfermo que los aguante. (There is no illness that will last one hundred years nor a person that can withstand illness for so long). Everything passes in time.

Panza llena; corazón contento. (A full tummy makes a happy person). When one is full of food one is content. Literally: Full gut; happy heart.

Perro que ladra no muerde. (Dog that barks does not bite). Said of someone who puts up a front but is really harmless.

Tanto va el cántaro al agua hasta que se quiebra. (The water jar that goes to the water well often will eventually break). If a person is exposed to danger enough times he or she will eventually get hurt.

Uno no puede repicar y andar en la procesion. (One cannot be ringing the bells and marching in the procession). One cannot be in two places at the same time.

- Personal collection learned from my grandmother Susana Escamilla de Tarango.

PROVERBIAL EXPRESSIONS: COMPARISONS AND EXAGGERATIONS

Abuela: *más vieja que mi abuela la tuerta* (as old as my one-eyed grandmother)

Aceituna: *tan flaca y tan flaca que si se traga una aceituna parece que está preñada.* (so skinny, so skinny that if she swallows an olive it looks as though she's pregnant)

agua: *más claro que el agua.* (as clear as water)

agua: *está como agua para chocolate* (he's like water for making chocolate—meaning ready to explode, angry, heated.)

aguja: *era tan flaco que se acuesta en una abuja y se arropa con la hebra.* (he's so skinny that he lies down on a needle and covers himself with the thread)

alma: *como alma que se lleva el Diablo* (like a soul being carried off by the devil—meaning taking off fast; someone leaving rapidly).

banqueta: *era tan chaparrita que se sentaba en la banqueta y le colgaban los pies* (she was so short that when she sat on the sidewalk her feet would dangle.)

boca: *es tan perezoso que no come por no abrir la boca* (he's so lazy that he won't eat so as not to open his mouth)

cabra: *más loco que una cabra en el desierto* (as crazy as a goat in the desert)

cabra: *es más loco que una cabra en patines* (as crazy as a goat on skates)

cacahuate: *no vale un cacahuate* (it's not worth [as much as] a peanut.)

cochino: *más sucio que un cochino* (as dirty as a pig)

dolor: *es tan feo como un dolor de estógamo* [estómago] (as ugly as a stomach ache).

estampilla: *es tan pequeño que se sienta en una estampilla y le sobran los pies* (he's so small that he sits on a postage stamp and his feet hang over the edge.)

estrella: *más alto que las estrellas* (taller than the stars)

frijol: *eres como los frijoles, al primer hervor te arrugas* (you're like beans: at the first boil you wrinkle up) Meaning that at the first sign of trouble you give up.

gallina: *más cobarde que una gallina* (as cowardly as a hen).

gallo: *más claro no canta un gallo* (a rooster doesn't crow more clearly—meaning it is very clear.)

guitarra: *más tocada que una guitarra* (more played than a guitar—meaning the woman has been touched by many men).

hipo: *es tan feo, que quita el hipo* (he's so ulgy that he cures the hiccups).

melon: *más pelón que un melón* (as bald as a melon).

pedrada: *me cayó como pedrada en ojo tuerto* (it suited me like a stone thrown in a blind eye). Meaning I took it very badly.

perico: *hablar más que un perico* (to talk more than a parrot).

visita: *fue como visita de médico* (like a doctor's visit). Very quick.

- Shirley Arora. *Proverbial Comparisons and Related Expressions in Spanish.* Berkeley: University of California Press, 1977.

Caló [Jargon]

agüitar (get depressed, sad)

al alba (be smart; quick; sharp)

bato / bata (dude/ chick)

bote (jail)

birria (beer)

cantón (house)

carcacha (car)

carnal (brother as in bro')

carnales (brothers as in close friends)

Chale (No. No way)

de aquellas (great; super)

están muy verdes (they are too green, as in immature)

filero (knife)

gabacho (Anglo-American, gringo)

garras (clothes)

güisa (girlfriend)

Hay los vidrios (see you later)

jaina (girlfriend)

jando (money)

jefa (mother)

jefe (father)

lisa (shirt)

Nel (no)

pisto (alcoholic drink)

ponte trucha (be sharp; on the lookout)

puchar (to push)

ramfla (car)

refinar (to eat)

ruca (girlfriend)

Simón (yes)

vato, also *bato* (dude)

watchar (to watch)

- Personal collection. See also George C. Baker. "Pachuco: An American-Spanish Argot and Its Social Function in Tucson Arizona." In *El Lenguaje de los Chicanos: Regional and Social Characteristics of Language Used by Mexican Americans,* edited by Eduardo Hernández-Chávez, Andrew D. Cohen, and Anthony F. Beltramo. Arlington, VA: Center for Applied Linguistics, 1975.

Commentary

Chicanos and Chicanas have developed a type of Chicano Spanish and English characterized by (1) bilingualism, (2) using standard Spanish in a different context, (3) adopting English words and making them into Spanish words, (4) code-switching from one language to another at different points in a speech act. Some Chicanos/as tend to use this type of Spanish/English more than others; in particular marginalized youth, youth from low income neighborhoods, prisoners, gang members, and other disenfranchised youth and adults.

RIDDLES

Conundrum

A conundrum is a riddle containing its own answer:

Agua pasa por mi casa Cate de mi corazón, si no me adivinas ésta—eres puro burro cabezón. Respuesta: el aguacate.

[Water passes by my house, Cate dear to my heart, if you do not know the answer to this you are a big-headed donkey. Answer: the avocado. the Spanish words "agua" and "cate" (*aguacate* means *avocado*) are within the sentence.]

True Riddles

A. Comparison to a living creature:

Anda y no tiene pies, habla y no tiene boca y adivina lo que es? Respuesta: La carta. [It travels but has no feet, it talks but has no mouth and guess what it is? Answer: the letter.]

B. Comparison to an animal:

Paso por la casa. Voy a la cocina. Meneándo la cola como una gallina. Respuesta: La escoba. [I pass through the house. I go to the kitchen wagging my tail like a chicken. Answer: the broom.]

C. Comparison to several animals:

Tengo un par de caballitos que cuando los amarro se van y cuando los suelto aquí están. Respuesta: los zapatos. [I have a pair of ponies that when I tie them they leave, and when I let them loose, they stay. Answer: shoes.]

D. Comparison to a person:

Una vieja larga y seca que le escurre la manteca. Respuesta: la vela [A skinny old lady and all her lard is draining out. Answer: a candle]

E. Comparison to several persons:

Son hermanos muy unidos, donde quieren van juntitos. Respuesta: los dedos. [They are brothers very united; wherever they go they go together. Answer: fingers.]

F. Comparison to plants:

Tengo una adivinanza que se pela por la panza: Respuesta: la naranja [I have a riddle that you peel through its stomach. Answer: naval orange]

G. Comparison to things:

Lana sube; lana baja. Respuesta: la navaja. [Wool rises and wool comes down. Answer: the knife.]

H. Enumeration of comparisons:

Chiquito como un ratón; pero cuida más su casa que un león. Respuesta: el candado. [Small like a mouse but guards his house like a lion. Answer: a lock.]

I. Enumeration in terms of form and function.

Sombrero sobre sombrero, sombrero de rico pano; el que me adivine esta tiene de termino un año. Respuesta: la cebolla. [Hat upon hat; hat of rich cloth. Who guesses this riddle wins his goal in a year. Answer: an onion.

J. Enumeration in terms of color.

Blanco ha sido mi vestido y amarillo mi corazón. Respuesta: el huevo. [White is my dress, and yellow is my heart. Answer: an egg.]

K. Enumeration in terms of acts.

Sube al cerro y baja y siempre está en el mismo lugar. Respuesta: el camino. [It goes up the hill and comes down the hill and it is always in the same place. Answer: the road.]

Riddle Problems

Estos eran cuatro gatos, cada gato en su rincón, cada gato veía tres gatos, adivina cuántos gatos son. Respuesta: cuatro gatos.

[There were four cats, each cat in its corner, each cat saw three cats. Tell me how many cats there were. Answer: four cats]

Riddling Questions

¿En que se parece el café al autobús? Respuesta: en los asientos.
[How are coffee and a bus alike? Answer: in the grounds (i.e. seats).] In Spanish, the word *asientos* means both *seats* and *coffee grounds*.

¿Cuántas estrellas hay en el cielo? Respuesta: Cincuenta; es decir—sin cuenta.
[How many stars are there in the sky? answer: Fifty or countless.] This is a play on the words *cincuenta* (meaning *fifty*) and *sin cuenta* (meaning *infinite*).

Pretended Obscene Riddles

¿Qué le mete el hombre a la mujer cuando se casa? Respuesta: el anillo.

[What does a man put on (or insert in) a woman when he marries her? Answer: a ring.]

Riddling Wellerisms

This type of riddles involve the question *¿Qué le dijo . . . ?* [What did so and so say . . .]

¿Qué le dijo el piojo al calvo? Respuesta: No te agaches porque me caigo.
[What did the louse say to the bald man? Answer: Don't bend over or I'll fall off.]

- John O. West. *Mexican-American Folklore: Legends, Songs, Festivals, Proverbs, Crafts, Tales of Saints, of Revolutionaries, and More.* Little Rock, AR: August House, Inc. 1989. Riddles were taken from Mark Glazer. *Flour from Another Sack.* Edinburg, TX: Pan American University, 1984. María Herrera-Sobek. Personal collection.

CHILDREN'S SONGS AND GAMES

Lullabies

A la ruru nene	Ruru baby
duérmase me ya	Go to sleep now
porque viene el Viejo	Because the bogeyman will come
y se lo llevará.	And take you away.

Señora Santa Ana	Lady Saint Ann
Por qué llora el niño	Why does the child cry?
Por una manzana	Because an apple
que se le ha perdido.	He has lost.

Iremos al huerto	We shall go to the orchard
cortaremos dos	We will cut two
Uno para el niño	One for the baby
y otro para vos.	And another for you.

Toddler's Games: Finger Games

"Niño Chiquito"

Niño chiquito (little finger)	Little boy
señor de anillito (ring finger)	Mr. Ringman
tonto loco (middle finger)	Crazy and wild
lambe cazuelas (index finger)	Licks the pots
y mata el piojo. (thumb)	Kills lice

"Este Se Hayó un Huevito"

Este se halló un huevito	This [little finger] found an egg
Este dijo lo freiremos	This [ring finger] said: we'll fry it.

este puso la cazuela	This [middle finger] brought the frying pan.
este lo frió	This [index finger] fried it.
y este dedo gordo se lo comió.	This [thumb] fat finger ate it.

"La Arañita"

"The Little Spider"

Esta era una arañita	There was a little spider [*adult plays with child's palm of hand and twirls fingers inside palm*]
comenzó a llover	It started to rain [*adult takes hand and moves it up the arm of the child toward his/her underarms*]
y se metió en su cuevita.	And hid in her cave. [*tickles child's underarms*]

"Tilín Campana"

"Ringing Bell"

Tilín Campana	Ringing Bell
cayó en la cama	Fell down in bed
por darle un beso	Because he kissed
a la Americana.	An American girl.

[The game is played with the baby or toddler sitting on top of a bed and being rocked back and forth by an adult singing the song until the adult gently lets the baby down on the bed at the end of the song.]

"Los Maderos de San Juan"

"The Lumberjacks from San Juan"

Los maderos de San Juan	The lumberjacks from San Juan
piden pan y no les dan	Ask for some bread and they don't get it
piden queso y les dan un hueso	As for some cheese and they get a bone
en el mero pescuezo.	Behind their neck.

[The baby or toddler is gently rocked back and forth in bed with the adult sitting beside him or her and singing the song. At the end of the song the adult gently taps the child neck as if hitting him with a bone.]

Counting out Rhymes

"Tín Marín"

Tin Marín de don pingué

cúcara mácara títere fue

yo no fui; fue teté

pégale, pégale que ella fue.

[The preceding rhymes are mostly nonsense syllables. They are counting rhymes, similar to "eeny, meeny, miny, moe . . ."]

"Ring around the Rosy" Games

"Naranja Dulce"

Naranja dulce
limón partido
dame un abrazo
que yo te pido.

Si fueran falsos
mis juramentos
en otros tiempos
se olvidarán.

Toca la marcha
Mi pecho llora
adiós señora,
yo ya me voy
a mi casita de Sololoy
a comer tacos
y no les doy.

"Sweet Orange"

Sweet orange
Lemon slice
Give me a hug
That I request from you.

If my vows
Were false
With time
They will be forgotten.

Play the marching song
My heart does cry
Good-bye my lady,
I am leaving
To my little house of plastic.
To eat tacos
And I will not give any.

"A La Rueda de San Miguel"

A la rueda de San Miguel,
   San Miguel
Todos traen su copa de miel
A lo maduro, a lo maduro
   que se voltié
[name of child] de burro.

"The Ring of San Miguel"

To the ring of San Miguel, San Miguel

All have their cup of honey
Let it ripe, let it ripe, let
turn around
[name of child] as a donkey.

"Arroz con Leche"

Arroz con leche
   me quiero casar
con una mexicana
   que sepa bailar.

"Rice Pudding"

Rice pudding I want to get married

With a Mexican girl who knows how to
   dance.

con esta sí, con esta no
con esta mero me caso yo.

With this one yes, with this one no
With this one I will marry her.

Children's Songs

"La Muñeca"

"The Doll"

Tengo una muñeca vestida de azul
con sus zapatitos y su velo tul.

I have a doll dressed in blue
with her little shoes and a veil of lace.

La llevé a la plaza se me
    constipó.
La llevé a la casa y la niña
    murió.

I took her to the town square and
    she caught a cold.
I took her home and the child died.

Dos y dos son cuatro
cuatro y dos son seis
seis y dos son ocho
y ocho diez y seis.

Two plus two are four
four plus two are six
six plus two are eight
and eight plus eight are sixteen.

Brinca la tablita yo ya la
    brinqué
bríncala de vuelta yo ya
    me cansé.

Jump the little wooden board I already
    jumped it
Jump it again I am now tired.

- María Herrera-Sobek. Personal collection learned when I was a child living in Rio Hondo, Texas in the 1950s.

FOLK ART AND ARTISANS

El Platero (The Silversmith)

Sources of information: José Gurulé, Patricio Gallegos, Dave Trujillo. José Gurulé was a small child when old Narvez made jewelry for the people of Las Placitas. He knew how the old man made it and what it looked like. Patricio Gallegos recalled seeing the ruins of the little smelter near the old Montezuma Mine and remembers how it was built. Dave Trujillo knew from his parents that silver and other ores taken from the old Montezuma Mine were smelted nearby and made into jewelry, though he could not remember the name of the silversmith.

El Platero (The Silversmith)

In the long-ago days of Las Placitas when the barest necessities were obtained only through hard work, many long hours of it, the women somehow managed to work a little harder to raise surplus commodities in order to barter for *prendería* [jewelry]. Those precious treasures of personal adornment, which were made of silver, of copper, of iron, were all hand-wrought.

In those days old Narvez (none living today remember his family name) gladdened the hearts of the feminine members of the village with his handiwork. Whether his rings and bracelets were of silver (few could afford the silver), or copper or iron, they were all works of art, crude though they were, and they all bore designs, and never were two ornaments carved alike. To keep a piece of stolen jewelry made by old Narvez was almost impossible. By the design on it, the owner was certain to know it. Old Narvez lived at Algodones, but much of his time was spent at or near Las Placitas, for there he found his materials: metals, a whole mine of them the fabled old Montezuma Mine, and there he found coal which he could reduce to *coque* (coke), and there he found *barro* (clay) of just the right kind and there he found plenty of *piñón* wood abounding in *resina* (pitch) to raise the heat units of his fire, which he must have in his *fundidor* (smelt). Narvez dug a very shallow place in the ground large as he wished the base to be. He lined it with rock and clay, then built it to the desired height, making it with thick walls and using plenty of adobe mud to hold the rocks together. He molded a bowl-shaped *crisol* (crucible) of the clay, and when it was finished, it was as hard as rock and no degree of heat could damage it, that is, the highest degree of heat he needed for his smelting. The *crisol* became the top of the *fundidor*. Two small holes were made at the base of the *fundidor*. They were directly opposite each other and permitted free circulation of air, which fanned the fire to greater heat.

When his *fundidor* was ready and his ore piled near it for fusion or smelting, Narvez piled up his fuel. He had cut down an abundance of *piñón* wood and cut it into proper lengths with his *hacheta* (small stone axe). That wood was full of *resina* (pitch), which would raise the heat units of his fire. A mound of *coque* (coke), which he had made by burning the coal until combustion was greatly reduced, was ready and some dirt and clay. Narvez laid brush and dry leaves in the bottom of his smelter; on that he piled the pieces of piñón and covered them with coke. He knew how to sprinkle adobe dirt over the top to compact the fuel space, and how to set the *crisol* and pack the clay about it to hold it firm. He struck his flints together, ignited the dry brush at the bottom of the smelter, and his fire was built. Into the *crisol* went the intended ore and the melting process was on.

Old Narvez made most of the jewelry of iron because there was much greater demand for it, even for rings. But into that iron went pyrites, both of iron and copper. Those pyrites glitter like gold; in fact, they are known as fool's gold. When they were smelted into the iron, rings and bracelets made of it dazzled in the sunlight and the candlelight. Then Narvez dropped pieces of copper ore and little chunks of silver ore into the *crisol* with the iron and got daily flecked molted stuff from which to hammer and cut out rings and bracelets.

As different metals required different heats to melt them, they were in different states of molten mass. But when in an adorning piece of jewelry, that roughness, knobby appearance, and general mixed-upness added to its worth and beauty.

When his molten mass was ready, Narvez poured it out on a flat smooth stone as he kneaded it and tooled it and cut it with stone tools. Upon the rings and bracelets he carved figures of animals, birds, reptiles, flowers and geometric symbols. The plain pieces made from iron alone were carved with the same skill and artistic touch as those rings and bracelets which would bring him more beans, chili, peas (both black-eyed and Spanish), and wheat or blue corn. The silver rings were beyond all but a few, unless they were to be bought at great sacrifice. But there were those who made the sacrifices and adorned themselves with silver rings, silver bracelets, and even silver earrings, which were all highly polished and carved. Narvez used pumice for polishing as well as smoothing down his melted metals. After he had labored with sand or pumice, even the roughest rings and bracelets took on a finished appearance.

In those old days there was a demand for rings of iron and the iron made to glitter by the addition of pyrites, for it was the custom of the day for engaged couples to exchange rings in a dance called *la prendería* given at the home of the bride, or some place chosen by her family, on the night preceding the wedding. A tragedy it was for a girl's family not to provide her with a ring to give her husband-to-be on that great night amid festivities and the eyes of friends. Then the young man would be a poor lover if he did not bring a ring to slip on the finger of his wife-to-be as they both moved to the center of the floor in the dance and came very close together to exchange rings. That ceremony meant much to all concerned and rings must be had for it. That old custom brought happiness to brides and developed the art of making jewelry in the village of long ago. Narvez has long since passed away but his memory still lives among those who are left who wore his precious jewelry, or those who saw some of it bought by barter by their ancestors. Sad it is that the artistic work of *el platero viejo* (the old silversmith) can no longer be found in Las Placitas. Like other things from the hands of the artists and craftsmen of old Las Placitas, his creations, crude but beautiful, have disappeared and newer, modern machine-made ornaments of personal adornment have taken their place.

- Tey Diana Rebolledo and María Teresa Márquez. *Women's Tales from the New Mexico WPA: La Diabla a Pie.* Houston: Arte Público Press, 2000. Pp. 349–351.

FOLK THEATER

Las Cuatro Apariciones de Nuestra Señora de Guadalupe [The Four Apparitions of Our Lady of Guadalupe]

Coro:

Para comenzar, señores,
Pido me déis atención
Y veréis que Dios no quiere
Más que un limpio corazón.
Qué aplauso, señores, es éste?
¿Qué música, qué alegría?
Es que esta noche celebramos
La aparición de María.

. . . .

Letra:

Hoy rendidos a tus plantas
Sagrada Virgen María
Felicitamos el día
De María Guadalupana.
(Se oye música; aparece
    la Virgen)

Juan:

¿Qué es ésto?¡Dios!
¡Qué asombro!
    ¡Qué confusión!
¡Qué ruido tan soberano!
Esto del cielo ha bajado.
¿Dónde está? no lo veo
No lo percibo, no lo alcanzo.

Virgen:

Aquí estoy Juan,
    ¿Qué no lo ves?
Llega a mi, pues,
    Hijo amado.

Choir:

In order to begin, Gentlemen
I ask for your attention
And you will see that God does not desire
More than a clean heart.
What applause, gentlemen, is this?
What music, what joyfulness?
It is that tonight we celebrate
María's apparition.

Music:

Today kneeling at your feet
Most sacred Virgin Mary
We celebrate the day
Of the feast of María Guadalupe.
(Music is heard; the Virgin appears)

Juan:

What is this? God save me!
What fright!
    What confusion!
What majestic sounds
Are emanating from Heaven.
Where is she? I cannot see.
I cannot behold, I cannot see.

Virgin:

I am here, Juan.
    Can't you see me?
Come here,
    my beloved son.

Juan:

Ahora es peor mi confusión
Que hasta mi nombre
   ha llamado,
¿Quién puede ser
   que me llama
En esto tan solitario?

Virgen:

Yo soy, Juan. ¿Qué no tú ves?
Llega a mis pies, hijo amado.

Juan:

Por allí lo anda
   una luz muy soberana.
Quizá será alguna parida
Que se lo vino de Méjico
Mas, llegaré a saludarla
Pues es linda como el cielo.
Tente quinquí (A solas):
Dime ¿qué lo andas haciendo
Tan temprano en este monte?

Virgen:

Párate, hijo y atiende
A ti te busco, Juan Diego.
Ya sé que a Méjico vas
Y luego en llegando
Te vas para el Obispado
Y le dices al Arzobispo
Que en este lugar
   te he hablado.
Le dirás como soy;
Las señas que me has mirado
Y que en este sitio quiero,
Siendo de gran agrado,
Que se me fabrique un
   templo

Juan:

Now my confusion is even worse
She is even calling
   my name.
Who can it be
   that is calling me
In this deserted place?

Virgin:

It is me, Juan. Can't you see?
Come to my feet, my beloved son.

Juan:

Over there is
   a majestic light
Maybe it is someone
Who came from Mexico
I will go and greet her
She is as beautiful as heaven.
Stop (To himself)
Tell me, what are you doing
So early in this forest?

Virgin:

Stop my son and listen
I am looking for you, Juan Diego.
I know you are going to Mexico
And when you arrive there
Go to the Bishop's rectory
And inform the Archbishop
That I spoke to you
   in this spot
Tell him how I look
As a sign that you have seen me
And that in this place I desire
Being that it is very pleasant
That a temple be built here

Que he de venir a visitarlo
a este reino mexicano
A amparar a sus moradores
Y a los que buscan mi amparo.
Y así, véte ya, hijo mío,
No tienes que estar dudando
Que me tienes a mi
Y me tendrás a tu lado.

Juan:

¡Alabado sea mi Señor!
Y ¿por qué, Cosa tan buena,
Te quieres venir aquí
En este tan solitario cerro?

Virgen:

Porque esta es propia
   morada de los Indios
Y yo quiero vivir entre ellos.

Juan:

Cuan mucho te lo agradezco.
Pero, Señora Madre,
Siento mucho el que no puedo
Porque Señor Arzobispo
   me dirá
Que soy un mentiroso
Y que no le ande
   con cuentos
Porque me pondrá la picota
Y me dará los *doscientos.*

Virgen:

Anda, hijo, que yo te mando
Y he de ser amparo vuestro.

Juan:

Pero, Señora Madre,

That I will be coming to visit
This Mexican lands
To protect its inhabitants
And others who seek my protection.
So therefore, go my son.
You do not have to be doubting
Since you have me
And you will have me by your side.

Juan:

Praise be the Lord!
And tell me, Beautiful Virgin
Do you want to come here
To this deserted hill?

Virgin

Because this is where
   the Indians reside
And I want to live among them.

Juan:

I am very grateful for that
But my Dear Mother
I am so sorry I cannot do it
Because the Archbishop
   will tell me
That I am a liar
And not to go around
   telling lies
Otherwise he will whip me
Will give me two hundred lashes.

Virgin:

Go my son, for I request it
And I will protect you.

Juan:

But my Dear Mother

Una duda entre cuidado lo tengo
Y te quiero preguntar
¿Por qué dejaste lo cielo
Y lo veniste a buscar aquí?

Virgen:

Por tí lo dejé, Juan Diego.
A buscar vengo a los Indios
Y quiero quedarme entre ellos
Hasta que con todos suba
A la corte celestial.

Juan:

Cuando no me ha de cuadrar.
'Stá bueno, pero mira,
Señora Madre,
Tú lo andas volando
y lo llegarás más presto
A ver a Señor arzobispo.
Yo, en verdad, tengo miedo.

Virgen:

No temas que con mi auxilio
En todo tendrás acierto.
Vé y cuenta lo que te pasa
Y vuelve aquí.
Te espero.

Juan:

Pues, voy camino corriendo
Allí se quede tu musicada.
Estate divertida. Ten cuidado,
no te espines.
¡Hasta luego!

Virgen:

Mi Hijo guíe tus pasos.

I have great doubts and worries
I would like to ask you
Why did you leave heaven
And came to look for it here?

Virgin:

For your sake, Juan Diego.
I came to look for the Indians
And I want to stay with them.
Until I take all of them with me
To Heaven.

Juan:

How can that not please me?
Alright, but look,
Dear Mother
You can fly
and will get there faster
To see the Archbishop
To tell you the truth, I am afraid.

Virgin:

Do not be afraid you have my aid
You will not fail in anything.
Go and tell what you have seen
And come back here.
I'll wait for you.

Juan:

Very well, I will go quickly
I leave you with your music
Entertain yourself. Be careful
do not prick yourself (with the thorns).
Good-bye!

Virgin:

May my Son guide your steps.

Telón	Curtain
....	....

[Juan Diego goes to the cathedral in Mexico City to deliver the message to the Archbishop, but just as he had predicted he is unable to talk to the Archbishop because the priests at the door do not believe him and send him away.]

(Sale el portero)

Aquí empieza la carabana.

(Al Padre)

Que lo tenga usted muy bien,
Su Reverencia.
Que me alegro que esté bien.

Padre Chico:

Bueno es, Juan.
   ¿Qué andas haciendo?

Juan (A solas):

Lo mismo que lo pensé.

(Al Padre)

Bien, ¿Cómo le va a usted?

Padre:

¿Que se te ofrece?

Juan (A solas):

Yo se lo dije a Nana Virgen
Que había de perder
  la tiempo
Y no me lo habían de creer.

Padre:

¿Que Virgen?

(the doorman comes out)

Here my troubles begin.

(To the priest)

May you be well today
Your Reverence.
I am glad you are fine.

Small Father:

Good Juan.
   What brings you here?

Juan (to himself)

Just as I thought.

(To the Priest)

I'm fine, how are you?

Priest:

What can I do for you?

Juan (to himself)

I already told Mother Virgin
That I was going to waste
  my time
And they were not going to believe me.

Priest:

What Virgin?

Juan:

La del cerro
Una que me hallé
   esta mañana
Más hermosa que uno lucero
Y que me dijo
   que venía a vivir
En compañía vuestra.

Padre:

¡Quítate de mi presencia
Indio, brujo, hechicero!
¡Qué virgen te había
   de hablar a tí,
perro chuchumeco?

Juan:

Mira, Señor, te lo juro.
(Haciendo la *señal de la cruz)*

Padre:

¿Qué juramento es ese?

Juan:

De mi padre, de mi madre
De mis abuelitos y hermanitos.

Padre:

Ya te puedes ir mudando
Con tus soflanas y cuentos
Porque si mi amo lo sabe
Te manda dar los 'doscientos.'

Juan (A solas):

Ya yo tenía noticias
Desde allá desde lo cerro

Juan:

The one on the hill.
One that I met
   this morning
More beautiful than a star
And who said
   she was coming to live
With you.

Priest:

Get out of my sight!
You Indian, witch, sorcerer
What Virgin would want
   to talk to you!
You street dog!

Juan:

Look, Sire, I swear to it.
(Making a the sign of the cross)

Priest:

And what do you swear to?

Juan:

Upon my father and mother,
My grandparents and my brothers.

Priest:

You can leave now.
With your make believe stories and lies
Because if my master hears of this
Will give you 200 whip lashes.

Juan (To himself):

I already knew this
Would happen even at the hill

Pero antes que me los den	But before they whip me
Voy para estufa, ya vuelvo.	I will leave and will return.
(Al Padre)	**(To the Priest):**
Su mano, su Reverencia,	Your hand, your Reverence,
Me alegro que esté bueno.	I am glad you are doing fine.
(Se Va)	(He leaves)

[Juan Diego returns to inform the Virgin of Guadalupe of his failed mission and the Virgin asks him to deliver the message again. This happens four times in all until the Virgin sends a sign and the Archbishop finally is convinced of the truthfulness of Juan Diego's message.]

- Aurora Lucero-White Lea. "Las Cuatro apariciones de Nuestra Señora de Guadalupe." *Literary Folklore of the Hispanic Southwest.* San Antonio, TX: The Naylor Company, 1953. pp. 86–89.

Commentary

The Four Apparitions of Our Lady of Guadalupe is an example of Chicano/a folk theater. There are many other plays that are under the category of religious folk theater and basically narrate episodes from the bible which depict the life of Jesus Christ on earth. These plays revolve around the Christmas season and the Easter and Lent holidays.

There are also a few secular plays dating from the colonial period and dealing mainly with battles fought against Native Americans such as *Los Comanches*. Folk plays from the nineteenth and early twentieth century are generally one act plays or skits of the humorous, picaresque type. They depict the daily life of the Chicano/a worker using comedy as a main element in the skits. Both colonial period plays as well as those from the nineteenth and early twentieth century had a great influence on the development and structure of the Teatro Campesino which was formed in 1965 at the inception of the Chicano movement.

FOLK FOOD

Nopalitos (tender cactus leaves) with dry shrimp albondigas (six servings)

Ingredients for shrimp albondigas

1   envelope of dried, powdered shrimp (Mexican food section of grocery store)

2   eggs

3   tablespoons of cooking oil for frying shrimp albondigas

Shrimp albondigas:

Beat two eggs until fluffy; add dried shrimp and mix.

Spoon about one tablespoon of mixture one at a time until all mixture is used up into hot oil and fry a minute or two on each side until lightly brown. Take out of oil and set aside.

Red Chile salsa:

4 red dried chiles boil in water for about 15 minutes until tender

6 green tomatillos boiled in water for about 15 minutes or until tender

Put both tomatillos and chiles in blender and blend.

Nopalitos:

2 cups of clean and cut nopalitos (cut cactus leaves into one-inch squares)

1 quart of water

1 tablespoon of cooking oil

1 onion chopped

1 teaspoon oregano

1 clove of garlic finely chopped

1 1/2 cups of red chile salsa

Salt and pepper to taste

Boil fresh nopalitos in one quart of water for about thirty minutes.

Drain and rinse about three times to take away sticky substance from boiled nopalitos.

In frying pan place one tablespoon of cooking oil

Add nopalitos, garlic, and onions and fry until onions are tender about 3–5 minutes

Add 1 1/2 cups of red chile salsa.

Add fried albondigas.

Cook salsa, fried albondigas and nopalitos for about 10 minutes to blend in the taste of all ingredients.

- María Herrera-Sobek, family recipe from grandmother Susana Escamilla de Tarango.

Capirotada (bread pudding) (six servings)

Grease with vegetable oil a Pyrex (oven proof) large bowl and have ready)

Ingredients:

Four large buns of French style bread cut into small cubes or pieces and toasted in pan with butter or oil

eight small corn tortillas (toasted lightly in grill over stove or in oven)

1 cup of peanuts

1 1/2 cups of sliced bananas

1 cup raisins

1 1/2 cups of cheese cubes (Monterrey Jack or Longhorn cheese is fine)

2 sticks of cinnamon

1 cup of small, hard, colorful candy (small pieces)

2 cups of brown sugar

1 cup of water

Boil water, cinnamon, and brown sugar to make a sweet liquid mixture.

Line large glass bowl with tortillas

Mix raisins, cheese, peanuts, bread, sliced bananas, and colorful candy and place mixture in bowl.

Pour sweet brown sugar liquid mixture over ingredients to moisten them.

Put in 350 degree oven for 1/2 hour or until cheese is slightly melted.

- María Herrera-Sobek family recipe given to her by grandmother Susana Escamilla de Tarango.

Four
Scholarship and Approaches

The study of Chicano/a folklore can be divided into four separate eras of folklore scholarship and four distinct generations of scholars who have devoted their lives to collecting, analyzing, and interpreting Hispanic/Mexican American/Chicano oral traditions. The first generation or Hispanist generation dates from 1893 to 1930 and focused mainly on collecting and archiving folk genres. The main thrust of this scholarship centers on the diffusionist and comparativist theories of the day and were concerned with the Spanish origins of Hispanic folklore found in the United States. Aurelio Macedonio Espinosa is the leading figure of this generation. The second generation of folklorists focusing on the oral traditions of the Spanish-speaking people of the United States took a 180-degree turn and viewed this folklore production as not emanating directly from Spain but from Mexico: This was the Mexicanist generation as opposed to the Hispanist generation. This second generation of scholars began to focus on the Mexican character of U.S. Spanish language folklore and dates from 1930 to 1950, the decades when they published their major scholarly contributions. Its major figure is Arthur León Campa, who argued for the Mexican origins theory of Mexican American folklore. The third generation, dating from 1950 to 1970, was dominated by the figure of Américo Paredes, who diverged from studying folklore and its origins to the analysis of folklore in context and as the cultural production of a people in conflict and culturally battling the hegemonic society who had conquered and colonized them. In other words, Paredes adds the concept of race and class to the hermeneutics of folklore. His work introduces the study of folklore with a contemporary lens and definitely departs from the collecting and archiving of folklore texts, as race and class become important elements in analyzing the various genres. He veers towards the theoretical analysis of the numerous folklore genres as performative, racially marked political acts in the Chicano/a struggle for self-determination and cultural survival.

The present generation of folklore scholars, or fourth generation, dates from 1970 to the present. They continue to study folklore more in line with the theoretical paradigms (mostly postcolonial) first posited and delineated by Paredes but, in addition, this most recent generation has underscored the vectors of gender, sexuality, and feminist theories to the study of Chicano/a folklore. Chicana folklorists, in particular, have focused extensively on gender and feminist issues and added this important dimension to the study of this scholarly discipline. In the pages that follow the four generations are further delineated and studied. Each generation is highlighted citing the major figures of the period, their publications, and the contributions these scholars made and continue to make to the study of folklore.

I. FIRST-GENERATION FOLKLORISTS: 1893–1930

Chicano folklore scholarship has a relatively long history: One of the first published articles in the *Journal of American Folklore* (hereafter *JAF*) date from 1893. John G. Bourke wrote an essay titled "The Miracle Play of the Rio Grande," which appeared in one of the early volumes of the *Journal of American Folklore* (volume 6). He followed this study with three essays focusing on Mexican American oral traditions: "Popular Medicine, Customs, and Superstitions of the Rio Grande" (*JAF* volume 7), "The Folk-Foods of the Rio Grande Valley and of Northern Mexico" (*JAF* volume 8), and "Notes on the Language and Folk-Usage of the Rio Grande Valley" (*JAF* volume 9). This last article, interestingly enough, actually deals with tracing vestiges of Arab customs in the Mexican American community in Southeastern Texas near the cities of Brownsville, Harlingen, and McAllen area. These essays are significant for being the very first articles published in the earliest volumes of the prestigious *JAF*, which was founded in 1882.

An interesting, albeit controversial, early figure who focused on the study of Mexican American folklore and particularly folk music was Charles F. Lummis. Lummis had a long career in publishing articles on the songs and folklore of the Spanish-speaking population of New Mexico and California. One of his first articles that focused on this topic appeared in May 1896, in the popular magazine *The Land of Sunshine*. The essay commented on the religious order known as the *penitentes* [penitents] from New Mexico. The *penitentes* is a religious organization, still functioning today, steeped in folklore and characterized by the harsh punishing blows they administer to their own bodies, particularly during the Easter season. Lummis's interest leaned toward exploring musical traditions, and in this article he includes some of the music played during the *penitentes* procession associated with Lent. This early article from the nineteenth century marks the beginning of Lummis's interest in Hispanic folklore, which he kept for more than half a century, as evidenced by the publications of one of his landmark books, *The Land of Poco Tiempo* (1952), a work that provided an overall view of the folk traditions of New Mexico, particularly the *penitentes* and the folk songs of the area. Lummis continued his interest in Mexican American folk music, as evidenced by his article titled "A New Mexican Folk-Song" published in 1901 in *The Land of Sunshine* and later reprinted in his collection of Mexican American folk songs from California, *Spanish Songs of Old California* (1923).

Although Lummis achieved prominence in the United States for his writings on Mexican American folklore, he was more of a popular magazine writer and not a scholar; he did not undertake in-depth analysis of the material he collected. His articles appealed to the general public, and he was perceived as a popularizer and disseminator of Mexican American culture. Although he is a controversial figure, since he is viewed by some Chicano scholars as a man who used the New Mexican people by appropriating their folklore and using it for his own personal aggrandizement, his work as a collector of folk songs is appreciated: He amassed several hundred folk songs and recorded numerous folksongs in cylinder form. His collection of recorded songs can be found in the Museum of the Southwest in Los Angeles, California.

The first bona fide Hispanic scholar to direct his attention to Chicano folklore was Aurelio Macedonio Espinosa (1880–1958) from the state of New Mexico. Espinosa's folklore studies covered a wide spectrum of folklore genres in the numerous books and articles he wrote, such as *The Spanish Language in New Mexico* and *Southern Colorado*, (1911), *Estudios sobre el español de Nuevo México* [Studies on New Mexican Spanish] (1934), and *Romancero de Nuevo Méjico* [New Mexican Spanish Ballads] (1953). However, he concentrated his scholarly work on New Mexico and, to a lesser extent, California. He collected numerous folklore traditions such as children's songs and games, riddles, folk tales, ballads, customs, folk beliefs, proverbs, comparisons, and so forth. Nevertheless, he greatly distinguished himself for the linguistic studies he undertook on New Mexican Spanish. His published works on the Spanish *romances* (ballads) found in New Mexico and California provide valuable insights on New Mexican balladry, with respect to its close connections to Spain. Aurelio M. Espinosa's work on the linguistic characteristics of New Mexican Spanish has been highly lauded and was based on his folktale collections. Aside from the landmark studies he published on Hispanic folklore of the Southwest between 1909 and 1917, including the two books cited previously, he published several works in the 1920s and 1930s. He had a long and productive career; he continued publishing up until the 1950s. One of his last works was an article titled *"Folklore infantil de Nuevo Méjico"* in 1954.

A collection of Aurelio M. Espinosa's works was edited and published by his son José Manuel Espinosa under the title *The Folklore of Spain in the American Southwest: Traditional Spanish Folk Literature in Northern New Mexico and Southern Colorado* (1985). José Manuel followed in the footsteps of the elder Espinosa and continued the tradition of undertaking research on New Mexican oral traditions.

In spite of his distinguished scholarly career, Aurelio M. Espinosa has been highly criticized, first by Arthur León Campa and later by Chicano scholars, regarding his theories on the origins of New Mexican folklore. Whereas A. M. Espinosa posited the strong influence of Spain on the folklore of New Mexico, other scholars such as Américo Paredes, have pointed out that a more realistic source of New Mexican folklore was from Mexico since colonization and settlement of that state came from Mexico (under the Spanish Crown in the late 1500 and early 1600s). New Mexican folklore was further reinforced by subsequent waves of Mexican immigrants in later periods. Arthur L. Campa and Américo Paredes agree that the origins and diffusion of Chicano folklore was through Mexico and did not come directly from Spain.

Other notable scholars working on Chicano folklore in the first two decades of the twentieth century include the well-known Texas folklorist John A. Lomax and his son Alan Lomax, who collected folksongs of the Texas Mexican cowboys. John A. Lomax's article "Two Songs of Mexican Cowboys from the Rio Grande Border" appeared as early as 1915 in the *JAF.* Folk songs and folk drama were the two most popular genres studied and collected by early twentieth century folklorists. Eleanor Hague, for example, was one of the first woman folklorists who focused on California folk songs. One of her first published article appeared as early as 1911 and consists of 15 songs—all in Spanish—collected from the Los Angeles and San Francisco areas. Her books *Spanish American Folk Songs* (1917) and *Early Spanish California Folksongs* (1922) evidenced an interest in the folksong tradition, although she also published some essays on Mexican dances.

A second female folklorist from the first generation of scholars concentrating their work on Mexican American folklore was Mary Austin. Austin was basically interested in folk drama, although her first essay published in 1919 focused on another genre: "New Mexico Folk Poetry" as the title indicates. Her later work, appearing in the 1927–1934 period, dealt with folk dramas from New Mexico evidencing her interest in archiving and preserving Southwestern Hispanic folk plays. She firmly believed this was an important area of American cultural production and did not see it as quaint regional folklore. Some of her published works include "Native Drama of New Mexico" (1929) and "Folk Plays of the Southwest" (1933).

Two other women folklorists from this early period at the beginning of the twentieth century were Barbara Freire-Marreco, who wrote "New Mexican Spanish Folklore" (1916) and Elsie Clews Parson who explored connections between Pueblo-Indian and New Mexican folk tales in 1918 in her essay "Pueblo-Indian Folktales."

II. SECOND-GENERATION FOLKLORISTS: 1930–1950

The second-generation folklorists are those who published their major works in the 1930–1950 decades. Among this generation are three Mexican American scholars who made their mark mainly in the 1930s and 1940s although some continued publishing up until the 1970s. These scholars include Jovita González (1904–1983), Arthur León Campa (1905–1978), and Juan B. Rael (1900–1993). Jovita González, an upper middle class woman from Texas, actually published her first article, "Folk-Lore of the Texas Mexican Vaquero," in 1927. She was the first Chicana to belong to the American Folklore Society and continued her scholarly work in the 1930s with such articles as "Tales and Songs of the Texas-Mexican" (1930), "Among My People" (1932), and "The Bullet Swallower" (1935). González was interested in collecting the folklore of the Texas Mexicans, and she had a strong desire to preserve the cultural contributions of her people even though she belonged to the upper middle class, she identified with the general Texas-Mexican population and conveyed an ethnic pride that is evident in her writings. Her last article, "Stories of My People," appeared in 1954; the title again conveys a strong ethnic identification with her Texas Mexican community. In the past few years there has been a renewed interest in González and her articles, novels and memoirs have been published by Arte Público Press under the Recovering the U.S. Hispanic Literary Heritage Project. Some of these works include *Caballero* (1996), *Dew on the Thorn* (1997), and *The Woman Who Lost Her Soul and Other Stories* (2000).

Juan B. Rael and Arthur León Campa are two scholars who concentrated their folklore studies in the New Mexico area although Rael also wrote on the folk tales of Colorado. Rael began his folklore scholarly career with the publication of his article "The Theme of the Theft of Food by Playing Godfather in New Mexico Folklore" in 1937. His second article, "Cuentos Españoles de

Colorado y de Nuevo México," published in 1939, was later transformed into a book bearing the title *Cuentos Españoles de Colorado y Nuevo Méjico* (1940), a two-volume collection of folk tales from the two states. Rael later branched out to study *pastorelas* or Christmas nativity plays as exemplified by his major work in this area, *The Sources and Diffusion of the Mexican Shepherds Plays* (1965). This study was a major undertaking of identifying and classifying, analyzing, and comparing pastorelas from the Mexican and Chicano traditions. Other areas Rael studied were the New Mexican *alabado* [religious folk song] and New Mexican wedding songs. His work, nevertheless, consisted of collecting and classifying New Mexican and Colorado folk tales and Mexican/Chicano *pastorelas* from Mexico and the American Southwest. The question of origins and diffusion of these folklore genres was an important element in his scholarly writings.

Arthur León Campa was by far the most prolific of the 1930s generation of folklorists. Like his predecessor, Aurelio Macedonio Espinosa, Campa had a relatively long scholarly life, starting from 1929 with his first publication "Spanish Folklore in New Mexico" until his last publication in 1972: "Cultural Differences that Cause Conflict and Misunderstanding in the Spanish Southwest." His major contribution to folklore studies is in collecting New Mexican folklore focusing on folk songs and folk theater. He later branched out to collecting folktales and other oral traditions from the Southwest as the title of his 1963 book indicates: *Treasure of the Sangre de Cristo. Tales and Traditions of the Spanish Southwest* (1963). Campa's studies are significant not only for the contribution he made in collecting a large number of folksongs in "The Spanish Folksong in the Southwest" (1933) and folk poetry published in his book *Spanish Folk-Poetry in New Mexico* (1946), but also for his theory regarding the origins of New Mexican folklore. His position was that New Mexican folklore is basically derived from Mexican folklore and did not come directly from Spain, as Aurelio M. Espinosa had posited in previous scholarly works. Campa challenges the Spanish heritage myth and provides logical arguments for a Mexican origins of New Mexican folklore. His studies on religious theater include *Religious Spanish Folk-Drama in New Mexico* (1931), *The Spanish Religious Folktheater in the Southwest (First Cycle)* (1934), and *The Spanish Religious Folktheater in the Southwest (Second Cycle)* (1934), are particularly important since they are collections of complete religious plays with introductory, explanatory notes. In addition, he has made the folk play *Comanches: A New Mexican Folk Drama* relatively easy to obtain. This folk play is based on the battle fought between Native Americans and Spaniards that took place toward the end of the eighteenth century. It highlights the defeat of a group of Native Americans by Spanish troops and the conversion of the Indian leader to Catholicism. Again Campa provides ample background history and explanatory notes for the play.

Anglo-American folklorists active in the 1930–1950 decades include Frank J. Dobie, Mody C. Boatright, Ralph Steele Boggs, George Carpenter Barker, and Mary R. Van Stone. Frank J. Dobie edited the landmark collection of articles *Puro Mexicano* in 1935, although his interest in Mexican American folklore, particularly Texan Mexican folklore, began in the 1920s with the publication of three articles on border music and lore and a book on *Legends of Texas* (1924). In 1930 he also published *Coronado's Children: Tales of Lost Mines and Buried Treasures of the Southwest.*

Three Hispanic women from New Mexico are particularly noteworthy for their writings during the time period 1930–1950: Fabiola Cabeza de Vaca Gilbert centered her attention on the traditions of New Mexico in her books *The Good Life: New Mexico Traditions and Food* (1949) and *We Fed Them Cactus* (1954), Cleofas Jaramillo (1878–1956), who wrote *Cuentos del Hogar* (1939), *The Genuine New Mexico Tasty Recipes: Pasajes Sabrosos* (1939), and *Shadows of the Past/Sombras del Pasado* (1941). Jaramillo's work, *Shadows of the Past,* is more of a memoir than a bona fide collection of folklore since the central topic of her book is life as a young girl as she lived it in New Mexico. Nevertheless, her recollections bring to bear the numerous oral traditions her family practiced in her ranch. The tone of the book exhibits a strong regret for the passing of time and the transformations New Mexico is experiencing at the hands of a new cultural group—the Anglo-Americans who have recently "discovered" the charms of New Mexico and are migrating in large numbers to that state. The Mexican traditions are evaporating under the new regime, and Jaramillo evidences nostalgia for the Hispanic past. The work of Cabeza de Vaca Gilbert is in a similar vein to that of Jaramillo. Both women wrote about the loss of a traditional New Mexican way of life.

More highly recognized for her folklore collections is Aurora Lucero-White Lea (1894–1965). Aurora Lucero-White Lea probably had the same nostalgia for the past and sensed there was a great need and urgency for preserving some of the literary folklore that was fast disappearing. She began collecting folklore in the New Mexican area and published her first book, *The Folklore of New Mexico,* in 1941. She continued collecting oral traditions from New Mexico, and in 1947 her work *Los Hispanos: Five Essays on the Folkways of the Hispanos as Seen Through the Eyes of One of Them* appeared; this was followed by her excellent collection titled *Literary Folklore from the Hispanic Southwest* (1953), a work which included folk songs, folk theater, and other literary folklore genres.

III. THIRD-GENERATION FOLKLORISTS: 1950–1970

The figure of Américo Paredes (1915–1999) dominates the scholarly writings of the 1950–1970 period. He is the key scholar who literally placed Chicano folklore studies on the map. Américo Paredes Manzano, or Don Américo, as he is affectionately known by his friends and admirers, was a brilliant and original thinker who left a body of solid scholarly work in folklore as well as a significant corpus of creative writings: novels, poetry, and short stories. This work has influenced a generation of Chicano scholars such as José Saldívar, Ramón Saldívar, José Limón, John H. McDowell, Richard Bauman, Manuel Peña, and numerous others including this author. He is recognized as the dean of Chicano studies, having been at the forefront of Chicano scholarship positing a series of theoretical paradigms in the 1950s used in the interpretation, understanding, and analysis of the Chicano experience and its cultural production.

Américo Paredes, one of the most outstanding and prolific Chicano scholars of this century, was born on September 3, 1915 in Brownsville, Texas, a city located in an area known as the Rio Grande Valley in the southern tip of Texas. A descendent of a family that traced its origins to the original Spanish settlers of Nuevo Santander, as the area was named in the first half of the eighteenth century (1749), Paredes was particularly well qualified to write about this part of Texas. Paredes grew up in a family environment where Mexican and Mexican American traditional customs were observed and cherished and where both English and Spanish were spoken. Of particular interest to Paredes was the musical tradition, which in south Texas has always been very strong. In his groundbreaking book *"With His Pistol in His Hand": A Border Ballad and Its Hero* (1958), Paredes recalled how "in the ranches when men gathered at night to talk in the cool dark, sitting in a circle, smoking and listening to the old songs and the tales of other days" (33).

Paredes's first interest had been as a journalist; however, after the 1950s his journalistic efforts became secondary, for it was in these years that Don Américo returned to school in Texas, eventually graduating *summa cum laude* from the University of Texas at Austin in 1951. He continued his education at this same institution and in 1953 obtained a master's degree in English and Spanish. Three years later, Paredes was awarded a doctorate from the Department of English and the Department of Spanish, once again from the University of Texas, at Austin. After receiving his doctorate, he worked for a year at Texas Western College (now the University of Texas, El Paso). He became assistant professor at the University of Texas in the English Department in 1957, where he taught courses in folklore and Mexican-American Studies. Professor Paredes was the key figure in organizing a Folklore Studies Program at the University of Texas in 1957 and was head of the Program until he became Director of the Center for Mexican American Studies, a post he held until 1978. Professor Paredes continued his research and writing until his death on May 5, 1999.

Paredes's fame rests squarely on his scholarly career, which began with the publication of his article "The Mexico-Texas *Corrido*" in the *Southwest Review* in 1942. This essay offers a general overview of the topics that would develop into full-blown articles and books in later years, particularly topics related to *corridos* popular along the border area of Texas and Mexico. In this first scholarly piece Paredes posits a concise definition of the *corrido:* "The Mexican *corrido* is, like the British ballad, a song, of the people, composed by the people as a folksong in their moments of relaxation, and records past events of interest. It's prime quality is simplicity and lack of artistry" (Paredes 1942, 470). A description of the rhythm of the *corrido* and the general structure of this type of folksong are further offered. Paredes delineates three types of Texas-Mexican *corridos:* (1) the heroic type, (2) the adventure and travel type, and (3) the tragedy type. The first one derives its thematic matter from the physical clashes and culture conflict that took place in the Texas-Mexican border area after the Mexican American War of 1848. During this time, border heroes such as Gregorio Cortez surface *"defendiendo su derecho con su pistola en la mano."* [defending his rights with his pistol in his hand]. This thematic matter, of course, will form the basis of his book " *With His Pistol in His Hand*": *A Border Ballad and Its Hero* (1958). The article, well-structured and well-written, contains the many kernels that will yield a crop of important scholarly works in later years.

Paredes's second article, "The Love Tragedy in Texas Mexican Ballads" written in 1956, provides an analysis of the *tragedia* type *corrido.* Love-tragedy *corridos* generally told of crimes committed during dances; in particular the killing of young women by men who had been rejected by these women at local dances or fandangos.

The article describes the geographic and social conditions under which the incidents that served as subject matter for this type of love-tragedy *corridos* arose. According to the author, the Texas Mexican living in isolated ranches in the Lower Rio Grande gathered at "fandangos" or dances whenever possible. During these dances, men, flushed from drinking, their tempers rising and sensitive feelings easily hurt, would eventually become involved in some type of altercation in the course of the night. This type of incidents gave rise to a series of *tragedias* (tragedies), one of the most famous being "Rosita Alvírez," which Paredes describes in detail.

This article, although written at the inception of Paredes's folkloristic career, evidences the characteristics that would predominate in his later works; these include an intimate knowledge of the social, political, historical, and economic conditions under which the folklore entity developed and the contextual environment under which the folk performance took place. In this respect, he would antedate by a decade or more the "new folkloristics," whose theory of folklore emphasizes not motif counting nor the tracing of a folk element from its origins to its present state (geographic-historic method or Finnish method) but the "content and context" of the folk performance. In other words, Paredes was one of the first folklorists to reorient himself, as another well-known folklorist, Richard Bauman (Paredes and Bauman, 1972, xi), puts it, "from the traditional focus upon folklore as 'item'—the things of folklore—to a conceptualization of folklore as 'event'—the doing of folklore. In particular, there is an emphasis upon performance as an organizing principle that comprehends within a single conceptual framework artistic act, expressive form, and aesthetic response, and that does so in terms of locally defined culture—specific categories and contexts."

It is important to point out that Paredes very early on focused on the analysis, performance, and social significance of the folklore event. Proponents of the "new folkloristics" such as Dan Ben-Amos, Roger Abrahams, and Richard Bauman argued in the 1970s and 1980s for a reconceptualization of folklore in terms of performance and communicative process, a reconceptualization that Paredes had begun in his first two articles in the 1950s.

In 1957, he published one of his most outstanding article focusing on the historical antecedents of the *corrido* titled "The Mexican *Corrido:* Its Rise and Fall." This work explores the historical background of the *corrido* and the controversy surrounding it—that is, whether there is a direct unbroken line of descent from the Spanish *romances,* as previously postulated by such authorities as Vicente T. Mendoza, the Mexican ballad scholar, or whether the *corrido* first surfaced after a hiatus in the Lower Rio Grande area in Texas. Paredes posits the hypothesis that there was a hiatus in *corrido* production both in the Greater Mexican area and in the Lower Rio Grande Mexican area. The hiatus was due to the takeover of the popular *décima* (ten-line stanzas) and the *copla* (four-line stanzas). He asserts, "Thus, for a period covering at least a century, the *décima* was the dominant ballad form among widely separated folk groups of Spanish America" (98). Paredes further proposes in this article the controversial thesis that the Mexican *corrido* first emerged as a ballad tradition in South Texas as a result of the culture clash and culture conflict experienced after the Texas-Mexican War of 1836 and the Mexican United States War of 1848. He argues that the corrido replaced the *décima* in the second half of the nineteenth century as a preferred form of musical expression (Paredes 1957, 98–99).

Paredes based his thesis on the fact that scholars (such as Mendoza) did not find true *corridos* before the 1880s. It is a well-known fact, however, that the oldest Texas-Mexican *corrido,* which is found basically intact in the "El *corrido* de Kiansis," detailing the early cattle drives from South Texas to Kansas and dates from the late 1860s or early 1870s, a decade before the rise of the true *corrido* in Greater Mexico. Paredes's flint-sharp mind examines the different variables related to the historical antecedents of the *corrido* and arrives at the conclusion that border conflict and cultural clash between Anglo-Americans and Mexican Americans are the primary ingredients giving rise to the Texas-Mexican *corrido.* Such *corrido* border-conflict heroes as Juan Nepomuceno Cortina (1850s) and Gregorio Cortez (b. 1870) antedated the heroes of the Mexican Revolution of 1910 and served as prototypes for the revolutionary heroes of Mexico. In this article we find the theoretical model for the analysis of what would be called by later scholars and critics in the 1980s the "literature of resistance"—that is to say, a literature that arises out of the conflict between an oppressed cultural group and its oppressor. For Paredes, much of Chicano cultural production has arisen out of the culture clash and cultural conflicts that arose after the United States–Mexican War of 1848.

The Texas-Mexican folklorist further posits in "The Mexican *Corrido:* Its Rise and Fall" that "Either the Lower Border *corrido* owes its existence to the Greater Mexican form, or the Greater Mexican *corrido* is indebted to the more localized Texas-Mexican ballad. Until true *corridos* are collected in Greater Mexico that go back farther than Cortina's raid on Brownsville and the cattle drives to Kansas, the theory that the development of the Greater Mexican *corrido* has been influenced by Texas-Mexican balladry is a plausible one" (Paredes 1957, 105).

Américo Paredes's position as a folklore scholar solidifies with the publication of his first book *"With His Pistol in His Hand": A Border Ballad and Its Hero* in 1958. The book was Paredes's doctoral dissertation, and it is a meticulous and brilliantly executed scholarly analysis of a legend and its hero, Gregorio Cortez. The author, a native of the area from where Cortez came (the lower Rio Grande area in the southernmost tip of Texas), has the advantage of intimately knowing the land and its people. With such a background, Paredes can speak authoritatively about the attitudes and the "facts" as the people knew them surrounding such legendary figures as Gregorio Cortez. Paredes's study entailed the weaving of the various strands related to the Cortez legend; these included archival material such as historical records, court records, and newspaper accounts, the oral narratives surrounding the legend and the numerous Gregorio Cortez *corridos*. In this manner he was able to write the outstanding piece of scholarly work that *"With His Pistol in His Hand"* turned out to be.

The book is divided into two parts. Part I consists of four chapters. These chapters describe the geographical features of Nuevo Santander (the Lower Rio Grande Valley area). They describe the customs, the values, and traditions of the people living there and the resultant culture clash that ensued after the Mexican American War of 1848. Paredes points out this was in a sense inevitable given the contrast between catholic Mexicans and protestant Anglo Saxons the language factor—English versus Spanish—and the long animosity already existing between Anglo Saxons and Spaniards in Europe. There is a section in Part I describing the Texas Rangers and the lore surrounding them. Paredes does not paint a very flattering picture of this police force. The Texas Rangers were instituted to "pacify" the border area, but they in fact exacerbated the clash of cultures. Mexican Americans viewed the Texas Ranger, or *rinches* as they were called, as bullies who abused their position of power by beating and even killing innocent people of Mexican descent. This clash of cultures eventually gave rise to a series of heroes who refused to submit to tyranny and humiliation and "with their pistol in their hand" defended their rights to the bitter end. Such a hero was Gregorio Cortez. Section I also narrates the legend related to Gregorio: how he happened to move to the Kenedy area in Karnes County in Texas; how his brother Román traded a horse to an *Americano* and the results of this trade; Cortez's eventual shooting of Sheriff Morris, his escape and flight to the border, his capture, and imprisonment. Finally the legend details the release of Cortez from prison and his eventual death.

Paredes provides a description of Cortez: his physical, moral and spiritual characteristics. Section I ends with the different variations of the Cortez legend and the eventual canonization of Cortez as a folk hero.

In Part II of *"With His Pistol in His Hand"* Paredes discusses the numerous *corridos* collected thematizing the Cortez legend; he contextualizes the *corrido* with the Mexican ballad tradition in general and also includes a structural and stylistic analysis of the corrido with respect to language, rhythm, versification, verbal usage, structure, imagery, and other corrido conventions. He further contextualizes the *corrido* within the international ballad tradition. Mention is made of the similarities among Russian, Greek, and Spanish frontier ballads, particularly with the Scottish ballad.

"With His Pistol in His Hand" makes several outstanding contributions to the study of folklore: First, it develops a methodology for the in-depth

study of a *corrido*. It provides a model that incorporates all the variables of a legend together into a cohesive whole. Second, it provides meaningful insights into the culture, history, and political and social situation of the Mexican American in the 1850–1901 time span. And third, it posits again the startling thesis discussed earlier that the modern *corrido* as known today has its rebirth in the Lower Rio Grande Valley of Texas and not in the Greater Mexican area. This of course departs from other well-known scholars' hypothesis of the origins of the *corrido* such as Vicente T. Mendoza and Merle T. Simmons. The controversy resulting from Paredes's position was aired in an article by Don Américo titled "The Ancestry of Mexico's *Corridos:* A Matter of Definition" (1963).

The book *"With His Pistol in His Hand"* is a seminal study about a culture hero and the historical period in which he lived. It has been reprinted numerous times, and in 1982 a film was made based on the book titled *The Ballad of Gregorio Cortez*. It was first aired on PBS on 19 June, 1982.

Américo Paredes's interest in examining and documenting the points of convergence between Mexican and Hispanic Anglo-American society is evident in his article "The Bury-Me-Not Theme in the Southwest." This study, published in 1959 compares and contrasts the similarities and differences between the "bury-me-not" motif in the American cowboy and European balladry and the "bury-me-not-in holy-ground" motif which appeared in Spanish, Portuguese and Latin American (particularly Mexican) balladry. The analysis of the two closely related themes led Paredes to conclude, "It seems then that the two bury-me-not traditions in the southwest, arriving from different directions but having a common source in medieval Europe, have inevitably crossed paths and, existing side by side, have reacted upon one another. It is not strange that the Mexican *vaquero* and the American cowboy should have found some things in common when both rode the Kansas Trail" (Paredes 1959, 92).

Paredes's interest in highlighting contributions and finding commonalities in cultural production between Mexicans and Anglo-Americans once again is evident in his article published in 1960 titled "Luis Inclán: First of the Cowboy Writers." Paredes points out that he is not suggesting "that American Western writers are indebted to Inclán in the same manner that the American cowboy is indebted to the Mexican vaquero; no cowboy writer as far as we know ever read *Astucia* (Inclán's novel). But the same conditions that produced Western writing made of Inclán a veritable 'cowboy' writer, a forerunner of men writing in another language but sharing his methods and his outlook, as well as his subject matter" (Paredes 1960, 66). The article details in a most meticulous scholarly manner the life and works of the Mexican writer. Luis Gonzaga

Inclán (June 21, 1816–1875) wrote about ranch life in Mexico during the second half of the nineteenth century. Some of the stylistic characteristics of the works of this author, together with the subject matter extant in his work, are compared with North American Western writers.

The decade of the 1960s was an extremely productive time for Don Américo. During this period he collaborated with Edward Larocque Tinker in the production of the excellent work *Corridos and Calaveras: Mirrors of the Mind of the People* (1961) by providing the translations and notes for the book. His other studies in folklore took two major forms: (1) the study of the theoretical framework upon which folklore rests in Latin America and the United States and (2) he continued his scholarly study of folklore as an important field that revealed the racial and cultural attitudes of the two groups coming into culture conflict in Texas: the Mexican and the Anglo. In addition to these two major areas of emphasis, Paredes published two articles on the *décima* and held the following important posts: bibliographer for the respected folklore journal the *Southern Folklore Quarterly* for the years 1960–1965, book review editor for the *JAF* (1964–1965), editor of this same journal (1968–1973), member of the editorial board of *Folklore Americas* (1966–1968), and contributing editor for the *Handbook of Latin American Studies* (1968).

In "Folklore and History," published in *Singers and Storytellers* (1961), edited by Mody C. Boatright, Wilson M. Hudson, and Allen Maxwell, Paredes argues, and very persuasively indeed, for historians to reevaluate their concept of folklore (or at the very least be cognizant of its existence) and examine folklore and its implications for the study of a historical period. He points out that much that is called history (for example, events related to the Alamo in Texas) is actually folklore and much that is folklore affords the historian an excellent opportunity to examine the "attitudes and feelings, undercurrents of emotion in the masses of people, which are not recorded in official documents but which may have a profound effect upon events" (Paredes 1961, 62). The author gives two concrete examples of historical facts recorded in two folksongs, "A Grant" and "A Zaragoza," which narrate the deeds of these two historical figures. Paredes translated this article into Spanish and published it in an expanded form in *"Folklore e historia: Dos cantares de la frontera del Norte"* in *25 Estudios del folklore* edited by Fernando Anaya Monroy in 1971. Paredes's insistence on history being one more "fictional" narrative subject to the ideological standpoint of the writer would be fully explored by internationally respected theorists such as Hayden White in later decades.

"Folklore and History" was followed by the publication of "On Gringo, Greaser and Other Neighborly Names" (1961). The article is an interesting and illuminating study of the etymology of the Spanish word *gringo*, one of the many names Mexican use to call North Americans. Don Américo traces *gringo*, to its original Spanish meaning of "stranger," "barbarian" or "foreigner." He further comments on the other epithets the two cultures coming in conflict (Mexican and American) have hurled at each other throughout the century such as *greaser, bolillo* and *gabacho.*

Paredes's intimate knowledge of the cultural, historical, and even psychological working of the Texas-Mexican coupled with an equally close knowledge of American culture made him an excellent folklore scholar who was able to explore, analyze, and examine the different facets related to the cultural conflict existing between the two groups in his native state of Texas.

In the incisive article "Texas' Third Man: The Texas-Mexican" (1963) Don Américo perceptively explains the political and cultural position in which the Texas Mexican finds himself vis-à-vis the "white" or Anglo-Saxon man and the black man. He posits the thesis that as far as the Anglo-Texan is concerned there are three races of human beings: white, black, and Mexican. Furthermore, this classification is not so much based on color (with respect to the Mexican) being that a blond, blue-eyed, Spanish-speaking person will be classified Latin American (a euphemism for Mexican) and not white.

However, overt racism and discrimination (such as nonadmittance to swimming pools and restaurants) no longer exist in Texas. According to Paredes, the most subtle forms of discrimination exist in the economic sphere; it is here that the Mexican-American feels racism the most. The Texas scholar demonstrates in this article that gains made in the human dignity sphere are due in part to Mexico's protests against the violations of the bracero workers who came to work in the United States through a bilateral agreement between the two governments and lasted from 1942–1964. More covert areas of racism such as job discrimination, political gains, and educational reform are areas in which Mexico has not shown an interest in protecting. And it is here where the more subtle and less dramatic forms of discrimination continue to exist.

By the middle of the 1960s Don Américo had achieved international fame as a folklore scholar. He contributed four pieces to the collection of folklore studies published in *Buying the Wind: Regional Folklore in the United States* (1964) edited by Richard M. Dorson: "*Pastorela* to Celebrate the Birth of Our Lord Jesus Christ" (466–479), "Corrido de Jacinto Treviño" (483–485), "Corrido de Gregorio Cortez" (480–483), and some humorous anecdotes.

In 1964, his article on "Some Aspects of Folk Poetry" examined the controversial issue of literary criticism and folklore. Paredes proposed in this essay that there are some aspects of literary criticism that can be fruitfully applied to the study of folk poetry. He argues that: "There is, of course, no reason why folklore should not be subjected to critical analysis" (Paredes 1964, 214). But he cautions that this literary analysis of folk poetry should be based "on its own terms rather than on those sophisticated literature, while maintaining some common ground with modern criticism" (214). Paredes proceeds to illustrate this assertion by examining "language, structure, and tone in folk poetry" (214). He analyzes the English ballad, the *corrido,* and the proverb applying principles of literary criticism. Such aspects of folk poetry as the binary nature of the structure of the folk poems and their rhythm, metaphor, rhyme (texture) of the poems are highlighted. The author also underscores the importance of the performative act, the context of the performance, and the performer of folk poetry. These areas of folkloristics would be fully explored after the 1960s and continues to be a very important aspect of folkloristics and critical literary theory. Paredes in this article was once again ahead of his time.

With characteristic thoroughness Paredes analyzed in 1965 the history and folkloristic nature of the Argentine *gaucho* and American cowboy in the article *"El cowboy norteamericano en el folklore y la literatura."* A comparison is made between the Argentine *gaucho* and the American cowboy with emphasis on the origins (both etymological and historical) and their status as folklore entities. Paredes very successfully related the popularity and subsequent diffusion of cowboy "folklore" with the historical, social, and political events of the emerging American nation. Paredes views both "cowboy" and "gaucho" as foundational narratives used in the construction of the respective nations to which each entity belonged: Argentine and the United States. His theories coincide with those of Benedict Anderson's as expressed in his highly influential book *Imagined Communities* (1983). Again, Paredes anticipates in this study theories that would become commonplace in later decades vis-à-vis foundational narratives and their importance in the construction (or imagining) of a nation.

Don Américo attributes the "mythification" and spread in popularity of the "folklore" of the cowboy to the tremendous publicity it received through works of fiction, advertising, the press, and, more recently, the movies. An explanation for the immediate acceptance of the cowboy and his folklore is found in the nationalistic fervor of the new nation (i.e. the United States) to find its own identity.

In 1966 Paredes published four articles, two dealing with the *décima:* "The *Décima* on the Texas-Mexican Border: Folksong as an Adjunct to Legend" (coauthored with George Foss) and "The *Décima Cantada* in the Texas-Mexican Border: Four Examples." Both of these articles follow the general type of analysis exhibited in his book *"With His Pistol in His Hand."*

In the essay "The Anglo-American in Mexican Folklore," Paredes analyzes the attitudes of Mexican toward Anglos as reflected in Mexican folklore, specifically as these attitudes are mirrored in *corridos* and in prose narratives. Open attitudes of hostility are more commonly expressed in the Mexican ballad, particularly in the border-conflict type *corridos,* whereas a more veiled or disguised hostility is evident in the anecdote "in which the Anglo-American plays the simpleton within a framework of slapstick or low comedy" (Paredes 1966, 118).

In 1966 Paredes wrote another seminal article: *"El Folklore de los grupos de origin Mexicano en Estados Unidos,"* later translated as "The Folklore of Groups of Mexican Origin in the United States" and appearing in the collection of articles written by Paredes and edited by Richard Bauman *Folklore and Culture on the Texas-Mexican Border* (1993). Paredes pinpoints three main lines of thought with respect to the origin of Mexican American folklore: (1) Hispanophile, those that trace Mexican American folklore back to the Spanish Peninsula; (2) diffusionist, those scholars who believe such Mexican American folklore found in the United States is merely that coming from Mexico; and (3) the regionalist those maintaining that Mexican American folklore is regional folklore pertaining to the United States with its roots in Mexico views (3–4).

The article *"El Folklore de los grupos de origen mexicano en Estados Unidos"* was revised and translated with the new title of "Tributaries to the Mainstream: The Ethnic Groups" and appeared in Tristram P. Coffin's anthology *Traditions: An Introduction to American Folklore* (1968). Paredes again centers his scholarly attention on the folklore of Mexican Americans: He describes the early origins of this folklore and the differences and similarities with Mexican folklore. This article makes a significant contribution in the analysis, clarification, and identification of Mexican American folklore. In addition, Paredes provides a useful classification system for Chicano folklore. He divides Mexican American folklore into three general categories: regional, rural or semirural, and urban.

In 1966 the Thirty-seventh International Congress of Latin Americanists took place in Buenos Aires, Argentina. This event stimulated heated discussions and a vigorous exchange of ideas regarding the basic concept of folklore. As a result of this intellectual give and take in Buenos Aires, Paredes wrote the article *"Divergencias en el concepto del folklore y el contexto cultural,"* which was later translated and published as "Concepts about Folklore in Latin America and in the United States" in the *Journal of the Folklore Institute* (1969). This article examines the differences (and similarities) found in the conceptualization of what folklore is between Latin American folklorists and their North American counterparts.

Basically, Paredes pointed out how the two groups of folklorists perceive each other through stereotypical lenses. The Latin American scholars see North Americans as empiricists, non–theory oriented, and "mistaking" what in reality belongs to ethnography (folklore of "primitive" groups) and what belongs to sociology (urban folklore) for "real" and "authentic" folklore. In contrast, North American folklore scholars stereotype their counterparts in Latin American as "anti-democratic,' theory oriented, without a good scientific basis of collected data, "backward" in their conception of what folklore is, and "ignorant" of the new trends in folklore. They view them as still involved and bogged down in the old discredited theories of folklore as "survivals." Paredes sought a middle point between these two extreme perspectives, noting that although there are diehard scholars who adhere to the two extremes cited, there are many more in both countries who share similar views and methodologies.

The groundbreaking article "Folk Medicine and the Intercultural Jest" appeared in the anthology edited by June Helm *Spanish-Speaking People in the United States* (1968). The study examines the jest with respect to the attitudes Mexicans and Mexican-Americans reveal toward the United States and toward cultural transformations. The author found that since the interviewees were highly acculturated Mexican Americans belonging to the middle class in Brownsville, Texas, the jests, all related to folk medicine and *curanderismo,* expressed both resentment toward the dominant Anglo culture and at the same time an exasperation at the Mexican American's attachment to old traditions such as the *curandero* and folk medicine.

A perceptive analysis of *machismo* [exaggerated male characteristics] is found in the article published in 1967 titled *"Estados Unidos, México y el machismo."* Ever the careful scholar, Paredes challenges with historical data the idea that *machismo* is a Mexican phenomenon. He challenges the Freudian (Oedipal Complex) hypothesis and theories posited by Samuel Ramos, Octavio Paz, and even Vicente T. Mendoza with respect to the image of the Mexican macho and the psychological forces that produced him. He maintains that the figure of the macho man is popular throughout the world, and it was not until the advent of the celluloid screen and cowboy movies, which were imported from the United States, that machismo in its present form came into full being. He particularly challenges anyone to find the word *macho* in any of the songs or *corridos* prior to the 1940s. A comparative historical analysis of the growth of machismo in the United States with that in Mexico is further developed in the article. With characteristic carefulness and scholarship Paredes discards yet another stereotype about Mexican people.

In the article "José Mosqueda and the Folklorization of Actual Events" (1973), Paredes reexamines the *corrido* of José Mosqueda from historical, folk legend, and *corrido* perspectives. According to Paredes, a reexamination of the ballad was prompted by (1) documentary materials from the records at the Cameron County (Texas) courthouse not available previously; (2) publications of the memoirs of William A. Neale of Brownsville, containing a chapter titled "The Rio Grande Railroad Robbery"; (3) collection of variants of the Mosqueda corrido that include stanzas not found in the Lomax variant; and (4) a tape recording of an especially interesting version of the Mosqueda legend from Matamoros, Tamaulipas done in 1962. The new materials make the Mosqueda matter worth reconsidering from two viewpoints: as an example of the *corrido*-legend process and of what Latin American folklorists often call the "folklorization of historical events" (Paredes 1973, 2).

Gloria Anzaldúa's seminal study *Borderlands/La Frontera: The New Mestiza* (1987) brought to the attention of the world her concept of *mestizo/a* consciousness. In an early article titled "Mexican Lengendry and the Rise of the *Mestizo:* A Survey," published in 1971, Paredes explores the *mestizo* as an entity in Mexican politics and this hybrid population's rise to power after the Mexican Wars of Independence in 1810–1821. In the article the Chicano scholar posits that "the rise of the *mestizo* as representative of the Mexican nationality may be illuminated by the study of Mexican legendry" (98). He bases his thesis on three premises: "that the general category 'legend' may be distinguished in the history of Mexican folklore, that it serves to express or project certain sets a attitudes, and thirdly that the preference for certain kinds of legendry at certain periods in Mexican history reflects changes in the historical process resulting in the emergence of modern Mexico" (98).

Legends popular before the "rise of the *mestizo,*" that is, before the nineteenth century, generally depicted the life and miracles of saints. These early legends concentrated on the miraculous, but as the *mestizo* came into his own socially and politically speaking toward the end of the nineteenth century and beginning of the twentieth century, there was a change in the legends' subject matter. *Mestizo* legends focused on the real, the here and now; they depicted flesh and blood heroes such as Heraclio Bernal and later on the heroes of the Mexican Revolution of 1910–1917.

In *"El concepto de la 'médula emotiva' aplicado al corrido mexicano 'Benjamín Argumendo'"* (1971–72), Paredes ably demonstrates the validity of Tristam P. Coffin's hypothesis that ballads retain an "emotional core," which form the basis for the subsequent versions elaborated as time passes. At one time it was assumed that shorter ballads were the original ballads from which the "corrupted" longer texts later derived. Paredes finds evidence to support an opposite view in the Mexican *corrido* "Benjamín Argumedo" by examining texts from six different versions he collected, one from Mexico city and five from local folk singers from the Rio Grande Valley. Specific information as to the recording of the corridos and background on the interviewees is detailed in this study. Later on in the article, Paredes does an exhaustive scholarly comparison between the different versions in order to ascertain the validity of the "emotional core" hypothesis. The author concludes that there is indeed an "emotional core" in the *corrido* "Benjamín Argumedo" that is common to all the variants collected.

In the "Preface" to his book *A Texas-Mexican Cancionero: Folksongs of the Lower Border* (1976) Paredes states: "Although *cancionero* means 'songbook,' it may refer to a corpus of folksongs. *A Texas-Mexican Cancionero* pretends to be both: a songbook and a representative collection of the folksong corpus of a Texas-Mexican area (the Lower Rio Grande Border) at a particular period in history (1750–1960). While not all-inclusive, it does attempt to give example of the main forms and the principal themes in Texas-Mexican folksong" (xiii).

Paredes's excellent *Cancionero* is not only a mere collection of folksongs, but also provides a scholarly background regarding historical, sociological, political, and cultural antecedents of the songs and of the period and people that composed and sang these songs. Of added value, especially for those interested in the musical aspect, are the musical transcriptions preceding each song. Through the folksong, Paredes again aptly presents the views, attitudes, and the social conditions of the Texas Mexican people.

Paredes's "On Ethnographic work Among Minority Groups: A Folklorist's Perspective," (1977) is concerned with the research undertaken by anthropologists and sociologists in minority communities in general and more specifically, Mexican American communities in particular, without previous training in that ethnic group's folklore and culture. The folklore scholar perceives this lack of training in the important field of folklore as being one of the primary reasons social science scholars have been instrumental, even though perhaps unwittingly so, in propagating many of the stereotypes attributed to Mexican Americans.

Paredes edited several outstanding books that have received consistent high praise for their superior scholarship and for the contribution they make in the various fields covered. One of the first books he edited was the highly acclaimed *Folktales of Mexico* (1972)—an anthology that is part of Richard M. Dorson's series "Folktales of the World." The collection of Mexican folktales included in the volume has been praised for its content and for the excellent rendition of them in the English language. Paredes's background as a creative writer, no doubt, served him well in translating the folktales into English without making the Mexican characters sound like dime-store or Hollywood Mexicans.

In 1971, a volume of essays appeared edited by Paredes and Ellen J. Stekert titled *The Urban Experience and Folk Tradition*. The collection of scholarly works on "folklore in the city" focus on the urban environment and offers interdisciplinary perspectives from scholars specializing in various fields of research.

In 1972, Don Américo was involved with the production of yet another important theoretical work on folklore. In conjunction with Richard Bauman, Paredes edited *Toward New Perspectives in Folklore*, a book consisting of a collection of articles written by some of the most prominent folklorists, such as Dan Ben-Amos, Roger D. Abrahams, Dell Hymes, Elli Kongas Maranda, Alan Dundes, and others. And as the title indicates, the articles focus on the examination of current trends in folklore theory in the United States and suggest new theoretical models and perspectives toward the study of folklore.

Paredes's 11 most significant articles from the viewpoint of the editors appear in the anthology titled *Folklore and Culture on the Texas-Mexican Border* (1993). The essays explore issues of identity as well as the nature and origins of Chicano folklore. A fundamental thesis running through these articles is the theory of cultural resistance and cultural conflict as key to the production of Chicano folklore. *Folklore and Culture* underscores the outstanding contributions Paredes made to folkloristics and Chicano studies. His articles anticipated many of the theories in folklore and Chicano studies that are more extensively developed and popularized in the 1970s–1990s decades.

Paredes's book *Uncle Remus Con Chile* (1993) features a collection of 217 Mexican American jokes. The texts were collected during fieldwork undertaken in the 1963–93 period in the Rio Grande Valley; some of the jokes are completely rendered in Spanish, whereas others are offered in English. Many of the jokes are bilingual and contain both Spanish and English and base their humor on the misinterpretation of English or Spanish within the context of the joke; for example, joke #123, "Huevos rancheros," reads as follows:

A pretty little gringa walked into a restaurant here in Mexico City and ordered breakfast. She was served eggs, scrambled with tomatoes and chile and onion, you know, and she liked them very much.

When she was through she asked what they were called, and the waiter told her, "Huevos rancheros."

Next morning she came back and told the waiter, "Déme huevos de ranche-ros, por favor." (Paredes 1993, 94–95)

The joke is on the Anglo-American woman, who confuses scrambled eggs for "ranchers' testicles." Cultural conflict is evident in joke #34, "Dogs Allowed":

"Now that you mention these little towns in central Texas. There was one in which they had a restaurant with a sign that said, "No dogs or Mexicans Allowed."

So down the street just a little ways was another restaurant run by some Mexican people, and they put up a sign: "Dogs Allowed. Gringos Too." (Paredes 1993, 43)

The vast majority of the jokes are based on cultural conflicts between Anglos and Chicanos, and they support Paredes's thesis on the genesis and development of Mexican American folklore—that much of it is based on the conflictual relationships between the two groups in the United States.

Other folklorists forming part of the 1950s–1970 generation include Stanley Robe, Merle Simmons, and Vicente T. Mendoza. Robe focused on the folktale and published such works as *Antología del saber popular: A Selection from Various Genres of Mexican Folklore across Borders* (1971) and *Hispanic Legends from New Mexico: Narratives from the R.D. Jameson Collection.* (1980). John Donald Robb, in contrast, collected folk songs from New Mexico and published them as *Hispanic Folk Songs of Hispanic new Mexico* (1954) and *Hispanic Folk Music of New Mexico and the Southwest: A Self-Portrait of a People* (1980). Simmons researched the Spanish *romance* and Mexican *corrido*. Even though Vicente T. Mendoza is more of a Mexican folklore scholar with outstanding works on the Spanish *romance* and on the *corrido,* he does have a comprehensive volume on the *canción* from New Mexico titled *Estudio y clasificación de la música tradicional hispánica de Nuevo México* (1986). While all three scholars did more than collect folklore items, their work is still very much in the vein of folklore collections. Vicente T. Mendoza is highly acclaimed for his work on Mexican folklore, in which, in addition to collecting a great number of folklore items, he also interpreted and analyzed the folklore collected.

IV. FOURTH-GENERATION FOLKLORISTS: 1970–PRESENT

The Chicano Movement elicited a new interest in Chicano/a culture and a renewed commitment to the study of oral traditions inherited from past generations. The Chicano generation of folklore scholars was also influenced by a general new focus in folklore that had surfaced in the late 1950s and

1960s with such folk singers as Bob Dylan; Joan Baez; Judy Collins; Woody Guthrie; Peter, Paul, and Mary; Simon and Garfunkel; and numerous other folk singers of the counterculture revolution or the "hippie" era. Américo Paredes influenced scholars such as José Reyna, John H. McDowell, José Limón, Manuel Peña, and María Herrera-Sobek. Herrera-Sobek and Limón focused much of their scholarly attention on the *corrido* (although writing on other genres of folklore such as jokes (Limón and Herrera-Sobek) and *pastorelas* (Herrera-Sobek), while McDowell wrote on the *corrido* and on children's riddling. Enrique Lamadrid, aside from his studies on the *corrido*, also branched out to explore New Mexican traditions and other types of

María Herrera-Sobek.

folksongs such as the *indita*. Some of his most recent works include *Tesoros del Espíritu: A Portrait in Sound of Hispanic New Mexico* (with Jack Loeffler) (1994), *La Música de los Viejitos: Hispano Folk Music of the Río Grande del Norte* (with Jack Loeffler and Katherine Loeffler) (1999) and *Hermanitos Comanchitos: Indo-Hispano Rituals of Captivity and Redemption* (2003). José Reyna wrote his 1972 dissertation on the intercultural jest and published it in under the title *Raza Humor: Chicano Joke Tradition in Texas*. Manuel Peña has written extensively on the Texas Mexican *conjunto* type music in such works as *The Texas-Mexican Conjunto: History of a Working Class Music* (1985) and *Música Tejana,* 1999. Contemporary scholars such as Peter García are surfacing in the twentieth-first century. His work on ethnomusicology is an excellent example of the new work that is being done in folklore studies today.

Fourth Generation Folklorists and Gender Studies

While Américo Paredes's research brilliantly transitioned from the comparativist-diffusionist critical folkloristics type of scholarly work to critical cultural studies that specifically encompassed and highlighted race and class, he did not focus on gender studies or include feminist theoretical paradigms in his analysis and interpretation of Chicano folklore. It was up to the fourth generation of folklore scholars to bring into focus these new feminist perspectives. Herrera-Sobek was the first scholar to apply feminist theories surfacing in the 1970s to the study of Mexican and Chicano folksongs, particularly the *corrido*. One of her first presentations evidencing this application of feminist theory to *corrido* studies was "Mothers, Lovers, and Soldiers: Images of Women in the Mexican *Corrido*," which was read at the American Folklore Society Annual Meeting held in Detroit, Michigan in 1977. Two years later, the article appeared in the University of Pennsylvania's *Keystone Folklore Journal* (1979, 53–77). Several scholarly essays written by Herrera-Sobek centering on the representation of women in the Mexican ballad were read at various national and international conferences during the 1970s and 1980s and were subsequently published. Some of these articles include "The Treacherous Woman Archetype: Structuring Agent in the *Corrido*" (1982); "The Acculturation Process of the Chicana in the *Corrido*" (1982), and "La Delgadina: Incest and Patriarchal Structure in a Spanish/Chicano Romance-*Corrido*," (1986). Herrera-Sobek's work in gender studies and *corridos* culminated in her book-length study, *The Mexican Corrido: A Feminist Analysis* (1990). For a complete listing of gender studies and the *corrido*, see the bibliography.

José Limón.
Source: Courtesy of José Limón.

Herrera-Sobek's work on gender issues and folklore has not been limited exclusively to the *corrido* tradition but has included studies on *décimas, pastorelas* or shepherds' plays, and cowboy songs. An article published in 1987 focused on the Chicano *décima:* "Discourse on Love and *Despecho:* Representation of Women in the Chicano *Décima*" (1987). Her study on *pastorelas,* "The Defiant Voice: Gender Conflict in Mexican/Chicano *Pastorela* Drama," appeared in *Gestos* (1991). She branched out into cowboy songs and gender in 1993 with the publication of "The Pretty *Señorita* Motif: Territorial Conquest and Interracial Love in Cowboy Ballads" (Herrera-Sobek 1993). In 1991 she also published the book *Gender and Print Culture: New Perspectives on International*

Norma Cantú.
Source: Courtesy of Norma Cantú. Photograph by
Michael Short.

Ballad Studies, which is composed of a collection of articles dedicated to the
study of women in European and American ballads.

In the twenty-first century, her scholarly work includes an article on
patriarchal structures and children's songs and games. This study was
published as "Danger! Children at Play: Patriarchal Ideology and the
Construction of Gender in Spanish Language Hispanic/Chicano Children's
Songs and Games" in *Chicana Traditions: Continuity and Change* (2002). Her
most recent work related to folklore, published in 2005, analyzes the mythic
figure of La Malinche: "In Search of La Malinche: Pictorial Representations
of a Mytho-historical Figure" (Romero 2005).

Olga Nájera-Ramírez.
Source: Courtesy of Olga Nájera-Ramírez.

The study of folklore and literature has also been a hallmark of Herrera-Sobek's scholarly production. In her book *The Bracero Experience: Elitelore Versus Folklore* (1979) she analyzed the *bracero* (Mexican immigrant worker) via three venues: folklore (*corridos*), literature, and oral history interviews. In her book *Northward Bound: The Mexican Immigrant Experience in Ballad and Song* (1993), she traced the history of Mexican immigration through Mexican *corridos* and popular songs. This was in line with the new cultural studies that were providing new paradigms for the study of ethnic groups in the United States. Other publications such as "Social Protest, Folklore, and Feminist Ideology in Chicana Prose and Poetry" (Preston 1995) examined folklore in Chicana literary production.

Peter García.
Source: Courtesy of Peter García.

Other Chicano scholars are concentrating their studies in various areas of folklore scholarship such as Yolanda González-Broyles, who has written on the *canción ranchera* and on singer Lydia Mendoza and the theater tradition: *El Teatro Campesino: Theater in the Chicano Movement* (1994). Her study of Lydia Mendoza's work, *Lydia Mendoza's Life in Music/La historia de Lydia Mendoza: Norteño Tejano Legacies* (2001) has been highly praised. Norma Cantú wrote her dissertation on the Texas *pastorelas* and more recently edited a book with Olga Nájera–Ramírez on Chicana oral traditions, *Chicana Traditions: Continuity and Change* (2002). Included are several younger scholars such as Helen R. Lucero, Brenda M. Romero, Domino Renee Pérez, Cynthia L. Vidaurri, Leonor Xóchitl Pérez, Cándida F. Jáquez, Deborah R.

Vargas, and Tey Marianna Nunn. In addition to Cantú and Broyles-González, Richard R. Flores and María Herrera-Sobek have done extensive work on the *pastorela* (shepherds' plays) tradition in the southwest. Flores published the excellent study *Los Pastores: History and Performance in the Mexican Shepherd's Play of South Texas* in 1995.

Studies on the *corrido* have evolved from examining older forms of these texts to applying contemporary critical theories to their interpretation and analysis. Herrera-Sobek, Helena Simonett, Elijah Wald, and Mark Cameron Edberg have all written in-depth studies on the *corrido* and its most recent form, the *narcocorrido*. Simonett's book *Banda: Mexican Musical Life Across Borders* (2001) did a thorough study on contemporary banda music, including the *narcocorrido* and the *quebradita*, a type of dancing and music that swept the Southwest and northern Mexico in the 1980s and 1990s. Wald published his book *Narcocorrido: A Journey into the Music of Drugs, Guns and Guerrillas* in 2001, and Edberg followed in 2004 with his work *El Narcotraficante: Narcocorridos and the Construction of a Cultural Persona on the U.S.-Mexico Border.* All of these studies on the *narcocorrido* seek to interpret the socio-cultural aspects of the genre and are not a mere compilation of the songs.

Herrera-Sobek's work on the *corrido* has focused on feminist studies, new historicism, postcolonial studies, and sociological studies such as *The Bracero Experience: Elitelore Versus Folklore* (1979), *The Mexican Corrido: A Feminist Analysis* (1990), and *Northward Bound: The Mexican Immigrant Experience in Ballad and Song* (1993). She has also written several articles on the *narcocorrido* such as "The Transnational Imaginary and 'Narcocorridos'—Violence, Drugs and Transgressive Discourse in Mexican Ballads" published in *Violence and Transgression in World Minority Literatures* (2005).

Excellent bibliographic work was carried out in the 1970s by Michael Heisley, which he published as *Chicano Folklore: An Annotated Bibliography of Chicano folklore of the Southwestern United States* (1977) and a dictionary of folk terms was compiled by Rafaela G. Castro: *Chicano Folklore: A Guide to the Folktales, Traditions, Rituals, and Religious Practices of Mexican-Americans* (2001). This latter work includes an extensive bibliography on Chicano folklore.

For folk belief, particularly folk medicine and folk legend, Mark Glazer from Pan American University in Edinburg, Texas, has an extensive archival collection. His collection of legends on La Llorona is outstanding, and he is planning to have the archival collection online in the near future. Shirley Arora from the University of California, Los Angeles, did extensive work on the proverb and proverbial expressions in the 1970s and Luis Leal from Santa Barbara, California has done work on the *corrido* as well as published the

Luis Leal.
Source: Courtesy of Luis Leal.

outstanding collection of myths and legends: *Mitos y Leyendas de México: Myths and Legends of Mexico* (2002). In addition he has published articles on La Llorona and on the *corrido*.

Both José Limón and John H. McDowell have published brilliant studies on the *corrido*. McDowell's book, *Poetry and Violence: The Ballad Tradition of Mexico's Costa Chica* (2000), as well as his article, "The Corrido of Greater Mexico as Discourse, Music and Event" (1981), are excellent incursions in *corrido* hermeneutics. Equally impressive is Limón's work *Mexican Ballads, Chicano Poems: History and Influence in Mexican American Social Poetry* (1992). Additionally, Limón has written studies on Chicano jokes and a landmark study on the Weeping Woman legend, "La Llorona, the Third Legend of Greater Mexico: Cultural Symbols, Women, and the Political Unconscious" (1988).

Important work on the *corrido* was also done by the late Guillermo Hernández, best known for his work *Canciones de la Raza* (1978). His work on setting up the digitizing of more than 30,000 *corridos* and *canciones* with the aid of the Los Tigres del Norte Foundation grant at the University of California, Los Angeles is a great contribution to *corrido* studies.

APPROACHES TO THE STUDY OF CHICANO FOLKLORE

Approaches to the study of Chicano folklore mirror those that have been extant in general folklore studies. The early works of scholars such as Aurelio Macedonio Espinosa (first generation, 1900–1930) focused on aspects of collecting, comparing, and classifying and an interest in origins and diffusion. There was a general feeling that oral traditions were fast disappearing under the impetus of modernity and these cherished traditions would be lost forever. The dynamic nature of folklore was not perceived at all at this point in time. The linguistic approach was favored by some of the top folklore scholars of the era such as Aurelio M. Espinosa. His early works focused on the linguistic characteristics of the Spanish from New Mexico as found in the folktales and other folk narratives from the region. Another early approach favored was the comparative approach. Again, Aurelio M. Espinosa was very keen in proving the direct relationship between New Mexican folklore and the Spanish Peninsula.

The second generation of folklorists (1930–1950) continued to focus on collecting and classifying. A new interest developed on the connection between Mexican folklore and the Mexican American folklore of the Southwest as exemplified by the major figure of this generation Arthur León Campa. A comparative approach was still popular with this generation of folklorists.

The third generation of folklorists (1950–1970) was dominated by the outstanding work of Don Américo Paredes. He can rightly be called the "father" of contemporary Chicano folklore, since he brought a new theoretical paradigm for the study of Chicano folklore. His theoretical framework for the study of Chicano folklore is directly linked to what later developed as new historicism, cultural studies, and postcolonial studies. Paredes posited the theory that much of Chicano folklore arose from the culture clash between Anglo-Americans and Chicanos, citing the Mexican *corrido* and the intercultural jest as examples of this phenomenon. Paredes's contribution is in diverting our scholarly attention from merely collecting and comparing to positing theoretical models for the analysis and interpretations of the folklore items as they exist in a historical and social context. In particular, he infused the study of folklore, taking into account the political, historical, economic, and social context in which it was produced. His landmark studies pointed to a new conceptualization of folkloristics, one that underscored the context in which the folklore item was embedded as well as the performative aspect in which folklore would manifest itself. The most distinguishing aspect of Paredes's folkloristics was his introduction of race and class to the study of folklore. He was, therefore, the first Chicano scholar to undertake cultural studies in the contemporary sense of the word.

Contemporary scholars avail themselves of critical theories that surfaced during the 1960s to the present. Feminist, postcolonial, anthropological, postmodern, semiotic, psychoanalytic, structuralist, and poststructuralist theories are the most commonly used in Chicano/a folkloristics today. Postcolonial theories are particularly relevant to the study of Chicano/a folklore, as are feminist theories, and Chicano/a scholars avail themselves of these theoretical frameworks in the hermeneutics of this ethnic group's folklore production.

REFERENCES

Anderson, Benedict. 1983. *Imagined Communities: Reflections on the Origin and Spread of Nationalism*. London: Verso.

Herrera-Sobek, María. 1979. "Mothers, Lovers, and Soldiers: Images of Women in the Mexican *Corrido*." *Keystone Folklore Journal* 23, no. 1:53–77.

———. 1979. *The Bracero Experience: Elitelore versus Folklore*. Los Angeles: UCLA Latin American Publications, University of California, Los Angeles.

———. 1982. "The Treacherous Woman Archetype: Structuring Agent in the *Corrido*." *Aztlán: International Journal of Chicano Studies Research* 13 (Spring):136–147.

———. 1986. "'La Delgadina': Incest and Patriarchal Structure in a Spanish/ Chicano Romance—Corrido." *Studies in Latin American Popular Culture Journal* 5 (Spring,):90–107.

———. 1987. "Discourse on Love and *Despecho:* Representation of Women in the Chicano *Décima*." *Aztlán:*69–82.

———. 1990. *The Mexican Corrido: A Feminist Analysis*. Bloomington: Indiana University Press.

———. 1991. "The Defiant Voice: Gender Conflict in a Mexican/Chicano *Pastorela* Drama." *Gestos:*63–77.

————. 1991. *Gender and Print Culture: New Perspectives on International Ballad Studies.* Madison, Wisconsin: Impressions, Kommision Für Volksdictung-Société International D'Ethnologie et de Folklore.

————. 1993. *Northward Bound: The Mexican Immigrant Experience in Ballad and Song.* Bloomington: Indiana University Press.

————. 1993. "The Pretty *Señorita* Motif: Territorial Conquest and Interracial Love in Cowboy Ballads." In *III Hispanic Cultures in the U.S.A.: Gender, Self and Society,* ed. Renate von Bardeleben. Germershiem, Germany, 191–202.

————. 1995. "Social Protest, Folklore, and Feminist Ideology in Chicana Prose and Poetry." In *Folklore, Literature, and Cultural Theory: Collected Essays,* ed. Cathy Lynn Preston. New York: Garland Publishing.

————. 2002. "Danger! Children at Play: Patriarchal Ideology and the Construction of Gender in Spanish Language Hispanic/Chicano Children's Songs and Games." In *Chicana Changing Traditions,* eds. Norma Cantú and Olga Nájera-Rámirez. Urbana: University of Illinois Press, 81–99.

————. 2005. "In Search of La Malinche: Pictorial Representations of a Mytho-Historical Figure." In *Feminism, Nation and Myth: La Malinche,* ed. Rolando Romero and Amanda Nolacea Harris. Houston: Arte Público Press, 2005, 112–133.

————. 2005. "The Transnational Imaginary and 'Narcocorridos' -Violence, Drugs and Transgressive Discourse in Mexican Ballads." In *Violence and Transgression in World Minority Literatures.* eds. Rüdiger Ahrens, María Herrera-Sobek, Karin Ikas and Francisco Lomelí. Heidelberg, Germany; Universitats Verlag Winter GmbH.

Paredes, Américo. 1957. "The Mexican *Corrido:* Its Rise and Fall." In *Madstones and Twister*s, eds., Mody C. Boatright, Wilson M. Hudson, and Allen Maxwell. Dallas and Austin: Texas Folklore Society Publications, Number 28, 91–105.

————. 1958. *"With His Pistol in His Hand:" A Border Ballad and Its Hero.* Austin: University of Texas Press.

————.1960. "Luis Inclán, First of the Cowboy Writers." *American Quarterly* 12, no. 1:55–70.

————. 1960. "The Bury-Me-Not Theme in the Southwest." In *And Horns on the Toads,* eds., Mody C. Boatright, Wilson M. Hudson and Allen Maxwell. Dallas and Austin: Texas Folklore Society Publications Number 29, 55–70.

————. 1961. "Folklore and History." In *Singers and Storytellers,* eds., Mody C. Boatright, Wilson M. Hudson, and Allen Maxwell. Dallas and Austin: Texas Folklore Society Publications, Number 30.

————. 1961. "On Gringo, Greaser and Other Neighborly Names. In *Singers and Storytellers,* eds., Mody C. Boatright, Wilson M. Hudson, and Allen Maxwell. Dallas and Austin: Texas Folklore Society Publications, Number 30, 285–290.

————. 1963. "Texas' Third Man: Texas-Mexican." Race: *The Journal of the Institute of Race Relations,* 4, no. 2 (May):49–58.

————. 1963 "The Ancestry of Mexico's Corridos: A Matter of Definition." *JAF,* 76, no. 301 (July–September):231–235.

———. 1964. "Corrido de Gregorio Cortez." In *Buying the Wind: Regional Folklore in the United States,* ed. Richard M. Dorson. Chicago: University of Chicago Press, 480–483.

———. 1964. "Corrido de Jacinto Treviño." In *Buying the Wind: Regional Folklore in the United States,* ed. Richard M. Dorson. Chicago: University of Chicago Press, 483–485.

———. 1964. "'No Estiendo,' 'Moochers,' and 'La Flora y la Fauna.'" In *Buying the Wind: Regional Folklore in the United States,* ed. Richard M. Dorson. Chicago: University of Chicago Press, 452–454.

———. 1964. "Pastorela to Celebrate the Birth of Our Lord Jesus Christ." In *Buying the Wind: Regional Folklore in the United States,* ed. Richard M. Dorson. Chicago: University of Chicago Press, 466–479.

———. 1964. "Some Aspects of Folk Poetry." *University of Texas Studies in Literature and Language,* 6, no. 2 (Summer):213–225.

———. 1965. "El cowboy norteamericano en el folklore y la literatura." *Cuadernos del Instituto Nacional de Antropología* (Buenos Aires) 0:227–240.

———. 1966. "El folklore de los grupos de origin mexicano en Estados Unidos." *Folklore Americano* 14, no. 34:146–163.

———. 1966. "The Anglo-American in Mexican Folklore." In *New Voices in American Studies.* Lafayette, Indiana: Purdue University Studies, 113–127.

———. 1966. "The Décima on the Texas-Mexican Border: Folksong as an Adjunct to Legend." *Journal of the Folklore Institute* 3, no. 2 (August):154–167.

———. 1968. "Tributaries to the Mainstream: The Ethnic Groups." In *Our Living Traditions: An Introduction to American Folklore,* ed. Tristram P. Coffin. New York: Basic Books, 70–80.

———. 1971. "Folklore e historia: Dos cantares de la frontera del Norte." In *25 Estudios del Folklore,* ed. Fernando Anaya Monroy. Mexico City: Universidad Autónoma de México, Estudios de Folklore No. 4, 290–222.

———. 1971. "Mexican Legendry and the Rise of the Mestizo: A Survey." In *American Folk Legend: A Symposium,* ed. with a preface by Wayland D Hand. Berkely: University of California Press.

———. 1972. "The Mexico-Texan *Corrido.*" *Southwest Review* (Summer): 470–481.

———. 1993. "The Folklore of Groups of Mexican Origin in the United States." In *Folklore and Culture on the Texas-Mexican Border,* ed. Richard Bauman. Austin: Center for Mexican American Studies, University of Texas.

Paredes, Américo and George Foss. 1966. "The *Décima Cantada* on the Texas-Mexican Border: Four Examples." *Journal of the Folklore Institute* 3, no. 2 (August):91–115.

Paredes, Américo and Richard Bauman. 1972. *Toward New Perspectives in Folklore.* Austin: University of Texas Press.

Five

Contexts

FOLKLORE AND CHICANO POLITICAL IDEOLOGY

Folklore is an integral part of Chicano/a cultural production. From the very inception of the Chicano movement in the 1960s folklore was a source of inspiration for all areas of artistic creativity and for political thought. The Chicano/a intelligentsia was highly steeped in Mexican history and the philosophical writings of José Vasconcelos, the Mexican Secretary of Education during the 1920s. Previous to the Mexican Revolution of 1910–1917, during the colonial period and the nineteenth century, the issue of Mexican identity had been vigorously contested. The ruling *criollo* (Spaniards born in Latin America and Mexico) elite preferred a European identity, and therefore the value systems instituted during those centuries were of Western Europe; in other words, the privileging of white skin, the Spanish language, the Catholic church, and other aspects of European culture were firmly established in Mexico to the exclusion or near exclusion of other modes of being. The indigenous cultures and the imported African cultures were generally devalued and marginalized; for example, black and brown skin and the indigenous languages were viewed as inferior, and religious practices were outright abolished. These European values were so entrenched that even in the nineteenth and early twentieth centuries, after Spain was defeated in the Wars of Independence (1810–1821), the Mexican President, Porfirio Díaz, who ruled for more than 30 years (1880–1910), was still a strong proponent of transforming Mexico into a "white" country and erasing the indigenous groups of people from the landscape. The Mexican Revolution (1910–1917) brought a new perspective on the value of the autochthonous cultures present in Mexico and on the nature of the *mestizo* (mixed blood) population which made up most of the country. The new nationalist wave enveloping the nation after the Revolution began to reimagine in a positive light Mexico and its glorious indigenous past—particularly that of the Aztecs and the Mayas. Vasconcelos was a committed nationalist and initiated reforms designed to refashion Mexican identity, believing that it was a crucible for the future of humanity with respect to racial mixture. In his extensive writings he developed the concept of *La Raza Cósmica*—the Cosmic Race, which consisted of a blending of white, Indian, Asian, and African peoples. Thereafter, a new emphasis and pride was placed on the great *mestizaje* or racial mixture that characterized Mexican identity. Vasconcelos sought to instill pride in Mexican identity; to achieve this goal, Mexico's Indian heritage had to be rescued and reconceptualized. Indigenous myths and legends were recuperated and taught in the schools and visual artists such as Diego Rivera, José Clemente Orozco, and David Alfaro Siqueiros glorified in their canvases the faces of the peasant *mestizos* and Indians. Poets and novelists, too, wrote about the Indian and the *mestizo*. A new valorization of the Indian and *mestizo* historical past was promulgated throughout the Mexican republic.

The Chicano movement was also a nationalist movement that sought to instill pride in the Mexican American population. The movement emphasized that to be Mexican and to be Indian was something to be proud of and not ashamed of as Anglo-American hegemonic society had proclaimed in the previous decades. Chicanos therefore went to the myths and legends of the ancient Aztecs and Mayas for inspiration; they perceived in these ancient narratives powerful tools for the education and consciousness-raising of the Chicano people, particularly college students and children. The myths and legends of ancient Indian civilizations were a great inspiration for intellectuals and artists and were seen as splendid means by which to build the self-esteem of the younger generation. The myth of Aztlán was deemed to be particularly relevant for Chicanos/as' self-knowledge regarding their historical roots in the American Southwest, since it posited that the Aztecs had lived in the Southwest for hundreds if not thousands of years before migrating south to found their city and empire in Tenochtitlan (Mexico City) as their God Huitzilopochtli had instructed them to do. Aztlán then became the original home of the Chicanos/as.

The myth of Aztlán was critical in affirming the self-esteem of Chicanos/as since it was a foundational myth of origins for the Chicano population. If the Chicanos/as' ancestors were deemed to be originally from the Southwest, then Chicanos/as, in an analogous manner to other Native Americans, were legitimate inhabitants of the Southwest and not "foreigners," as Anglo-America had always perceived Mexicans to be (even if they were American citizens and traced their ancestry to the 1600s). Not only were Chicanos the descendents of Spanish and Mexican explorers and settlers from the 1520s onward, but they could claim Southwest ancestry dating back to the original settlers of the Southwest—the Native American or Nahua-speaking peoples who migrated south in 1100–1200 AD to found the Aztec empire in Tenochtitlan. Aztlán, then, became the magic word for the Chicano political movement and the myth that bestowed legitimacy of residence in the Southwest to Mexican Americans. Through the myth of Aztlán, Chicanos began to see themselves not as interlopers, intruders, "illegals," but in fact the descendents of the original peoples of the Southwest.

The Chicano movement also received inspiration from the myth of Quetzalcóatl. Quetzalcóatl was a priest/God of the Toltecs, another indigenous group of people from Mesoamerica. Quetzalcóatl (the plumed serpent) was a kind, wise, and brilliant ruler who brought prosperity to his people, taught them arts and crafts and abolished human sacrifices. Chicanos saw a model ruler in this priest/God. For Chicanas, Coyolxauhqui, the Moon Goddess, offers a certain appeal with respect to male/female reconciliation. The Moon Goddess was displaced by her brother, Huitzilopochtli, the Sun God and also god of war. The myth has been interpreted as the vanquishing of matriarchy and the ascendancy of the patriarchal system. Huitzilopochtli was born fully grown from the breast of Coatlicue, the Earth Goddess. When Coyolxauhqui and her 400 brothers, the stars, tried to kill Coatlicue, Huitzilopochtli jumps out of Coatlicue fully dressed for battle and kills Coyolxauhqui, dismembering her in the process. For Chicanas, such as Cherríe Moraga and Irene Pérez, the healing process must begin with acknowledging the violence done on Coyolxauhqui (women). Irene Pérez paintings depict Coyolxauhqui not in her dismembered state but whole again—reconstituted and ready for battle.

Gloria Anzaldúa, another Chicana writer, focuses on Coatlicue, the Earth Mother Goddess and conceptualizes her as a source of inspiration, of creative energies. The "Coatlicue State" for Anzaldúa is a state of introspection, when the creative process is reconnecting with the cosmic forces of the universe. Upon one's return from the Coatlicue State of reflection, a person feels rejuvenated and filled with strong creative powers.

FOLKLORE AND CHICANO LITERATURE

For Chicano/a writers folklore has been an amazing source of raw material from which they have sculpted their literary worlds. In early Chicano poetry movement in the 1960–1980, the myths and legends of Mesoamerican indigenous populations were a great source of inspiration and thematic material and continue to be in the twenty-first century. Particularly partial to using myths and legends from the Aztec and Maya worlds was the poet Alurista (Alberto Urista). Alurista was heavily imbued with indigenous philosophical concepts and derived his political ideology and literary inspiration from Mesoamerican pre-Hispanic cultures. One of his earliest collections of poems, significantly titled *Nationchild Plumaroja* (1972) [Nationchild Red Feather] and published by a Chicano movement sponsored organization Toltecas en Aztlán Centro Cultural de la Raza [Toltecs in Aztlán The La Raza Cultural Center] bears the following philosophical goals inscribed in the dedication:

> . . . dedicated to Human Truth (Social, Economic, Political, Historical, and Ecological) and Chicano Harmony which in our belief can only be practiced through Mutual Self-Respect, Self-Determination in our endeavors and the Self-sacrifice of our individual differences for the sake of a Centro Cultural de la Raza where our indigenous ancestral spirit of brotherhood and sisterhood, justice and peace can flourish in contemporary Chicano art forms. (Alurista 1972, 2 given in the Aztec numerical system)

The collection of poems is imbued with Mesoamerican indigenous drawings and philosophical thought. For example, in the poem "A Child to Be Born" the concept of Aztlán is ever present:

> a child to be born
> pregnant is the continente
> el barro y la raza
> to bear Aztlán on our forehead
> el niño que como pájaro
> en su vuelo de colores cantos
> guió a Tenoch hacia el águila
> el niño dentro del vientre semilla
> una madretierraroja le acaricia
> Aztlán, Aztlán of the continent that bears child (Alurista 1972, 62)

> [a child to be born
> pregnant is the continent
> the clay of the race
> to bear Aztlán on our forehead
> the child as a bird
> in his flight and songs of many colors
> guided Tenoch towards the eagle
> the child inside the womb-seed
> a red-mother-earth loves him
> Aztlán, Aztlán of the continent that bears child]

Alurista was one of the first poets to underscore the Chicanos' Native American heritage and to use mythological motifs consistently in his creative writings.

Ana Castillo is another poet-novelist who uses folklore liberally in her literary production. Particularly salient is the folklore used in her second novel *So Far From God* (1993). The title of the novel is derived from a proverbial phrase attributed to the Mexican dictator Porfirio Díaz, who ruled from 1880 to 1910, and who is said to have uttered "Poor Mexico, so far from God; so near the United States." The novel incorporates folklore throughout the narrative and, in fact, Castillo's work is noted for its magic realism, which is structured mainly through folklore elements. For example, one of the principal characters, La Loca, possesses extraordinary powers such as flying, predicting the future, and healing the sick. Furthermore, La Loca is in constant communication with La Llorona and can predict when someone is going to die. Castillo also uses folk speech throughout the narrative as is evident in Chapter 9, which is structured with the use of proverbs and proverbial expressions. Chapter 3 is likewise structured with a large sprinkling of folk elements—in this case with folk remedies. This chapter goes into great detail regarding the different remedies used for various folk ailments such as *empacho* [gastrointestinal obstruction], *aigre* [aire = air or drafts], and *mal de ojo* [the evil eye]. Folk beliefs of a religious nature (as well as secular folk beliefs) are also an integral part of Castillo's novel. There is, for example, a pilgrimage to Chimayó, the sacred site in New Mexico. Castillo integrates the full spectrum of folk genres in her novel to great effect.

In Castillo's fourth novel, *Peel My Love Like an Onion* (1999), a major folk element structures the entire novel: the dance flamenco. The main character, Carmen "La Coja" Santos is physically challenged in one leg due to polio. In spite of her physical disability, she plans to be a flamenco dancer. The book comments continuously on the art of flamenco dancing and the ancient tradition of flamenco music.

Castillo's interest in writing on folk-related material continued in her nonfiction books, such as *Massacre of the Dreamers: Essays on Xicanisma* (1994) and *Goddess of the Americas/La Diosa de las Américas: Writings on the Virgin of Guadalupe* (1996). The latter is an anthology consisting of a collection of essays written by scholars and focusing on various aspects dealing with the legendary patron of Mexico. Her work *Massacre of the Dreamers* centers its attention on indigenous cultures from Mexico and their relationship to Chicano culture. Included are numerous indigenous traditions such as folk remedies still relevant to contemporary Chicanos/as.

Sandra Cisneros, likewise, nourishes her literary creativity from Mexican and Chicano folklore. In her book *Woman Hollering Creek and Other Stories*

Ex-voto of Juanita Limón, from *Miracles on the Border: Retablos of Mexican Migrants to the United States* by Jorge Durand and Douglas S. Massey.
Source: Copyright © 1995 The Arizona Board of Regents. Reprinted by permission of the University of Arizona Press.

(1991), the title refers to the La Llorona legend. The short story bearing the same title has as its subtext the La Llorona legend. In another short story included in the collection bearing the title "Little Miracles/Kept Promises" Cisneros integrates the folk tradition of the ex-voto or *retablo* into the whole format of that narrative. The short story, in fact, is a collection of creatively written ex-votos using the structure, thematic content, and speech register of the common people who actually write ex-votos in honor of a miracle granted to them by specific saint. Various folk beliefs are included in Cisneros's ex-votos, such as the belief in San Antonio's power to grant boyfriends to women asking him for that favor.

Folklore is equally important in her most recent book, *Caramelo* (2002), which narrates the life story of young Lala as she is growing up in two cultures Mexico and the United States. The word *caramelo*—meaning a specific type of candy made with milk—caramel, itself has multiple folklore connotations, as it can refer to a Mexican traditional candy as well as a specific type of rebozo or Mexican shawl. The *rebozo*, which is a folk garment traditionally used by Mexican women is an important motif in the structure of the novel as well as its feminist conceptualizations. Cisneros also uses folk speech throughout the narrative and includes folksongs in many of the chapters.

San Antonio (1994) by Ray Martín Abeyta.
Source: Courtesy of the National Hispanic
Cultural Center, Art Museum, Albuquerque,
New Mexico.

Rudolfo Anaya, a Chicano author from New Mexico in his first novel
Bless Me Ultima (1972), integrated folk traditions throughout the narrative.
Ultima, one of the principal characters in the novel, is a *curandera* or folk
healer. She is also perceived as a witch by some of the townsfolk. The narrative
includes numerous folk beliefs and folk practices such as the belief in witches
and beliefs associated with owls, folk remedies, folk ailments, bewitchments,
and so forth. Anaya has several novels; most of them are permeated with
folk beliefs and traditions. In particular, his detective novels, *Winter Shaman*
(1999) and *Zia Summer* (1999), make liberal use of folklore. Anaya's love and
reverence of folk traditions has led him to write children's books depicting

traditions of New Mexico. He has also written a book titled *The Legend of La Llorona* (1984), which includes a series of creatively elaborated Mexican, pre-Hispanic, and Spanish colonial-period legends.

Other Chicana writers have also incorporated folk motifs and folk traditions in their poetry and novels. Cordelia Candelaria has a poem on La Llorona, and Erlinda Gonzales-Berry has a novel titled *Paletitas de Guayaba* (1991), which includes a section on La Malinche. Alicia Gaspar de Alba has also written on La Malinche and La Llorona and in fact has a poetry-essay collection titled *La Llorona on the Longfellow Bridge* (2003). Pat Mora, a poet-novelist from El Paso, Texas, in her book *House of Houses* (1997) incorporates numerous folk elements within her excellent narrative. Moreover, one of her poems, "Cuarteto Mexicano," found in her poetry collection *Agua Santa/Holy Water* (1995) has as speaking characters Coatlicue, La Malinche, La Virgen de Guadalupe, and La Llorona (59–77).

Lucha Corpi, another Chicana poet and novelist, frequently uses folk elements throughout her narratives and in her poems. Her novel *Black Widow's Wardrobe* (1999) has as it subtext the legends of La Malinche and La Llorona.

CHICANO FOLKLORE AND VISUAL ARTS

Visual artists in a similar manner to literary authors find Chicano folklore a powerful, never-ending source of inspiration. From the very inception of the Chicano movement, Chicano/a visual artists took folk motifs, particularly from Mesoamerican indigenous cultures, and incorporated them in their artwork. Mythic figures such as Quetzalcóatl, Tonantiuh, Huitzilopochtli, the serpent motif, and so forth began to appear throughout the murals painted on the walls of buildings in Southwestern cities. The Virgin of Guadalupe became a popular icon as the defender of Chicano rights and as a symbol of social justice. Chicana artists commenced to use indigenous goddesses such as Coatlicue, Coyolxauhqui, Tonantzin, and of course the Virgin of Guadalupe. Chicanas did not slavishly copy rescued images from the past but creatively transformed them to meet the needs of the new generation. Yolanda M. López was at the forefront of this movement with the re-created images of the Virgin of Guadalupe. López began by first cutting the traditional Virgin of Guadalupe's robe which completely covers the Virgin's feet, impeding her from moving. Her reconceptualization freed her from the static position in which she had been imprisoned and made it possible for the Virgin to move. The new Guadalupe version featured her image wearing midcalf robes and walking in high heels. This of course created an uproar in some sectors of Mexican and Chicano society, but her transformed Guadalupe spoke to a new, active, not passive, generation of women. López's triptych further liberated the Virgin of Guadalupe and featured paintings of her grandmother, her mother as a seamstress, and the artist herself as a jogger in tennis shoes and mini skirt. Equally arresting is Ester Hernández's black and white drawing of the Virgin of Guadalupe. Hernández early drawing of the Virgin of Guadalupe has her dressed in a karate outfit and in a karate-like pose (i.e. one leg extended outward and with fists clenched ready to fight). The caption *"La Virgen de Guadalupe*

Portrait of the Artist as the Virgin of Guadalupe (1978) by Yolanda M. López.
Source: Courtesy of Yolanda M. López.

defendiendo los derechos de los chicanos" (1986) [The Virgin of Guadalupe Defending the Rights of Chicanos] encapsulates the ideology behind it: The divine is on the side of Chicanos' struggle for self-determination and human rights. Her other Guadalupe paintings inhabit the world of the marginalized (e.g., lesbians, the working poor).

The Virgin of Guadalupe icon became a touchstone for a myriad of interpretations and transformations. César González portrayed her as the Mona Lisa, Rosa M. featured her as the Statue of Liberty, and Alma López from Los Angeles, California, the most controversial, painted the Virgin of Guadalupe in a bikini. Alma López received a barrage of death threats for her unusual and provocative renderings of Guadalupe.

The Virgin of Guadalupe has been reconfigured by Santa Barraza, an artist from Kingsville Texas and well-known for her work on Guadalupe images. Barraza's series of Guadalupe paintings have the Virgin appear as her sister and her mother. While presenting Guadalupe in a more traditional stance than Yolanda M. López, her Guadalupe series all project a powerful, modern Guadalupe who looks straight at the viewer with unflinching eyes. Other visual artists such as Irene Pérez from San Francisco, California, focused on other Aztec goddesses such as Coyolxauhqui. Pérez's conceptualization reconfigures the Coyolxauhqui myth: the dismembered Coyolxauhqui portraying her as a reconstituted woman. Coyolxauhqui had been dismembered (i.e., her head, arms, and legs were cut off after her defeat at the hands of her brother, the War God Huitzilopochtli). Pérez believes that in order for the gender divide to heal Coyolxauhqui must heal; thus she reconstitutes Coyolxauhqui and features her ready to fight for the rights of all Chicanos.

Maya González also delves deep into Aztec mythological themes and icons. Her paintings feature La Llorona figures as well as the Virgin of Guadalupe. Her latest work includes the motif of the rabbit, a fertility symbol as well as a prominent icon in Aztec codices.

FOLKLORE AND CHICANO THEATER

Chicano theater has made ample use of folk motifs and folk genres within its performances. The traveling tent theaters or *teatros de carpa* from the nineteenth century and early twentieth centuries used folk speech as well as jokes within their short skits. The Teatro Campesino in the 1960s incorporated much of the techniques initiated in tent theater in the development of their repertoire. The Teatro Campesino relied heavily on folk music, principally the *corrido*, folk speech *(caló)*, jokes, and folk stock characters such as El Diablo and La Muerte. Some of the major works include *Corridos: Tales of Passion and Revolution* (1987), which was based on the performances of the plots of the following *corridos*: "La Delgadina," Rosita Alvírez," "La Adelita," and "El Lavaplatos"; and *Zoot Suit*, based on the folk icons of El Pachuco. Luis Valdez's plays such as *The Myth of Queztalcóatl* and *Bernabé* have as their subtext mythological themes of the Priest God Quetzalcóatl and Mother Earth. His two plays performed in San Juan Bautista, California, alternating each year are also based on folk theater: *La Pastorela (the Shepherds' Play)*, which he also turned into a video production, and *Las Cuatro Apariciones de la Virgen de Guadalupe*. As is evident Luis Valdez and the Teatro Campesino make ample use of folklore to develop their theatrical plays and performances.

CHICANO FOLKLORE AND FILMS

Although there are not a great number of Chicano films, the impact folklore has had on them is highly significant. Chicano films can be divided into films and documentaries. With respect to films, one of the most obvious one in which folklore is an integral part is *The Ballad of Gregorio Cortez* (1988). The film by Moctezuma Esparza was based on the true story of a Texas Mexican, Gregorio Cortez, accused of having killed a sheriff in 1901 in Texas. Cortez's escape from the Texas Rangers, his long saga in trying to fool the Texas Rangers as he led them across the Texas countryside, and his eventual capture are all detailed in the film following the narrative line of the *corrido* and Américo Paredes's book *"With His Pistol in His Hand": A Border Ballad and Its Hero*. The book served as the primary source of information, and the *corrido* itself served as the background music for the film.

A second major film using folk images is *Zoot Suit* (1981). The film is based on a true story regarding a murder at the Sleepy Lagoon in East Los Angeles, California, and the accusation and eventual incarceration of Chicano young men. The film, however, makes liberal use of folklore in the music that is played throughout, the *caló* or folk speech used, and the title itself, *Zoot Suit*, which refers to specific garments worn by the Chicano youth in the 1930–1950 decades.

La Bamba: The Ritchie Valens Story (1987) is a third major Chicano film; it was based on the short life of pop singer Richard Valenzuela, who shortened his name to Ritchie Valens to appeal to a larger segment of the population who might not be too keen on a Mexican singer. The title of the film is taken from Valen's major musical hit "La Bamba," which was a rock and roll rendition of a traditional folk song from Veracruz bearing the same name.

Two videos, *Corridos: Tales of Passion and Revolution* (1987) and *La Pastorela: The Shepherds' Tale* (1991), have been produced by the Luis Valdez and the Teatro Campesino. Both are based on folk traditions—one on the ballad tradition and the second on the folk theater traditions. Regarding documentaries, there are several that are based on folklore themes and/or icons. Dan Banda produced the documentary *Indigenous Always: La Malinche* in 2000; it explores the life of La Malinche and questions her status in contemporary Mexican and Chicano society. Interviews are carried out with both Mexican and Chicano/a scholars as well as working-class people. Lourdes Portillo, a Chicana filmmaker produced and directed a documentary based on the Day of the Dead (November 1 and 2), *La Ofrenda; Day of the Dead* (1990). The documentary explores the spiritual meaning of the Day of the Dead and portrays the various traditions associated with this sacred holiday.

CHICANO FOLKLORE AND COMMUNITY CELEBRATIONS

Chicano folklore has permeated the U.S. consciousness in such a decisive manner that two holidays—one secular (Cinco de Mayo) and one sacred (Día de los Muertos)—that they are fast becoming part of the national holiday celebration scene. The Cinco de Mayo, or May 5, holiday commemorates the battle between Mexican forces and French forces. The French, under the leadership of Napoleon III, had wanted to establish an empire in Mexico in the 1860s. They arrived in Veracruz in January 1862 together with British forces, who later withdrew from their alliance with the French and Spanish in an effort to take over Mexico as a response to nonpayment of the debt owed to them by Mexico. Spain also withdrew and the French were left alone to carve out a desired empire, which they mistakenly believed would be easy to do. They erroneously thought the people of Mexico would welcome them heartily as saviors. As it turned out, only the military, the upper conservative elites, and the conservative Catholic Church clergy supported a French monarchy. The rest of the population was fiercely against it and fought until the French were ousted from Mexico. The first major victory for the Mexicans occurred on May 5, 1862, when the superior and finely trained French troops were defeated by the Mexican troops in the city of Puebla. It is this military victory that the Chicanos celebrate each year on May 5. The French recuperated their losses and went on to defeat Mexican troops and to establish their empire. Napoleon III installed Archduke Maximilian of Austria as Emperor of Mexico in July 1863. He reigned for a few years until June 19, 1867 when he was captured and executed at the Cerro de Las Campanas in Querétaro, Mexico.

The significance of Cinco de Mayo is in the psychological dimension the battle that transpired on that day offers the poor and downtrodden. The victory of a poor, ragtag army against the powerful French Empire gave sustenance and hope to those who feel politically and economically oppressed. Any victory, however small, in the struggle to gain freedom is always a cause for celebration. The Chicano movement reintroduced the celebration of Cinco de Mayo in a more pronounced manner and has spread this celebration across the Southwest. Due to the mass media's interest in the holiday, it has become a well-known celebration across the country. In fact, the holiday has become so mainstream that some Chicanos/as bemoan its appropriation, especially by beer companies and bars across America, and by mainstream commercial interests.

Cinco de Mayo is typically celebrated with family gatherings, picnics, and parties. At schools festivities include food bazaars and Mexican folk dancing, and small towns and cities may produce full fledged festivals with food, dancing, music, and commercial enterprises selling all types of products.

Día de los Muertos, or Day of the Dead, in contrast, is a religious celebration reserving a specific day or days to remember and rejoice in the memory of the dearly departed. The Day of the Dead is derived from two cultural strands: the Indigenous and the European (Spanish). Mesoamerican Indians reserved two days of the year, August 8 and August 28, to honor their dead. The first date was designated for children that had died and the second date was for adults. Both dates were celebrated with food and drink and with visits to the graves of the deceased relatives. The observances were marked by a serious respect for the departed and did not have the humor, satire, ribbing, and general irreverence that today's holidays have. The second strand, the Spanish one was the source of this contemporary jocosity and laughter in the face of death. When the Spaniards came they brought the Catholic tradition of observing All Saints Day (November 1) and All Souls Day (November 2). It is obvious that the holidays blended perfectly with each other. From Medieval Europe, particularly Spain, came the irreverence and was retained throughout the centuries. Even today, the feast of Carnaval (or farewell to flesh) has its origins in medieval Europe (González 2002, 7). It was during carnival that hierarchies were deconstructed and the classes and genders blended and mingled with each other.

In the late nineteenth century a talented engraver from Aguascalientes, Mexico, José Guadalupe Posada (1852–1913), introduced the artistic engravings of calaveras or skeletons. The skeletons depicted people engaged in all walks of life doing their daily chores as if they were not dead: students, priests, merchants, politicians, and so forth became fair game for Posada's satire. The encoded message was that death is the great leveler: power,

Day of the Dead Altar.
Source: Photo by and courtesy of Carmen Flys-Junquera.

money, prestige, class position, luxuries, and so forth are all for naught at the hour of death. We all leave this world as we came—with nothing. The phrase "You cannot take it with you" resonates well with the *calaveras vivientes* [live skulls]. And so Posada's calaveras are often portrayed enjoying life: singing, dancing, drinking, and so forth. Urbanization in Mexico began to weaken some of the traditions associated with the Day of the Dead. However the Chicano movement has brought back into focus this specific holiday. As a possible response to the Anglo-American tradition of Halloween celebrated on October 31, Chicanos rallied around the Day of the Dead celebration, finding it more meaningful and spiritual. They reintroduced the celebration in the Southwest and for whatever reason, the mainstream community has begun to embrace this tradition. Evidence of this acceptance is that museums and other institutions such as colleges and community centers sponsor the construction and display of Día de los Muertos altars. Altars are artistically designed spaces that consist of flowers, especially marigolds, food, fruits, drink, pictures of the departed, candles, and other objects that the departed particularly was fond of. The

Day of the Dead Altar.
Source: Photo by and courtesy of Carmen Flys-Junquera.

spread of some aspects of this tradition of the Day of the Dead is most spectacularly seen in the use of "memorials" dedicated to people who die tragically in some accident. Previous to the 1960s the custom of decorating a space where people perished due to some tragic accident were not seen at all in the United States. Today, anytime a tragedy occurs, that is, where a child or an adult loses his or her life, a "memorial' or altar is enacted. Toys, flowers, letters, notes, candles, pictures of the deceased, and other objects decorate the spot where the tragic even took place, or in the case of famous people that perish far or outside the country, a memorial space is created near or in front of their house. This has happened in the case of Princess Diana and John F. Kennedy Jr. And during the tragic events of September 11, 2001 when the Twin Towers in New York fell after the attack by Al Qaeda operatives, memorials surfaced near Ground Zero.

Chicano folklore has had and continues to have a great impact on mainstream society. The acceptance of the Chicanos/as cultural traditions speaks volumes regarding the power of some of these folk customs, which date back hundreds of years ago to pre-Hispanic cultures. The continued expansion of the Chicano and Latino population in the United States guarantees that more and more Chicano folk traditions will become part of the cultural landscape of the entire United States.

REFERENCES

Alurista (Alberto Urista). 1972. *Nationchild Plumaroja.* San Diego, CA: Toltecas en Aztlán.

González, Rafael Jesús. 2002. *Días de los Muertos/Days of the Dead.* Berkeley, CA: Dragonfly Press.

Glossary

Aarne-Thompson (A-T). Classificatory system for the folktale devised first by Antti Aarne and later expanded by Stith Thompson to include American folktales. This classificatory system allows scholars to compare folktales from all over the world.

Abuelo. **Literally** *abuelo,* **or grandfather**; in folklore tradition it is one of the principal protagonists in the "La Malinche" dance from New Mexico. He appears as a terrifying figure with a horrible mask and a whip. He is also used as a bogeyman to frighten children into good behavior. In folk speech it is also written and pronounced as *agüelo.* In New Mexico, it is synonymous with the "El Coco" and the "Cucuy"; also bogeyman.

Adobada. As in *carne adobada* [marinated meat], a marinade made with red chili powder. The chili paste is then spread on the meat and left overnight to marinate before cooking it.

Adelitas. From the Mexican ballad "La Adelita," made famous during the Mexican Revolution (1910–1917); word used to refer to Mexican women participating in the Mexican Revolution. It acquired new meaning in the 1960s–1970s in reference to Chicanas supporting the male Chicano movement leadership.

Adivinanza. Riddle; a folklore genre that has two parts: a question and an answer.

Adobe. Mud bricks; folk technology related to making houses with mud and straw.

Aesop. One of the first persons to collect folktales, particularly animal tales, that includes a moral at the end of the narrative.

Agringado. Acquiring the characteristics of Anglo-Americans; becoming assimilated.

Agüero. Omen, sign. It can be a bad omen (*mal agüero*) or a good omen (*buen agüero*).

Aguinaldo. Christmas present; gift.

Ahijado/a. Godson or goddaughter.

Alabado. Sacred religious song; hymn.

Alabanzas. Religious folk songs whose main theme is praise.

Alambrista. Usually undocumented worker who crosses the border in the area where the dividing line is a wire fence, such as in California near the San Ysidro border area (near San Diego).

Albricias. Gift; reward for good news.

Albur. Pun; play on words; using words with double meaning.

Alma en pena. A soul doing penance; the folk expression *andar como alma en pena* means to be with great anxiety, distressed.

Altar. A special decoration involving a table and religious objects plus candles and flowers. For the Day of the Dead *(Día de los Muertos)* the altars built can be very elaborate.

Americano. folk speech; refers to Anglo-Americans; white people from the United States.

Amuleto. A good luck charm; a charm to ward off evil or to bring good luck.

Animal tales. Folktales in which the main protagonist is an animal—for example, the coyote folktales from the Southwest.

Animism. The belief in some cultures that all matter in the universe is alive and possesses a spirit—for example, the belief that plants, rocks, trees, and other inanimate objects in the world are alive and that humans can communicate with them.

Anthropomorphic. Attributing human characteristics to animals and inanimate objects. For example, plants and animals have the ability to talk in some folktales.

Aphorism. Proverb, maxim.

Archetype. According to Jungian psychology, archetypes are structures of the subconscious and can manifest themselves in certain contexts.

Asado. A roast, either beef or pork.

Asustado. *Estar asustado* is to have the folk ailment of *susto* or to be in psychological shock. The folk ailment manifests itself as a real physical illness such as having fever, vomiting, and feeling weak.

Atole. gruel made with corn meal, water, sugar, and milk.

Aztlán. (in Nahuatl it means "land of the herons"). Mythical land of the Aztecs. It is supposedly located in the area comprising the present day American Southwest. During the Chicano Movement, Chicanos revived the concept and claimed it as their original homeland.

Bailes. Dances.

Ballad. A folksong that narrates a story; see *corrido.*

Ballet folklórico. Regional dances of Mexico and the Southwest; they became popular in the Southwest during the Chicano Movement in the 1960s and continue to be very popular today.

Barbacoa. Barbecue; folk food made with any type of meat cooked slowly in a pit filled with hot coals.

Barrio. Chicano neighborhood; in the United States it is perceived as a ghetto.

Bato. dude; Chicano *caló* or slang for a male

Bautismo. Baptism; the rite of baptizing a child.

Belief. Folk belief; people may believe in the supernatural, folk ailments, and folk remedies; they may believe in witches, ogres, monsters, ghosts, and other supernatural beings; they may believe in miracles, hexes, curses, and other evil doings.

Bilis. A folk ailment characterized by indigestion and a bad taste in the mouth; usually occurs when a person suffers from emotional trauma such as being angry and upset.

Birria. Goat meat cooked in a slow oven.

Bizcocho. Small biscuits.

Bogeyman. A scary character used to frighten children into proper behavior.

Bolillo(s). Word for bread, particularly French style bread or bread rolls; used as a slang word for Anglo-Americans; similar to *gringo*.

Broadside. Ballads or narratives that have been published on leaflets and distributed to people in the streets of cities and towns, at fairs, festivals, and other places where folks gather by the singers of the ballads.

Bracero(s). Word denoting a farm worker; later was used for contract workers from Mexico who came to work in the United States under a 1942 World War II emergency agreement known as the Bracero Program, which lasted until 1964.

Bruja (o). Witch.

Brujería. Witchcraft.

Bulto. An undefined object or mass that exhibits supernatural characteristics such as moving about in the air; usually appears at night and is perceived to be evil—perhaps the devil.

Buñuelo. A Mexican/Chicano pastry made like a thin flour tortilla fried and dusted with cinnamon and sugar. *Buñuelos* were traditionally made and eaten for Christmas and New Year, but they can be found now at anytime in grocery stores specializing in selling Mexican foods.

Burrito. Folk food; tortilla wraps; a tortilla typically containing beans, rice, beef, or poultry with cheese, lettuce, and tomatoes and rolled up; may contain other types of filling.

Cabrito. Kid goat; may be roasted or broiled and eaten as a delicacy.

Caída de mollera (**also called** ***mollera caída***)**.** Fallen fontanel (soft spot on a baby's head) believed to happen when a baby falls from bed or one's arms or is not handled gently. Usually a folk healer (*curandera/o*) will take water into their mouths and suck at the top of a baby's head in order to "lift" the fallen fontanel.

Calabasas. Squash or pumpkin; can also be used in folk speech such as *dar calabasas*—to be jilted by a boyfriend or girlfriend.

Calavera. Literally skull, but also includes the skeleton in folk art. José Guadalupe Posada popularized the calavera or skull and skeleton in folk art with his dancing calaveras. He sought to poke fun at any human arrogance by making a statement that all will be dead someday no matter how rich or famous. The Chicano Movement incorporated the calavera in its art and its theater particularly in the Teatro Campesino.

Calaifa. Mythical queen of the Amazons supposedly residing in the area that is now California. The state is named after her.

Califas. Chicano slang (folk speech) for California.

Caló. Chicano folk speech; the argot of the underclass, the marginalized, especially the *pachucos* (youth from the 1940 that dressed in a specific style with baggy pants and long baggy coats; see *Zoot suit*) and the *cholos* or urban, poor, Chicano/Latino youth who also dress in a particular manner: gabardine, baggy, beige pants and Pendleton shirts. *Caló* words make use of standard Spanish and English but may use the words with different meanings, such as *garras*, which means rags for clothes. They also convert English verbs into Spanish by adding the suffix *ar* to the ending such as push = *pushar* ; watch = *watchar*. Nouns are also converted into Spanish such as nickel = *nicle*; quarter = *cuora*.

Canción. Song; there are various categories of *canciones* such as *canción romántica* and *canción ranchera*.

Capirotada. Mexican bread pudding. It is made with tortillas; dried, cubed, oven toasted bread; bananas; peanuts; candy; cheese; and brown sugar. The tortillas line the dish in which the rest of the ingredients rest and the other ingredients are cut up in small cubes and mixed. The mixture is sweetened with brown sugar (which has been mixed with water) poured over the ingredients and baked in an oven. The word is also used humorously to denote a mixture of any kind.

Carne asada. Grilled meat.

Carne seca. Folk food—dried meat or beef jerky.

Cascarones. Decorated egg shells filled with confetti. The decorated egg is broken on top of a persons head in a playful manner. This is usually done during Easter.

Caso. A folk narrative detailing a supernatural, such as seeing a ghost or a miraculous recovery from an illness.

Casorios. Weddings.

Cautionary tale. Similar to *exemplum*. A tale whose main function is to provide a moral or example of what is proper behavior.

Cautiva. White or Hispanic women captured by Native American tribes and kept as slaves or servants or even as wives.

Chamuco. Another name for the devil. The *chamuco* refers to the devil in its "burnt" state, caused by his living in the eternal fires of hell.

Chanes. Mythical water spirits.

Charreada. Mexican rodeo featuring *charros* and women dressed Jalisco style with colorful wide skirts and big-brimmed Mexican *charro* hats. They do exhibition horseback riding for the audiences as well as other rodeo type of tricks.

Charro. A man dressed in the regional costume typical of the state of Jalisco: wide-brimmed fancy hat, tight pants decorated with braiding and silver and a jacket equally decorated with braiding and silver. His dress is typical of a horseman.

Chicano/a. a person of Mexican descent born or raised in the United States and with a political consciousness regarding the history of Mexican Americans.

Chicharrones. Pork rinds.

Child ballad. A classificatory system for ballads devised by Francis James Child in his *English and Scottish Popular Ballad (1882–1898)*. Child classified 305 different ballad types.

Chile. Hot pepper.

Chile Colorado. Red hot peppers.

Chile con queso. Hot peppers with melted cheese.

Chile relleno. Stuffed peppers.

Chili. As in chili con carne—red chili sauce with beef.

Chile verde. Green hot peppers; also the sauce made with green chiles.

Chimichanga. Fried burritos—that is, flour tortillas stuffed with beef or chicken and beans and fried.

Chiste. Joke.

Chirrionera. Mythical snake.

Cholo(a). Urban youth from the barrios sporting a specific way of dressing and talking.

Chorizo. Mexican style sausage.

Ciboleros. Buffalo hunters.

Cinco de Mayo. (May 5). The date celebrates the initial victory Mexicans had over the French troops in 1862 in Puebla, when the Emperor Maximillian and his wife Carlota tried to establish an empire in Mexico.

Coco (El Coco). Bogeyman; a scary character used to socialize children into proper behavior.

Cofradía. A religious group of people; brotherhood.

Colchas. Quilts made by Chicana women from bits and pieces of fabric. Many of these specimens are beautiful works of art.

Comadre **(female) and** ***Compadre*** **(male).** Fictive kinship used in Latin America and the Hispanic Southwest. The fictive kinship is formed when a person participates in a religious ritual as sponsor, such as a godfather or godmother of a child for baptism, confirmation, first communion, or weddings. In folk speech *comadre* and *compadre* have come to mean a good friend.

Comanches (Los). The folk theater play *Los Comanches* details the 1774 battle between Spanish troops and a Comanche tribe and their leader, Cuerno Verde. Cuerno Verde and his people are defeated and converted into Catholicism. The play, supposedly written in around 1780, is reenacted in New Mexico once a year.

Conjunto music. Music typical of Texas (known as Tex-Mex music) and northern Mexico (aka *norteño* music). Generally played by a small group of musicians composed of a drummer, guitar, accordion, *bajo sexto*, (12-string guitar), and a bass, The most typical music played and sung are polkas, *corridos, canciones*, especially *canciones rancheras*. It is associated with the working class.

Con safos. A ritual signature that is supposed to grant protection to the site bearing the signature. It means "do not disturb or else bad luck will fall upon you."

Copla. Couplet.

Corridista. *Corrido* singer.

Corrido. Mexican ballad.

Coyotes. Canine mammal related to the wolf and dog indigenous to the Southwest. He appears in many folktales and is a main character, a trickster figure, in Native American folklore.

Curandera(o). Folk healer.

Curanderismo. Folk healing and its practitioners.

Custom *(costumbre).* A cultural form of behavior that has been in existence in a particular culture for many generations. It thus has the force of tradition behind it and is a very powerful socializing agent.

Dancing with the devil. Folk legend related to the belief that the devil dances with young ladies at local dances. At midnight the young women dancing with him realize he has feet resembling those of roosters and/or hoofs.

Danza. A ritual dance.

Danzante. Usually refers to a folk dancer, but can be any dancer.

Day of the Dead *(Día de los Muertos).* November 1 and 2. All Souls Day and All Saints Day. It is believed that those who have died return to visit the living on that day. The living receive them with their favorite beverages, food, and music.

Death *(La Muerte).* A folk character who comes to take the living to the beyond.

Death cart. The folk character Death comes with her folk cart to take the living away.

Décimas. Poetry that has a characteristic 10-line stanza with a specific rhyme scheme. The *décima* can be sung or recited and was especially popular during the eighteenth and nineteenth centuries.

Descansos. Memorials generally at roadsides usually composed of candles and flowers perhaps with a religious object. It memorializes the death of a person who died on the spot where the memorial is erected.

Despedida. Leave-taking; farewell; the closing stanza of a Mexican ballad.

Devil. Folk character popular in folklore legends and other folk genres.

Día de fiesta. Holiday; feast day.

Dichos. Literally sayings; proverbs, axioms.

Diez y Seis de Septiembre **(September 16).** Mexican national holiday celebrating Mexico's independence from Spain.

Diffusion. Explanatory theory for the origins of folklore. This theory posits that folklore originated in one geographic spot and spread to the rest of the world.

Don Cacahuate **(Mr. Peanut).** Popular folk character in jokes.

Doña Marina **(see La Malinche).** The Indian maiden given to the conquistador Hernán Cortez and perceived by nineteenth and twentieth century Mexican scholars as a traitor for having aided Cortez in the conquest of the Aztecs. Marina was the Christian name given to her when she was baptized. The word *Doña* was a title denoting respect.

Doña Sebastiana. A manifestation of Death in Mexican/Chicano folklore. It is believed that death comes in the form of an old woman.

Double entendre. Double meaning; a phrase or word said with the intention of having a different meaning from the normal.

Duende. A tiny mischievous supernatural being similar to a leprechaun.

Empacho. A folk ailment in which the symptoms are similar to indigestion. The belief is that if you ate something that did not agree with you it becomes a dense ball of food that does not digest and clings to the walls of your stomach and it can only be cured with folk remedies.

Empanada. Pastry similar to a turnover. It has a pocket inside and can be filled with different types of meat, poultry, or fish. Sweet empanadas are filled with sweet fruits.

Enchilada. Folk food made with tortillas dipped in red chili sauce filled with cheese and beef or poultry.

Endless story. An endless story is a short narrative that has no ending but keeps repeating itself over and over. It is also called a *chain tale* or *round.*

Entriega. A ritual related to weddings; when the bride is given to the groom.

Epic. A narrative song or story related to the deeds of heroes. Heroic type of song or narrative.

Espanto. Folk ailment similar to susto. When a person sees a ghost or supernatural being he/she is said to have seen an *espanto* and become *espantado/a.*

Espiritista. Spiritualist; a person who is supposed to be able to communicate with the beyond or with people who have died.

Evil eye (mal de ojo). Folk belief; a belief that a person has very strong vision and can cause illness or harm just by looking at someone or something. Causes a folk illness of *mal de ojo.*

Exemplary tale. A tale that has a strong message of moral comportment within its structure; in other words, the person that commits a transgression usually receives a terrible punishment.

Exemplum (pl. exempla). From example; a narrative in folktale or song that has a strong moral structured within the plot.

Fable (*fábula*). A folk tale or narrative.

Fairy (*hada*). A supernatural being, usually kind, but can be evil also.

Fajita. Literally small belt or strip. It is now a popular Mexican food and can be made with beef or poultry. It is fried with green peppers, onions, and tomatoes and served with flour or corn tortillas.

Fandango. Word popular in the nineteenth and early twentieth century for dance or festivity. The word *baile* is more commonly used now.

Fiesta. A holiday; a festive occasion; a celebration.

Fifteenth birthday (*quinceañera*). A rite of passage for a young lady celebrating her fifteenth birthday. The girl is presented at church with her court of honor, and a mass is said. After the church ritual, a dance and banquet are held.

Fifth of May. (see *Cinco de Mayo*).

Finnish school. Geographic-historic method of folktale scholarship.

Flan. Custard; Hispanic desert found in all the Spanish-speaking countries.

Folk drama. Folk theater; performances that come from oral traditions. There are secular folk dramas and religious or sacred folk dramas.

Folklore. Oral traditions including folk narratives, myths, folktales, legends, jests, rounds, folksongs, folk dances, folk food, folk belief, folk speech, folk ailments, folk medicine, folk dress, folk architecture, folk art, folk technology, riddles, proverbs, proverbial expressions, children's songs and games, folk customs, and so forth.

Folktale. Folk narrative.

Formula. A phrase that is repeated in numerous texts.

Formulaic. When a genre is composed of phrases that are used repeatedly through various texts it is said to be formulaic. The *corrido,* or Mexican ballad, is formulaic.

***Gavacho* (also spelled *gabacho*).** pejorative term to designate Anglo-Americans. Similar to the word *gringo.*

Genízaro. Assimilated Native American into Spanish culture. Spaniards would buy or capture Native American children and youths and acculturate them to the Spanish culture.

Genre. A category or division.

Geographic-historic method. The geographic-historic method of folklore study focuses on the tracing of origins and diffusion of folklore genres and motifs throughout the world.

Gesture. Body movements with special significance, such as waving good-bye, saying hello by shaking hands, winking, and so on.

Ghost story. Folk narratives that have ghosts in their plot.

Gorda. Tortillas that are thick. The word means *fat* in Spanish.

Gordita. Thick tortillas filled with beans, meat, poultry, cheese, or other foods inside it.

Graffiti. Writings on walls particularly in urban areas using highly stylized forms of writing and folk speech related to urban youth. They write political messages to the world or to each other, particularly if they are in gangs. Graffiti is seen by many as urban art, though others see it as a defacement of property.

Greaser. A derogatory term used to refer to Mexicans and Chicanos.

Gringo. A derogatory term used to refer to Anglo-Americans

Guacamole. Folk food made with mashed avocados, chopped onions, hot peppers, and tomatoes.

Hada. (see *fairy*), as in *cuento de hadas* (fairy tales).

Hero tale. A folk narrative with a hero as the main protagonist.

Hispano. a person of Hispanic descent. Usually refers to people from New Mexico who believe they are the direct descendents of the Spanish conquistadors.

Horno. Traditional oven made with adobes outside the house. It is also used to designate contemporary stove ovens.

Huesero. A folk healer specializing in setting broken bones or sprains.

Huevos Rancheros. A Mexican food made with fried eggs, hot pepper sauce, and fried tortillas on the bottom.

Indita. A folk song from New Mexico that uses the word *indita,* or Indian, in its lyrics.

Jaina. *Caló* word for girlfriend.

Jamaica. Weekend bazaars or festivals.

Jaripeo. Mexican rodeo.

Jerky. Beef jerky.

Jest. Joke.

Jungian. Refers to the theories Carl Gustav Jung, Swiss psychologist and psychiatrist, regarding collective unconscious archetypes.

Kermés. A dance; a festival that includes dancing.

Klicas. From the word *clique* or *gang;* urban gang.

Leitmotif. From German *leiten* (to lead) and *Motiv* (theme, motive, or subject); recurring theme.

Limpia. Folk remedy; the word literally means "cleaning," to clean a person from a folk illness. Generally branches of the peppertree are used, or a *limpia* can also be done with an egg. A prayer is said while the folk healer "cleans" the person with an egg or with peppertree branches.

Low rider. A car that has been transformed so that it rides very, very close to the pavement. The car has been restored and highly decorated inside and out. The person driving the car is called a low rider as well.

Luminarias. A type of bonfire found especially in New Mexico during the Christmas season.

Machismo. Folk speech used today to designate a male who exhibits exaggerated male characteristics. It is also applied to a womanizer who fancies himself a ladies' man. In the first half of the twentieth century and previous centuries the word did not have the connotation it has today. It was applied to a highly responsible, fearless, masculine individual who took care of his family.

Madrina. Godmother.

Magic. Supernatural events or actions; magic events are common in folktales, in which supernatural powers in both evil characters and the hero protagonist are common. In folk belief people believe some persons possess supernatural knowledge to do both evil and good (black magic and white magic).

Maleficio. Spell; witchcraft practiced on someone.

Mandas. Promises to saints for a special favor done to the person making the promise. For example if a person is ill he or she may promise the Virgin of Guadalupe to pay her a visit in Mexico City at her shrine if he or she gets well. If the favor is granted the person is obligated to do as promised.

Manzanilla. Chamomile tea; used in many folk remedies, especially related to headaches or stomachaches.

Märchen. German word designating folktales, as differentiated from fairy tales.

Mariachi. a group of singers and musicians wearing charro outfits. They sing all types of songs, although they especially play *canciones rancheras,* romantic-type *canciones, corridos, boleros,* and *sones.*

Memorate. folk narratives in which the main topic are family stories.

Menudo. Mexican soup made with tripe, spices such as oregano and red chile, and hominy. This folk food is also thought to cure hangovers.

Metate. Grinding stone to grind cooked corn to make corn dough *(masa)* for making tortillas in the traditional manner.

Migra. Abbreviated word for Immigration Officer or the Border Patrol, which deports undocumented workers.

Mojado. folk speech for an undocumented worker. It literally means *wet* and derives from the fact that undocumented people crossed the Rio Grande River by swimming it and would arrive to the other side soaking wet. The English term *wetback* is a pejorative term used to designate these people.

Mole. Traditional Mexican sauce made originally from the Aztec culture. It is made with chocolate, peanuts, almonds, brown sugar, and red chiles. It is used with poultry.

Monogenesis. The term used to designate the theory that folktales came from only one original place, as opposed to polygenesis, which posits the folktale had different origins.

Monomyth. The theory that posits there is one central universal structure for a myth.

Morada. The gathering place of the *cofradía* or brotherhood (such as the penitents); usually a cottage in an isolated area where the meeting would take place and religious rites enacted.

Moral. The message inscribed in a folktale.

Motif. The smallest recognizable unit in a folk narrative or ballad.

Música norteña. Country music typical of northern Mexico and Texas. It is associated with conjunto type music, in which the accordion, guitar, and drums predominate.

Música tropical. Music with a strong tropical rhythm such as merengue, mambo, chacha, rumba, cumbia, salsa, and so forth. This type of music has a strong African influence.

Myth. In folklore, designates a sacred story that is believed by members of a society.

Nacimiento. Nativity scene made during the Christmas season. It is composed of Mary, Joseph, and the baby Jesus in a manger. It also has the animals surrounding the baby Jesus and may also include shepherds coming to worship the newborn baby.

Nicho. Niche; a small recess in a wall that can be used to place sacred statues in traditional homes.

Nursery Rhyme *(canción de cuna).* Babies' songs or chants often used to put babies to sleep or to play with them.

Ofrenda. Offering for the Day of the Dead. The offering could be flowers, food, drink, music, or a favorite object the dead person was particularly fond of.

Pachuco(s). Usually young men who dressed in a certain style in the 1930s–1950s. The style was to wear long coats with baggy pants and a long chain on the side of the pants. They were perceived by hegemonic society as marginalized delinquents. Chicanos view them as heroic figures who were resisting total assimilation into Anglo-American society.

Padrino. Godfather.

Partera. Midwife.

Pastorela. Nativity play; depicts the birth of Christ and the shepherds' attempt to go worship the newborn Jesus after the archangel announced His birth to them in the countryside where they were taking care of their sheep. The devil is the main character in the play trying to prevent the shepherds from reaching their destination, Bethlehem.

Pedro de Urdemalas. Literally Peter Who Does Mischief. A trickster type figure in folktales and jokes in the Hispanic culture.

Piñata. Brightly colored and decorated papier-mâché object in the shape of animals, humans, or other objects such as stars, jars, balloons, and so on used at parties. The children are blindfolded, one at a time, and with a big stick try to break the piñata that is being held above their heads and moved around with a rope. The piñata is filled with candy, and the children try to break it so they can get at the candy which spills to the ground when broken.

Pintos. Prisoners; persons in jail.

Platero. silversmith; a jewelry maker specializing in silver.

Pochismos. Spanish words that have been invented by Chicanos and Mexican Americans.

Pocho(a). A pejorative term used by Mexicans for Mexican Americans and Chicanos.

Polygenesis. The theory positing that folktales had their origins at different places at the same time. This theory is opposed to the monogenesis theory, which posits one origin for a folktale and a diffusion theory—that is, the folktale spread from one point of origin to the rest of the world.

Posadas (Las Posadas). traditional Christmas singing activity much like caroling. The singers go from house to house asking for shelter but are refused (repeating the Joseph and Mary journey and their being refused room at an inn). At the end of the singing, a designated house lets them in and they have a party. This is done nine days before Christmas.

Pozole. Stew; traditional food made with pork, hominy, and red chile like a stew.

Promesa. Promise; usually related to the promise made to a saint if the saint grants a favor to the person asking for it. See also *manda.*

Proverb. A short succinct sentence in which is inscribed a wise message.

Ranchera. Literally "from the countryside." It implies a person is from the country as oppose to the city. It is applied to songs that country folk like.

Rascuache (also found with the spelling *rasquache*). Old, dilapidated. Art critic Tomás Ybarra-Frausto posited the theory of Chicano *rascuache* art which meant that Chicano/as used whatever objects they could find (recycled) and made art from them such as garden planters from old tires, vases from jars.

Raza. A word which literally means "race" but which in folk speech means "people" especially belonging to the working class.

Rebozo. Mexican shawl.

Relajo. Literally means relax but also has the meaning of a party; loud festive event.

Remedies. Folk medicine, remedies used to cure ailments.

Retablos. Ex-votos; folk art related to *promesas* (promises) made to a saint for granting a favor. Usually the favor or miracle granted is depicted on a small tin plate (the size of a license plate) by a folk artist. A text is at the bottom of the painting explaining the miracle that was granted by the saint. The ex-voto bears witness to the saint's efficacy and power to grant miracles or favors to those that ask them.

Rezador. A person who knows the traditional way of praying at special occasions such as wakes, when a person is ill, or when a person wants a special favor (e.g., rain for the crops).

Riddle. A short narrative consisting of two parts: a question and an answer to the question.

Rinches. Texas Rangers; a police force instituted in Texas during the second half of the nineteenth century to quell the Mexican American uprisings that were frequent during that period after the United States–Mexican War of 1848. *Rinches* is the Spanish pronunciation of the word *rangers*.

Romance. Spanish ballad precursor of the Mexican and Chicano *corrido*.

Romancero. A collection of Spanish ballads (romances).

Saint's Day. A saint's holiday; the day that the saint is honored. A person who is named after that saint also celebrates that day with a party. It is almost like a birthday party, because in the past many people were given the name of the saint corresponding to the date they happened to be born.

Santero(a). A person who carves or makes saint statutes from wood or clay.

Santo. Saint.

Sarape. A colorful blanket.

Sobador. A folk healer specializing in giving massages to those who are ill, especially related to a muscle strain.

Sopapillas. pastries made with dough and fried in hot oil. After they are taken out, they are sprinkled with powdered sugar.

Spanglish. A word used to designate Chicano Spanish, which mixes Spanish and English.

Superstition. Pejorative term for folk belief.

Taco. a word designating almost any snack, although people associate it with food made with a corn tortilla and with beef, pork, fish, or poultry inside (the round tortilla is folded after ingredients are placed inside). Lettuce, tomatoes, cheese and hot sauce is also added.

Tamales. Mexican food originally came from the Aztecs. Corn dough with meat inside and steam cooked.

Tio taco. A sell-out; one who betrays his own people for money or other type of personal gain. Similar to Uncle Tom.

Tonantzin. Literally "Our Mother," an Aztec Earth Goddess.

Tortillas. Mexican bread derived from corn; originally came from the Aztecs. A round bread made from corn and cooked on a griddle.

Trovador. troubadour; one that wrote and/or sang folk songs, especially *décimas.*

Urban legend. legends found in today's urban society.

Variant. another version of a text.

Vaqueros. Mexican cowboys.

Vato loco. crazy dude.

Velorio. wake.

Vida loca or *la vida loca.* living the crazy life usually associated with youth who take drugs and party all the time.

Witchcraft. folk belief in the power of a person to do evil—cast a hex, make a person ill, have bad luck, and so on.

Yerbabuena. mint used for teas and folk remedies

Zoot suit. the type of suit a *pachuco* wore.

Filmography

The Ballad of Gregorio Cortez. Directed by Robert Young. Beverly Hills, CA: Moctesuma Esparza Productions, Inc. 1982.

Chulas Fronteras and *Del Mero Corazón.* Directed by Les Blank and Chris Strachwitz. El Cerrito, CA: Brazos Films, 1976. (Also in CD #425).

Chulas Fronteras. Directed by Les Blank and Chris Strachwitz, El Cerrito, CA: Brazos Films, 1976.

Corridos: Tales of Passion and Revolution. Directed by Luis Valdez. San Francisco, CA: KQED and El Teatro Campesino, 1987.

Indigenous Always: The Legend of La Malinche and the Conquest of Mexico. Directed by Dan Banda. Milwaukee, WI: Bandana Productions, 2000.

La Bamba: The Ritchie Valens Story. Directed by Luis Valdez. CA: Columbia Pictures, 1987.

La Ofrenda: The Days of the Dead. 50-mm. videorecording. Directed by Lourdes Portillo and Susana Muñoz. San Francisco, CA: Xochitl Films, 1990.

"La Pastorela/The Shepherds' Tale." Video. Written and directed by Luis Valdez, produced by Richard D. Soro. San Juan Bautista, CA: El Teatro Carnpesino, 1991.

Zoot Suit. Written and directed by Luis Valdez; produced by Peter Burrell. Los Angeles: Universal Pictures, 1981.

Bibliography

ABBREVIATIONS USED FOR JOURNALS

JAF	Journal of American Folklore
PTFS	Publications of the Texas Folklore Society
CFQ	California Folklore Quarterly
WF	Western Folklore
NMFR	New Mexico Folklore Record
SFQ	Southern Folklore Quarterly
JFI	Journal of the Folklore Institute

BIBLIOGRAPHIES

Arora, Shirley. "A Critical Bibliography of Mexican American Proverbs." *Aztlán: International Journal of Chicano Studies Research* 13 (1982a): 71–80.

Bibliography of Spanish Ballads in Spanish America in Homenaje a Menéndez Pidal, 3 vols., Madrid, 1925, vol. 1, l99–260.

Boggs, Ralph Steele. *Bibliografía Completa, Clasificada y Comentada, de los Artículos de Mexican. Folkways, con Indice.* Mexico City, 1945.

———. *Bibliografía del Folklore Mexicano.* Mexico City: Instituto Panamericano de Geografía e Historia, 1939.

———. *Bibliography of Latin American Folklore.* New York: The H. W. Wilson Co., 1940; republished Detroit: Blame Ethridge, 1971.

———. *Folklore Bibliography 1937–1959.* Jacksonville: University of Florida, 1938–1959.

Chabrán, Richard. "Folklore del Chicano," *Selected Collections of the Chicano Studies Library.* Vol. 3. Berkeley: University of California, 1974.

Chase, Gilbert. "United States." In *A Guide to the Music of Latin America.* Washington, DC: Pan American Union, 1962, pp. 348–57.

Haywood, Charles. *A Bibliography of North American Folklore and Folksong,* 2nd revised edition. New York: Dover Publications, 1961. 2 vols.

Heisley, Michael. *An Annotated Bibliography of Chicano Folklore from the Southwestern United States.* Los Angeles: Center for the Study of Comparative Folklore and Mythology, University of California, Los Angeles, 1977.

Huerta, Jorge A., ed. *A Bibliography of Chicano and Mexican Dance, Drama, and Music.* Oxnard, CA: Colegio Quetzalcoatl, 1972.

Igo, John. *Los Pastores: An Annotated Bibliography with an Introduction.* San Antonio, TX: San Antonio College Library, 1967.

Lesser, Arthur. "Bibliography of Spanish American Folklore." *JAF* 41 (1928): 37–45.

Moreno, Joseph A. Clark. "A Bibliography of Bibliographies Relating to Studies of Mexican-Americans." *El Grito* 2 (Winter, 1971–1972): 47–59.

Peterson, Anaya. *Mexican Dance Forms: A Bibliography with Annotations.* Palo Alto, CA: Institute for the Study of Contemporary Cultures of the Institute of International Relations. Stanford University, 1967.

Robe, Stanley L., comp. *Index of Mexican Folktales: Including Narrative Texts from Mexico, Central America, and the Hispanic United States,* Folklore Studies 26. Berkeley and Los Angeles: The University of California Press, 1973.

———. "Selective Bibliography of Folk Drama in Hispanic America." *Western Folklore* 16 (1957): 287–89.

Saunders, Lyle, comp. *Spanish-Speaking Americans and Mexican-Americans in the United States: A Selected Bibliography.* New York: Bureau for Intercultural Education, 1944. Also reprinted in *Mexican American Bibliographies.* New York: Arno Press, 1974.

Simmons, Merle E. *A Bibliograpy of the Romance and Related Forms in Spanish America.* Indiana University Folklore Series, 18. Bloomington: Indiana University Press, 1963.

Tully, Marjorie F., and Juan B. Rael, comps. *An Annotated Bibliography of Spanish Folklore in New Mexico and Southern Colorado.* The University of New Mexico Publications in Language and Literature, 3. Albuquerque: University of New Mexico Publications, 1950.

GENERAL WORKS

Abernethy, Francis Edward. *Folk Art in Texas.* Dallas: Methodist University Press, 1985.

Abeyta, Ray Martín. *Cuentos y encuentros.* Albuquerque, NM: National Hispanic Cultural Center, 2003.

Aceves, J. Jesús Rodríguez. *Danzas de Moros y Cristianos.* Guadalajara, Jalisco, México: Gobierno de Jalisco, Secretaria General Unidad Editorial, 1988.

Ahlborn, Richard E. *The Penitente Moradas of Abiquiu.* Contributions from the Museum of History and Technology, Paper 63. Washington, DC: The Smithsonian Institution Press, 1968.

Aiken, Riley. "Fifteen Mexican Tales." In *A Good Tale and Bonny Tune,* eds. Mody C. Boatright, Wilson M. Hudson, and Allen Maxwell. *PTFS* 32 (1964): 3–56.

———. "A Pack Load of Mexican Tales." In *Texas Folk and Folklore,* eds. Mody C. Boatright, Wilson M. Hudson, and Allen Maxwell. *PTFS* 26 (1954): 224–38.

Alarcón, Norma. "Traddutora, *Traditora:* A Paradigmatic Figure of Chicana Feminism." *Cultural Critique* 13(1989): 57–87.

Alexander, Frances, ed. and trans. *Mother Goose on the Rio Grande.* Dallas, TX: Upshaw and Company, 1944.

Alurista (pseudonym) Urista Heredia, Alberto Baltazar, "Chicano Art, Dance and Music." Show # 15 in *Chicano: Mexican Americans.* Burbank, CA: KNBC TV, n.d. RISC TV on September 25, 1972.

———. *Nationchild Plumaroja.* San Diego, CA: Toltecas en Aztlán, 1972.

Amon Carter Museum of Western Art. *Santos: An Exhibition of the Religious Folk Art of New Mexico.* Fort Worth, TX, 1964.

Anaya, Rudolfo A. *The Farolitos of Christmas.* New York: Hyperion Books, 1995.

———. *The Legend of La Llorona.* Berkeley, CA: Tonatiuh-Quinto Sol International, Inc., 1984.

———."*La Llorona,* El *Kookoóee,* and Sexuality." In *The Anaya Reader,* ed. César González. New York: Warner Books, 1995.

Anaya, Rudolfo, Denise Chávez, and Juan Estevan Arellano. *Descansos: An Interrupted Journey, Tres Voces.* Photographs by Juan Estevan Arellano. Albuquerque, NM: Academia/El Norte Publications, 1995.

Anaya, Rudolfo A., and Francisco A. Lomelí, eds. *Aztlán: Essays on the Chicano Homeland.* Albuquerque, NM: Academia/El Norte Publications, 1989.

Anderson, Reed. "Early Secular Theater in New Mexico." In *Pasó por Aquí: Critical Essays on the New Mexican Literary Tradition, 1542–1988,* ed. Erlinda Gonzales-Berry. Albuquerque: University of New Mexico, 1989.

Anonymous. "Los Hermanos Penitentes," *El Palacio* 8 (1920): 3–20.

Anonymous. "California Spanish Proverbs and Adages." *CFQ* 3 (1944): 121–23.

Applegate, Betty. "Los Hermanos Penitentes," *Southwest Review* 17:1 (Autumn 1931): 100–107.

Applegate, Frank. "New Mexico Legends," *Southwest Review* 17:2 (Winter 1932): 199–208.

Applewhite, Steven Lozano. "*Curanderismo:* Demystifying the Health Beliefs and Practices of Elderly Mexican Americans." *Health and Social Work* 20 (1995): 247–54.

Aranda, Charles. *Dichos: Proverbs and Sayings from the Spanish.* Santa Fe, NM: Sunset One Press, 1977.

Arbuckle, H. C., III. "Don José and Don Pedrito." *The Folklore of Texan Cultures,* ed. Francis Edward Abernethy. *PTFS* 38 (1974): 84–87.

Arellano, Anselmo F., and Julian Josue Vigil, eds. *Arthur L. Campa.* Las Vegas, NV: Editorial Telaraña, 1980.

Arellano, Estevan. "*Descansos.*" *New Mexico Magazine,* February 1986, 42–45.

Arora, Shirley L. "Como La Carabina De Ambrosio." *Proverbium* 15 (1970): 428–30.

———. "La Llorona: The Naturalization of a Legend." *Southwest Folklore* 5 (1981): 23–40.

————. "More Spanish Proverbial Exaggerations from California." *WF* 30 (1971): 105–18.

————. *Proverbial Comparisons and Related Expressions in Spanish.* Berkeley: University of California Press, 1977.

————. "Proverbial Exaggerations in English and Spanish." *Proverbium* 18 (1972): 675–83.

————. "Proverbs in Mexican American Tradition." *Aztlán: International Journal of Chicano Studies Research* 13 (1982b): 43–69.

————. "'El Que Nace Para Tamal … ': A Study in Proverb Patterning." *Folklore Americas* 28:2 (1968): 55–79.

————. "Some Spanish Proverbial Comparisons from California," *WF* 20 (1961): 229–37.

————. "Spanish Proverbial Exaggerations from California," *WF,* 27, (1968), 229–53.

Arqueología Mexicana: Investigaciones recientes en el Templo Mayor. 6: 31 (mayo-junio 1998).

Arroyo, Ronald D. "La Raza Influence in Jazz," *El Grito* 5:4 (1972): 80–84.

Arteaga, Alfred. "Aesthetics of Sex and Race." In *Feminism, Nation and Myth: La Malinche,* ed. Rolando Romero and Amanda Nolacea Harris. Houston, TX: Arte Público Press, 2005, pp. 60–66.

————. "The Chicano Mexican Corrido." *Journal of Ethnic Studies* 13 (Summer 1985): 75–105.

Astorga, Luis A. *Mitología del 'narcotraficante' en México.* Mexico City: Plaza y Valdés Editores, 1996.

Atkinson, William C. "The Chronology of Spanish Ballad Origins." *Modern Review* 32 (1937): 44–61.

Atwood, E. Bagby. *The Regional Vocabulary of Texas.* Austin, TX: The University of Texas Press, 1962.

Austin-Applegate Manuscript on *Spanish Colonial Art.* "New Mexico Santeros." *NMFR* 1 (1946–47): 9–10.

Austin, Mary. "Native Drama in New Mexico." *Theater Arts Monthly* 13:8 (1929): 564–67.

————. "New Mexico Folk Poetry." *El Palacio* 7 (1919): 146–154.

————. "Native Drama in Our Southwest." *Nation* 124: 322 (1927): 437–40.

————. "Spanish Manuscripts in the Southwest." *Southwest Review* 19 (1934): 402–9.

Austin, Mary, and John H. McNeely. "Francisco Villa in Folk-Songs," *Arizona Quarterly* (Tucson, Arizona) 10:1 (Spring 1954): 5–16.

Awalt, Barbe. *Our Saints among Us/Nuestros Santos entre Nosotros: 400 Years of New Mexican Devotional Art.* Albuquerque, NM: LPD Press, 1998.

Bach, Marcus. "Los Pastores." *Theater Arts Monthly* 24 (1940): 282–88.

Baer, Roberta D., and María Bustillo. "Susto and Mal Ojo among Florida Farmworkers: Emic and Etic Perspectives." *Medical Anthropology Quarterly* 7 (1993): 90–100.

Bandini, Arturo. *Navidad:* A *Christmas Day with the Early Californians. Pastorela, A Shepherds' Play.* Trans. y Gladys Louise Williams. San Francisco: California Historical Society, 1958.

Barker, George Carpenter. *Pachuco: An American-Spanish Argot and Its Social Functions in Tucson, Arizona.* Tucson: University of Arizona Press, 1974.

Barakat, Robert A. "Aztec Motifs in 'La Llorona.'" *SFQ* 29 (1965): 288–96.

———. "The Bear's Son Tale in Northern Mexico." *JAF* 78 (1965): 330–36.

Barrera, Alberto. "Mexican-American Roadside Crosses in Starr County." In *Hecho en Texas: Texas-Mexican Folk Arts and Crafts,* ed. Joe S. Graham. Denton: University of Texas Press, 1991.

Bascom, William. "The Forms of Folklore: Prose Narrative." *Journal of American Folklore* 78, no. 307 (January–March 1965): 3–20.

Bauman, Richard, and Roger D. Abrahams. *"And Other Neighborly Names": Social Process and Cultural Image in Texas Folklore.* Austin: University of Texas Press, 1981.

Bauman, Richard, and Américo Paredes. *Toward New Perspectives in Folklore.* Austin: University of Texas Press, 1972.

Bevans, Charles I., ed. *Treaties and Other International Agreements of the United States of America, 1776–1949.* Vol. 9. Washington, DC: Department of State, 1972.

Blea, Irene I. *"Brujería:* A Sociological Analysis of Mexican American Witches." In *Sex Roles, Language: Selected Papers 1979.* Berkeley, CA: Tonatiuh-Quinto Sol, 1980.

Bloom, Maude McFie. "Holy Ghost Canyon." In *Puro Mexicano,* ed. J. Frank Dobie. *PTFS* 12 (1935); reissued in 1969: 175–83.

Boatright, Mody C. "The Devil's Grotto." In *Texas and Southwestern Lore,* ed. J. Frank Dobie, *PTFS* 6 (1927): 102–6.

Boggs, R.S. "To Love Like Salt: A New Mexican Folktale." *NMFR* 2 (1947–1948): 20–23.

———. "La Adivinanza." *Folklore Americas* 21: 1–2 (1963): 1–22.

Bonfil, Alicia Olveira de. *La literatura Cristera.* Mexico City: Instituto de Antropología e Historia, 1970.

Bourke, John G. "The Folk-Foods of the Rio Grande Valley and of Northern Mexico." *JAF* 8 (1895): 41–71; also reprinted in *Southwestern Lore,* ed. J. Frank Dobie. *PTFS* 9 (1931): 85–117.

Boyd, E. *Saints and Saint Makers of New Mexico.* Santa Fe, NM: Laboratory of Anthropology, 1946.

Boydstun, Laurence C. "The Classification and Analysis of the Spanish-American Versions of the Tar-Baby Story." unpublished masters thesis, Stanford University, 1947.

Braddy, Haldeen. *Cock of the Walk: The Legend of Pancho Villa.* Albuquerque, NM: The University of New Mexico Press, 1955.

Brewer, Fred Meza. "Los Pastores: A Problem in Sources, Language, and Folk Theater." *NMFR* 2 (1947–48): 46–57.

Briggs, Charles L. *Competence in Performance: The Creativity of Tradition in Mexicano Verbal Art.* Philadelphia: University of Pennsylvania Press, 1988.

————. "The Role of Mexicano Artists and the Anglo Elite in the Emergence of a Contemporary Folk Art." In *Folk Art and Art Worlds,* ed. John Michael Vlach and Simon J. Bronner. Ann Arbor, Ml: UMI Research Press, 1986.

————. *The Wood Carvers of Cordova, New Mexico: Social Dimensions of an Artistic Revival.* Knoxville: University of Tennessee Press, 1980.

Briggs, Charles L., and Julian Josue Vigil. *The Lost Gold Mine of Juan Mondragón: A Legend from New Mexico Performed by Melaquías Romero.* Tucson, AZ: University of Arizona Press, 1990.

Bright, Brenda Jo. "Remappings: Los Angeles Low Riders." In *Looking High and Low: Art and Cultural Identity,* ed. Brenda Jo Bright and Liza Bakewell. Tucson: University of Arizona, 1995.

Brito, Aristeo. *The Devil in Texas/El Diablo en Texas.* Trans. David William Foster. Tempe, AZ: Bilingual Press, 1990.

Brown, Lorin W. *Hispano Folklife of New Mexico: The Lorin W. Brown Federal Writers' Project Manuscripts.* Albuquerque, NM: University of New Mexico, 1978.

Brown, M. H. de La Peña. "*Una Tamalada:* The Special Event." *Western Folklore* 40 (1981): 64–71.

Broyles-González, Yolanda. *El Teatro Campesino: Theater in the Chicano Movement.* Austin: University of Texas Press, 1994.

————. *Lydia Mendoza's Life in Music: La historia de Lydia Mendoza—Norteño Legacies.* New York: Oxford University Press, 2001.

Brundage, Burr Cartwright. *The Fifth Sun: Aztec Gods, Aztec World.* Austin: University of Texas Press, 1979.

Buss, Fran Leeper. *La Partera: Story of a Midwife.* Ann Arbor: University of Michigan Press, 1980.

Cabello-Argandoña, Roberto. *Brief History of Cinco de Mayo.* Encino, CA: Floricanto Press, 1993.

Cabeza de Baca, Fabiola. *The Good Life: New Mexico Traditions and Food.* Santa Fe, NM: Museum of New Mexico Press, 1982.

————. *We Fed Them Cactus.* Albuquerque, NM: University of New Mexico Press, 1954.

Campa, Arthur L. "Bernal Frances y La Esposa Infiel," *Folklore: Boletin del Departmento de Folklore del Instituto de Cooperación Universitaria* (Buenos Aires) 2 (1941): 35–36.

————. "A Bibliography of Spanish Folk-Lore in New Mexico." *The University of New Mexico Bulletin* 2:3 Language Series. Albuquerque: University of New Mexico Press, 1930.

————. "Chili in New Mexico." *New Mexico Business Review* 3 (1934): 61–63.

————. "*Los Comanches:* A New Mexican Folk Drama." *The University of New Mexico Bulletin* 7:1 (1942): 5–42.

————. *Hispanic Culture in the Southwest.* Norman: University of Oklahoma Press, 1979.

————. *Hipanic Folklore Studies of Arthur L. Campa.* New York: Arno Press, 1976.

———. "The New Mexican Spanish Folktheater." *SFQ* 5 (1941): 127–31.

———. "New Mexico Spanish Folk-Tales." unpublished masters thesis, University of New Mexico, Albuquerque.

———. "El Origen y la Naturaleza del Drama Folklórico." *Folklore Américas* 20:2 (1960): 13–48.

———. "Religious Spanish Folk-Drama in New Mexico." *New Mexico Quarterly* 1 (February 1931): 3–13.

———. "Sayings and Riddles in New Mexico." *The University of New Mexico Bulletin*, Language Series, 6:2 (1937): 3–67.

———. "Some Herbs and Plants of Early California." *WF* 9 (1950): 338–47.

———. "Spanish-American Folksongs from the Collection of Leonora Curtin, Santa Fe, New Mexico," Albuquerque, New Mexico, n.d.

———. *Spanish Folk-Poetry in New Mexico.* Albuquerque: The University of New Mexico Press, 1946.

———. "The Spanish Folksong in the Southwest." *The University of New Mexico Bulletin* 4:1 (1933): 5–67.

———. "Spanish Folksongs in Metropolitan Denver." SFQ 24 (1960): 179–92 *Southern Folklore Quaterly (SFQ).*

———. "The Spanish Language in the Southwest." In *Humanidad: Essays in Honor of George I. Sanchez,* ed. Américo Paredes. Los Angeles: Chicano Studies Center Publications, University of California, 1977.

———. "Spanish Traditional Tales in the Southwest." *WF* 6 (1947): 322–34.

———. "Spanish Religious Folktheater in the Southwest (Second Cycle)." *The University of New Mexico Bulletin*, Language Series, 5:2 (June 15, 1934): 5–157.

———. "Today's Troubadours.": *New Mexico* (Santa Fe) 14:9 (September 1936): 16–17, 49–50.

———. *Treasure of the Sangre de Cristo: Tales and Traditions of the Spanish Southwest.* Norman: University of Oklahoma Press, 1963.

Campos, Anthony John, ed. and trans. *Mexican Folk Tales.* Illustrated by Mark Sanders. Tucson: University of Arizona Press, 1977.

Candelaria, Cordelia. "Letting La Llorona Go: In: Re/reading History's Tender Mercies." *Heresies* 7 (1993): 111–15.

Cantú, Norma. "Chicana Life-Cycle Rituals." In *Chicana Traditions: Continuity and Change,* ed. Norma E. Cantú and Olga Nájera-Ramírez. Urbana: University of Illinois Press, 2002.

———. "Costume as Cultural Resistance and Affirmation: The Case of a South Texas Community." In *Hecho en Tejas: Texas Mexican Folk Arts and Crafts,* ed. Joe S. Graham. Denton: University of North Texas Press, 1991.

———. "*Los Matachines de La Santa Cruz de La Ladrillera:* Notes toward a Socio-Literary Analysis." In *Feasts and Celebrations in North American Ethnic Communities,* ed. Ramón A. Gutiérrez and Genevieve Fabré. Albuquerque: University of New Mexico Press, 1995.

————. "The Mexican-American Quilting Traditions of Laredo, San Ygnacio, and Zapata." In *Hecho en Tejas: Texas-American Folk Arts and Crafts*, ed. Joe S. Graham. Denton: University of Texas Press, 1991.

Cantú, Norma and Olga Nájera-Ramírez. *Chicana Traditions: Continuity and Change.* Urbana: University of Illinois Press, 2002.

Cardozo-Freeman, Inez. "Games Mexican Girls Play." *JAF* 88 (1975): 12–24.

Carmichael, Elizabeth, and Chloe Sayer. *The Skeleton at the Feast: The Day of the Dead in Mexico.* London: British Museum Press, 1999.

Carpenter, Ann. "Scratches on the Bedpost: Vestiges of the Lechuza." In *The Folklore of Texan Cultures,* ed. Francis Edward Abernethy. *PTFS* 38 (1974): 75–78.

Carrasco, David. *Quetzalcóatl and the Irony of Empire: Myths and Prophecies in the Aztec Tradition.* Chicago: University of Chicago Press, 1992.

Carter, George F. "A California Account of Uses of Medical Herbs," *WF* 6 (1947): 199–203.

Cash, Marie Romero. *Living Shrines: Home Altars of New Mexico.* Santa Fe: Museum of New Mexico Press, 1998.

————. *Santos: Enduring Images of Northern New Mexican Village Churches.* Boulder: University Press of Colorado, 1999.

Castañeda, Antonia I. "Malinche, Calafia y Toypurina: Of Myths, Monsters and Embodied History." In *Feminism, Nation and Myth: La Malinche,* ed. Rolando Romero and Amanda Nolacea Harris. Houston, TX: Arte Público Press, 2005.

Castillo, Ana, ed. *Goddess of the Americas/La Diosa de las Américas: Writings on the Virgin of Guadalupe.* New York: Riverhead Books, 1996.

————. *Massacre of the Dreamers: Essays on Xicanisma.* Albuquerque: University of New Mexico, 1994.

Castillo, Bernal Díaz del. *Historia verdadera de la conquista de la Nueva España.* [1632].Mexico City: Editorial Porrúa,1967.

Castillo, Debra A. "Coagulated Words: Gaspar de Alba's Malinche." In *Feminism, Nation and Myth: La Malinche,* ed. Rolando Romero and Amanda Nolacea Harris. Houston, TX: Arte Público Press, 2005.

Castillo, Pedro, and Albert Camarillo, eds. *Furia y Muerte: Los Bandidos Chicanos.* Monograph No. 4. Los Angeles, CA: Aztlán Publications, UCLA Chicano Studies Research Center, 1973.

Castro, Rafaela G. *Chicano Folklore: A Guide to the Folktales, Traditions, Rituals, and Religious Practices of Mexican-Americans.* Oxford: Oxford University Press, 2001.

————. "Mexican Women's Sexual Jokes." *Aztlán: International Journal of Chicano Studies Research* 13 (1982): 275–93.

Champe, Flavia Waters. *The Matachines Dance of the Upper Rio Grande: History, Music, and Choreography.* Lincoln: University of Nebraska Press, 1983.

Chávez, Tibo J. *New Mexican Folklore of the Rio Abajo.* Portales, New Mexico: Bishop Printing Co., 1972.

Chávez, Tomas Jr. *Quinceañera: A Liturgy in the Reformed Tradition.* San Angelo, TX: Presbytery of Tres Ríos, 1983.

Clark, Margaret. *Health in the Mexican-American Culture, A Community Study,* 2nd ed. Berkeley and Los Angeles: The University of California Press, 1970.

Clark, Walter Aaron, ed. *From Tejano to Tango: Latin American Popular Music.* New York: Routledge, 2002.

Cobos, Ruben. *A Dictionary of New Mexico and Southern Colorado Spanish.* Santa Fe: Museum of New Mexico Press, 1983.

———. *Music in the Ruben Cobos Collection of Spanish New Mexican Folklore: A Descriptive Catalogue,* ed. Victoria Lindsay Levine and Amanda Chase. Colorado Springs, CO: The Hulbert Center Press of the Colorado College, 1999.

———. "New Mexican Spanish Proverbs." *NMFR* 12 (1969–1970): 7–11.

———. *Refranes: Southwestern Spanish Proverbs.* Santa Fe: Museum of New Mexico Press, 1985.

Cole, M.R. *Los Pastores: A Mexican Play of the Nativity.* Memoirs of the American Folklore Society, 9, 1907.

Cordova, Gabriel. "Black and White Magic on the Texas-Mexican Border." In *Folk Travelers: Ballads, Tales, and Talk,* eds. Mody C. Boatright, Wilson M. Hudson, and Allen Maxwell. *PTFS* 25 (1953): 195–99.

de la Cotona, Juan. *100 Adivinanzas picarescas.* Mexico City: Gómez, Gómez Hermanos, 1977.

Coutrer, Lane. *New Mexican Tinwork, 1840 1940.* Albuquerque: University of New Mexico Press, 1990.

Creson, D. L., Cameron McKinley, and Richard Evans. "Folk Medicine in Mexican-American Sub-Culture." *A Practical Journal on Psychiatry and Neurology* 30:1 (1969): 264–66.

Crews, Mildred T. "Saint Maker from Taos." *Americas* 21:3 (March, 1969): 33–37.

Crook, Alice M. "Old Times New Mexican Usages." In *Puro Mexicano,* ed. J. Frank Dobie. *PTFS* 12 (1935): 184–89.

Cunningham, Keith K. "Ethnocuisine: Arizona Mexican American." *Southwest Folklore* 21 (1980): 58–60.

Curtin, L.S.M. *Healing Herbs of the Upper Rio Grande.* Santa Fe, NM: Laboratory of Anthropology, 1947.

———. "Spanish and Indian Witchcraft in New Mexico." *Masterkey,* 45:3 (July-September 1971): 89–101.

Curtis, F. S., Jr. "Spanish Folk-Poetry in the Southwest." *Southwest Review* 10:2 (January 1925): 68–73.

Dávalos, Karen Mary. "'La Quinceañera': Making Gender and Ethnic Identities." *Frontiers* 16 (Spring and Summer 1996): 101–28.

Day, Mark. *Forty Acres: César Chávez and the Farm Workers.* New York: Praeger, 1971.

Del Castillo, Adelaida R. "Malintzin Tenépal: A Preliminary Look into a New Perspective." In *Essays on La Mujer,* ed. Rosaura Sánchez and Rosa Martínez Cruz

Sánchez: Chicano Studies Center Publications, Anthology No. 1. Los Angeles: University of California, 1977.

Del Castillo, Bernal Díaz. *Historia verdadera de la conquista de la Nueva España [1568]*. Mexico City: Editorial Porrúa, 1967.

———. *The True History of the Conquest of Mexico*. [1568] Trans. Maurice Keatinge, Esq. La Jolla, CA: Renaissance Press (reprinted from the 1800 John Dean, London edition), 1979.

Delgado, Edmundo R. *Witch Stories of New Mexico, Folklore of New Spain/Cuentos de Brujas de Nuevo Mexico, Folklore de La Nueva España*. Santa Fe, NM: Works Progress Administration, 1994.

Demarest, Donald, and Coley Taylor. *The Dark Virgin: The Book of Our Lady of Guadalupe*. Freeport, ME: Coley Taylor Inc., 1956.

Demello, Margo. "The Convict Body: Tattooing among Male American Prisoners." *Anthropology Today* 9 (1993): 10–13.

Día de los Muertos: An Illustrated Essay and Bibliography. Santa Barbara, CA: Center for Chicano Studies and Colección Tloque Nahuaque, University Library, 1983.

Dickey, Dan William. *The Kennedy Corridos: A Study of the Ballads of a Mexican American Hero*. Austin: Center for Mexican American Studies, University of Texas Press, 1978.

Dobie, J. Frank. *Coronado's Children: Tales of Lost Mines and Buried Treasures of the Southwest*. Dallas: The Southwest Press, 1930.

———. *Guide to Life and Literature of the Southwest, with a Few Observations*. Austin: The University of Texas Press, 1943; republished by the Southern Methodist University Press, 1952.

———, ed. *Legends of Texas*. 2nd edition. *PTFS* 3 (1924).

———. "Weather Wisdom of the Texas-Mexican Border." *Coffee in the Gourd*, ed. J. Frank Dobie. *PTFS* 2 (1923): 87–99.

Dodson, Ruth. "The *Curandero* of Los Olmos." In *Texas Folk and Folklore*, eds. Mody C. Boatright, Wilson M. Hudson, and Allen Maxwell. *PTFS* 26 (1954): 264–70.

———. "Don Pedrito Jaramillo: The *Curandero* of Los Olmos." In *The Healer of Los Olmos and Other Mexican Lore*, ed. Wilson Mathis Hudson. *PTFS* 24 (1951): 9–70.

———. "Folk-Curing among the Mexicans." In *Tone the Bell Easy*, ed. J. Frank Dobie. *PTFS* 10 (1932): 82–98.

———. "Tortilla Making." In *In the Shadow of History*, eds. J. Frank Dobie, Mody C. Boatright, and Harry H. Ransom. *PTFS* 15 (1939): 137–41.

Domínguez, Miguel. "Coplas from East Los Angeles." *Southwest Folklore* 5 (1981): 41–54.

Dorson, Richard M. *American Folklore*. Chicago: University of Chicago Press, 1959.

———. "Latino Folklore in the Region." In *Forging a Community: The Latino Experience in Northwest Indiana, 1919–1975*, ed. James B. Lane and Edward J. Escobar. Chicago: Cattails Press, 1987.

———, ed. "Southwest Mexicans." In *Buying the Wind: Regional Folklore in the United States*. Chicago: University of Chicago Press, 1964.

————. "Spanish New Mexico," in *American Folklore*. Chicago: University of Chicago Press, 1959.

Duffy, Karen M. "Tracing the Gift: Aurelio M. Espinosa, 1880–1958." *The Folklore Historian* 12 (1995): 39–53.

Dundes, Alan. *Analytic Essays in Folklore*. The Hague: Mouton, 1975.

————, ed. *The Evil Eye: A Casebook*. Madison: University of Wisconsin Press, 1992.

————. "What Is Folklore?" In *The Study of Folklore*, ed. Alan Dundes. Englewood Cliffs, NJ: Prentice-Hall, Inc., 1965.

Durán, Fray Diego. *Historia de Las Indias de Nueva España e Islas de Tierra Firme*. Mexico City: Consejo Nacional para la Cultura y las Artes, 1995.

Durand, Jorge, and Douglas S. Massey. *Doy Gracias: Iconografía de la Emigración México—Estados Unidos*. Guadalajara, Jalisco, México: Programa de Estudios Jaliscienses, Universidad de Guadalajara, 1990.

————. *Miracles on the Border: Retablos of Mexican Migrants to the United States*. Tucson: University of Arizona Press, 1995.

Ebinger, Virginia Nylander. *Niñez: Spanish Songs, Games, and Stories of Childhood*. Santa Fe, NM: Sunstone Press, 1993.

Edbert, Mark Cameron. *El Narcotraficante: Narcocorridos and the Construction of a Cultural Persona on the U.S.–Mexico Border*. Austin: University of Texas Press, 2004.

Egan, Martha. *Milagros: Votive Offerings from the Americas*. Santa Fe: Museum of New Mexico Press, 1991.

Elizondo, Virgil. "Our Lady of Guadalupe as a Cultural Symbol: 'The Power of the Powerless.'" In *Liturgy and Cultural Religious Traditions*, ed. Herman Schmidt and David Power. New York: Seabury Press, 1977.

Ellis, Florence Hawley. "Saints in Wood." *New Mexico Magazine* 31 (November 1931): 17, 40–41.

El Teatro Campesino: The Evolution of America's First Chicano Theatre Company, 1965–1985. San Juan Bautista, CA: El Teatro Campesino, 1985.

Engh, Michael S. "Companion of the Immigrants: Devotion to Our Lady of Guadalupe among Mexicans in the Los Angeles Area, 1900–1940." *Journal of Hispanic Latino Ideology* 5 (1997): 37–43.

Englekirk, John E. "Notes on the Repertoire of the New Mexican Spanish Folktheater." *SFQ* 4 (1940): 227–37.

————. "The Passion Play in New Mexico." *WF* 25 (1966): 17–33, 105–21.

————. "The Source and Dating of New Mexican Spanish Folk Plays." *WF* 16 (1957): 232–55.

————. "El Teatro Folklórico Hispanoamericano." *Folklore Americas* 17:1 (1957): 1–36.

Erevia, Angela. *Quinceañera*. San Antonio, TX: Mexican American Cultural Center, 1980.

Escalera, José. "Curanderos in Our Time." In *Chicano Border Culture and Folklore*, ed. José Villarino and Arturo Ramírez. San Diego, CA: Mann Publications, 1992.

Espinel, Luisa. *Canciones de Mi Padre*. Tucson: University of Arizona Press, 1946.

Espinosa, Aurelio Macedonio. "California Spanish Folklore Riddles." *CFQ* 3 (1944): 293–98.

———. "Comparative Notes on New-Mexican Spanish Folk-tales." *JAF,* 27 (1914): 211–31.

———. *Cuentos Populares Españoles, Recogidos de la Tradición Oral de España.* 3 vols. Madrid: S. Aguirre, 1946–1947.

———. "Cuentitos Populares Nuevo-Mejicanos y su Transcripción Fonética," *Bulletin de Dialectologie Romane* 4 (1912): 97–115.

———. *Estudio Sobre el Español de Nuevo México.* Buenos Aires: Imprenta de la Universidad de Buenos Aires, 1934.

———. "The Field of Spanish Folklore in America." *SFQ* 5 (1941): 29–35.

———. "Folklore Infantil de Nuevo Méjico." *Revista de Dialectología y Tradiciones Populares,* 10:4 (1954): 499–547.

———. *The Folklore of Spain in the American Southwest: Traditional Spanish Folk Literature in Northern New Mexico and Southern Colorado,* ed. J. Manuel Espinosa. Norman: University of Oklahoma Press, 1985.

———. "Hispanic Versions of the Tale of the Corpse Many Times Killed." *JAF* 49 (1936): 181–93.

———. "Los Comanches: A Spanish Heroic Play of the Year Seventeen Hundred and Eighty." *The University of New Mexico Bulletin,* Language Series, 1:1 (1907): 1–46.

———. "New Mexican Spanish Folklore: I. Myths." *JAF* 23 (1910): 395–404.

———. "New Mexican Spanish Folklore: II. Superstitions and Beliefs." *JAF* 23 (1910): 405–18.

———. "New Mexican Spanish Folklore: III. Folk-Tales." *JAF* 24 (1911): 397–444.

———. "New-Mexican Spanish Folklore: IV. Proverbs." *JAF* 26 (1913): 97–114.

———. "New-Mexican Spanish Folklore: V. Popular Comparisons." *JAF* 26 (1913): 114–22.

———. "New-Mexican Spanish Folklore: VII. More Folk-Tales." *JAF* 27 (1914): 119–42.

———. "New-Mexican Spanish Folklore: VIII. Short Folktales and Anecdotes." *JAF* 27 (1914): 142–47.

———. "New-Mexican Spanish Folklore: IX. Riddles." *JAF* 28 (1915): 319–52.

———. "New-Mexican Spanish Folklore: X. Children's Games." *JAF* 29 (1916): 505–19.

———. "New Mexican-Spanish Folklore: XI. Nursery Rhymes & Children's Songs." *JAF* 29 (1916): 519–35.

———. "Spanish-American Folklore." *JAF* 60 (1947): 373–77.

———. "Spanish and Spanish-American Folk Tales." *JAF* 64 (1951): 151–62.

———. "Spanish Folktales from California." *Hispania* 22:1 (February 1940): 121–44.

———. *The Spanish Language in New Mexico and Southern Colorado.* Publications of the Historical Society of New Mexico, 16 (1911).

———. "Speech-Mixture in New Mexico." In *The Pacific Ocean in History,* eds. H. M. Stephens and H. E. Bolton. New York: The Macmillan Company, 1917.

————. *Studies in New Mexican Spanish.* New Mexico University Language Series, 1:2. Albuquerque: New Mexico University, 1909.

Espinosa, Aurelio M., and J. Manuel Espinosa. "The Texans: A New Mexican Folk Play of the Middle Nineteenth Century." *The New Mexico Quarterly Review* 13:3 (Autumn 1943): 299–309.

Espinosa, Gilberto. *Heroes, Hexes, and Haunted Halls.* Albuquerque: Calvin Hall, 1972.

Espinosa, José Edmundo. *Saints in the Valley: Christian Sacred Images in the History, Life, and Folk Art of Spanish New Mexico,* revised edition. Albuquerque: University of New Mexico Press, 1967.

Espinosa, José Manuel. *Cuentos de Cuanto Hay/Tales from Spanish New Mexico,* ed. and trans. by Joe Hayes. Albuquerque: University of New Mexico Press, 1998.

————. "Spanish Folklore in the Southwest: The Pioneer Studies of Aurelio M. Espinosa." *The Americas* 35 (1978): 219–37.

————. *Spanish Folk-Tales from New Mexico.* New York: Publications of the American Folklore Society, Memoir Series, Volume 30 (1937).

Fernández Mines, Rosa. "Hispanic Wedding Customs in New Mexico: Yesterday and Today." *Selected Proceedings of the 3rd Annual Conference on Minority Studies,* Vol. 3, April 1975. In *Essays on Minority Folklore.* La Crosse: University of Wisconsin Press, 1977.

Ferriss, Susan, and Ricardo Sandoval. *The Fight in the Fields: César Chávez and the Farm Workers Movement.* New York: Harcourt Brace, 1997.

Fisher, Nora. *Rio Grande Textiles.* Santa Fe: Museum of New Mexico Press, 1994.

Flores, Richard R. "The Corrido and the Emergence of Texas-Mexican Social Identity." *Journal of American Folklore* 105 (1992): 166–82.

————. *Los Pastores: History and Performance in the Mexican Shepherd's Play of South Texas.* Washington, DC: Smithsonian Institution Press, 1995.

Florescano, Enrique. *The Myth of Quetzalcoatl,* trans. Raul Velázquez. Baltimore, MD: Johns Hopkins University Press, 1999.

Folktales from the Patagonia Area, Santa Cruz County, Arizona. Tucson: University of Arizona General Bulletin, 13, 1949.

Ford, Karen Cowan. *Las Yerbas de Ia Gente: A Study of Hispano-American Medicinal Plants.* Anthropological Papers No. 60, Museum of Anthropology. Ann Arbor: University of Michigan Press , 1975.

Foster, George M. "Relationships between Spanish and Spanish-American Folk Medicine." *JAF* 66 (1953): 201–17.

Foster, Nelson, and Linda S. Cordell. *Chiles to Chocolate: Food the Americas Gave the World.* Tucson: University of Arizona Press, 1992.

Freedman, Samuel G. "Los Lobos: Hot North-of-the-Border Mexican Rock." *Utne Reader* 22 (July–August 1987): 92–98.

Freire-Marreco, Barbara. "New-Mexican Spanish Folklore." *JAF* 29 (1916): 536–46.

Freud, Sigmund. *Jokes and Their Relation to the Unconscious.* New York: Norton, 1960.

Fuentes, Dagoberto, and José A. López. *Barrio Language: First Dictionary of Caló.* Los Angeles: Southland Press, 1974.

Fuson, Robert H. "The Origin of the Word *Gringo.*" *Singers and Storytellers,* eds. Mody C. Boatright, Wilson M. Hudson, and Allen Maxwell. *PTFS* 30 (1961): 282–84.

Galindo, Letticia D. "Dispelling the Male-Only Myth: Chicanas and Caló." *The Bilingual Review/La Revista Bilingüe* 17 (1992): 3–35.

———. "The Language of Gangs, Drugs, and Prison Life among Chicanas." *Latino Studies Journal* (September 1993): 23–43.

Gallegos, Esperanza. "The Piñata-Making Tradition in Laredo." In *Hecho en Tejas: Texas-American Folk Arts and Crafts,* ed. Joe S. Graham. Denton: University of Texas Press, 1991.

Galván, Roberto A., and Richard V. Teschner. *El Diccionario del Español Chicano/ The Dictionary of the Chicano Spanish.* Lincolnwood, IL: National Textbook Company, 1985.

Gamio, Manuel. *Mexican Immigration to the United States: A Study of Human Migration and Adjustment.* Chicago, 1930/New York: Dover Publications, 1970.

García, Nasario. *Recuerdos de los Viejitos. Tales of the Río Puerco.* Albuquerque: University of New Mexico Press, 1992.

———. *Comadres: Hispanic Women of the Río Puerco Valley.* Albuquerque: University of New Mexico Press, 1997.

———. *Más Antes: Hispanic Folklore of the Río Puerco Valley.* Santa Fe: Museum of New Mexico Press, 1997.

———. *Tales of Witchcraft and the Supernatural in the Pecos Valley.* Santa Fe, New Mexico: Western Edge Press, 1999.

García, Richard A. "César Chávez: A Personal and Historical Testimony." *Pacific Historical Review* 63 (May 1994): 225–34.

Garza, Humberto. "Owl-Bewitchment in the Lower Rio Grande Valley." In *Singers and Storytellers,* eds. Mody C. Boatright, Wilson N. Hudson, and Allen Maxwell. *PTFS,* 30 (1961): 218–25.

de la Garza, Sarah Amira. *María Speaks: Journeys into the Mysteries of the Mother in my Life as a Chicana.* New York: Peter Lang Publishing Inc., 2004.

Gaspar de Alba, Alicia. "Malinche's Revenge." In *Feminism, Nation and Myth: La Malinche,* ed. Rolando Romero and Amanda Nolacea Harris. Houston: Arte Público Press, 2005.

———. "Malinchista, A Myth Revised." In *Feminism, Nation and Myth: La Malinche.* ed. Rolando Romero and Amanda Nolacea Harris. Houston: Arte Público Press, 2005.

Gil, Carlos B. "Lydia Mendoza: Houstonian and First Lady of Mexican American Song." In *Chicano Border Culture and Folklore,* ed. José Villarino and Arturo Ramírez. San Diego, CA: Marin Publications, Inc., 1992.

Gillmor, Frances, ed. "*Los Pastores* Number: Folk Plays of Hispanic America-Foreword." *WF* 16 (1957): 229–31.

Glantz, Margo, ed. *La Malinche, Sus Padres y Sus Hijos.* Mexico City: Facultad de Filosofía y Letras, Universidad Nacional Autónoma de México, 1994.

Glazer, Mark. "Continuity and Change in Legends: Two Mexican American Examples." In *Perspectives on Contemporary Legend: Proceedings of the Conference on Contemporary Legend.* Conference Papers Series No. 4, ed. Jillian Bennet and Paul Smith. Sheffield, UK: Center for English Cultural Tradition and Language (CECTAL), 1984.

———. A *Dictionary of Mexican American Proverbs.* New York: Greenwood Press, 1987.

———. *Flour from Another Sack and Other Proverbs, Folk Beliefs, Tales, Riddles, and Recipes,* revised edition. Edinburg, TX: Pan American University Press, 1994.

———. "Mexican-American Culture and Urban Legend: The Case of the Vanishing Hitchhiker." *Urban Resources* 4 (1987b): 31–36.

———. "The Mexican American Legend in the Rio Grande Valley: An Overview." *Borderlands* 10 (Fall 1986): 143–160.

———. "La Muerte: Continuity and Social Organization in a Chicano Legend." *Southwest Folklore* 4 (Winter 1980): 1–13.

———. "The Rio Grande Folklore Archive: A Summary of Methods of Collection, of Classification, and of Holdings." *Southwest Folklore* 5 (1981a): 16–23.

———. "*La Sirena del Mar:* An Interpretation of Symbolism, Disobedience, and Transformation in a Mexican-American Example." *Southwest Folklore* 5 (1981): 55–69.

Goldberg, Julia. "Rita Younis: The Next Generation in the Delgado Tin Tradition." *Spanish Market* (July 1994): 20–21.

Gonzales, Alicia María. "Murals—Fine, Popular, or Folk Art?" *Aztlán: International Journal of Chicano Studies Research* 13 (1982): 149–63.

Gonzales, Dolores, ed. *Canciones y Juegos de Nuevo Mexico/Songs and Games of New Mexico.* Writers' Program of the Works Progress Administration, New Mexico. South Brunswick, NJ: A. S. Barnes, 1974.

———. "Mexican Popular Music at Mid-Century: The Role of José Alfredo Jiménez and the Canción Ranchera." *Studies in Latin American Popular Culture* 2 (1983): 99114.

Gonzales, Jovita. "The Bullet Swallower," in *Puro Mexicano,* ed. J. Frank Dobie. *PTFS* 12 (1935): 107–14.

———. *Dew on the Thorn,* ed. and introduced by Jose E. Limón. Houston, TX: Arte Público Press, 1997.

———. "Folk-Lore of the Texas Mexican *Vaquero,*" in *Texas and Southwestern Lore,* ed, J. Frank Dobie. *PTFS,* 6 (1927), 7–22. Also reprinted in *Aztlán: An Anthology of Mexican-American Literature,* eds. Luis Valdez and Stan Steiner. New York: Vintage Books, 1972.

———. "Tales and Songs of the Texas-Mexicans," in *Man, Bird, and Beast,* ed. J. Frank Dobie. *PTFS* 8 (1930): 86–116.

———. *The Woman Who Lost Her Soul and Other Stories.* Houston: Arte Público Press, 2000.

Gonzales, Rafael Jesús. "Pachuco: The Birth of a Creole Language." *Arizona Quarterly* (Tucson, Arizona) 23:4 (Winter 1967): 343–56.

Gonzales, René Abelardo. "The *Pastorelas* of Rio Grande City and Hebbronville, Texas," *Folklore Annual of the University Folklore Association,* 4 and 5 (1972–1973).

Published by Austin: the Center for Intercultural Studies in Folklore and Oral History, University of Texas at Austin, 10–22.

González, Deena. "Malinche Triangulated, Historically Speaking." In *Feminism, Nation and Myth: La Malinche,* Ed. Rolando Romero and Amanda Nolacea Harris. Houston: Arte Público Press, 2005.

Goodwyn, Frank. "Folklore of the King Ranch Mexicans." In *Southwestern Lore,* ed. J. Frank Dobie. *PTFS* 9 (1931): 48–63.

———. "An Interpretation of the Hispanic Folk Hero, Pedro de Urdemalas," unpublished dissertation, Romance Literature, University of Texas, 1946.

Graham, Joe S. "The *Caso:* An Emic Genre of Folk Narrative." In *"And Other Neighborly Names": Social Process and Cultural Image in Texas Folklore,* ed. Richard Bauman and Roger D. Abrahams. Austin: University of Texas Press, 1981.

———. "Folk Medicine and Intracultural Diversity among West Texas Mexican Americans." *Western Folklore* 49 (1985): 168–93.

———, ed. *Hecho en Tejas: Texas-Mexican Folk Arts and Crafts.* Denton: University of North Texas Press, 1993.

———. *Hispanic-American Material Culture: An Annotated Directory of Collections, Sites, Archives, and Festivals in the Unite States.* New York: Greenwood Press, 1989.

———. "The Jacal in South Texas: The Origins and Form of a Folk House." In *Hecho en Tejas: Texas-Mexican Folk Arts and Crafts,* ed. Joe S. Graham, Denton: University of North Texts Press, 1991.

———. *El Rancho in South Texas: Continuity and Change from 1750.* Denton: University of North Texas Press, 1993.

———. "The Role of the *Curandero* in the Mexican American Folk Medicine System in West Texas," in *American Folk Medicine: A Symposium,* ed. Wayland D. Hand, Publications of the UCLA Center for the Study of Comparative Folklore and Mythology, 4. Berkeley and Los Angeles: University of California Press, 1976.

———. *Tejano Folk Arts and Crafts in South Texas/Artesanía Tejana.* Kingsville, TX: John E. Conner Museum, 1990.

Granger, Byrd Howell. "Witchcraft in the Southwest." *Western Review* (Silver City, NM) 5:1 (Summer 1968): 3–12.

Green, Thomas A. *Folklore: An Encyclopedia of Beliefs, Customs, Tales, Music, and Art.* Vols. 1 and 2. Santa Barbara: ABC-CLIO, 1997.

Grider, Sylvia Ann. "Con Safos: Mexican-Americans, Names and Graffiti." *JAF* 88 (1975): 132–42.

Griffith, James S. *Beliefs and Holy Places: A Spiritual Geography of the Pimería Alta.* Tucson: University of Arizona Press, 1992.

———. "Cascarones: A Folk Art Form of Southern Arizona." *International Folklore Review: Folklore Studies from Overseas* 9 (1993): 34–40.

———. "Quetzalcoatl on the Border? Mestizo Water Serpent Beliefs of the Pimería Alta." *Western Folklore* 49 (October 1990): 391–400.

———. *A Shared Space: Folklife in the Arizona-Sonora Borderlands.* Logan: Utah State University Press, 1995.

Griswold del Castillo, Richard, and Richard A. García. *César Chávez: A Life of Struggle and Sacrifice.* Norman: University of Oklahoma Press, 1995.

Griswold del Castillo, Richard, and Rita Sánchez. "The Corrido de César Estrada Chávez: A Need to Remember." In *Aztlán Chicano Culture and Folklore: An Anthology,* ed. José Pepe Villarino and Arturo Ramírez. New York: McGraw- Hill Companies, Inc., 1997.

Guerra, Fermina. "Mexican Animal Tales." In *Backwoods to Border,* eds. Mody C. Boatright and Donald Day. *PTFS* 18 (1943): 188–94.

Guevara, Ruben. "The View from the Sixth Street Bridge: The History of Chicano Rock." In *The First Rock & Roll Confidential Report,* ed. Dave Marsh. New York: Pantheon Books, 1985.

Gutiérrez, Ramón A. "The Politics of Theater in Colonial New Mexico." In *Reconstructing a Chicano/a Literary Heritage: Hispanic Colonial Literature of the Southwest,* ed. María Herrera-Sobek. Tucson: University of Arizona Press, 1993.

———. "El Santuario de Chimayó: A Syncretic Shrine in New Mexico." In *Feasts and Celebrations in North American Ethnic Communities,* ed. Ramón A. Gutiérrez and Genevieve Fabré. Albuquerque: University of New Mexico Press, 1995.

Gutiérrez, Ramón A., and Genevieve Fabré, eds. *Feasts and Celebrations in North American Ethnic Communities.* Albuquerque: University of New Mexico Press, 1995.

Hall, Douglas Kent. "Los Matachines: Dancers Keep Old World Tradition Alive." *New Mexico Magazine,* December 1986, 42–47.

Hallenbeck, Cleve, and Juanita H. Williams. *Legends of the Spanish Southwest.* Glendale, California: The Arthur H. Clark Company, 1938.

Halseth, Odd. "*Santos* of the Southwest." *El Palacio* 25 (1968): 436–39.

Hand, Wayland D. *American Folk Legend.* Berkeley: University of California Press, 1979.

———. "The Evil-Eye in Its Folk Medical Aspects: A Survey of North America." In *The Evil Eye: A Folklore Casebook,* ed. Alan Dundes. New York: Garland Publishing, Inc., 1981.

Haralson, Marianne. "Joyful Customs Reign at Mexican Weddings." *San Antonio Express News,* June 15, 1980.

Harmeyer, Alice J. "Devil Stories from Las Vegas, New Mexico." *Hoosier Folklore* 6 (1947): 37–39.

Harpole, Patricia. *Los Mariachis! An Introduction to Mexican Mariachi Music.* Danbury, CT: World Music Press, 1990.

Harris, Mary G. *Cholas: Latino Girls and Gangs.* New York: AMS Press, 1988.

Harris, Max. "Muhammed and the Virgin: Folk Dramatizations of Battles between Moors and Christians in Modern Spain." *The Drama Review* (Cambridge, MA) 38 (Spring 1994): 45–62.

———. "Moctezuma's Daughter: The Role of La Malinche in Mesoamerican Dance." *Journal of American Folklore* 109 (Spring 1996): 149–77.

————."The Return of Moctezuma: Oaxaca's 'Danza de la Pluma' and New Mexico's 'Danza de los Matachines.'" *The Drama Review* (Cambridge, MA) 41 (Spring 1997): 106–35.

Harwell, Thomas Meade. *Studies in Texan Folklore, Rio Grande Valley Lore: Twelve Folklore Studies with introductions, Commentaries and a Bounty of Notes.* Lewiston, ID: E. Mellen Press, 1997.

Hatch, E. Le Roy, M.D. "Home Remedies Mexican Style." *WF* 28 (1969): 163–68.

Hattersley-Drayton, Karana, Joyce M. Bishop, and Tomás Ybarra-Frausto, eds. *From the Inside Out: Perspectives on Mexican and Mexican-American Folk Art.* San Francisco: The Mexican Museum, 1989.

Hawes, Bess Lomax. "La Llorona in Juvenile Hall." *WF* 27 (1968): 153–70.

Heisley, Michael. "Lummis and Mexican-American Folklore." In *Charles. F. Lummis: The Centennial Exhibition Commemorating His Tramp across the Continent,* ed. Daniela P. Moneta. Los Angeles: Southwest Museum, 1985.

Heisley, Michael, and Mary MacGregor-Villarreal. *More Than a Tradition: Mexican American Nacimientos in Los Angeles.* Los Angeles: Southwest Museum, 1991.

Helm, June, ed. *Spanish-Speaking People in the United States.* Proceedings of the 1968. Annual Spring Meeting of the American Ethnological Society. Seattle: University of Washington Press, 1968.

Henderson, Alice Corbin. *Brothers of Light: The Penitentes of the Southwest.* New York: Harcourt, Brace, and Co., 1937/Chicago: Rio Grande Press, 1962.

Hernández, Guillermo. *Canciones de La Raza.* Berkeley, CA: El Fuego de Aztlán, 1978.

Herrera-Sobek, María. "Américo Paredes: A Tribute." *Mexican Studies/Estudios Mexicanos* 16:2 (Winter 2000): 235–62.

————. "Américo Paredes." *Encyclopedia Dictionary of Chicano Literature.* Ed. Julio Martínez and Francisco A. Lomelí. Westport CT: Greenwood Press, 1985.

————. "The Acculturation Process of the Chicana in the *Corrido.*" *De Colores Journal* 6 (1982): 7–16. Shorter version published in *Proceedings of the Pacific Coast Council of Latin American Studies* 9 (1982): 25–34.

————. *The Bracero Experience: Elitelore versus Folklore.* Los Angeles: University of California Press, 1979.

————. "Bride Rape in the *Corrido*: A Feminist Analysis." *Scandinavian Yearbook of Folklore* 48 (1992):127–44.

————. "Canción Ranchera." In *Encyclopedia of Latin American History and Culture.* New York: Charles Scribner's Sons, 1996.

————. "Chicano/a Oral Traditions." In *Teaching Oral Traditions,* ed. Michael Foley. New York: Modern Language Association Publication Series, 1999, 216–24.

————."Chicano Literary Folklore." In *Chicano Studies: A Multi-disciplinary Approach,* ed. Eugene E. García, Francisco A. Lomelí, and Isidro Ortiz García. New York: Teachers College Press, 1984.

————. "The *Comedia de Adán y Eva* and Language Acquisition." In *Reconstructing a Chicano/a Literary Heritage: Hispanic Colonial Literature of the Southwest,* ed. María Herrera-Sobek. Tucson: University of Arizona Press, 1993.

————. "The Corrido as Hypertext: Undocumented Mexican Immigrant Films and the Mexican/Chicano Ballad." In *Culture across Borders: Mexican Immigration and Popular Culture,* ed. David R. Maciel and María Herrera-Sobek. Tucson: University of Arizona Press, 1998.

————. "Corridos de la Frontera: La Representación del Emigrante en corridos contemporáneos de la frontera." México City: Archivo Nacional de la Historia de México, 2000.

————. "Critical *Mestizaje* and National Identity: Discourse on Difference in Américo Paredes." *Journal of American Studies, Turkey* 20 (2004): 3–16.

————. "Danger! Children at Play: Patriarchal Ideology and the Construction of Gender in Spanish Language Hispanic/Chicano Children's Songs and Games." In *Chicana Changing Traditions*, eds. Olga Nájera-Rámirez and Norma Cantú. Urbana: University of Illinois Press, 2002.

————. "Décimas de *Amor* y *Despecho*: Representation of Women in the Chicano *Décima*." *Aztlán: International Journal of Chicano Studies*, 1989.

————. "'La Delgadina': Incest and Patriarchal Structure in a Spanish/Chicano Romance-Corrido." *Studies in Latin American Popular Culture Journal* 5 (Spring, 1986): 90–107.

————. "Death of an Immigrant." In *Encuentro Internacional de la Literatura de la Frontera /Borderlands Literature: Towards an Integrated Perspective*, eds. Harry Polkingorn, José Manuel Di Bella, and Rogelio Reyes. Mexicali, Baja California: XIII Ayuntamiento de Mexicali, 1990.

————. "The Defiant Voice: Gender Conflict in a Mexican/Chicano *Pastorela* Drama." *Gestos* (1991): 63–77.

————. "The Devil in the Discotheque: A Semiotic Analysis of a Contemporary Legend." In *Monsters with Iron Teeth: Perspectives on Contemporary Legend,* vol. 3, ed. Jillian Bennet and Paul Smith. Sheffield, UK: Sheffield Academic Press, for the International Society for Contemporary Legend Research in Association with the Centre for English Cultural Tradition and Language, 1988.

————. "The Discourse of Love and Despecho: Representations of Women in the Chicano Décima." *Aztlán, International Journal of Chicano Studies Research* 18 (Spring 1987): 69–82.

————. "Drama: The Spanish Borderlands." In *Encyclopedia of the North American Colonies*, vol. III. New York: Charles Scribner's Sons, 1993.

————. "Folkore and Politics and the Construction of Magic Realism in Ana Castillo's *So Far From God.*" In *Literatura Chicana: Reflexiones y ensayos críticos*, eds. Rosa Murillo Sánchez and Manuel Villar Raso. Granada, Spain: Editorial Comares, 2000. 193–202.

————. "From *Adelitas* to Farm Workers: The Representation of Chicanas in Painting and Folksong." In *Ballads and Boundaries: Narrative Singing in an Intercultural Context*, ed. James Porter. Los Angeles, CA: Department of Ethnomusicology and Systematic Musicology, 1995. 119–29.

————. *Gender and Print Culture: New Perspectives on International Ballad Studies.* Madison, WI: Impressions, Kommision Für Volksdictung—Société International D'Ethnologie et de Folklore, 1991.

———. "Gender and Rhetorical Strategies in Mexican Ballads and Songs: Plant and Mineral Metaphors." *Lore and Language: The Journal of the Centre for English Cultural Tradition and Language* 12:1–2, (1994): 97–112.

———. "'Heraclio Bernal': the Hero Monomyth Structure in the Mexican Ballad." *Scandinavian Yearbook of Folklore* 43 (1988): 89–107. A shorter version of this article appeared in *Ballads and Other Genres: Balladen Und Andere Gattungen*. Zagrab, Yugoslavia: Institute of Folklore Research, 1988, 53–67.

———. "Hispanic Oral Traditions: Form and Content." In *Handbook of Hispanic Cultures in the United States: Literature and Art*, ed. Francisco Lomelí. Madrid, Spain: Arte Publico Press, 1993, 226–33.

———. "Indio, Gringo and Gachupín: Ethnic Construction in the Mexican Ballad." In 27th International Ballad Conference. Ed. Marjetka Golez. Ljubljana, Slovenia: Institute of Ethnomusicology Scientific Research Centre of the Slovenian Academy of Sciences and Arts, 1999.

———. "In Search of La Malinche: Pictorial Representations of a Mytho-Historical Figure." In *Feminism, Nation and Myth: La Malinche,* ed. Rolando Romero and Amanda Nolacea Harris. Houston: Arte Público Press, 2005.

———. "Joaquín Murieta: Mito, leyenda e historia." In *Entre la magia y la historia*, ed. Manuel Valenzuela. Tijuana, Baja California: El Colegio de la Frontera Norte, Programa Cultural de las Fronteras, 1992.

———. "Luis Valdez's *La Pastorela:* 'The Shepherd's Tale': Tradition, Hybridity, and Transformation." *Estudios Ingleses* 43 (2001): 133–44.

———. "Memory, Folklore, Reader's Response, and Community Construction in *Mi abuela fumaba puros/My Grandma Smoked Cigars*." In *Sabine R. Ulibarrí: Critical Essays*, ed. María Duke Dos Santos and Patricia de la Fuente. Albuquerque: University of New Mexico Press, 1995.

———. "The Mexican/Chicano Pastorela: Toward a Theory of the Evolution of a Folk Play." In *Feasts and Celebrations in North American Ethnic Communities,* ed. Ramón A. Gutiérrez and Genevieve Fabré. Albuquerque: University of New Mexico Press, 1995.

———. *The Mexican Corrido: A Feminist Analysis*. Bloomington: Indiana University Press, 1990.

———. "Mexican Immigration and Petroleum: A Folklorist's Perspective." *New Scholar* 9 (1984): 99–110. Issue reprinted 1986.

———. "The Mexican Manda: Structure and Social Function of a Religious Folk Narrative." Proceedings of the 8th Congress of the International Society for Folk Narrative Research. Bergen, Norway: 1986.

———. "Mica, Migra, and Coyotes: Contemporary Issues in Mexican Immigrant Corridos and Canciones." In *Creative Ethnicity: Symbols and Strategies of Contemporary Ethnic Life,* ed. Stephen Stearn and John Allan Cicala. Logan: Utah State University Press, 1991.

———. "Mothers, Lovers, and Soldiers: Images of Women in the Mexican *Corrido*." *Keystone Folklore Journal* 23:1 (1979): 53–77.

————. "La mujer traidora: Arquetipo estructurante en el corrido." *Cuadernos Americanos* 235 (marzo-abril, 1981): 230–42

————. "Mules, Chickens, and Toads: Animal Metaphors, Women and Humor in the Mexican *Corrido*." In *Recent Ballad Research.* Vol. 1. London, UK: Folklore Society Library Publications, No. 4. 1990, 19–33.

————. "Myths, Murals and Motherhood: Global Nature of Chicana Artistic Production." In *The Borders in All of Us*, eds. William A. Little, Selase W. Williams, Irene Vásquez, Munashe Furusa, and Jung-Sun Park. Northridge, CA: New World African Press, 2006, 248–64.

————. *Northward Bound: The Mexican Immigrant Experience in Ballad and Song.* Bloomington: Indiana University Press, 1993.

————. "Los parricidas: El mito de Edipo y las confrontaciones padre e hijo en el corrido." *Estudios de Folklore y Literatura dedicados a Mercedes Díaz Roig,* eds. Beatriz Garza Cuarón and Yvette Jiménez de Báez. México City: Centro de Estudios Lingüísticos y Literarios, El Colegio de México, 1992, 573–90.

————. "The Pretty *Señorita* Motif: Territorial Conquest and Interracial Love in Cowboy Ballads." In *III Hispanic Cultures in the U.S.A.: Gender, Self and Society,* ed. Renate von Bardeleben. Germershiem, Germany, 1993, 191–202.

————. "Protesta social, folklore e ideología feminista en escritoras chicanas." In *El poder hispano,* ed. Alberto Moncada Lorenzo, Carmen Flys Junquera, and José Antonio Gurpegui Palacios. Alcalá de Henares, Spain: Universidad de Alcalá, Centro de Estudios Norteamericanos, 1994, 455–63.

————. "Protesta social e ideología socialista en el corrido." In *Pensamiento y Literatura en América Latina,* Memoria del XX Congreso del IILI, ed. Matyas Horanyi. Budapest, Hungary: Departamento de Español de la Universidad Eotvos Lorand 1982, 287–302.

————. *Reconstructing a Chicano/a Literary Heritage: Hispanic Colonial Literature of the Southwest.* Tucson: University of Arizona Press, 1993.

————. "'Rosita Alvírez': Gender Conflict and the Medieval Exemplum in the Corrido." *Centro* 3:2 (Spring, 1991): 105–10.

————. *Santa Barraza: Artist of the Borderlands.* College Station: Texas A&M University Press, 2001.

————. "Social Protest, Folklore, and Feminist Ideology in Chicana Prose and Poetry." In *Folklore, Literature, and Cultural Theory: Collected Essays,* ed. Cathy Lynn Preston. New York: Garland Publishing, Inc., 1995.

————. "Toward the Promised Land: La Frontera as Myth and Reality in Ballad and Song." *Aztlán: International Journal of Chicano Studies Research* 21 (1–2) (1992–1996): 227–261.

————. "The Theme of Drug-Smuggling in the Mexican *Corrido*." *Revista Chicano-Riqueña* 7:4 (1979): 49–61.

————. "Transformaciones Culturales: La Tradición Oral Mexicana y la Literatura de Escritoras Chicanas." *Foro Hispánico: Revista hispánica de los países bajos.* No. 8 (Julio, 1995): 53–61.

———. "The Transnational Imaginary and Narcocorridos: Violence, Drugs, and Transgressive Discourse in Mexican Ballads." In *Violence and Transgression in World Minority Literatures,* ed. Rüdiger Ahrens, María Herrera-Sobek, Karin Ikas, and Francisco A. Lomelí. Heidelberg: Universitätsverlag, Winter, 2005.

———. "The Treacherous Woman Archetype: Structuring Agent in the *Corrido.*" *Aztlán: International Journal of Chicano Studies Research* 13 (Spring, 1982): 136–47.

———. "Verbal Play in Mexican Immigrant Jokes." *Southwest Folklore Journal* 4 (1980): 14–22.

———. *Violence and Transgression in World Minority Literatures,* ed. Rüdiger Ahrens, María Herrera-Sobek, Karin Ikas and Francisco A. Lomelí. Heidelberg, Germany: Universitatsverlag, 2005.

Herrera-Sobek, María, James Wilkie, and Edna Monzón de Wilkie. "The Theory of Elitelore and Folklore: *One Hundred Years of Solitude* as a Test Case." *Journal of Latin American Lore* 4 (Winter, l979): l83–223.

Herrera-Sobek, María, and Virginia Sánchez-Korrol, eds. *Recovering the U.S. Hispanic Literary Heritage. Volume IV.* Houston: Arte Público Press, 2000.

Hinckle, Catherine J. "The Devil in New Mexican Spanish Lore." *WF* 8 (l949): 123–25.

Hinojosa, Francisco G. "Notes on the Pachuco: Stereotypes, History, and Dialect." *Atisbos: Journal of Chicano Research* (Summer 1975): 53–65.

Hobsbawn, Eric. *Bandits.* New York: Delacorte Press, 1969.

Holmes, Urban Tigner. "Origin of 'Guarache.'" *American Notes and Queries* 60:822 (1942): 58–59.

Holscher, Louis M., Celestino Fernández, and Laura L. Cummings. "From Local Tradition to International Phenomenon: 'La Bamba.'" *Renato Rosaldo Lecture Series Monograph Series 1989-I 990,* no. 7. Tucson: Mexican American Studies and Research Center, University of Arizona, 1991.

———. *Homenaje a Nuestras Curanderas/Honoring Our Healers,* ed. Luz Alvarez. Oakland, CA: Latina Press, 1996.

Holt, Roy. "Frijoles," in *Texan Stomping Grounds,* eds. J. Frank Dobie, Mody C. Boatright, and Harry H. Ransom. *PTFS* 17 (1941): 49–58.

Horowitz, Ruth. "The Power of Ritual in a Chicano Community: A Young Woman's Status and Expanding Family Ties." *Marriage and Family Review* 19 (Winter 1993): 257–81.

Howe, Charles E. B. "Joaquín Murieta de Castillo." In *California Gold-Rush Plays,* ed. and introduced by Glenn Loney. New York: Performing Arts Journal Publications, 1983.

Hudson, Wilson M. "The Fisherman and the Snake of Many Colors." In *The Healer of Las Olmos and Other Mexican Lore,* ed. Wilson M. Hudson. *PTFS* 24 (1951): 132–36.

———. "To Whom God Wishes to Give He Will Give," in *Texas Folk and Folklore,* eds. Mody C. Boatright, Wilson M. Hudson, and Allen Maxwell. *PTFS* 26 (1954): 46–49.

———. "The Twelve Truths in the Spanish Southwest," in *Mesquite and Willow,* eds. Mody C. Boatright, Wilson M. Hudson, and Allen Maxwell. Dallas, TX: Southern Methodist University Press, 1957.

Huerta, Jorge A. "Chicano Teatro: A Background." *Aztlán* 2:2 (1971): 63–78.

Hurt, Wesley R, and Herbert W. Dick. "Spanish-American Pottery from New Mexico." *El Palacio* 53 (1946): 280–88, 307–12.

Husband, Eliza. *Geography of a Symbol: The Hispanic Yard Shrines of Tucson,* Arizona. Tucson: University of Arizona, 1985.

Igo, John. "Julia Nott Waugh on *Los Pastores.*" In *Diamond Bessie and the Shepherds,* ed. Wilson M. Hudson. *PTFS* 36 (1972): 15–25.

———. *Los Pastores: An Annotated Bibliography with an Introduction.* San Antonio, TX: San Antonio College Library, 1967

———. "Los Pastores: A Triple Tradition." *Journal of Popular Culture* 19 (Winter 1985): 131–38.

Ives, Ronald L. "The Sonoran 'Primer Montezuma' Legends." *WF* 9 (1950): 321–25.

Ingalls, Zoe. "Studying New Mexico's 'Saddest Songs.'" *Chronicle of Higher Education,* September 13, 1996, B11.

Jackson, Joseph Henry. *Bad Company: The Story of California's Legendary and Actual Stage-robbers, Bandits, Highwaymen and Outlaws from the Fifties to the Eighties.* New York: Harcourt, Brace and Co., 1949.

Jaquith, James R. "Cowboy de Medianoche: Mexican Highway Folklore," *The New Scholar,* 5:1 (1975), 39–72.

Jaramillo, Cleofas M. *The Genuine New Mexico Tasty Recipes.* Santa Fe, NM: Ancient City Press, 1981.

———. *Romance of a Little Village Girl.* San Antonio, TX: Naylor Co, 1955.

———. *Shadows of the Past (Sombras del Pasado).* Santa Fe: Seton Village Press, 1941.

Jasper, Pat, and Kay Turner, eds. *Art among Us/Arte entre Nosotros: Mexican American Folk Art of San Antonio.* San Antonio, TX: San Antonio Museum of Art, 1986.

Jente, Richard. "El Refrán." *Folklore Américas* 7:1–2 (1947): 1–11.

Jiménez, Baldeman A. "Cuentos de Susto,.." In *The Golden Log,* eds. Mody C. Boatright, Wilson M. Hudson, and Allen Maxwell. *PTFS,* 31 (1962): 156–64.

Jiménez, Carlos M. *The Mexican American Heritage.* Berkeley, CA: TQS Publications. 1992.

Johnson, William Templeton. "Bell Towers and Capitals." *Survey Graphic* 19:2 (1931): 158–59.

Johnston, Francis W. "Tension and Speech Play in Mexican-American Folklore." In *And Other Neighborly Names: Social Process and Cultural Image in Texas Folklore,* ed. Richard Bauman and Roger D. Abrahams. Austin: University of Texas Press, 1981.

———. "The Vaginal Serpent and Other Themes from Mexican-American Women's Lore." In *Women's Folklore, Women's Culture,* ed. Rosan A. Jordan and Susan J. Kalcik. Publications of the American Folklore & Society New Series. Philadelphia: University of Pennsylvania Press, 1985.

———. *The Wonder of Guadalupe: The Origin and Cult of the Miraculous Image of the Blessed Virgin in Mexico.* Chulmleigh, Devon, UK: Augustine Pub. Co., 1981.

Jones, Hester. "New Mexico Embroidered Bedspreads." *El Palacio* 37 (1934): 97–104.

Jones, Jack. *Vásquez: California's Forgotten Bandit.* Carlsbad, CA: Akira Press, 1996.

Jordan, Terry G. *Texas Graveyards: A Cultural Legacy.* Austin: University of Texas Press, 1982.

Jordan De Caro, Rosan A. "Ethnic Identity and the Lore of the Supernatural." *JAF* 88 (1975): 370–82.

———. "Language Loyalty and Folklore Studies: The Mexican-American." *WF* 31 (1972): 77–86.

Kahn, David, "Chicano Street Murals: People's Art in the East Los Angeles *Barrio.*" *Aztlan* 6:1 (1975): 117–21.

Kalb, Laurie Beth. *Crafting Devotions: Tradition in Contemporary New Mexico Santos.* Albuquerque: University of New Mexico Press, 1994.

Kanellos, Nicolás. *A History of Hispanic Theatre in the United States: Origins to 1940.* Austin: University of Texas Press, 1990.

———. *Mexican American Theater: Legacy and Reality.* Pittsburgh, PA: Latin American Literary Review Press, 1987.

———, ed. *Mexican American Theatre: Then and Now.* Houston, TX: Arte Publico Press, 1983.

Kany, Charles E. *American-Spanish Euphemisms.* Berkeley and Los Angeles: University of California Press, 1960.

Kaplan, Lawrence, and Lucille N. Kaplan. "Beans of the Americas." In *Chilies to Chocolate: Food the Americas Gave the World,* ed. Nelson and Linda S. Cordell Foster. Tucson: University of Arizona Press, 1992.

Kany, Charles E. "American-Spanish *no más.*" *Hispanic Review* 13 (l945): 72–79.

———. "American-Spanish *recién.*" *Hispanic Review* 13 (1945): 169–73.

———. "American-Spanish *Amalaya* to Express a Wish." *Hispanic Review* 11 (1943): 333–37.

———. *American-Spanish Euphemisms.* Berkeley and Los Angeles: University of California Press, 1960,

———. *American-Spanish Semantics.* Berkeley and Los Angeles: University of California Press, 1960.

Kay, Margarita Artschwager. "Health and Illness in a Mexican American Barrio." In *Ethnic Medicine in the Southwest,* ed. Edward H. Spicer. Tucson: University of Arizona Press, 1977.

Kearney, Michael. "La Llorona as a Social Symbol." *WF* 28 (1969): 199–206.

————. "A World-View Explanation of the Evil Eye." In *The Evil Eye,* ed. Clarence Maloney. New York: Columbia University Press, 1976.

Keller, John Esten. "El cuento folklórico en España y en Hispanoamérica," *Folklore Américas* 14 (1954): 1–14.

Keller, Randall D. "The Past in the Present: The Literary Continuity of Hispanic Folklore in New Mexico and the Southwest." *Bilingual Review* 16 (1991): 99–157.

Kennedy, Diana. *The Tortilla Book.* New York: Harper & Row, 1975.

Kennedy, Mary Jean. "The Gold Cap of Joaquín Murieta." *WF* 13 (1954): 98–100.

Kerchville, F. M., comp. *A Preliminary Glossary of New Mexican Spanish . . . Some Semantic and Philological Facts of the Spanish Spoken in Chilili, New Mexico.* New Mexico University Language Series, 5:3. Albuquerque: New Mexico University, 1934.

Kiev, Ari. *Curanderismo: Mexican-American Folk Psychiatry.* New York: The Free Press, 1968.

Kim, Sojin. *Chicano Graffiti and Murals: The Neighborhood Art of Peter Quezada.* Jackson: University Press of Mississippi, 1995.

Kirtley, Bacil F. "'La Llorona' and Related Themes." *WF* 19 (1960): 155–68.

Kitchener, Amy V. "La Cadena Que no Se Corta: Las Artes Tradicionales de la Comunidad México-Americana de Tucson/The Unbroken Chain: The Traditional Arts of Tucson's Mexican-American Community." *Journal of American Folklore* 110 (1997): 320–23.

————. *The Holiday Yards of Florencio Morales: El Hombre de Las Banderas.* Jackson: University Press of Mississippi, 1994.

————. "Windows into the Past: Mexican American Yardscapes in the Southwest," unpublished paper, Tucson, AZ: Small Manuscripts Collection, Southwest Folklore Center, University of Arizona Library, December 19, 1987.

Klette, Ernest. *The Crimson Trail of Joaquín Murieta.* Los Angeles: Weed Publishing Co., 1928.

Kraul, Edward García and Judith Beatty. *The Weeping Woman: Encounters with La Llorona.* Santa Fe, NM: The Word Process, 1988.

Kuri-Aldana, Mario y Vicente Mendoza Martínez. *Cancionero popular mexicano.* Tomo Uno y Dos. Mexico City: Consejo Nacional para la Cultura y las Artes, 2001.

Lafaye, Jacques. "Mexican Castas Painting." *Artes de México: La Pintura de Castas.* 8 (1998): 81–82.

————. *Quetzalcóatl y Guadalupe: La Formación de la Conciencia en México 1531–1813.* México: Fondo de Cultura Económica, 1983.

Lamadrid, Enrique R. "*Entre Cíbolos Criado:* Images of Native Americans in the Popular Culture of Colonial New Mexico." In *Reconstructing a Chicano/a Literary Heritage: Hispanic Colonial Literature of the Southwest,* ed. Maria Herrera-Sobek. Tucson: University of Arizona Press, 1993.

————. *Hermanitos Comanchitos: Indo-Hispano Rituals of Captivity and Redemption.* Albuquerque: University of New Mexico Press, 2003.

———."The Rogue's Progress: Journeys of the Pícaro from Oral Tradition to Contemporary Chicano Literature of New Mexico." *Multi-Ethnic Literature of the United States* 20 (Summer 1995): 15–35.

———. *Tesoros del Espíritu: A Portrait in Sound of Hispanic New Mexico.* Embudo, NM: El Norte/Academia Publications, 1994.

Latorre, Guisela. "Agustín Casasola's Soldaderas: Malinchismo and the Chicana/o Artist." In *Feminism, Nation and Myth: La Malinche,* ed. Rolando Romero and Amanda Nolacea Harris. Houston: Arte Público Press, 2005.

Laval, Ramón A. *Cuentos de Pedro Urdemales.* Santiago de Chile: Cruz del Sur, 1943.

LaWare, Margaret R. "Encountering Visions of Aztlán: Arguments for Ethnic Pride, Community Activism and Cultural Revitalization in Chicano Murals." *Argumentation and Advocacy* 34 (Winter 1998): 140–54.

Leal, Luis. "Américo Paredes and Modern Mexican American Scholarship." *Ethnic Affairs* 1 (Fall 1987): 1–11.

———. "Joaquín Murrieta in Literature." In *Aztlán: Chicano Culture and Folklore: An Anthology,* ed. José Pepe Villarino and Arturo Ramírez. New York: McCraw-Hill Companies, Inc., 1997.

———. "The Malinche-Llorona Dichotomy: The Evolution of a Myth." In *Feminism, Nation and Myth: La Malinche,* ed. Rolando Romero and Amanda Nolacea Harris. Houston: Arte Público Press, 2005.

———. *Mitos y leyendas de México/Myths and Legends from Mexico.* Santa Barbara: University of California, Santa Barbara, Center for Chicano Studies, 2002.

———. *No Longer Voiceless.* San Diego, CA: Marin Publications, 1995.

Leddy, Betty. "La Llorona Again." *WF* 9 (1950): 363–65.

———. "La Llorona in Southern Arizona." *Western Folklore* 7 (1948): 272–77.

León Portilla, Miguel. *Los Antiguos Mexicanos: A Través de Sus Crónicas y Cantares.* Mexico City: Fondo de Cultura Económica, 1961.

Levy, Jacques E. *César Chávez: Autobiography of La Causa.* New York: Norton, 1975.

Limón, José E. "Agringado Joking in Texas Mexican Society." *Perspectives in Mexican American Studies* 1 (1988): 109–27.

———. *American Encounters: Greater Mexico, the United States, and the Erotics of Culture.* Boston: Beacon Press, 1998.

———."Américo Paredes: A Man from the Border." *Revista Chicano-Riqueña* 8 (l980): 1–5.

———. *Dancing with the Devil: Society and Cultural Poetics in Mexican-American South Texas.* Madison: University of Wisconsin Press, 1994.

———. *Expressive Culture of a Chicano Student Group at the University of Texas at Austin, 1967–1975.* Austin: University of Texas, 1978.

———."Folklore, Gendered Repression, and Cultural Critique: The Case of Jovita González." *Texas Studies in Literature and Language* 35 (Winter 1993): 453–73.

———. "El Folklore y Los Mexicanos en Los Estados Unidos: Una Perspectiva Cultural Marxista." In *La Otra Cara de México: El Pueblo Chicano,* ed. David R. Maciel. Mexico City: Ediciones "El Caballito," 1977.

———."The Folk Performance of 'Chicano' and the Cultural Limits of Political Ideology." In *And Other Neighborly Names: Social Process and Cultural Image in Texas Folklore,* ed. Richard Bauman and Roger D. Abrahams. Austin: University of Texas Press, 1981.

———."History, Chicano Joking, and the Varieties of Higher Education: Tradition and Performance as Critical Symbolic Action." *Journal of the Folklore Institute* 19 (2–3) (1982): 141–66.

———."La Llorona, the Third Legend of Greater Mexico: Cultural Symbols, Women, and the Political Unconscious." In *Between Borders: Essays on Mexicana/Chicana History,* ed. Adelaida R. Castillo. Los Angeles, CA: Floricanto Press, 1988b.

———. *Mexican Ballads, Chicano Poems: History and Influence in Mexican American Social Poetry.* Berkeley: University of California Press, 1992.

———."Oral Tradition and Poetic Influence: Two Poets from Greater Mexico." In *Redefining American Literary History,* ed. A. Lavonne Brown and Jerry W. Ward Jr. New York: Modern Language Association of America, 1990.

———. *The Return of the Mexican Ballad: Américo Paredes and His Anthropological Text as Persuasive Political Performance.* Working Paper Series No, 16. Stanford, CA: Stanford Center for Chicano Research, 1986.

———. "Texas-Mexican Popular Music and Dancing: Some Notes on History and Symbolic Process." *Latin American Music Review* 4 (1983): 229–46.

———. "'La Vieja Inés: A Mexican Folkgame—A Research Note." In *Twice a Minority: Mexican American Women,* ed. Margarita B. Melville. St. Louis, MO: C. V. Mosby Company, 1980b.

Lipsitz, George. *Time Passages: Collective Memory and American Popular Culture.* Minneapolis: University of Minnesota Press, 1990.

Lockpez, Inverna, ed. *Chicano Expressions: A New View in American Art.* New York: INTAR Latin American Gallery, 1986.

Loeffler, Jack, Catherine Loeffler, and Enrique Lamadrid. *La Música de los Viejitos: Hispano Folk Music of the Río Grande del Norte.* Albuquerque: University of New Mexico Press, 1999.

Lomas, Juan. *Teoría y Práctica del Insulto Mexicano/Pueblo Mexicano: Una Recopilación de Juan Lomas.* Mexico City: Posada, 1974.

Lomas Garza, Carmen. *Making Magic Windows: Creating Papel Picado/Cut-Paper Art with Carmen Lomas Garza.* San Francisco: Children's Book Press/Libros para Niños, 1999.

López, Ella T. *Make Mine Menudo: Chicano Cook Book.* La Puente, CA: Sunburst Enterprises, 1976.

Los Pastores: A Christmas Drama of Old Mexico. San Antonio, TX: Treviño Brothers Printing Co., 1949.

Loza, Steven Joseph. *Barrio Rhythm: Mexican American Music in Los Angeles.* Urbana: University of Illinois Press, 1993.

———. *The Musical Life of the Mexican/Chicano People in Los Angeles, 1945–1985: A Study in Maintenance, Change, and Adaptation.* Los Angeles: University of California, 1985.

———. "Origins, Form, and Development of the Son Jarocho: Veracruz, Mexico." *Aztlán: International Journal of Chicano Studies Research* 13 (1982): 257–74.

Lucero-White, Aurora, ed. and trans. *Coloquios de Los Pastores.* Santa Fe, NM: Santa Fe Press, 1940.

———. *Folk-Dances of the Spanish-Colonials of New Mexico.* Santa Fe, NM: Examiner Publishing Co., 1940.

———, ed, *The Folklore of New Mexico, Volume One: Romances, Corridos, Cuentos, Proverbios, Dichos, Adivinanzas.* Santa Fe: Seton Village Press, 1941.

———. *Los Hispanos: Five Essays on the Folkways of the Hispanos as Seen through the Eyes of One of Them.* Denver: Sage Books, Inc., 1947.

———. *Literary Folklore of the Hispanic Southwest.* San Antonio: Naylor Co., 1953.

———. "More about the Matachines." *NMFR* 11 (1963–1964): 7–10.

Lummis, Charles F. *Spanish Songs of Old California.* Los Angeles: Charles F. Lummis, 1923.

———. *Stand Fast Santa Barbara: Save the Centuried Romance of old California in This, Its Last and Most Romantic Stronghold: Sense, Sentiment, Business.* Santa Barbara, CA: Community Arts Association, 1923.

MacAulay, Suzanne. *Colcha Embroidery along the Northern Rio Grande: The Aesthetics of Cultural Inversion in San Luis, Colorado.* Philadelphia: University of Pennsylvania, 1992.

MacGregor-Villarreal, Mary. "Celebrating Las Posadas in Los Angeles." *Western Folklore* 39 (1980): 71–105.

Maciel, David R. "Pochos and Other Extremes in Mexican Cinema: or, El Cine Mexicano Se Va de Bracero, 1922–1963." In *Chicanos and Film: Representation and Resistance,* ed. Chon A. Noriega. Minneapolis: University of Minnesota Press, 1992.

Maciel, David R., and María Herrera-Sobek. *Al otro lado de la frontera: Inmigración y cultura popular.* Mexico City: Siglo 21, 1999. This is translated version of *Culture Across Borders: The Popular Culture of Mexican Immigration.* Tucson: University of Arizona Press, 1998.

Macklin, June. "'All the Good and Bad in This World': Women, Traditional Medicine, and Mexican American Culture." In *Twice a Minority: Mexican American Women,* ed. Margarita B. Melville. St. Louis, MO: Mosby, 1980.

MacLean, Angus. *Legends of the California Bandidos.* Fresno, CA: Pioneer Publishing, 1977.

Madrid-Barela, Arturo. "Alambristas, Braceros, Mojados, Norteños: Aliens in Aztlán, An Interpretative Essay." *Aztlán: International Journal of Chicano Studies Research* 6 (Spring 1975): 27–42.

———. "Pochos: The Different Mexicans, An Interpretive Essay, Part I." *Aztlán: International Journal of Chicano Studies Research* 7 (Spring 1976): 51–64.

Madsen, William. "The Alcoholic Agringado." *American Anthropologist* 66 (1964): 356–57.

———. *A Guide to Mexican Witchcraft.* Mexico City: Editorial Minutiae Mexicana, 1969.

Maestas, José Griego y and Rudolfo A. Anaya. *Cuentos: Tales from the Hispanic Southwest.* Santa Fe: The Museum of New Mexico Press, 1980.

Marks, Susan Tosaw. "Low Riding: One Road to an Ethnic Identity." *Southwest Folklore* 4 (Winter 1980): 40–50.

Márquez, Mary, and Consuelo Pacheco. "Midwivery Lore in New Mexico." *American Journal of Nursing* (New York) 64:9 (September 1964): 81–84.

Martínez, Cervando, and Harry W. Martin. "Folk Diseases among Urban Mexican-Americans: Etiology, Symptoms, and Treatment." *Journal of the American Medical Association* 196 (April 11, 1966): 147–50.

Martínez, Yleana. "Cracking Cascarones." *Hispanic* (March 1996): 49–50.

Martínez-Chávez, Diana. "Quinceañeras." *Hispanic* (October 1989): 11–12.

———. *True West: Arts, Traditions, and Celebrations.* New York: C. Potter, 1992.

Mazón, Mauricio. *The Zoot-Suit Riots: The Psychology of Symbolic Annihilation.* Austin: University of Texas Press, 1984.

McDowell, John Holmes. *Children's Riddling.* Bloomington: Indiana University Press, 1979.

———. "The Corrido of Greater Mexico as Discourse, Music, and Event." In *"And Other Neighborly Names": Social Process and Cultural Image in Texas Folklore,* ed. Roger Abrahams and Richard Bauman. Austin: University of Texas Press. 1981.

———. "Folklore as Commemorative Discourse." *Journal of American Folklore,* 195 (1992): 403–23.

———. *Interrogative Routines in Mexican-American Children's Folklore.* Working Papers in Sociolinguistics, 20. Austin, Texas: Southwest Educational Development Educational Laboratory, 1974.

———. "The Mexican Corrido: Formula and Theme in a Ballad Tradition." *Journal of American Folklore* 85 (1972):205–20.

———. *Poetry and Violence: The Ballad Tradition of Mexico's Costa Chica.* Urbana: University of Illinois, 2000.

———, "The Speech Play and Verbal Art of Chicano Children: An Ethnographic and Sociolinguistic Study," unpublished doctoral dissertation, Cultural Anthropology, University of Texas at Austin, 1975.

McNutt, James Charles. *Beyond Regionalism: Texas Folklorists and the Emergence of a Post-Regional Identity.* Austin: University of Texas, 1982.

MeKellar, Sarah S. "Br'er Coyote," in *Puro Mexicano,* ed, J. Frank Dobie. *PTFS,* 12 (1935); reissued in 1969: 101–6.

Meléndez, Theresa. "The Coyote." In *American Wildlife in Symbol and Story,* ed. Angus K. Gillespie and Jay Mechling. Knoxville: University of Tennessee Press, 1987.

———. "Coyote: Towards a Definition of a Concept." *Aztlán: International Journal of Chicano Studies Research* 13(1982):295–307.

Melville, Margarita B. "The Mexican American and the Celebration of the Fiestas Patrias: An Ethnohistorical Analysis." *Grito del Sol* 3 (1978): 107–16.

Mendoza, Vicente T. *La Canción Mexicana: Ensayo de Clasificación y Antología.* Mexico City: Universidad Nacional Autónoma de Mexico City, 1961.

———. *La Décima en Mexico.* Buenos Aires: Instituto Nacional de la Tradición, 1947.

———. *Estudio y clasificación de la música tradicional hispánica de Nuevo México.* Mexico City: Universidad Nacional Autónoma de México, 1986.

———. *Glosas y Décimas de México.* Letras Mexicanas, 32. Mexico City: Fondo de Cultura Económica, 1957.

———. *Lírica Infantil de México.* Mexico City: El Colegio de México, 1951.

———. "Some Forms of the Mexican Canción." In *Singers and Storytellers,* ed. Mody C. Boatright. Dallas, TX: Southern Methodist University Press, 1961.

Mentes, Sherilyn Meece. *Lalo: My Life and Music.* Tucson: The University of Arizona Press, 2002.

Mesa-Bains, Amalia. "'Domesticana': The Sensibility of Chicana Rasquache." *Aztlán: Chicano Journal of the Social Sciences and the Arts* 24 (Fall 1999): 157–67.

Messinger Cypess, Sandra. *La Malinche in Mexican Literature: From History to Myth.* Austin: University of Texas Press, 1991.

———. "'Mother' Malinche and Allegories of Gender, Ethnicity and National Identity in Mexico." In *Feminism, Nation and Myth: La Malinche,* ed. Rolando Romero and Amanda Nolacea Harris. Houston: Arte Público Press, 2005.

Miller, Elaine K. *Mexican Folk Narratives from the Los Angeles Area.* Publications of the American Folklore Society, Memoirs series 5, no. 56. Austin: University of Texas Press, 1973.

Molera, Frances M. "California Spanish Proverbs." *WF* 6 (1947): 65–68.

Mondini-Ruiz, Franco. "Malinche Makeover: One Gay Latino's Perspective." In *Feminism, Nation and Myth: La Malinche,* ed. Rolando Romero and Amanda Nolacea Harris. Houston: Arte Público Press, 2005.

Monsalvo, Sergio C. *La Canción del Inmigrante: De Aztlán a Los Lobos.* Mexico City: Tinta Negra Editores, 1989.

Montano, Mario. *The History of Mexican Folk Foodways of South Texas: Street Vendors, Offal Foods, and Barbacoa de Cabeza.* Pittsburgh: University of Pennsylvania Press, 1992.

Montaño, Mary. *Tradiciones Nuevomexicanas: Hispano Arts and Cultures of New Mexico.* Albuquerque: The University of New Mexico Press, 2001.

Montoya, José. *José Montoya's Pachuco Art: A Historical Update.* Sacramento, CA: Royal Chicano Air Force, 1977.

Montoya, Lori J. "El Kookoóee Destroys Fear at Festival de Otoño." *New Mexico Daily Lobo,* "In Sync," October 12, 1994.

Moore, Michael. *Los Remedios: Traditional Herbal Remedies of the Southwest.* Santa Fe, NM: Red Crane Books, 1990.

Morrison, Suzanne Shumate. *Mexico's "Day of the Dead" in San Francisco, California: A Study of Continuity and Change in a Popular Religious Festival.* Berkeley, CA: Graduate Theological Union, 1992.

Muñoz, Carlos Jr. "Reclaiming Our Heritage: Carlos Muñoz, Jr. Discusses Cinco de Mayo and the Politics of Identity." *CrossRoads* 10 (May 1991): 2–4.

Muñoz Camargo, Diego, ca. 1529—1599. *Descripción de La Ciudad y Provincia de Tlaxcala de las Indias y del Mar Oceano para el Buen Gobierno y ennoblecimiento dellas.* Mexico City: Instituto de Investigaciones Filológicas, Universidad Nacional Autónoma de México, 1981.

Museum of International Folk Art. *Spanish Textile Tradition of New Mexico and Colorado.* Series in Southwestern Culture. Santa Fe: Museum of New Mexico Press, 1979.

Myers, Joan. *Santiago: Saint of Two Worlds.* Albuquerque: University of New Mexico, 1991.

Nájera-Ramírez, Olga. "La Charreada! Rodeo a la Mexicana." San Jose, CA: UCSC/KTEH Production, 1997.

———. "Engendering Nationalism: Identity, Discourse, and the Mexican Charro." *Anthropological Quarterly* 67 (1994a): 1–14.

———. "Fiestas Hispánicas: Dimensions of Hispanic Festivals and Celebrations," in *Handbook of Hispanic Cultures in the United States,* edited and introduced by Thomas Weaver; ed. Nicolas Kanellos and Claudio Esteva-Fabregat. Houston, TX: Arte Público Press. Madrid: Instituto de Cooperación Iberoamericana, 1994.

———. "Greater Mexican Folklore in the United States: An Annotated Bibliography." *Ethnic Affairs* 1 (Fall 1987): 64–115.

———. "The Racialization of a Debate: The Charreada as Tradition or Torture." *American Anthropologist* 98 (September 1996): 505–11.

———. "Social and Political Dimensions of Folklórico Dance: The Binational Dialectic of Residual and Emergent Culture." *Western Folklore* 48 (January 1989): 15–32.

Neruda, Pablo. *Fulgor y Muerte de Joaquín Murrieta, Bandido Chileno Injusticiado en California el 23 de Julio de 1853.* Santiago de Chile: Zig-Zag, 1966.

Nieto-Gómez, Anna. "Women in Mexican History: 'Cinco de Mayo.'" *SOMOS* 2 (May 1979): 16–20.

Nieto-Phillips, John M. *The Language of Blood: The Making of Spanish-American Identity in New Mexico, 1880s–1930s.* Albuquerque: University of New Mexico Press, 2004.

Niggli, Josephina. *Mexican Folk Plays*. Chapel Hill: University of North Carolina, 1938.

Nolacea Harris, Amanda. "La Malinche and Post-Movement Feminism." In *Feminism, Nation and Myth: La Malinche,* ed. Rolando Romero and Amanda Nolacea Harris. Houston: Arte Público Press, 2005.

Oktavec, Eileen. *Answered Prayers: Miracles and Milagros along the Border.* Tucson: University of Arizona, 1995.

Orona-Córdova, Roberta. "Zoot Suits and the Pachuco Phenomenon: An Interview with Luis Valdez." In *Chicano Border Culture and Folklore,* ed. José "Pepe" Villarino and Arturo Ramírez. San Diego, CA: Mann Publications, Inc., 1992.

Ortega, Adolfo. *Caló Tapestry.* Berkeley, CA: Editorial Justa Publications, Inc., 1977.

Ortega, Pedro Ribera. *Christmas in Old Santa Fe.* Santa Fe, NM: Sunstone Press, 1973.

Ortiz, Almudena. *Fiesta de Quinceañera: Queen for a Day.* Berkeley: University of California, 1992.

Ortiz de Monetilano, Bernard. "Caída de Mollera: Aztec Sources for a Mesoamerican Disease of Alleged Spanish Origin." *Ethnohistory* 34 (Fall 1987): 381–99.

Ortiz y Pino, Yolanda. *Original Native New Mexican Cooking.* Santa Fe, NM: Sunstone Press, 1993.

Ortiz y Pino de Dinkel, Reynalda, and Dora Gonzales de Martínez, comps. *Una Colección de Adivinanzas y Diseños de Colcha/A Collection of Riddles and Colcha Designs.* Santa Fe, NM: Sunstone Press, 1988.

Otero, Nina. *Old Spain in Our Southwest.* New York: Harcourt, Brace and Company, 1936.

Paredes, Américo. "Ancestry of Mexico's Corridos: A Matter of Definitions." *Journal of American Folklore* 76 (1963): 231–35.

———. "The Anglo-American in Mexican Folklore," in *New Voices in American Studies,* eds. Ray B. Browne, Donald M. Winkelman, and Allen Hayman. West Lafayette, IN: C.E. Pauley and Company for Purdue University Studies, 1966.

———. "Ballads of the Lower Border." unpublished masters thesis, University of Texas, 1953.

———. "Concepts about Folklore in Latin America," *JFI* 6 (1969): 20–39.

———. "El Corrido de Gregorio Cortez: A Ballad of Border Conflict." Unpublished Dissertation, English, University of Texas, 1956.

———. "Corrido de Jacinto Treviño," "Dichos," and "The Legend of Gregorio Cortez," in *Mexican-American Authors,* eds. Américo Paredes and Raymund Paredes. Boston: Houghton Mifflin Company, 1972, pp. 5–7, 27–34, and 35–50.

———. "El Cowboy Norteamericano en el Folklore y la Literatura," *Cuadernos del Instituto de Antropología,* 4 (1963), 227–240.

———. "Dichos," in *Mexican American Authors,* eds. Américo Paredes and Raymund Paredes. Boston: Houghton Mifflin Co., 1972.

———. "Ethnographic Work among Minority Groups: A Folklorist's Perspective." In *New Directions in Chicano Scholarship,* eds. Ricardo Romo and Raymund Paredes. La Jolla: Chicano Studies Center, University of California, San Diego, 1978.

———. *Folklore and Culture on the Texas-Mexican Border,* ed. and introduced by Richard Bauman. Austin: Center for Mexican American Studies, University of Texas, 1993.

———. "El folklore de los grupos de origin mexicano en Estados Unidos." *Folklore Americano* 14 (1966): 146–63.

———. "Folk Medicine and the Intercultural Jest," in *Spanish-Speaking People in the United States,* ed. June Helm. Proceedings of the 1968 Annual Spring Meeting of the American Ethnological Society, Seattle and London: University of Washington Press, 1968.

———, ed. *Folktales of Mexico.* Chicago and London: University of Chicago Press, 1970.

———. "The Legend of Gregorio Cortez," in *Mesquite and Willow,* eds. Mody C. Boatright, Wilson M. Hudson, and Allen Maxwell. *PTFS* 27 (1957): 3–22.

———. "Mexican Legendry and the Rise of the Mestizo: A Survey." In *American Folk Legend: A Symposium,* ed. with a preface by Wayland D. Hand. Berkeley: University of California Press, 1971.

———. "On Gringo, Greaser, and Other Neighborly Names." in *Singers and Storytellers,* eds. Mody C. Boatright, Wilson M. Hudson, and Allen Maxwell. *PTFS,* 30 (1961), 285–90.

———. "Proverbs and Ethnic Stereotype." *Proverbium* 15 (1970): 95–97.

———. "Spanish Folklore." *WF* 9 (1950): 295–301.

———. *A Texas-Mexican Canionero: Folksongs of the Lower Border.* Urbana: University of Illinois Press, 1976.

———. *Uncle Remus con Chile.* Houston: Arte Público Press, 1993.

———. *"With His Pistol in His Hand": A Border Ballad and Its Hero.* Austin: University of Texas, 1958.

Parsons, Elsie Clews. "Fiesta of Santa Ana, New Mexico." *Scientific Monthly,* 16 (1923), 177–83.

Parsons, Jack. *Low 'n Slow: Lowriding in New Mexico.* Text by Carmella Padilla; poetry by Juan Estevan Arellano. Santa Fe: Museum of New Mexico Press, 1999.

———. *Straight from the Heart: Portraits of Traditional Hispanic Musicians.* Essay by Jim Sagel. Albuquerque: University of New Mexico Press, 1990.

Paz, Octavio. *The Labyrinth of Solitude: Life and Thought in Mexico.* New York: Grove Press, 1961.

Pearce, T. M. "The Bad Son (El Mal Hijo) in Southwestern Spanish Folklore." *WF* 9 (1950): 295–301.

———. "*Los Moros y los Cristianos:* Early American Play." *NMFR* 2 (1947–48): 58–65.

———. "The New Mexican Shepherds' Play." *WF* 15 (1956): 77–88.

———. "Tracing a New Mexico Folk Play." *NMFR* 9 (1954–55): 20–27.

Pearlman, Steven Ray. *Mariachi Music in Los Angeles.* Los Angeles: University of California, 1988.

Peña, Manuel. "Class, Gender, and Machismo: The 'Treacherous-Woman' Folklore of Mexican Male Workers." *Gender and Society* 5(1991): 30–46.

———. "Conjunto Music: The First Fifty Years." *Puro Conjunto: An Album in Words and Pictures.* San Antonio, TX: Guadalupe Cultural Arts Center, 2001, 13–30.

———. "The Emergence of Conjunto Music, 1935–1955." In *"And Other Neighborly Names": Social Process and Cultural Image in Texas Folklore,* ed. Richard Bauman and Roger D. Abrahams. Austin: University of Texas Press, 1981.

———. "From Ranchero to Jaitón: Ethnicity and Class in Texas-Mexican Music (Two Styles in the Form of a Pair)." *Ethnomusicology* 29 (Winter 1985): 29–55.

———. *The Mexican American Orquesta.* Austin: University of Texas Press, 1999.

———. "*Música Fronteriza* /Border Music." *Aztlán: International Journal of Chicano Studies Research* 21 (1992–1996): 191–226.

———. *Música Tejana: The Cultural Economy of Artistic Transformation.* College Station: Texas A&M University Press, 1999.

———. "Notes toward an Interpretive History of California-Mexican Music." In *From the Inside Out: Perspectives on Mexican and Mexican-American Folk Art,* ed. Karana Hattersley-Drayton, Joyce M. Bishop, and Tornás Ybarra-Frausto. San Francisco: The Mexican Museum, 1989.

———. "Ritual Structure in a Chicano Dance." *Latin American Music Review* 1 (1980): 47–73.

———. *The Texas-Mexican Conjunto: History of a Working Class Music.* Austin: University of Texas Press, 1985.

Peñuelos, Marcelino C. *El Español en el Suroeste de los Estados Unidos.* Madrid: Ediciones Cultura Hispánica, 1964.

———. *The New Mexican Alabado,* Stanford University Series, Language and Literature, 9:3 (1951).

———. "New Mexican Wedding Songs," *SFQ* 4 (1940): 55–72.

Pérez, Domino Renee. "Caminando con La Llorona: Traditional and Contemporary Narratives." In *Chicana Traditions: Continuity and Change,* ed. Norma Cantú and Olga Nájera-Ramírez. Urbana: University of Illinois Press, 2002.

Pérez, Leonor Xóchitl. "Transgressing the Taboo: A Chicana's Voice in the Mariachi World." In *Chicana Traditions: Continuity and Change,* ed. Norma Cantú and Olga Nájera-Ramírez. Urbana: University of Illinois Press, 2002.

Pérez, Soledad. "Mexican Folklore from Austin, Texas." In *The Healer of Los Olmos and Other Mexican Lore,* ed. Wilson Mathis Hudson. *PTFS* 24 (1951): 71–127.

———. "*Dichos* from Austin." In *Texas Folk and Folklore,* eds. Mody C Boatright, Wilson M. Hudson, and Allen Maxwell. *PTFS,* 26 (1954), 223–29.

———. "Ratoncito Pérez." In *Texas Folk and Folklore,* eds. Mody C. Boatright, Wilson M. Hudson, and Allen Maxwell, *PTFS,* 26 (1954), 77–79.

———. "The Weeping Woman." In *Texas Folk and Folklore,* eds. Mody C. Boatright, Wilson M. Hudson, and Allen Maxwell. *PTFS* 26 (1954): 127–30.

Periman, Kenneth I. *"Don Cacahuate to La Bruja:* Hispanic Folklore of the Four Corners." *Western Review* 6:2 (Winter 1969): 64–70.

———. "New Mexican Folk Tales." *WF* 10 (1951): 63–71.

Perl, Lila. *Piñatas and Paper Flowers.* Trans. Alma Flor Ada. New York: Clarion Books, 1983.

Perrone, Bobette. *Medicine Women, Curanderas, and Women Doctors.* Norman: University of Oklahoma Press, 1989.

Perry, Ann. "Tejano Festivals: Celebrations of History and Community." In *Hispanic Texas: A Historical Guide,* ed. Helen Simons and Cathryn A. Hoyt. Austin: University of Texas Press, 1992.

Peyton, James W. *La Cocina de la Frontera: Mexican-American Cooking from the Southwest.* Santa Fe, NM: Red Crane Books, 1994.

Phillips, Susan A. *Wallbaggin': Graffiti and Gangs in L.A.* Chicago: University of Chicago Press, 1999.

Pierce, Donna, ed. "Santa Fe's Fiesta." *El Palacio* 91 (Spring 1985): 7–17.

Pilcher, Jeffrey M. *Qué Vivan los Tamales!: Food and the Making of Mexican Identity.* Albuquerque: University of New Mexico Press, 1998.

Pill, Albert Seymur. "Mexican Regional Dance for the Elementary School," unpublished masters thesis, Education, University of California, Los Angeles, 1963.

Pitt, Leonard. *The Decline of the Califonios: A Social History of the Spanish-Speaking Californians,* 1846–1890. Berkeley: University of California Press, 1966.

Place, Edwin B. "A Group of Mystery Plays Found in a Spanish-Speaking Region of Southern Colorado." *The University of Colorado Studies, Series A: General Studies,* 18 (1930), 1–9.

Plascencia, Luis F. "Low Riding in the Southwest: Cultural Symbols in the Mexican Community." In *History, Culture, and Society: Chicano Studies in the 1980s,* ed. Mario García et al. Ypsilanti, MI: Bilingual Press/Editorial Bilingüe, 1983.

Ponce, Mary Helen. *Hoyt Street.* Albuquerque, NM: University of New Mexico Press, 1993.

———. *The Wedding.* Houston: Arte Publico Press, 1989.

Ponce, Merrihelen. *The Lives and Works of Five Hispanic New Mexican Women Writers,* 1878–1991. Albuquerque: Southwest Hispanic Research Institute, University of New Mexico, 1992.

Portilla, Jorge. *Fenomenología del Relajo, y Otros Ensayos.* Mexico City: Ediciones Era, 1966.

Post, Anita C. *Southern Arizona Spanish Phonology.* University of Arizona Humanities Bulletin, 1. Tucson, 1934.

Quiriarte, Jacinto. "Sources of Chicano Art: Our Lady of Guadalupe." *Explorations in Ethnic Studies* 15(1992): 13–26.

Rael, Juan B. "Cuentos Españoles de Colorado y de Nuevo Méjico." *JAF* 52 (1939): 227–323.

———. "Cuentos Españoles de Colorado y de Nuevo Méjico." *JAF* 55 (1942): 1–120.

———. *Cuentos Españoles de Colorado y de Nuevo Méjico*. 2 volumes, Stanford, CA, 1940.

———. "More Light on the Origin of *Los Pastores*." *NMFR* 6 (1951–52): 1–6.

———. "New Mexican Spanish Feasts," *CFQ*, 1 (1942), 83–90.

———. *The Sources and Diffusion of the Mexican Shepherds' Plays*. Guadalajara: Librería de Joyita, 1965.

———. "A Study of the Phonology and Morphology of New Mexican Spanish Based on a Collection of 410 Folk Tales," unpublished doctoral dissertation, Radcliffe College, 1937.

———. "The Theme of the Theft of Food by Playing Godfather in New Mexican Folklore." *Hispania* 20:3 (October 1937): 231–34.

Rapp, Mrs. I.H. "*Los Pastores* Is Gem of Miracle Plays." *El Palacio* 11 (1921): 151–63.

Rebolledo, Tey Diana and María Teresa Márquez. *Women's Tales from the New Mexico WPA: La Diabla a Pie*. Houston: Arte Público Press, 2000.

Rebolledo, Tey Diana, and Eliana S. Rivero. *Infinite Divisions: An Anthology of Chicana Literature*. Tucson: University of Arizona Press, 1993.

Reindorp, Reginald C. *La Décima de Nuevo Méjico*. San Salvador (?), 1946.

Reyna, José Reynaldo. *Folklore Chicano del Valle de San Luis, Colorado*. San Antonio, TX: Penca Books, 1980.

———. *Mexican-American Prose Narrative: The Jest and Anecdote*. San Antonio, TX: Penca Books, n.d.

———. *Modismos de Tejas*. San Antonio, TX: Penca Books, 1980.

———. *Raza Humor: Chicano Joke Tradition in Texas*. San Antonio: Penca Books, n.d.

Reyna, José R., and María Herrera-Sobek. "Jokelore, Cultural Differences, and Linguistic Dexterity: The Construction of the Mexican Immigrant in Chicano Humor." In *Culture across Borders: Mexican Immigration and Popular Culture*, ed. David R. Maciel and María Herrera-Sobek. Tucson: University of Arizona, 1998.

Ribera-Ortega, Peter. "*Las Posadas*." *El Palacio* 75:4 (Winter 1968): 5–10.

Rickard, J. A. "Riddles of Texas Mexican Children." In *Backwoods to Border*, eds. Mody C. Boatright and Donald Day, *PTFS* 18 (1943): 181–87.

Ridge, John Rollin (Yellow Bird). *The History of Joaquín Murieta: The King of California Outlaws, Whose Band Ravaged the State in the Early Fifties*. Hollister, CA: Evening Free Lance, 1927.

———. *The Life and Adventures of Joaquín Murieta, the Celebrated Bandit*. San Francisco, 1854.

———. *Joaquín Murieta*. Norman: University of Oklahoma Press, 1986.

Riedel, Johannes. *Dale Kranque: Chicano Music and Art in South Texas*. St. Paul: University Media Resources, Dept. of Independent Study, Continuing Education and Extension, University of Minnesota, 1982.

Riley, Michael. "The Dangerous Mime: Historical Photographs, Narratives, and Cultural Representations." In *Collectanea: Papers in Folklore, Popular, and Expressive Culture.* Austin: Center for Intercultural Studies in Folklore and Ethnomusicology, University of Texas , 1990.

Rivera, Tomás. "*... Y No Se lo Tragó la Tierra ... And the Earth Did Not Devour Him,"* 2nd ed. Translated by Evangelina Vigil-Piñon. Houston, TX: Arte Público Press, 1992.

Robb, John Donald. *Hispanic Folk Music of New Mexico and the Southwest: A Self Portrait of a People.* Norman: University of Oklahoma Press, 1980.

———. *Hispanic Folk Songs of New Mexico.* University of New Mexico Publications in the Fine Arts, l. Albuquerque: University of New Mexico Press, 1954.

———. "The J. D. Robb Collection of Folk Music Recordings," *NMFR,* 7 (1952–1953), 6–20.

———. "The Matachines Dance—A Ritual Folk Dance, *WF* 20 (1961): 87–101.

———. "The Music of *Los Pastores,*" *WF,* 16 (1957), 263–280.

Robe, Stanley L., ed. *Antología Del Saber Popular: A Selection from Various Genres of Mexican Folklore Across Borders.* Monograph, 2, Los Angeles: Aztlán Publications, Chicano Studies Center, University of California, Los Angeles, 1971.

———. "Four Mexican *Exempla* about the Devil," *WF* 10 (1951): 310–15.

———, ed. *Hispanic Legends from New Mexico: Narratives from the R. D. Jameson Collection.* University of California Publications. Folklore and Mythology Studies, no. 31. Los Angeles: University of California Press, 1980.

———. "Problems in Mexican-American Folk Tradition: The Southern California Scene." In *Contemporary Mexico: Papers of the IV International Congress of Mexican History,* eds. James W. Wilkie, Michael C. Meyer, and Stanley L. Robe. "The Relationship of *Los Pastores* to Other Spanish-America Folk Drama." *WF* 16 (1957): 281–89.

———. "Selective Bibliography of Folk Drama in Hispanic America." *WF* 16 (1957): 287–89.

Roberts, Don L. "The Archive of Southwestern Music." *The Folklore and Folk Music Archivist* 9:2 (1966–1967): 47–52.

Robertiello, Jack. "All Wrapped up in Tamales." *Americas* (English Edition) 48 (March–April 1996): 58–60.

Robinson, Willard B. "Colonial Ranch Architecture in Spanish-Mexican Tradition." *Southwestern Historical Quarterly* (October 1979): 123–50.

Rodríguez, Jeanette. Our *Lady of Guadalupe: Faith and Empowerment among Mexican-American Women.* Austin: University of Texas Press, 1994.

Rodríguez, Sylvia. "Defended Boundaries, Precarious Elites: The Arroyo Seco Matachines Dance." *Journal of American Folklore* 107 (Spring 1994): 248–67.

———. *The Matachines Dance: Ritual Symbolism and Interethnic Relations in the Upper Rio Grande Valley.* Albuquerque: University of New Mexico Press, 1996.

Roeder, Beatrice A. *Chicano Folk Medicine from Los Angeles, California,* Folklore and Mythology Studies, Vol. 34. Berkeley: University of California Press, 1988.

Rojas, Arnold R. *California Vaquero.* Fresno, CA: Academy Library Guild, 1953.

Romero, Brenda. "The Indita Genre of New Mexico: Gender and Cultural Identification." In *Chicana Traditions: Continuity and Change,* ed. Norma E. Cantú and Olga Nájera-Ramírez. Urbana: University of Illinois Press, 2002.

———. *The Matachines Music and Dance in San Juan Pueblo and Alcalde, New Mexico: Context and Meanings.* Los Angeles: University of California, 1993.

Romero, Orlando, and David Larkin. *Adobe: Building and Living with Earth.* New York: Houghton Mifflin Co., 1994.

Romero, Philomena. *New Mexico Dishes.* Los Alamos, NM: Philomena Romero, 1970.

Romero, Rolando J. "Foundational Motherhood: Malinche/Guadalupe in Contemporary Mexican and Chicana/Chicano Culture." In *Feminism, Nation and Myth: La Malinche,* ed. Rolando Romero and Amanda Nolacea Harris. Houston: Arte Público Press, 2005.

Romero Salinas, Joel. *La Pastorela Mexicana: Origen y Evolución.* México: Cultura Fondo Nacional para el Fomento de las Artesanías, Fonart, 1984.

Romo, Tere. "La Malinche as Metaphor." In *Feminism, Nation and Myth: La Malinche,* ed. Rolando Romero and Amanda Nolacea Harris. Houston: Arte Público Press, 2005.

Rubel, Arthur J., Carl W. O'Neill, and Rolando Collado-Ardón. *Susto, A Folk Illness.* Berkeley: University of California Press, 1984.

Rubio, Darío. *Refranes, Proverbios, Dichos Dicharachos Mexicanos.* Mexico City: Editorial A.P. Márquez, 1937.

Rush, Phillip. *Some Old Ranchos and Adobes.* San Diego: Neyenesch Printers, Inc. 1965

Ryan, Hellen Chandler, Supervisor. *Spanish American Singing Games of New Mexico.* Albuquerque, NM: New Mexico Music and Writers' Projects, Work Progress Administration, 1940.

Sagel, Jim. "La Comadre Sebastiana: The Flip Side of Death." *New Mexico Magazine* 70 (September 1992): 78–83.

Sahagún, Fray Bernardino. *Florentine Codex: General History of the Things of New Spain,* 2nd. ed. Trans. Arthur J. O. Anderson and Charles Dibble. Salt Lake City: University of Utah/ Santa Fe, NM: The School of American Research, Museum of New Mexico, 1953–1982.

Salas, Elizabeth. *Soldaderas in the Mexican Military: Myth and History.* Austin: University of Texas Press, 1990.

Salcedo, Michele. *Quinceañerita! The Essential Guide to Planning the Perfect Sweet Fifteen Celebration.* New York: Henry Holt and Company, 1997.

Salem, Zack, Jim Nicolopulos, and Chris Strachwitz. Linernotes, *Tejano Roots: The Women* (Berkeley, CA: Arhoolie Records), 1991.

Salinas-Norman, Bobbi. *Indo-Hispanic Folk Art Traditions: A Book of Culturally-Based, Year-Round Activities with an Emphasis on the Day of the Dead.* Oakland, CA: Piñata Publications, 1988.

Samora, Julián, Joe Bernal, and Albert Peña. *Gunpowder Justice: A Reassessment of the Texas Rangers.* South Bend, IN: University of Notre Dame, 1979.

Sanborn, Laura Sue. "Camposantos: Sacred Places of the Southwest." *Markers VI: The Journal of the Association for Gravestone Studies* 6 (1989): 158–79.

Sánchez, Louis. "Some Unclassic Myths of California." *California Folklore Quarterly* 4 (1945): 58–63.

Sánchez, Rosaura. "Spanish Codes in the Southwest." In *Modern Chicano Writers: A Collection of Critical Essays,* ed. Joseph Sommers and Tomas Ybarra-Frausto. Englewood Cliffs, NJ: Prentice-Hall, Inc., 1979.

Sánchez-Tranquilino, Marcos. "Space, Power, and Youth Culture: Mexican American Graffiti and Chicano Murals in East Los Angeles, 1972–1978." In *Looking High and Low: Art and Cultural Identity,* ed. Brenda Jo Bright and Liza Bakewell. Tucson: University of Arizona, 1995.

Sanders, Clinton R. *Customizing the Body: 'The Art and Culture of Tattooing.* Philadelphia: Temple University Press, 1989.

Sandoval, Annette. *Homegrown Healing: Traditional Home Remedies from Mexico.* New York: Berkley Books, 1998.

Sandoval, Ruben. *Games, Games, Games/Juegos, Juegos, Juegos: Chicano Children at Play-Games and Rhymes.* Garden City, NY: Doubleday & Co., Inc., 1977.

Sands, Kathleen M. *Charrería Mexicana: An Equestrian Folk Tradition.* Tucson: University of Arizona Press, 1993.

———. "Charreada: Performance and Interpretation of an Equestrian Folk Tradition in Mexico and the United States." *Studies in Latin American Popular Culture* 13 (1994): 77–100.

Santamaría, Francisco Javier. *Diccionario de Mejicanismos, Razonado: Comprobado con citas de Autoridades, Comparado con citas de Americanismos y con los Vocabularios Provinciales de los Mas Distinguidos Diccionaristas Hispano-Americanos.* Mexico City: Editorial Porrúa, 1978.

Sawin, Patricia. *La Entrega de los Novios: Ritual and Resistance in 19th Century New Mexico.* Austin: University of Texas, 1985.

Schander, Mary Lea. *Songs in the Air: Music of Early California.* Pasadena, CA: Hammers and Picks Publications, 1994.

Sedillo, Mela. *Mexican and New Mexican Folkdances,* 2nd revised edition. Albuquerque: The University of New Mexico Press, 1950.

Seriff, Suzanne, and José E. Limón. "Bits and Pieces: The Mexican-American Folk Aesthetic." In *Art among Us/Arte Entre Nosotros: Mexican American Folk Art of San Antonio,* ed. Pat Jasper and Kay Turner. San Antonio, TX: San Antonio Museum of Art, 1986.

Sewell Linck, Ernestine, and Joyce Gibson Roach. *Eats: A Folk History of Texas Foods.* Fort Worth: Texas Christian University Press, 1989.

Shalkop, Robert. *Wooden Saints: The Santos of New Mexico.* Colorado Springs, CO: The Taylor Museum of the Colorado Springs Fine Arts Center, 1967.

Shay, Anthony. "Fandangos and Bailes: Dancing and Dance Events in Early California." *Southern California Quarterly* 64 (Summer 1982): 99–113.

Sheehy, Daniel Edward. *The Son Jarocho: The History, Style, and Repertory of a Changing Musical Tradition.* Los Angeles: University of California, 1979.

Sheridan, Thomas E., and Joseph Noriega. "From Luisa Espinel to Lalo Guerrero: Tucson's Mexican Musicians before World War II." In *Frontier Tucson: Hispanic Contributions.* Tucson: Arizona Historical Society, 1987.

Siegal, Nina. "Reclaiming Vásquez's West (Luis Valdez's 'Bandido!')." *American Theater* 11 (July-August 1994): 10.

Silber, Irwin. "La Huelga!: Songs of the Delano Grape Strike." *Sing Out!* 18 (1968): 4–8.

Silverthorne, Elizabeth. *Christmas in Texas.* College Station: Texas A&M University Press, 1990.

Simmons, Marc. *Coronado's Land: Essays on Daily Life in Colonial* New *Mexico.* Albuquerque: University of New Mexico Press, 1991.

———. "La Mano Negra." *Santa Fe Reporter,* August 9–15, 1989, p. 2.

———. "Witchcraft and Black Magic: An Interpretive View." *El Palacio* 80 (1974): 5–11.

———. *Witchcraft in the Southwest: Spanish and Indian Supernaturalism on the Rio Grande.* Flagstaff, AZ: Northland Press, 1974.

Simmons, Merle E. "The Ancestry of Mexico's *Corridos." JAF* 76 (1963): 1–16.

———. "Attitudes toward the United States Revealed in Mexican Corridos," *Hispania,* 36:1 (1953), 34–42.

———. *A Bibliography of the Romance and Related Forms in Spanish America.* Indiana University Folklore Series, 18. Bloomington: Indiana University Press, 1963.

———. *The Mexican Corrido as a Source for Interpretative Study of Modern Mexico* (1870–1950). Indiana University Publications, Humanities Series, 38. Bloomington: Indiana University Press, 1957.

Simonett, Helena. *Banda: Mexican Musical Life across Borders.* Middletown, CT: Wesleyan University Press, 2001.

Skansie, Juli Ellen. "Death Is for All: Death and Death Related Beliefs of Rural Spanish Americans," unpublished doctoral dissertation, Anthropology, Northwestern University, 1974.

Smethurst, James. "The Figure of the 'Vato Loco' and the Representation of Ethnicity in the Narratives of Oscar Z. Acosta." *Multi-Ethnic Literature of the United States* 20 (Summer 1995): 119–33.

Soloman, Madelyn Loes. *Some Mexican Folk Dances Found in Los Angeles.* Los Angeles: University of California, 1941.

Sommers, Laurie Kay. "Symbol and Style in 'Cinco de Mayo.'" *Journal of American Folklore* 98 (October–December 1985): 476–82.

———. *Fiesta, Fe, y Cultura: Celebrations of Faith and Culture in Detroit's Colonia Mexicana.* Detroit: Casa de Unidad Cultural Arts and Media Center and Michigan State University, 1995.

Sonnichsen, Charles L. "Mexican Ghosts from El Paso." In *Texas Folk and Folklore,* eds. Mody C. Boatright, Wilson M. Hudson, and Allen Maxwell. *PTFS* 26 (1954): 118–24.

Sonnichsen, Phillip. "Chicano Music." In *The Folk Music Sourcebook,* eds. Larry Sandberg and Dick Weissman. New York: Alfred A. Knopf, 1976.

———. "Lalo Guerrero: Pioneer in Mexican American Music." *La Luz* 6 (May 1977): 11–14.

———. "Texas-Mexican Border Music, Vols. 2 & 3; Corridos Parts 1 & 2," notes accompanying *Una Historia de la Música de la Frontera: Texas Mexican Border Music Vol. 3* (Folklyric Records 9005), ed. Chris Strachwitz. Berkeley, CA: Arhoolie Records, 1975.

Soto, Shirlene. "*Tres Modelos Culturales: La Virgern de Guadalupe, La Malinche y La Llorona.*" *Fem* 48 (October–November 1986): 13–16.

Spanish Colonial Arts Society. *Spanish New Mexico: The Spanish Colonial Arts Society Collection.* 2 Vols. Ed. Donna Pierce and Marta Weigle; foreword by Anita Gonzales Thomas; photographs by Jack Parsons. Santa Fe: Museum of New Mexico Press, 1996.

Spicer, Edward H. *Ethnic Medicine in the Southwest.* Tucson: University of Arizona Press, 1977.

Sprott, Robert O.F.M. *Making up What Is Lacking: Towards an Interpretation of the Penitentes.* Working Paper Series No. 110. Albuquerque: Southwest Hispanic Research Institute, University of New Mexico, 1984.

Stark, Louisa A. "The Origin of the *Penitente* 'Death Cart.'" *JAF* 84 (1971): 304–10.

Stark, Richard Boies. *Music of the Spanish Folk Plays in New Mexico.* Santa Fe: Museum of New Mexico Press, 1969.

Stavans, Ilan. *Spanglish: The Making of a New American Language.* New York: HarperCollins Publishers, 2003.

Steckmesser, Kent L. "Joaquín Murieta and Billy the Kid." *WF* 21 (1962): 77–82.

Steele, Thomas. *Hispanic Los Agüelos and Pueblo Tsave-Yohs.* Working Paper Series No. 120. Albuquerque: Southwest Hispanic Research Institute, University of New Mexico, 1992.

Steele, Thomas J., S.J., and Rowena A. Rivera. *Penitente Self-Government: Brotherhoods and Councils, 1797–1947.* Santa Fe, NM: Ancient City Press, 1985.

Stewart, Marcus A. *Rosita: A California Tale.* San Jose, CA: Mercury Steam Print, 1882.

Stoller, Marianne L. "Traditional Hispanic Arts and Crafts in the San Luis Valley of Colorado." In *Hispanic Crafts of the Southwest: An Exhibition Catalogue,* ed. William Worth. Colorado Springs, CO: The Taylor Museum of the Colorado Springs Fine Arts Center, 1977.

Stone, Michael Cutler, " *Bajito y Sauvecito* (Low and Slow): Low Riding and the 'Class' of Class." *Studies in Latin American Popular Culture* 9 (1990): 85–126.

Strachwitz, Chris. "The 'Golden Age' of the Recorded Corrido." Liner notes, *Texas Mexican BorderMusic Vols. 2 and 3; Corridos Parts 1 and 2* (Folklyric Records 9005), ed. Christ Strachwitz. Berkeley, CA: Arhoolie Records, 1975.

————. "Texas-Mexican Border Music, Vol. 1: An Introduction 1930–1960," notes accompanying *Una Historia de la Música de La Frontera: Texas Mexican Border Music Vol. 1, An Introduction 1930–1960.* (Folklyric Records 9003), ed. Chris Strachwitz. Berkeley, CA: Arhoolie Records, 1974.

Swenson, Ed. "Mexican-American Tent Shows on Permanent Exhibit at Hertzherg Collection in San Antonio." *The White Tops* 71 (July/August 1998): 15.

Tales Told in Our Barrio. Tucson, AZ: Carrillo School, 1984.

Taylor, Paul S. "Deportados" and "Corrido de Texas." In *Texas Folk and Folklore,* eds. Mody C. Boatright, Wilson M, Hudson, and Allen Maxwell. *PTFS,* 26 (1954), 155–158.

————. "Songs of the Mexican Migration." In *Puro Mexicano,* ed. J. Frank Dobie. *PTFS* 12 (1935): 221–45.

Tejeda, Juan and Avelardo Valdez. *Puro Conjunto: An Album in Words and Pictures.* Austin: University of Texas, Center for Mexican American Studies and the Guadalupe Cultural Arts Center in San Antonio, Texas, 2001.

Thompson, Stith. *The Folktale.* Berkeley: University of California Press, 1977.

————. *Motif-Index of Folk-Literature: A Classification of Narrative Elements in Folktales, Ballads, Myths, Fables, Mediaeval Romances, Exempla, Fabliaux, Jestbooks, and Local Legends,* rev. and enl. ed. Bloomington: Indiana University Press, 1989.

Tijerina, Andrés. *Tejano Empire: Life on the South Texas Ranchos.* College Station: Texas A&M University Press, 1998.

Tinker, Edward Larocque. *Corridos y Calaveras.* Austin: University of Texas Press, 1961.

Tinkle, Lon J. *An American Original: The Life of J. Frank Dobie.* New York: Little, Brown, and Co., 1978.

Tolman, Ruth B. "Treasure Tales of the *Caballos.*" *WF* 20 (1961): 153–74.

Toor, Frances, ed. *Cancionero Mexicano.* Mexico, 1931.

————. "Mexican Folkways." *Southwest Review* 17:2 (Winter 1932): 230–37.

————. *Mexican Popular Arts.* Mexico City, 1939/Detroit: Blaine Ethridge Books, 1973.

————. *A Treasury of Mexican Folkways.* New York: Crown, 1947.

Torres, Eliseo. *The Folk Healer: The Mexican American Tradition of Curanderismo.* Kingsville, TX: Nieves Press, 1983a.

————. *Green Medicine: Traditional Mexican American Herbal Remedies.* Kingsville, TX: Nieves Press, 1983b.

Trager, George L. "Some Spanish Place Names of Colorado." *American Speech* 10:3 (l935): 203–7.

Treviño, Adrián. "El Corrido Mexicano," *Agenda* (Washington, DC, National Council of La Raza), Summer 1974, 18–21.

Trotter, R. T., II, and J. A. Chavira. *Curanderismo: Mexican American Folk Healing System,* rev. ed. Athens: University of Georgia Press, 1997.

Trotter, Robert T., Bernardo Ortiz de Montellano, and Michael H. Logan. "Fallen Fontanelle in the American Southwest: Its Origins, Epidemiology, and Possible Organic Causes." *Medical Anthropology* 10 (1989): 211–21.

Trujillo, Josue. "Spanish *Refranes* and Riddles of the Southwest," unpublished masters thesis, Spanish, University of New Mexico, 1933.

Tully, Marjorie F. *Annotated Bibliography of Spanish Folklore in New Mexico and Southern Colorado.* University of New Mexico Publications in Language and Literature, 3. Albuquerque: University of New Mexico Press, 1950.

Turbeville, Kay. "Proverbs of Spanish California." *Westways* 26 (1934): 25.

Turner, Kay F. *Beautiful Necessity: The Art and Meaning of Women's Altars.* London: Thames and Hudson, 1999.

———. *Mexican American Home Altars: The Art of Relationship.* Austin: University of Texas, 1990.

———. "Mexican American Home Altars: Toward Their Interpretation." *Aztlán: International Journal of Chicano Studies Research* 13 (1982): 209–327.

———. "La Vela Prendida: Mexican American Women's Home Altars." *Folklore Women's Communication* 25 (1981): 5–6.

Turner, Kay F., and Pat Jasper. "La Casa, la Calle y la Esquina: A Look at the Art among Us." In *Art among Us/Arte entre Nosotros: Mexican American Folk Art of San Antonio,* ed. Pat Jasper and Kay F. Turner. San Antonio, TX: San Antonio Museum Association, 1986.

Tushar, Olibama López. *The People of El Valle: A History of the Spanish Colonials in the San Luis Valley.* Pueblo, CO: El Escritorio, 1992.

Ulibarrí, Sabine R. *Mi abuela fumaba Puros/ My Grandma Smoked Cigars.* Berkeley, CA: Quinto Sol Publications, 1977.

———. *Tierra Amarilla: Stories of New Mexico, Cuentos de Nuevo México.* Trans. Thelma Campbell Mason. Albuquerque: University of New Mexico Press, 1971.

Utley, Francis Lee. "Folk Literature: An Operational Definition." In *The Study of Folklore,* ed. Alan Dundes. Englewood Cliffs, NJ: Prentice Hall, 1965.

Van Stone, Mary R., ed. *Los Pastores, Excerpts from an Old Christmas Play of the Southwest as Given Annually by the Griego Family, Santa Fe, New Mexico.* Cleveland: Gates Press, 1933.

———. and E. R. Simms. "Canto del Niño Perdido." In *Spur of the Cock,* ed. J. Frank Dobie. *PTFS* 11 (1933): 48–89.

Valdez, Luis. *Zoot Suit and Other Plays.* Houston, TX: Arte Público, 1992.

Valdez, Luis, and Stan Steiner. *Aztlán: An Anthology of Mexican American Literature.* New York: Alfred A. Knopf, 1972.

Valdez, Margarita. *Tradiciones del Pueblo: Traditions of Three Mexican Feast Days in Southwest Detroit.* Detroit: Casa de Unidad Cultural Arts and Media Center, 1990.

Valero Silva, José. *El Libro de La Charrería.* Mexico City: Ediciones Gacela, S.A., 1987.

Varley, James F. *The Legend of Joaquín Murrieta: California's Gold Rush Bandit.* Twin Falls, ID: Big Lost River Press, 1995.

Vásquez, Librado Keno, Dr., and María Enriqueta Vásquez. *Regional Dictionary of Chicano Slang.* Austin, TX: Jenkins Publishing Company, 1975.

———. "Jovita González, Una Voz de Resistencia Cultural en la Temprana Narrativa Chicana." In *Mujer y Literatura Mexicana y Chicana: Culturas en Contacto.* Mexico City: Colegio de la Frontera Norte, 1988.

Venegas, Daniel. *Las Aventuras de Don Chipote, o, Cuando los Pericos Mamen.* Introduction by Nicolás Kanellos. Mexico City: Secretaría de Educación Pública, Centro de Estudios Fronterizos del Norte de México, 1984.

Venegas, Sybil. *The Day of the Dead in Aztlán: Chicano Variations on the Theme of Life, Death and Self Preservation.* Los Angeles: University of California, 1993.

Vento, Arnoldo Carlos. *Mestizo: The History, Culture and Politics of the Mexican and the Chicano, The Emerging Mestizo-Americans.* Lanham, MD: University Press of America, 1998.

Verti, Sebastian. *Mexican Traditions.* Mexico City: Editorial Diana, 1993.

Vidaurri, Cynthia L. "Texas-American Religious Folk Art in Robstown, Texas." In *Hecho en Tejas: Texas-American Folk Arts and Crafts,* ed. Joe S. Graham. Denton: University of North Texas Press, 1991.

Vigil, Angel. *The Corn Woman: Stories and Legends of the Hispanic Southwest,* trans. Jennifer Audrey Lowell and Juan Francisco Mann. Greenwood, CT: Libraries Unlimited, Inc., 1994.

———. *Una Linda Raza: Cultural and Artistic Traditions of the Hispanic Southwest.* Golden, CO: Fulcrum, 1998.

Vigil, James Diego. "Chicano Gangs: One Response to Mexican Urban Adaptation in the Los Angeles Area." *Urban Anthropology 12* (1983): 45–75.

———. *Barrio Gangs: Street Life and Identity in Southern California.* Austin: University of Texas Press, 1988.

———. "Car Charros: Cruising and Low-Riding in the Barrios of East Los Angeles." *Latino Studies Journal 2* (May 1991): 71–79.

———. "Street Baptism: Chicano Gang Initiation." *Human Organization 55* (1996): 149–53.

Villanueva, Tino. "*Sobre el Termino 'Chicano.'*" *Cuadernos Hispano-Americano* (June 1978): 387–410.

Villarino, José Pepe, and Arturo Ramírez. *Chicano Border Culture and Folklore.* San Diego, CA: Mann Publications, Inc., 1992.

———. *Aztlán, Chicano Culture, and Folklore: An Anthology.* New York: McGraw-Hill Companies, Inc., 1998.

Wald, Elijah. *Narcocorrido: A Journey into the Music of Drugs, Guns, and Guerrillas.* New York: HarperCollins, 2001.

Wallis, Michael, and Craig Varjabedian. *En Divina Luz: The Penitente Moradas of New Mexico.* Albuquerque: University of New Mexico Press, 1994.

Wallrich, William Jones. "Five *Bruja* Tales from the San Luis Valley." *WF* 9 (1950). 359–62.

————. "The *Santero* Tradition in the San Luis Valley." *WF* 10 (l951): 153–61.

————. "Spanish American Devil Lore in Southern Colorado." *WF* 9 (1950): 50–55.

————. "Some Variants of the 'Demon Dancer.'" *WF* 9 (1950): 144–46.

Wardropper, Bruce W. "Fictional Prose, History, and Drama: Pedro de Urdemalas." In *Essays on Narrative Fiction in the Iberian Peninsula in Honour of Frank Pierce,* ed. R. B. Tate. Oxford: The Dolphin Book Co., Ltd., 1982.

Waterbury, Archie Francis. *Doña Rutilia: The Folk Belief System of a Mexican Herbalist.* Berkeley: University of California, 1974.

Watkins, Frances E. "The Charles F. Lummis Collection of Spanish California and Indian Songs in the Southwest Museum (of) Los Angeles." *CFQ* 1 (1942): 99–101.

————. "He Said It with Music: Spanish-California Folk Songs Recorded by Charles F. Lummis." *California Folklore Quarterly* 1 (1942): 359–67.

Waugh, Julia Nott. *The Silver Cradle.* Austin: University of Texas Press, 1955.

Weber, David J. *New Spain's Far Northern Frontier: Essays on Spain in the American West, 1540–1821.* Albuquerque: University of New Mexico, 1979.

Weigle, Marta. *Brothers of Light, Brothers of Blood.* Albuquerque: University of New Mexico Press, 1976.

————. "Ghostly Flagellants and Doña Sebastiana: Two Legends of the Penitente Brotherhood." *Western Folklore* 36 (1977): 135–47.

————. *The Penitentes of the Southwest.* Santa Fe, NM: Ancient City Press, 1970.

Weigle, Marta, and Claudia Larcombe, eds. *Hispanic Arts and Ethnohistory in the Southwest: New Papers Inspired by the Work of E. Boyd.* Santa Fe, NM: Ancient City Press, 1983.

Weigle, Marta, and Peter White. *The Lore of New Mexico.* Albuquerque: University of New Mexico Press, 1988.

Wesley, Howard D. "Ranchero Sayings of the Border." In *Puro Mexicano,* ed. J. Frank Dobie. *PTFS* 12 (1935): 211–20.

West, John O. "Grutas in the Spanish Southwest." In *Hecho en Tejas: Texas-Mexican Folk Arts and Crafts,* ed. Joe S. Graham. Denton: University of North Texas Press, 1991.

————. *Mexican American Folklore: Legends, Songs, Festivals, Proverbs, Crafts, Tales of Saints, of Revolutionaries and More.* Little Rock, AR: August House, 1988.

Whaley, Charlotte. *Nina Otero-Warren of Santa Fe.* Albuquerque: University of New Mexico Press, 1994.

Wilder, Mitchell A., and Edgar Breitenback. *Santos: The Religious Folk Art of New Mexico.* Colorado Springs, CO: Taylor Museum of the Colorado Springs Fine Arts Center, 1943.

Williams, Arthur Durword. *Spanish American Furniture.* Milwaukee, WI: The Bruce Publishing Co., 1941.

Williams, Brett. "Why Migrant Women Feed their Husbands Tamales: Foodways as a Basis for a Revisionist View of Tejano Family Life." In *Ethnic and Regional Foodways in the United States,* ed. Linda Keller Brown and Kay Mussell. Knoxville: University of Tennessee, 1984.

Wittliff, William D., and Joe B. Frantz. "*Vaquero:* Genesis of The Texas Cowboy." In *The Folklore of Texan Cultures,* ed. Francis Edward Abernethy. *PTFS* 38 (1974): 65–68.

Wolf, Eric R. "The Virgin of Guadalupe, A Mexican National Symbol." *JAF* 71 (l958): 34–39.

Work Projects Administration. Federal Music Project, Unit No. 1. *Spanish American Folk Songs.* New Mexico, 1936–1937.

Work Projects Administration. Federal Music Project, Unit No. 3. *Spanish American Singing Games.* Revised 1940.

Work Projects Administration in the State of Arizona, comps. "Folklore and Folkways." In *Arizona: A State Guide,* American Guide Series. New York: Hastings House, 1947.

Work Projects Administration in the State of New Mexico. "Fiestas in New Mexico." *El Palacio* 48 (1941): 239–45.

———. "Folklore," "Contributions to the Language," and "New Mexican Art." In *New Mexico: A Guide to the Colorful State,* American Guide Series. Albuquerque, NM: The University of New Mexico Press, 1945, pp. 98–106, 107–20, 156–70.

———. *The Spanish-American Song and Game Book.* New York: The A.S. Barnes and Company, 1942.

———. "Spanish American Wedding Customs." *El Palacio* 49 (1942): 1–6.

———. "Spanish Fiestas in New Mexico," *El Palacio* 51 (1944): 101–106.

Work Projects Administration in the State of Texas. "Folklore and Folkways," "Arts and Handicrafts," and "Little Mexicos." In *Texas: A Guide to The Lone Star State,* American Guide Series. New York: Hastings House, 1940, pp. 92–98, 141–48, 246–47.

Wroth, William. *Christian Images in Hispanic New Mexico.* Colorado Springs, CO: The Taylor Museum of the Colorado Fine Arts Center, 1982.

———, ed. *Hispanic Crafts of the Southwest: An Exhibition Catalogue.* Colorado Springs, CO: The Taylor Museum of the Colorado Fine Arts Center, 1977.

———. *Weaving and Colchas from the Hispanic Southwest.* Santa Fe, NM: Ancient City Press, 1985.

Ybarra-Frausto,Tomás. "Interview with Tomás Ybarra-Frausto: The Chicano Movement in a Multicultural/Multinational Society." In *On Edge: The Crisis of Contemporary Latin American Culture,* ed. Juan Flores, Jean Franco, and George Yudice. Minneapolis: University of Minnesota Press, 1992.

———. "Rasquachismo: A Chicano Sensibility." In *Chicano Art: Resistance and Affirmation, 1965–1985,* ed. Richard Griswold del Castillo, Teresa McKenna, and Yvonne Yarbro-Bejarano. Los Angeles: Wright Art Gallery, University of California, 1991.

Zabre, Alfonso Teja. *Guide to the History of Mexico: A Modern Interpretation.* New York: The Pemberton Press, 1935.

de Zavala, Adina. *History and Legends of the Alamo and Other Missions in and around San Antonio.* San Antonio, TX: Adina de Zavala, 1917.

Zavala, Bertha. *La Cocina Mexicana.* Mexico: Bertycel, 1990.

Zelayeta, Elena. *Elena's Secrets of Mexican Cooking.* Englewood Cliffs, NJ: Prentice-Hall, Inc., 1958.

Zinam, Oleg, and Ida Molina. "The Tyranny of the Myth: Doña Marina and the Chicano Search for Ethnic Identity." *Mankind Quarterly* 32 (Fall–Winter 1991): 3–18.

Zopf, Dorothy R. "The Hispanic Tradition of Quiltmaking in Taos County, New Mexico." In *On the Cutting Edge: Textile Collectors, Collections, and Traditions,* ed. Cecilia Oliver and Jeannette Lasansky. Lewisburg, PA: Oral Traditions Project of Union County Historical Society, 1994.

Zunser, Helen. "A New Mexican Village," *JAF* 48 (1935): 125–78.

Web Resources

This section provides the scholar with the numerous Web sites available for the various Chicano/a folklore genres discussed in this book. The Web sites are listed by genres, and the description of the Web site is taken from the Web site itself. When searching for Chicano folklore, it is advisable to search under the headings of both "Chicano" and "Mexican American." In addition, many sites do not differentiate between Mexican and Mexican American, listing them together. Although Mexican Web sites are cited in this section, the main emphasis is on Chicano folklore and Mexican American folklore and not on Mexican folklore.

The main search engine used was Google (www.google.com). It proved to be extremely useful and fairly thorough. There are other search engines, but because of the volume, I have limited the sites in this section to those found from Google..

I. FOLKLORE: GENERAL

1. Notable folklore books and journals
   http://afsnet.org/aboutfolklore/notablebooks.cfm

II. CHICANO FOLK LEGENDS

1. Leyendas and children's literature.
   http://retanet.unm.edu/article.pl?sid=03/05/18/2123111

2. Education Planet books for Mexican history
   Mexican-American Folklore: Legends, Songs, Festivals, Proverbs, Crafts, Tales of Saints, of Revolutionaries, and More.

http://www.educationplanet.com/search/search?keywords=Mexican+History+
Mexico&display=books&grade=all

3. Mexican American Studies: Selected reference sources
   This bibliography is intended as an introductory guide to a number of basic
   information and reference sources essential for the study of Mexican Americans.
   http://www.lib.utexas.edu/benson/mals/mexam_srs.html

4. Hispanic children's literature in the United States: Legends and folktales
   http://www.npl.org/Pages/ProgramsExhibits/Exhibits/habia.html

5. Leyendas urbanas
   http://club.telepolis.com/leyendasurbanas/creencias/

The Virgin of Guadalupe

1. The Virgin of Guadalupe—celebration in Oaxaca
   http://www.mexconnect.com/mex_/travel/blyons/blguadalupe1.html

2. La Virgen de Guadalupe—Mother of all Mexico
   http://www.mexconnect.com/mex_/travel/jking/jkguadalupe.html

3. La Virgen de Guadalupe
   http://www.corazones.org/maria/america/mexico_guadalupe.htm

4. The mystery of the Virgin of Guadalupe
   http://www.cancunsteve.com/guadalupe.htm

5. Links to La Virgen Morena
   http://www.ic.arizona.edu/~ws5001/links.html

6. Patron Saints index: Our Lady of Guadalupe
   http://www.catholic-forum.com/saints/mary0003.htm

7. Olvera-Street.com—Virgen de Guadalupe
   http://www.olvera-street.com/html/virgen_de_guadalupe.html

8. Virgen de Guadalupe—Black Madonna
   http://www.aquafemina.com/virgen-de-guadalupe.html

9. The Virgen of Guadalupe
   http://www.aquafemina.com/virgen-de-guadalupe.html

10. Virgen de Guadalupe
    http://www.aciprensa.com/Maria/Guadalupe/

La Malinche

1. La malinche
   http://www.mexconnect.com/mex_/history/malinche.html

2. La malinche, unrecognized heroine
   http://www.mexconnect.com/mex_/travel/slenchek/slmalinche.html

3. La malinche (article)
   http://www.emayzine.com/lectures/la.htm

4. La malinche: Creator or traitor?
   http://www.tihof.org/honors/malinche.htm

5. Malinche
   http://onesun.cc.geneseo.edu/~kintz/Malinche.html

6. La malinche
   http://www.lasculturas.com/lib/libMalinche.htm

7. La malinche—Wikipedia, the free encyclopedia
   http://en.wikipedia.org/wiki/La_Malinche

8. Cortes and La Malinche
   http://thedagger.com/archive/conquest/malinche.html

9. Malinche
   http://www.latinamericanstudies.org/malinche.htm

10. Reinterpreting Malinche
    http://userwww.sfsu.edu/~epf/2000/jt.html

La Llorona

1. The Spirit of La Llorona
   http://www.lallorona.com/

2. La Llorona—A Hispanic Legend
   http://www.literacynet.org/lp/hperspectives/llorona.html

3. La Llorona—Weeping Ghost of the Southwest
   http://www.legendsofamerica.com/HC-WeepingWoman1.html

4. La Llorona—Wikipedia, the free encyclopedia
   http://en.wikipedia.org/wiki/La_Llorona

5. SCORE: La Llorona—Teacher Guide
   http://www.sdcoe.k12.ca.us/score/rona/ronatg.html

6. La Llorona
   http://www.theoutlaws.com/ghosts3.htm

7. A Literary History of the American West
   http://www2.tcu.edu/depts/prs/amwest/html/wl1079.html

8. La Llorona: A New Mexico Ghost Story from American Folklore
   http://www.americanfolklore.net/folktales/nm3.html

9. The Llorona, Omen and Death
   http://www.americanfolklore.net/folktales/ca11.html

10. Obiwan's UFO-Free Paranormal Page, Ghosts and Hauntings FAQ
    http://www.ghosts.org/faq/4-1.html

11. La Llorona
    http://www.pantheon.org/articles/l/la_llorona.html

12. The Crying Woman—La Llorona
    http://www.castleofspirits.com/cryingwoman.html

13. Amazon.com: La Llorona: Music
    http://www.amazon.com/exec/obidos/tg/detail/-/B000009MV1?v=glance

14. MELUS: From Llorona to Gritona
    http://www.findarticles.com/p/articles/mi_m2278/is_2_24/ai_59211507

15. Navidad El Colombiano
    http://www.elcolombiano.terra.com.co/proyectos/navidad/2003/enmedellin/
    mitos-lallorona.htm

16. lapovertydept.org—La Llorona
    http://lapovertydept.org/urban-theater/La_Llorona/

17. La Llorona: Information from Answers.com
    http://www.answers.com/topic/la-llorona

18. kristyk.org, Blog Archive, La Llorona
    http://kristyk.org/?p=1320

19. NewPages Book Reviews—*La Llorona on the Longfellow Bridge*
    http://www.newpages.com/bookreviews/archive/reviews/lalloronaonthelong-
    fellowbridge.htm

20. Handbook of Texas Online: La Llorona
    http://www.tsha.utexas.edu/handbook/online/articles/LL/lxl1.html

21. Sunstone Press—La Llorona
    http://www.sunstonepress.com/cgi-bin/bookview.cgi?_recordnum=335

22. PRX, Pieces, La Llorona
    http://www.prx.org/pieces/7613

23. PRX, Reviews, La Llorona
    http://www.prx.org/review/5027

24. La Llorona, the Weeping Woman
    http://www.scifidimensions.com/Mar02/lallorona.htm

25. La Llorona
    http://ingeb.org/songs/lalloron.html

26. Tradiciones—Delegación Xochimilco
    http://www.xochimilco.df.gob.mx/tradiciones/ferias/llorona.html

27. sandiego.indymedia.org, (audio) Llorona Post 9-11
    http://sandiego.indymedia.org/en/2005/10/111332.shtml

28. Apocrypha Now! Archive: Milking a Legend—"La Llorona"
    http://urbanlegends.about.com/library/bl-an012202.htm

29. Duke City Fix, La Llorona Revisited
    http://www.dukecityfix.com/index.php?itemid=1077

30. BIG SALE: La Llorona's Children
    http://www.ucpress.edu/books/pages/8931.html

31. Walking the Walk, Talking the Talk—Mexican-moon-mother?
    http://www.mexconnect.com/mex_/travel/wdevlin/wdwalktalk20.html

III. CHICANO MYTHS

1. Indigenous peoples of Mexico
   This Web site describes the origins of various Chicano folk myths.
   http://www.indians.org/welker/mexmain1.htm

2. Chicano! History of the Mexican American Civil Rights Movement
   Discusses the Aztec myth of Aztlán.
   http://www.albany.edu/jmmh/vol3/chicano/chicano.html

3. In search of Aztlán
   Provides a discussion of Aztlán.
   http://www.insearchofaztlan.com/index2.html

4. Gloria Anzaldúa
   Anzaldúa revises andocentric myths of the Chicano homeland, Aztlán, and of La
   Llorona (the Weeping Woman).
   http://college.hmco.com/english/lauter/heath/4e/students/author_pages/
   contemporary/anzaldua_gl.html

5. Collecting Chicano literature
   This Web site lists various books which discuss Chicano myths.
   http://www.downtownbrown.com/collecting/collecting.htm

Aztlán

1. What is the meaning of the word Aztlán?
   http://www.azteca.net/aztec/aztlan.html

2. What is Aztlán, Raza and Mecha?
   http://www.mayorno.com/WhoIsMecha.html

3. El Plan de Aztlán.
   http://studentorgs.utexas.edu/mecha/archive/plan.html

4. Aztlán.
   http://www.sonorannews.com/aztlan.html

5. Barrios of Aztlán unite.
   http://www.barriowarriors.net/home.html

6. What is the meaning of the word Aztlán?
   http://www.public.iastate.edu/˜rjsalvad/scmfaq/AZTLAN

7. The road to Aztlán.
   http://boundless.org/2002_2003/features/a0000660.html

IV. FOLK TALES

1. Mexican folktales
   http://nancykeane.com/rl/682.htm

2. Magic tales of Mexico
   http://www.g-world.org/magictales/magictales.shtml

3. ales
   http://collaboratory.nunet.net/nssd112/oakterrace/imc/tales.html

4. Folktales
   http://www.folkart.com/home/tales.htm

5. Mexican folktales
   http://www.globecorner.com/t/t35/17543.php

6. Folktales from Mexico and Latin America
   http://www.surlalunefairytales.com/boardarchives/2002/jan2002/ftfrommexico_
   pg1.html

7. Listmania: Chicano folk tales and legends
   Horse Hooves and Chicken Feet
   http://www.houghtonmifflinbooks.com/catalog/titledetail.cfm?titleNumber=
   111156

8. Folktale links
   http://www2.muw.edu/˜kdunk/folk.html

9. Bibliographies of folktales for children
   http://books.valdosta.edu/bib/latiname.htm

10. Myths, folktales, and fairy tales
    http://teacher.scholastic.com/writewit/mff/folktale_almafolktale.htm

V. CHICANO JEST (JOKES)

See also "Mexican American Jokes."

1. Fishing jokes
   http://www.paralumun.com/jokesfishing.htm

2. The construction workers
   http://www.thehumorarchives.com/humor/0000685.html

3. Humor: ethnic jokes
   http://www.zenhex.com/jokes.php?joke=4814

4. HumorShack—Miscellaneous Jokes
   http://www.humorshack.com/archive/jokes/miscellaneous/49.shtml

5. Another Mexican joke from Sandrita
   http://www.spanish.bz/blog/2005/05/another-mexican-joke-from-sandrita.htm

6. Spicy Jokes—Mexican jokes
   http://www.spicyjoke.com/mexican_jokes.html

7. Office jokes
   http://officediversions.com/discover/modules/wfsection/article.php?articleid=114

8. Just Advance
   http://www.justadvance.com/p_jokes.html

9. Mexican jokes: Funny clean jokes about Mexicans
   http://www.basicjokes.com/mexican.php

10. Lots of Jokes: original jokes
    http://www.lotsofjokes.com/cat_109.htm

VI. CHICANO FOLK MEDICINE

1. Curanderismo: Folk healing in the Mexican American community.
   http://www.lib.utexas.edu/benson/bibnot/bn-101.html

2. Curanderismo: Resources available at the San Antonio Central Library
   http://www.sat.lib.tx.us/Latino/curand.htm

3. Curandera practicing traditional Mexican/Chicano Folk Medicine (Elena Avila)
   http://www.elena-curandera.com/Elena-Vita.htm

4. The Curanderismo Forum
   http://www.alt-med-ed.com/practices/curanderismo.htm

5. UCLA Chicano Studies Research Center
   http://www.chicano.ucla.edu/library/crcpamphlets.htm

6. California State University, Long Beach, Chicano and Latino Studies Research Guide
   http://www.csulb.edu/~sluevano/CHLS_REV/CHLS_COAST.htm

7. Aspectos Culturales
   http://www.aspectosculturales.com/books.html

8. *Encyclopedia: Culture of Mexico*
   http://www.nationmaster.com/encyclopedia/Culture-of-Mexico

VII. CHICANO FOLK DANCE

1. Noroeste Chicano Folk Music
   http://www.alegria.org/Ubb/Forum4/HTML/000304.html

2. Peter Garcia's Web page

3. Hispano Folk Music of the Río Grande del Norte
   http://www.asu.edu/clas/chicana/garcia.html

4. Aztlán Academy

5. Aztlán Academy was founded in 1972 to promote cultural awareness and pride through the teaching and performance of Mexican and Chicano folkloric arts.
   http://www.sanjosearts.com/aztlan.html

6. Alegría—Mexican folk dance directory
   http://www.alegria.org/body_dirUSA-M-Z.html

7. Aztec Academy home page
   The Aztlán Academy-San José, Inc. is a non-profit cultural entity dedicated to the advancement of Mexican and Chicano Folk Arts including art, music, dance, literature and drama.
   http://aztlanacademy.org/aztlanAcademyHome.htm

8. Latino Program for libraries
   Here you'll find basic contact information for storytellers, musicians, dance troupes, puppeteers, artists, and more.
   http://www.bibliotecasparalagente.org/program.html

VIII. CHICANO THEATER

1. El Teatro Campesino: The Evolution of America's first Chicano theatre Company.
   http://home.earthlink.net/~brinac/LatinaoPerform.htm

2. Chicano Theatre: books on Chicano Theatre
   http://www.campusi.com/keyword_Chicano_Theatre.htm

3. Chicano Theatre Bibliography: Archive, Hemispheric Institute
   http://hemi.nyu.edu/archive/bib/pineda/chicano.shtml

4. Chicano Theatre: Themes and Forms
   http://www.asu.edu/brp/backlist/cinema/JHue1c.html

5. Our Mission
   http://www.suteatro.org/suhistory/

6. Code-switching In Chicano Theatre
   http://www.diva-portal.org/diva/getDocument?urn_nbn_se_umu_diva-498-2__fulltext.pdf

7. Amazon: Listmania!—View List "Chicano Studies and Theatre"
   http://www.amazon.com/exec/obidos/tg/listmania/list-browse/2VUS3YVAAX1V6

8. Hispanic Heritage—Biographies: Luis Valdez
   http://www.galegroup.com/free_resources/chh/bio/valdez_l.htm

9. PAL: Luis Valdez (1940–)
   http://www.csustan.edu/english/reuben/pal/chap8/valdez.html

10. Ford Foundation: Hispanic Theatre in the United States and Puerto Rico
    http://www.fordfound.org/elibrary/documents/0146/037.cfm

IX. CHICANO FOLK COSTUMES

1. Art of Mexico—Latin American Art
   http://www.princetonol.com/groups/iad/lessons/middle/mexico.htm

2. Mexican American Association of Baile Folklórico
   The association promotes Mexican dances and costumes as close as possible to its roots.
   http://mexican-folk-dancing-in-seattle.info.hosting.domaindirect.com/

3. Open Directory Project
   http://dmoz.org/Shopping/Ethnic_and_Regional/North_American/Mexican/

4. Latin American Festival
   http://www.bazaardelmundo.com/events/LatinFest04.html

5. Chicano Web page
   Chicano/Hispanic-Americans/Latino Groups: Library Resources
   University of Illinois at Urbana-Champaign
   http://www.library.uiuc.edu/mdx/latinoweb/border.htm

6. Aztlan Sportswear
   http://www.chicanomall.com/

7. BrownPride.com
   A Web site dedicated to the Chicano/Mexican culture of California.
   http://www.brownpride.com/history/default.asp

8. Chicano Gear: CafePress.com
   http://www.cafepress.com/chicano

X. CHICANO FOLK FOOD

1 Chicano Foods: A Cultural Perspective of the Rio Grande Valley
   http://www.panam.edu/dept/lrgvarchive/foods.html

2. Food in Latin America
   Latin American Food & Cooking Carnegie Library of Pittsburgh Subject
   Guide
   http://lanic.utexas.edu/la/region/food/

3. Food Timeline: History Notes, Mexican and Tex Mex food
   http://www.foodtimeline.org/foodmexican.html

4. Hispanic American Influence on the U.S. Food Industry
   http://www.nal.usda.gov/outreach/HFood.html

5. Mexican food and cooking history
   A guide and bibliography of Mexican foods and cooking
   http://www.gourmetsleuth.com/mexicanfoodhistory.htm

6. Lo Mexicano: Mexican food, cooking and Mexican food recipes
   http://www.lomexicano.com/

7. Allrecipes: Fiesta foods for Cinco de Mayo
   http://allrecipes.com/advice/coll/all/articles/60P1.asp

8. Latin Merchant.com
   Latin food, Mexican food, Spanish food, South American food, and Caribbean
   Food
   http://www.latinmerchant.com/

Tamales

1. Tamales.
   http://www.sonofthesouth.net/tamales/

2. GourmetSleuth—Mexican Tamales
   http://www.gourmetsleuth.com/tamales.htm

3. Tamales.
   http://www.hotdamntamales.com/

4. Tamales: books.
   http://www.amazon.com/exec/obidos/tg/detail/-/0028613279/103–
   5030603–8524615?v = glance

5. Tamales norteños.
   http://mexicancooking.netrelief.com/tamales/how_to_make_hot_tamales_
   recipe.shtml

6. SCORE Teacher guide: "Too many tamales."
   http://www.sdcoe.k12.ca.us/score/too/tootg.html

7. Making tamales.
   http://www.mexgrocer.com/14994.html

8. How to make tamales.
   http://www.fabulousfoods.com/features/tamales/tamales.html

9. Recipe for Honduran Tamales.
   http://www.honduras.net/foods/tamales.html

10. Tamale: Wikipedia, the free encyclopedia.
    http://en.wikipedia.org/wiki/Tamal

Enchiladas

1. An excellent free recipe for enchiladas
   http://www.premiersystems.com/recipes/mexican/enchilada.html

2. Enchiladas recipes
   http://www.thatsmyhome.com/texmex/main/M_Enchiladas.htm

3. Mexican Recipe Index: enchiladas
   http://mexican.allrecipes.com/directory/3353.asp

4. Simply Recipes: Enchiladas recipes
   http://www.elise.com/recipes/archives/000055enchiladas.php

5. Chicken enchiladas recipe
   http://www.dianaskitchen.com/page/recipes03/081303chicken4.htm

6. Mexico: enchiladas with green sauce
   http://www.globalgourmet.com/destinations/mexico/enchverd.html

7. Beef enchiladas
   http://www.mex-recipes.com/beef-enchiladas.html

8. Cheese enchilada
   http://www.cooks.com/rec/search/0,1–0,cheese_enchiladas,FF.html

9. Recipe—cheese enchiladas
   http://www.texascooking.com/recipes/cheeseenchiladas.htm

10. Mexican style enchilada
    http://fancy.zecilia.se/enchilada/

Menudo

1. Menudo recipe
   http://www.vivacincodemayo.org/recipe.htm

2. The official menudo Web site
   http://www.menudo.com/

3. An excellent free recipe for menudo
   http://www.premiersystems.com/recipes/mexican/menudo.html

4. Food Network: menudo
   http://www.foodnetwork.com/food/cda/recipe_print/0,1946,FOOD_9936_
   3774_PRINT-RECIPE-4X6-CARD,00.html

5. Menudo—Mexican beef tripe soup
   http://www.mexgrocer.com/catagories-canned-foods-menudo.html

6. Menudo recipe
   http://homecooking.about.com/library/archive/blss18.htm

7. Veg-menudo recipe
   http://www.fatfree.com/recipes/mexican/veg-menudo

8. Menudo: An acquired taste
   http://www.heb.com/mealtime/celeb-traditionsMenudo.jsp

9. Menudo
   http://mexico.udg.mx/cocina/carnes/Menudo.html

10. Menudo recipe
    http://recipes.epicurean.com/recipedetail.jsp?recipe_no = 11455

Buñuelos

1. RecipeSource: Buñuelos
   http://www.recipesource.com/ethnic/americas/mexican/bunuelos1.html

2. Mexican dessert recipe buñuelos
   http://www.mex-recipes.com/mexican-dessert-recipe.html

3. All recipes: buñuelos
   http://cookie.allrecipes.com/AZ/Bunuelos.asp

4. Cooks.com: recipes, buñuelos
   http://www.cooks.com/rec/search/0,1–00,bunuelos,FF.html

5. Buñuelos: Mexican recipe
   http://www.mexgrocer.com/502-bunuelos-bunuelos.html

6. Buñuelos
   http://argentina.informatik.uni-muenchen.de/recetas/msg00838.html

7. Buñuelos (Christmas) recipe
   http://www.mrbreakfast.com/superdisplay.asp?recipeid = 734

Churros

1. Churros—favorite Spanish food recipe
   http://www.xmission.com/˜dderhak/recipe/churros.htm

2. GourmetSleuth—churros
   http://www.gourmetsleuth.com/recipe_churros.htm

3. Delicious churros
   http://www.churros.com/churros.htm

4. Churro: Wikipedia, the free encyclopedia
   http://en.wikipedia.org/wiki/Churro

5. Cooks.com: churros
   http://www.cooks.com/rec/search/0,1–0,churros,FF.html

6. Churros
   http://argentina.informatik.uni-muenchen.de/recetas/msg00013.html

7. Learn to make churros
   http://www.clic.es/churros_recipe.php

Chocolate

1. Mexican chocolate
   http://www.gourmetsleuth.com/mexicanchocolate.htm

2. Recipe for Mexican Hot chocolate
   http://www.gourmetsleuth.com/mexicanhotchocolate.htm

3. Collection: Mexican chocolate
   http://www.cs.cmu.edu/˜mjw/recipes/ethnic/mexican/mexican-chocolate-coll.
   html

4. Mexico Hot or Not: Mexican chocolate
   http://www.mexconnect.com/mex_/recipes/puebla/kgchoc.html

5. Chocolate: History of chocolate
   http://whatscookingamerica.net/Beverage/HotChocolate.htm

6. Mexican: Mexican chocolate
   http://www.recipecottage.com/mexican/mexican-chocolate01.html

Capirotada

1. Capirotada: Mexican food
   http://www.bellaonline.com/articles/art9217.asp

2. Capirotada
   http://mexico.udg.mx/cocina/postres/Capirotada.html

3. Capirotada: Mexican recipe
   http://www.mexgrocer.com/455-capirotada.html

4. Maria Elena's capirotada recipe
   http://www.thatsmyhome.com/texmex/desserts/caprid.htm

5. Capirotada
   http://www.gourmetsleuth.com/capirotada.htm

6. Capirotada
   http://www.rollybrook.com/capirotada.htm

7. Capirotada: Mexican bread pudding
   http://www.rollybrook.com/capirotada.htm

Atole

1. Recipe for Mexican atole
   http://www.gourmetsleuth.com/atole.htm

2. Recipe: Drinks, Mexican atole
   http://recipes.chef2chef.net/recipe-archive/3/A03205.shtml

3. Atole: Mexican milk beverage
   http://houseandhome.msn.com/food/recipes/RecipeDetail.aspx?rid = 578

4. Holiday Traditions, Mexico
   http://www.californiamall.com/holidaytraditions/traditions-mexico.htm

5. Atole
   http://www.mexgrocer.com/481-atole.html

6. Atole: Mexican milk
   http://www.adpi.org/recipes_mexmilk.asp

7. Atole de Zarzamora Recipe
   http://www.cdkitchen.com/recipes/recs/61/Atole_De_Zarzamora47615.shtml

8. Mexican, Latin American recipes
   http://www.elook.org/recipes/latin/mexican1.html

Tortillas

1. Tortillas:
   http://www.gourmetsleuth.com/mexicantortillasbreadsrecipes.htm

2. Mexican tortilla press
   http://www.gourmetsleuth.com/tortillapress.htm

3. Tortillas, maseca corn tortillas
   http://www.texmextogo.com/tortillas.htm

4. Mexican recipes, tortilla press
   http://www.texmextogo.com/Recipes_tortilla.htm

5. Mexican tortilla bake
   http://www.care2.com/channels/solutions/food/1584

6. Mexican casserole tortillas
   http://www.cooks.com/rec/search/0,1–0,mexican_casserole_tortillas,FF.html

7. Meals for you: Mexican tortillas
   http://www.mealsforyou.com/cgi-bin/recipe?id.1557

8. How are tortillas made?
   http://www.public.iastate.edu/~rjsalvad/scmfaq/tortilla.html

9. Authentic Mexican tortillas
   http://www.fortunecity.com/meltingpot/belgium/1029/tortillas.html

XI. CHICANO FOLK SONGS

Corridos

1. The Mexican corrido
   http://carriagehousebandb.ca/corido.html

2. Artsedge
   http://artsedge.kennedy-center.org/content/3742/

3. Narcocorrido, book on corridos, Mexican drug ballads, by Elijah Wald
   Detailed description of this book about the corrido music style, and the
   Mexican culture.
   http://www.elijahwald.com/corrido.html

4. The handbook of Texas online
   http://www.tsha.utexas.edu/handbook/online/articles/CC/lhc1.html

5. Corrido
   http://corrido.idoneos.com/

6. Thomson Gale
   http://www.gale.com/free_resources/chh/music/cancion.htm

7. CIENCIA ergo sum
   http://ergosum.uaemex.mx/marzo01/corridos.html

8. Another 50 years of the corrido: a reassessment
   http://fuentes.csh.udg.mx/CUCSH/Sincronia/nicolopulos.html

9. El corrido
   http://www-mcnair.berkeley.edu/2000journal/Hernandez/Hernandez.html

10. Let me sing you a story
    http://www.uh.edu/hti/cu/2002/v02/08.htm

Joaquín Murieta

1. Joaquin Murrieta
   http://www.ameri-land.com/joaquin.htm

2. Murrieta's Well Winery
   http://www.murrietaswell.com/joaquin.html

3. Joaquin Murrieta
   http://www.inn-california.com/sierramountains/TUOLUMNE/
   murrietabionotes.html

4. Joaquin Murrieta: Literary fiction or historical fact?
   http://www.cocohistory.com/essays-murrieta.html

5. Joaquin Murrieta
   http://www.columbiagazette.com/joaquin.html

6. Joaquin Murrieta
   http://www.picacho.org/interest/joaquin-murrieta.html

7. Joaquin Murrieta
   http://www.infoplease.com/ce6/people/A0834521.html

Gregorio Cortez

1. Gregorio Cortez, the Mexican fugitive
   http://www.texasescapes.com/MurrayMontgomeryLoneStarDiary/Mexican
   FugitiveGregorioCortez.htm

2. The Ballad of Gregorio Cortez
   http://www.imdb.com/title/tt0083613/

3. The Ballad of Gregorio Cortez

http://movies2.nytimes.com/gst/movies/movie.html?v_id = 3804

4. El corridor de Gregorio Cortez
   http://artsedge.kennedy-center.org/content/3742/3742_mexCor_cortez
   Cor.pdf

5. The Latino history project
   http://www.latinohistory.com/people.php?id = 95

6. Smithsonian Center for Latino Initiatives
   http://latino.si.edu/researchandmuseums/presentations/chewsanchesz_papers.
   html

7. A literary history of the American west
   http://www2.tcu.edu/depts/prs/amwest/html/wl1079.html

Narcocorrido

1. Baltimore City Paper: Music
   http://www.citypaper.com/music/recordreview.asp?id = 8413

2. Narco Pop's Bloody Polkas
   http://web.mit.edu/aaelenes/www/sinaloa/narco/narcocorrido3.html

3. The corridos Matrix
   http://kancrn.kckps.k12.ks.us/Harmon/breighm/narco1.html

4. Library Journal: Author of the hour: Arturo Perez-Reverte
   http://www.libraryjournal.com/article/CA262857.html?display=criticas&pub
   date=12%2F1%2F02

5. The Ballad of Chalino Sánchez
   http://web.mit.edu/aaelenes/www/musica/chalino/chal.html

6. Gangsta polkas
   http://www.villagevoice.com/music/0104,wondrich,21648,22.html

7. The observer: Death in the midday sun
   http://observer.guardian.co.uk/omm/story/0,13887,1304449,00.html

8. Drug Culture Eulogized by Musicians from the North
   http://www.banderasnews.com/0505/nr-narcocorrido.htm

9. en.wikipedia.org
   http://en.wikipedia.org/wiki/Narcocorrido

10. Noticias: Los Chalinillos
    http://www.chalino.com/noticias/los-chalinillos.asp

11. Bad subjects: Violent ballads as border representations
    http://bad.eserver.org/issues/2002/61/garcia.html

Mariachi

1. Welcome to Puro Mariachi
   Calendar of western U.S. concerts and events, directory of groups, and links to history and review sites.
   http://www.mariachi.org/

2. El Mariachi
   The Internet's most comprehensive Mariachi Web site.
   http://www.elmariachi.com/

3. History of Mariachi
   http://www.mexconnect.com/mex_/guadalajara/marhis.html

4. Fiesta del Mariachi
   The premiere spot for mariachis on the Web.
   http://www.geocities.com/Broadway/2626/

5. Welcome to Mariachi USA
   http://www.mariachiusa.com/

6. Mariachi Connection
   Clothing and accessories for mariachi. Instruments, strings, sheet music, and books.
   http://www.mariachiconnection.com/

7. Mariachi Publishing Company
   Offers Mariachi music transcriptions.
   http://www.sobrino.net/mpc/

8. Mariachi—Wikipedia, the free encyclopedia
   http://en.wikipedia.org/wiki/Mariachi

9. Mexican mariachi music and instruments
   http://www.sbgmusic.com/html/teacher/reference/cultures/mariachi.html

10. Mariachi radio—All mariachi—All the time
    The premiere Web site for all information related to mariachis on the Web.
    http://personal.linkline.com/dserrano/

11. KC Youth Mariachi Foundation
    Offers after school programs including music, mentoring, and family involvement.
    http://www.kernmariachi.com/

Banda

1. *Encyclopedia: Music of Mexico*
   http://www.nationmaster.com/encyclopedia/Music-of-Mexico

2. Bands show their best
   http://msnbc.msn.com/id/8812697/

3. Traditional music of Mexico
   Learn about some of the most popular forms of Mexican music including mariachi, banda, and ranchero.
   http://gomexico.about.com/cs/mexico/a/music.htm

4. The intelligence group/youth intelligence
   http://www.youthintelligence.com/company/yiArticle.asp?yiArticleId = 35

5. UPNE: Banda
   http://www.upne.com/0–8195–6429-X.html

6. Music of Mexico
   http://www.absoluteastronomy.com/encyclopedia/m/mu/music_of_mexico.htm

7. Mexican music
   http://www.mexfoldanco.org/music.htm

Décima

1. Décima and Rumba: Iberian formalism in the heart of AfroCuban song
   http://ietpd1.sowi.uni-mainz.de/~pseelig/pasmanick/

2. Jibaro singers
   http://www.cuatro-pr.org/Home/Eng/Instrmus/Genres/jibaro_singers.htm

3. Décima's Iberian genesis
   http://www.periodico26.cu/english_new/poetry/genesis.htm

4. Música de Puerto Rico: Música folklorica
   http://www.musicofpuertorico.com/es/genre_folk.html

5. What is décima?
   http://www.periodico26.cu/english_new/poetry/what.htm

6. AAW décima poetry
   http://www.ncteamericancollection.org/aaw_decima_poetry.htm

7. Topica Email List Directory
   http://lists.topica.com/lists/Temple2/read/message.html?mid=811252444&sort=d&start=1102

8. Décima-George Santayana Poems—poems and poetry
   http://www.poems-and-poetry.com/george-santayana/decima-poem.html

Canción Ranchera

1. Canción ranchera
   http://www.fortunecity.es/salsa/rap/552/cancionranchera.html

2. Ella" (Canción ranchera Mexicana)
   http://argentina.informatik.uni-muenchen.de/tangos/msg06851.html

3. Música y bailes de Morelos, México y todo el mundo
   http://infomorelos.com/cultura/mexmusic.html.

4. Beltrán, Lola
   http://www.lamusica.com/LolaBeltran.shtml

The Texas-Mexican Conjunto

http://www.folklife.si.edu/frontera/pena.htm

1. La música Mexicana
   http://www.geocities.com/ajzulic.geo/la_musica.html

2. Gale schools—celebrating Hispanic heritage
   http://www.gale.com/warehouse/chh/music/musnorte.htm

3. Orquesta Tejana
   http://www.lib.utexas.edu/benson/border/arhoolie2/orquesta.html

4. Valerio Longoria
   http://www.mp3.com/valerio-longoria-sr./artists/80358/biography.html

5. PBS: Accordion dreams—cultures of music and dance
   http://www.pbs.org/accordiondreams/cultures/

6. American musical traditions
   http://www.stg.brown.edu/projects/MusicAtlas/Volume5/playpagevol5ch10.html

7. Washington State Arts Commission
   http://www.arts.wa.gov/progFA/Gritos/faGritos6.html

8. Música fronteriza: border music
   http://www.lib.utexas.edu/benson/border/pena/

9. The roots of Tejano and Conjunto music
   http://www.lib.utexas.edu/benson/border/arhoolie2/raices.html

10. Border cultures: conjunto music
    http://www.lib.utexas.edu/benson/border/

11. PBS: Accordion dreams—all about conjunto
    http://www.pbs.org/accordiondreams/all/

12. San Antonio Public Library: Latino: Tejano conjunto music
    http://www.sat.lib.tx.us/Latino/tejano.htm

13. GCAC: History of conjunto music
    http://www.guadalupeculturalarts.org/xicanomusic/tcfhist.htm

14. Tejano-Conjunto music festival
   http://www.2camels.com/destination14.php3

15. Tejano—Conjunto music festival photographs
   http://lii.org/advanced?searchtype=subject;query=Conjunto+music;subsearch=
   Conjunto+music

16. SAPL: Latino collection——Tejano conjunto music
   http://www.sanantonio.gov/library/collections/latino/resTejano.asp?res=
   1280&ver = true

17. Los Lobos: living la vida NAFTA
   http://www.theglobalist.com/DBWeb/StoryId.aspx?StoryId = 2708

18. Smithsonian Folklife Festival
   http://www.folklife.si.edu/resources/Festival1998/conjunto.htm

19. Gale—Free Resources—Hispanic heritage
   http://www.gale.com/free_resources/chh/music/musnorte.htm

20. King of conjunto
   http://www.arguscourier.com/entertainment/stories/flaco050824.html

21. Tejano music history
   http://www.ondanet.com/tejano/tejhistory.html

22. Hacienda Artists
   http://www.haciendarecords.com/artists/bernal_madrigal_reyna_country.htm

23. Flaco Jiménez: The patron saint of conjunto music
   http://markguerrero.net/5.php

XII. FOLK SPEECH

Chicano Proverbs

1. Mexican proverbs
   http://oneproverb.net/bwfolder/mexicanbw.html

2. World of quotes
   http://www.worldofquotes.com/proverb/Mexican/1/

3. Creative proverbs from Mexico
   http://creativeproverbs.com/mx01.htm

4. Mexican proverb quotes
   http://en.thinkexist.com/quotes/mexican_proverb/

5. Bibliography of Mexican American proverbs
   http://info.utas.edu.au/docs/flonta/DP,1,2,95/MEXICAN_PROVERBS_
   BIBLIO.html

6. Pulplit—A tribute to clever Mexican proverbs
   http://www.pulplit.com/display/generic.php/372.html

7. Quotes about Mexican proverbs
   http://quotes.worldvillage.com/i/b/Mexican_proverbs_or_%22refranes%22

8. Mexican folklore
   http://www.lasculturas.com/lib/libFolklore.htm

9. Mexican proverbs
   http://www.tscholars.com/quote/Mexican_proverbs_or_%22refranes%22

10. Mexican lotería
    http://www.latinworksco.com/mexlotgam.html

Riddles (Adivinanzas)

1. Adivinanzas para niños.
   http://www.elhuevodechocolate.com/adivina1.html

2. Adivinanzas
   http://www.geocities.com/Athens/Thebes/6177/ws-riddles.htm

2. Adivinanzas: P
   http://www.pequenet.com/present/preadivina.asp

3. Welcome to adivinanzas.com
   http://www.adivinanzas.com/

4. Los mejores chistes de adivinanzas
   http://www.chistes.com/Clasificacion.asp?ID = 26

5. Abc de adivinanzas
   http://www.dichos.galeon.com/adivinanza.htm

6. BuscoAcertijos
   http://www.buscoacertijos.com/

7. Acertijolandia
   http://usuarios.lycos.es/acertijolandia/

XIII. CHICANO FOLK CELEBRATIONS

Quinceañeras

1. Quinceañeras
   Links and resources for Quinceañeras.
   http://www.partypop.com/planning/Quinceanera/quinceaneras.html

2. Caller.com: quinceañeras
   http://www.caller.com/ccct/people_quinceaneras

3. El sueño de las quinceañeras
   http://www.univision.com/content/content.jhtml?chid = 10&schid = 1948&secid = 1949&cid = 181211

4. The handbook of Texas online: quinceañeras
   http://www.tsha.utexas.edu/handbook/online/articles/QQ/ldq1.html

5. Las Vegas quinceañera
   http://www.lvweddingchapels.com/special_quinceaneras.html

6. A Hispanic's girl coming of age
   http://www.epcc.edu/ftp/Homes/monicaw/borderlands/10_a_hispanic_girl's.htm

7. Coming Events
   http://www.carts.org/artist_evaquincepup.html

8. HispanicPRWire—Quinceañeras, a dream come true.
   http://www.hispanicprwire.com/news_in.php?id = 4069&cha = 8

9. La quinceañera: towards an ethnographic analysis of a life
   http://colfa.utsa.edu/cantu/quinceaera.html

10. Dieta para quinceañeras
    http://www.alimentacion-sana.com.ar/informaciones/Dietas/quince.htm

Weddings (Bodas)

1. Bodas
   http://www.virtualbodas.com/etiqueta_y_protocolo_contenido.html

2. La organización de bodas en internet
   http://www.bodas.org/

3. Especial Bodas—El correo digital
   http://canales.elcorreodigital.com/especiales/bodas/

4. Bodas—Todo boda
   http://www.todoboda.es/

5. Bodas, boda
   http://www.publiboda.com/

6. Mexican wedding traditions
   Complete Wedding Planning and Honeymoon Information Guide.
   htp://www.weddingdetails.com/lore/mexican.cfm

7. Traditional Mexican weddings
   http://www.virtualvallarta.com/vallarta/articles/ss01-traditionalweddings.html

8. A Mexican wedding
   http://www.topics-mag.com/internatl/weddings/mexican-wedding.htm

9. MEXonline.com Mexican Wedding Planners Directory
   MexOnline.com Mexican wedding planners directory for couples who want to get married in Mexico.
   http://www.mexonline.com/wedding.htm

10. Modernbride.com
    Complete wedding planning site for the bride-to-be. Expert advice and local resources to help plan the wedding you've always wanted.
    http://www.modernbride.com/realweddings/outdoor/?rrwo_mexicombm0104.html

11. Mexican theme wedding and party guide
    http://www.askginka.com/nationality/mexican.htm

12. It takes more than "I do" to get married in Mexico
    http://www.mexconnect.com/MEX/jrose/jrmarriage.html

13. Articles
    Historical Perspective on a Traditional Mexican Wedding. http://www.muybueno.net/articles/mexicanwedding.htm

Birthdays

1. History of birthday celebrations
   Mexican birthday celebrations feature piñatas filled with candy and small toys.
   http://www.birthdayexpress.com/bexpress/planning/BirthdayCelebrations.asp

2. Lesson exchange: Mexican birthdays
   http://teachers.net/lessons/posts/1060.html

3. Mexican Americans, community, birthdays, sisters
   http://www.leeandlow.com/spanish/elbday.html

4. Mexico tourism, things to do in Mexico
   http://travelchannel.igougo.com/planning/journalEntryFreeForm.asp?journalID = 3986&entryID = 3677&n=Mexican+Birthday+Song

5. The piñata store—authentic Mexican party piñatas
   http://www.thepinatastore.com/

6. Mexican birthday dinner recipes
   http://www.razzledazzlerecipes.com/birthdays/mesdin.htm

Día de Santo

1. El día del santo
   http://pressroom.hallmark.com/el_dia_del_santo.html

Holiday Celebrations

1. Holiday and celebration in Oaxaca
   http://www.oaxacainfo.com/calendar.htm
2. Holidays and Fiestas in Mexico
   http://www.mexconnect.com/mex_/mexconctholidays.html
3. Santos
   http://www.aciprensa.com/santos/
4. El santo
   http://www.elalmanaque.com/santoral/SANTO.htm

Velorio (Wake)

1. Chistes de Velorio
   http://www.hablandopaja.com/velorio.html
2. Velando al velorio
   http://www.cortada.com/gallery/conceptual/velando-velorio.htm
3. The funeral
   http://www.timsbaja.com/nov02trip/nov02tripPFV.html
4. Modern and Ancient funeral rites on the Internet
   http://www.timsbaja.com/nov02trip/nov02tripPFV.html
5. Funeral customs
   http://www.emints.org/ethemes/resources/S00001505.shtml

Folk Celebrations: Religious

Christmas

1. Mexican Traditions, Christmas
   http://www.mexconnect.com/mex_/christmas.html
2. Traditional Mexican Christmas recipes
   http://www.inside-mexico.com/cocina4.htm
3. Holiday traditions: Mexico
   http://www.californiamall.com/holidaytraditions/traditions-mexico.htm
4. Mexican food history, Mexican Christmas tradition
   http://www.texmextogo.com/TexMexFoodHistory.htm
5. Fiesta Navidad
   http://www.geocities.com/Athens/Aegean/2221/mexico.html
6. How to celebrate a Mexican Christmas
   http://www.ehow.com/how_11722_celebrate-mexican-christmas.html

7. Mexican music: A Christmas tradition
   http://cnx.rice.edu/content/m12609/latest/

8. Mexican Christmas
   http://www.recipezaar.com/r/127/259

9. A Mexican Christmas, San Miguel, Mexico
   http://www.bedandbreakfastinmexico.com/a_Mexican_Christmas/a-mexican-christmas.htm

10. Mexican Christmas Ornaments and Decorations
    http://www.bedandbreakfastinmexico.com/a_Mexican_Christmas/a-mexican-christmas.htm

11. A red and green Mexican Christmas Fiesta
    http://www.mexgrocer.com/cocina-redgreen.html

12. Mexican Christmas Festival
    http://www.ci.austin.tx.us/library/posada2004.htm

13. Christmas Theme
    http://www.atozteacherstuff.com/Themes/Christmas/

Easter

1. Mexican Easter
   http://www.theholidayspot.com/easter/worldeaster/mexican_easter.htm

2. Easter in Mexico
   http://www.mexconnect.com/mex_/feature/easterindex.html

3. Mexican Tradition, Easter
   http://www.mexconnect.com/mex_/dppascua.html

4. Easter in Mexico is alive with tradition
   http://www.vivasancarlos.com/Easter.html

5. A Mexican Easter
   http://www.sofiaecho.com/article/a-mexican-easter/id_4239/catid_30

6. Country: Mexico: Traditions and Holiday
   http://www.emints.org/ethemes/resources/S00000209.shtml

7. Semana Santa in Mexico
   http://www.inside-mexico.com/Catalog/CatalogPages/6esemanasanta.htm

8. Easter
   http://re-xs.ucsm.ac.uk/re/religion/christianity/easter.html

9. Mexican Holidays
   http://www.ilcymex.com/mexican.htm

New Year

1. Mexican New Year—Just use it
   http://www.mexicannewyear.com/xoops/

2. Mexico City—traditional holidays
   http://www.mexicocity.com.mx/celebrat.html

3. Mexonline.com. Local festivals and fiestas in Mexico
   http://www.mexonline.com/festivals.htm

4. Mexican public holidays
   http://gomexico.about.com/cs/mexico/a/public_holidays.htm

5. Mexican traditions for Christmas
   http://www.nacnet.org/assunta/nacimnto.htm

6. Visite México
   http://www.visitmexico.com/wb2/Visitmexico/Visi_Home_Eventos

Día de los Muertos

1. Day of the Dead
   http://www.public.iastate.edu/~rjsalvad/scmfaq/muertos.html

2. Mexico's day of the dead
   http://www.mexconnect.com/mex_/feature/daydeadindex.html

3. azcentral.com: day of the dead
   http://www.azcentral.com/ent/dead/

4. Welcome to the day of the dead in Mexico
   http://www.dayofthedead.com/

5. Day of the dead
   Describes the celebration's history, spiritual significance, traditions, foods and decorations.
   The days of the dead. Explains the use of food and includes a recipe for traditional pan de muerto (bread of the dead).
   http://www.globalgourmet.com/food/egg/egg1096/daydead.html

7. Celebrating the day of the dead in Janitzio
   http://www.inside-mexico.com/featuredead.htm

8. Lesson Plan—day of the dead
   Teaching plan for teachers of grades 4–5. Includes a Spanish poem in Spanish and English.
   http://teacherlink.ed.usu.edu/tlresources/units/Byrnes-celebrations/Day.html

9. MEXonline—day of the dead holiday
   http://www.mexonline.com/dayofthedead.htm

10. Days of the dead on the net
    http://www.holidays.net/dayofthedead/

Folk Celebrations: National

1. Cinco de Mayo history
   http://www.vivacincodemayo.org/history.htm

2. History of Cinco de Mayo
   http://www.mexonline.com/cinco.htm

3. Cinco de Mayo
   http://www.nacnet.org/assunta/spa5may.htm

4. Cinco de Mayo Webquest
   http://www.zianet.com/cjcox/edutech4learning/cinco.html

5. Cinco de Mayo
   http://latino.sscnet.ucla.edu/demo/cinco.html

6. Cinco de Mayo, Fiesta 2003
   http://www.cincodemayo.net/

7. Cinco de Mayo
   http://www.inside-mexico.com/featurecinco.htm

8. Cinco de Mayo for Kids and Teachers
   http://www.kiddyhouse.com/Holidays/Cinco/

9. Celebrating Cinco de Mayo at The Holiday Zone
   http://www.theholidayzone.com/cinco/

XIV. CHICANO FOLK MEDICINE

1. Ritual mágico para quitar el mal de ojo [Magic ritual to cure the evil eye]
   http://www.thaisyjosef.com/ritualesdeproteccion/ritualquitarmaldeojo/
   ritualmagicoparaquitarelmaldeojo.htm

2. Protejerce del mal de ojo [Protection from the evil eye.]
   http://www.actuaciones.net/maldeojo.htm

3. Mal de ojo [evil eye]
   http://ar.geocities.com/argentinamisteriosa/maldeojo.htm

4. Mágia blanca y mal de ojo [White magic and the evil eye]
   http://www.anael.org/karma/magia.htm

5. Mal de ojo [Evil eye]
   http://www.aturquia.com/tradiciones/maldeojo.htm

6. Mal de ojo [Evil eye]
   http://www.editorialbitacora.com/bitacora/ojos02/ojos02.htm

7. Cuatro tratados médicos renacentistas sobre el mal de ojo [Four medical essays from the Renaissance to treat the evil eye.]
   http://www.agapea.com/Cuatro-tratados-medicos-renacentistas-sobre-el-mal-de-ojo-n48817i.htm

8. De nuestro folklore [From our folklore]
   http://lacapullana.tripod.com.pe/sullana_folklore.htm

Empacho (Indigestion)

1. Empacho: indigestion
   http://www.tuotromedico.com/temas/empacho_indigestion.htm

2. Empacho
   http://www.rice.edu/projects/HispanicHealth/Courses/mod7/empacho.html

3. Cultural aspects of treating Mexican patients
   http://www.findarticles.com/p/articles/mi_m0BUY/is_5_12/ai_87373532

4. El Periodista, última palabra
   http://www.elperiodista.cl/newtenberg/1435/article-36165.html

5. Cuidado doméstico: empacho
   http://www.sanitas.es/websanitas/web01.detalle_mensaje?v_id_mensaje = 17207&v_codigo = 1&v_id_idioma = 3

6. Empacho navideño
   http://octaedro.f2o.org/archives/2003/12/29/empacho-navideo/

7. El empacho, mal de ojo
   http://www.tlahui.com/medic/medic18/empacho1.htm

Mollera Caída (Fallen Fontanel)

1. Tía Josefa, the curandera
   http://www.tlahui.com/medic/medic18/empacho1.htm

2. Food, spices double as folk cures
   http://www.epcc.edu/ftp/Homes/monicaw/borderlands/09_food.htm

3. Contemporary pediatrics
   http://www.contemporarypediatrics.com/contpeds/article/articleDetail.jsp?id = 111743

4. Caída de mollera
   http://www.rice.edu/projects/HispanicHealth/Courses/mod7/caida.html

5. Where to find magical realism
   http://www.public.asu.edu/~aarios/resourcebank/03findmagicalrealism/

6. Caída de mollera among children of Mexican migrant workers
   http://www.ncbi.nlm.nih.gov/entrez/query.fcgi?cmd=Retrieve&db=PubMed
   &list_uids=9627925&dopt=Abstract

7. Cultural Facts
   http://www.clas-sd.org/culturalfacts.htm

8. Biblioteca virtual, caída de mollera
   http://www.uady.mx/sitios/editoria/biblioteca-virtual/miscelanea/ninos/
   parte3.html

9. The children's hospital, caring for our future
   http://www.thechildrenshospital.org/publications/cfof/2000/00fall/1.cfm

10. Latino health beliefs
    http://www.public.asu.edu/~squiroga/gutierre.HTM

Curandera (Folk Healer)

1. A Mexican curandera in Ojinaga, Chihuahua
   http://ojinaga.com/curandera/

2. The curandera's garden
   http://www.hgtv.com/hgtv/gl_herbs/article/0,1785,HGTV_3595_2251140,00.
   html

3. Elena Avila, curandera
   http://www.newtimes.org/issue/9901/99–01-avila.html

4. Curandera [folk healer]
   http://cam.utmb.edu/cases/Spina_bifida/curandera.asp

5. Josefina's curandera activity
   http://www.americangirl.com/agcn/josefina/game1_helping/

6. Poem: "Curandera."
   http://www.illyria.com/dusty/duscuran.html

7. ARTS online: curandera
   http://www.laep.org/artsonline/symbolism/curandera_wn.html

Embrujo (Bewitched)

1. La web de Vargas, "el brujo."
   http://www.embrujo.net/

2. El brujo [the witch]
   http://www.elbrujo.net/

3. Brujería [witchcraft]
   http://www.corazones.org/apologetica/practicas/brujeria.htm

4. Brujeria [witchcraft]
   http://www.ikuska.com/Africa/Etnologia/brujeria.htm

5. La inquisición y la brujería [the inquisition and witchcraft]
   http://www.archimadrid.es/princi/princip/otros/docum/iglebru/iglebru.htm

6. La brujería en la biblia [witchcraft in the bible]
   http://www.wzo.org.il/es/recursos/view.asp?id=573

7. Brujas, brujería [witches, witchcraft]
   http://www.actuaciones.net/brujas.htm

Susto (Shock)

1. Susto [shock]
   http://www.rice.edu/projects/HispanicHealth/Courses/mod7/susto.html

2. Susto: a folk illness
   http://www.ucpress.edu/books/pages/1851.html

3. Encyclopedia, susto
   http://www.nationmaster.com/encyclopedia/Susto

4. Barriendo de susto
   http://www.carmenlomasgarza.com/gallery/barriendo.html

5. Cultured Med
   http://www2.sunyit.edu/library/html/culturedmed/bib/tradmed/

6. Mexican American herbal remedies
   http://herbalgram.org/bodywise/herbalgram/articleview.asp?a=915&p=Y

XV. FOLK DRAMA

Pastorelas (Nativity Plays)

1. Las Pastorelas
   http://mexico.udg.mx/arte/posadas/pastorel.html

2. Posadas, Pastorelas and Nacimientos
   http://www.mexconnect.com/mex_/travel/ldumois/ldcposadas.html

3. Las pastorelas y la escencia del teatro
   http://redescolar.ilce.edu.m   x/redescolar/act_permanentes/teatro/segun_llama.htm

4. Las "pastorelas"
   http://redescolar.ilce.edu.mx/redescolar/efemerides/diciembre/trad-16–24c.htm

5. Pastorelas y posadas
   http://www.culturafronteriza.com/pastorelas.htm

6. Pastorelas
   http://buscador.hispavista.es/pastorelas/

7. La Navidad
   http://www.yucatan.com.mx/especiales/navidad/pastorelas.asp

8. Las pastorelas
   http://www.mexicodesconocido.com.mx/espanol/cultura_y_sociedad/
   religion/detalle.cfm?idpag=1037&idsec=19&idsub=0

9. Las pastorelas
   http://www.churchforum.org/info/Liturgia/Navidad/pastorelas.htm

10. Pastorelas
    http://www.sanbenito.k12.tx.us/schools/BertaCabaza/HSSB/Reading_
    Homepage/Pastorelas/Pastorelas.html

11. Mexico Desconocido
    http://www.mexicodesconocido.com.mx/espanol/cultura_y_sociedad/fiestas_
    y_tradiciones/detalle.cfm?idpag=3349&idsec=15&idsub=60

12. Pastorelas y fiestas navidenas
    http://www.edomexico.gob.mx/newweb/servicios/civica/pasajes/pastorelas.htm

13. Christmas in Mexico
    http://www.mexconnect.com/mex_/feature/xmasindex.html

14. Pastorela
    http://sepiensa.org.mx/contenidos/s_pastorelas/pastorelas.htm

15. Caminantetv.com
    http://www.caminantetv.com/caminante_dev/las_pastorelas.shtml

16. Pastorelas indigenas en Michoacan
    http://www.xiranhua.com/cultura/pastorela-04.htm

17. Pastorelas, tradiciones y tentaciones
    http://www.xiranhua.com/cultura/pastorela-04.htm

18. Catholic.net. Las pastorelas de Mexico
    http://es.catholic.net/turismoreligioso/659/1922/articulo.php?id=20006

19. Pastorelas, tradiciones, y tentaciones
    http://www.semanario.com.mx/2001/254–16122001/portada.html

20. Taller de pastorelas
    http://www.puentetheatre.ca/Spanish/taller_pastorelas.htm

Los Pastores

1. Los Pastores a Belen
   http://www.amorpostales.com/Los-Pastores-a-Belen.html

2. Catholic culture: Los pastores
   http://www.catholicculture.org/lit/activities/view.cfm?id=557

3. San Antonio Conservation Society
   http://www.saconservation.org/events/lospastores.htm

4. La adoración de los pastores en Murillo
   http://clio.rediris.es/fichas_arte/la_adoracion.htm

5. Los pastores a Belén
   http://ingeb.org/songs/lospasto.html

6. Los pastores
   http://www.navidadlatina.com/musica/letras/pastores.asp

7. Los pastores
   http://www.lib.utexas.edu/benson/lospastores/

8. Venezuela virtual—costumbres y tradiciones
   http://www.mipunto.com/venezuelavirtual/000/002/017/003/015.html

9. Los pastores
   http://www.trovadores.net/ctr.exe?NC=4321&FR=1

10. Villancico
    http://www.terra.es/personal/7sietes/pastor.htm

Las Posadas

1. Posadas in Mexico
   http://www.mexconnect.com/MEX/austin/posadas.html

2. Mexican traditions: Las posadas
   http://www.mexconnect.com/mex_/christmas.html

3. Mexico: Las posadas
   http://www.zuzu.org/mex.html

4. Las posadas
   http://mexico.udg.mx/arte/posadas/posadas2.html

5. Las posadas
   http://www.cinnamonhearts.com/LasPosadas.htm

6. Las posadas
   http://www.twilightbridge.com/hobbies/festivals/christmas/
   las_posadas/

7. Las posadas
   http://spanish.about.com/library/weekly/aa122099a.htm

8. Las posadas
   http://www.cinnamonhearts.com/LasPosadas03.htm

9. Olvera street.com—Las posadas
   http://www.olvera-street.com/html/las_posadas.html

10. Circle of Light—Las posadas
    http://www.circolite.com/lasposadas.htm

11. Las Posadas history
    http://www.brownielocks.com/posadas.html

12. Las posadas
    http://www.sahs.org/community/southoftheborder/lasposadas.htm

Los Moros y Cristianos

1. La fiesta de moros y cristianos de Alcoy
   http://www.uv.es/~pedrose/festes.html

2. Javea—Fiesta—Moros y Cristianos
   http://www.javea.net/01–05–02–07.htm

3. Las fiestas de moros y cristianos
   http://www.escuelai.com/spanish_culture/fiestas_espanolas/morosycristianos.html

4. Moros y cristianos Benissa
   http://www.morosicristians.com/benissa/

5. Fiestas mayores de moros y cristianos en el campello
   http://www.gulliveria.com/especiales/15.htm

6. Moros y cristianos en Ontinyent
   http://www.abc.es/abc/pg050821/prensa/noticias/Valencia/Valencia/200508/21/
   NAC-VAL-109.asp

7. Moros, cristianos y ateos
   http://www.webislam.com/numeros/2001/03_01/Articulos%2003_01/Moros_
   cristianos.htm

8. Arte y cultura: moros y cristianos
   http://www.pergaminovirtual.com.ar/categorias/Arte_y_Cultura_Festividades_
   Moros_y_Cristianos1.shtml

9. Petrer: moros y cristianos
   http://www.petrerenfestes.com/

10. Moros y cristianos
    http://www.antonioburgos.com/mundo/2004/03/re032904.html

11. Orihuela: Moros y cristianos
    http://www.orihueladigital.es/orihuela/moros_cristianos_300105.htm

12. Asociacion de San Jorge—Fiestas de moros y cristianos
    http://www.associaciosantjordi.org/fiesta.htm

13. Moros y cristianos—Ontinyen
    http://www.morosycristianos.com/fiestas-32.s.html

14. Fiestas de Moros y Cristianos en Villajollosa
    http://www.desembarco.com/fiestas_moros_cristianos.html

Los Comanches

1. The edge: "Los comanches"
   http://www.interculturalrelations.com/v1i2Spring1998/sp98gandert.htm

2. Portal de cultura Chicana—"Los comanches"
   http://www.cervantesvirtual.com/FichaObra.html?Ref=12572&
   portal=107

3. UNM Today: UNM celebrates "Los comanches en Nuevo Mexico"
   http://www.unm.edu/˜market/cgi-bin/archives/000523.html

4. Las tribus natives de Norteamerica: Los comanches
   http://personal.readysoft.es/jmcasasempere/comanche.htm

5. Marisa García-Verdugo: Dos muestras del teatro hispano
   http://www.ucm.es/info/especulo/numero19/teahispa.html

6. Los indios
   http://mx.geocities.com/presidial/losindios.htm

7. UNM Press: hermanitos comanchitos
   http://www.unmpress.com/Book.php?id=1629013098

8. Los comanches
   http://www.gazellebookservices.co.uk/ISBN/0826315488.htm

9. Nuevo México Profundo
   http://www.tfaoi.com/aa/3aa/3aa125.htm

10. Comanche Chiefs—the great chiefs of the Comanche nation
    http://www.comanchelodge.com/paraiboo.html

XVI. FOLK BELIEF AND SUPERSTITION

1. Creencias
   http://orbita.starmedia.com/alcozar-soria/creencias.htm

2. Leyendas Urbanas
   http://club.telepolis.com/leyendasurbanas/creencias/

3. Creencia—Wikipedia
   http://es.wikipedia.org/wiki/Creencia

4. Religion, mitos y supersticiones
   http://www.soygaucho.com/espanol/creencias/

5. Creencias y supersticiones
   http://www.elfolkloreargentino.com/creenciasysupersticiones.htm

6. Creencias de los pueblos indígenas
   http://virtual.finland.fi/finfo/espanja/aurora3.html

7. Credos y creencias
   http://www.prodiversitas.bioetica.org/credos.htm

Supersticiones

1. Supersticiones
   http://www.augustobriga.net/memoria/supersticiones.htm

2. Supersticiones
   http://espanol.geocities.com/sergiotacata/supersticiones.htm

3. Indice—Supersticiones
   http://web.madritel.es/personales/beamarciel/html/indice.htm

4. Supersticiones
   http://www.fut.es/~vne/supersticiones_1.htm

5. Supersticiones de boda
   http://www.publiboda.com/supersticiones/

6. La cruda realidad: supersticiones
   http://lacrudarealidad.blogsome.com/2005/08/02/supersticiones/

7. Supersticiones en el trabajo
   http://mifuturo.mujer.wanadoo.es/html/biblioteca/ocultismo5.html

Index

About the Author

MARÍA HERRERA-SOBEK holds the Luis Leal Endowed Chair in Chicano Studies at the University of California, Santa Barbara. Her many books include *The Bracero Experience: Elitelore versus Folklore* (1979), *The Mexican Corrido: A Feminist Analysis* (1990), and *Northward Bound: The Mexican Immigrant Experience in Ballad and Song* (1993). In addition, she has edited numerous anthologies and published more than one hundred articles.